FROMMER'S

FAMILY TRAVEL GUIDE

WASHINGTON, D.C., WITH KIDS

To Leslie Mick —
Thanks for
the encouragement
when I needed it most!
Beth Rubin

by Beth Rubin

PRENTICE HALL TRAVEL

NEW YORK • LONDON • TORONTO • SYDNEY • TOKYO • SINGAPORE

FROMMER BOOKS

Published by Prentice Hall General Reference
A division of Simon & Schuster Inc.
15 Columbus Circle
New York, NY 10023

ISBN 0-13-333360-4
ISSN 1058-4978

Design by Robert Bull Design
Maps by Geografix Inc. of New York

Manufactured in the United States of America

FROMMER'S WASHINGTON, D.C., WITH KIDS, '92–'93
Editor-in-Chief: Marilyn Wood
Senior Editor: Judith de Rubini
Editors: Alice Fellows, Paige Hughes, Theodore Stavrou
Assistant Editors: Peter Katucki, Lisa Renaud
Managing Editor: Leanne Coupe

CONTENTS

LIST OF MAPS

DEDICATION

For Ken—If it weren't for you, I'd probably still be stuck in New Jersey. For Rachel and Eric—Always my eager and enthusiastic travel companions, thanks for providing the inspiration for this book. It's been a trip.

THANK YOU

To my family and friends, thank you for sustaining me through this, my longest and most difficult pregnancy. Special thanks to Bubbles Fisher for believing I could do it, Marilyn Wood for giving me the green light, Judith de Rubini for dotting my "i's" and crossing my "t's," and Judi Scioli and Carole Ottesen for their unflagging encouragement, beneficial advice, and good humor.

INVITATION TO THE READERS

In researching this book, I have come across many wonderful establishments, the best of which I have included here. I am sure that many of you will also come across family-friendly hotels, inns, restaurants, guesthouses, shops, and attractions. Please don't keep them to yourself. Share your family's experiences, especially if you want to comment on places that have been included in this edition that have changed for the worse. You can address your letters to:

Beth Rubin
Frommer's Washington, D.C., with Kids
c/o Prentice Hall Travel
15 Columbus Circle
New York, NY 10023

A DISCLAIMER

Readers are advised that prices fluctuate in the course of time and travel information changes under the impact of the varied and volatile factors that affect the travel industry. Neither the authors nor the publisher can be held responsible for the experiences of readers while traveling. Readers are invited to write to the publisher with ideas, comments, and suggestions for future editions.

SAFETY ADVISORY

Whenever you're traveling in an unfamiliar city or country, stay alert. Be aware of your immediate surroundings. Wear a moneybelt and keep a close eye on your possessions. Be particularly careful with cameras, purses, and wallets, all favorite targets of thieves and pickpockets.

CHAPTER 1

PLANNING A FAMILY TRIP TO WASHINGTON, D.C.

Kids and Washington, D.C., go together like peanut butter and jelly. Little wonder that children of all ages come to know and love the exciting, accessible international playground that is the nation's capital. Packed into the 69¼-square-mile parcel of former swampland, "the District" or "D.C." offers a host of attractions, historic and new, waiting to be discovered and rediscovered. With its wide tree-lined boulevards, numerous parks and recreational areas, and multi-ethnic shops and restaurants, it's a natural for a family vacation. Families have been flocking to Washington in increasing numbers over the years, and for good reason. The capital city, which celebrated its bicentennial in 1991 and attracted 19 million visitors the previous year, continues to extend an ever-friendlier hand to families. Each year increasing numbers of hotels offer special family rates and restaurants go out of their way to please pint-size patrons.

Thousands of bus- and planeloads of schoolchildren visit annually from all over the world. Where else can kids visit the president's house, touch a moon rock, view the city from atop a 555-foot obelisk, and take a boat ride on the Potomac all in the same day? And that's just for openers!

Despite all the federal buildings and museums, Washington is like one enormous park. First-time visitors are quick to note the abundance of greenery and flora in the downtown area. In fact, grassy knolls, gardens, fountains, and parks hug most major sightseeing attractions. The area known as the Mall stretches for two miles from the Capitol to the Lincoln Memorial—the perfect site for pigeon-chasing or a family jog. Children who typically become bored or cranky after an hour or two cooped up in a museum can readily get rid of bottled-up energy in a flash.

For an urban area, Washington's skyline is surprisingly and pleasantly uncluttered. Because the original city planners declared that no building could be higher than the dome of the U.S. Capitol, the height of commercial buildings is strictly regulated to 110 feet, giving the city an open and expansive feeling. Compared to many metropolitan areas in the United States and abroad, Washington is also squeaky clean (we're not talking politics here).

Getting around D.C. is a breeze. All major attractions are accessible by Metro, the public rail/bus system. The subways are clean, efficient, safe, and surprisingly graffiti-free.

Prices for food, lodging, and entertainment compare favorably to other tourist meccas. If you've been to New York recently, you'll find Washington a relative bargain. Families can eat well in a wide variety of Washington's more than 3,500 restaurants and not break the bank. Best of all, for those watching their pocketbooks—and who isn't these days—most of the major attractions are free. Try that in New York or Paris!

Except for a few neighborhoods, where you're not apt to be in the first place, you can unleash older children to wander on their own. Teenagers, especially, should be allowed time to explore the District, particularly those areas uniquely appealing to this age group.

Tourism is the second largest industry in D.C. The first, as you may have guessed, is the federal government. The "natives" (sort of an inside joke, since so many residents come from somewhere else) are friendly, helpful, and eager to make visitors feel at home. Washington is, after all, everyone's home and engenders a sense of belonging to short-term guests as well as permanent residents. Those who live and work in D.C. share an immense feeling of pride. Chances are it will rub off on you and yours during your visit.

1. TOURIST INFORMATION

For a smooth-running, fun-filled vacation with kids, you have to plan, plan, plan. To do this well, first learn something about your destination before leaving home. After digesting as much information as you can, gather everyone around the kitchen table and talk about your priorities. For each day make a list of sights you *must* see and backups that you can live without. Don't leave anything but the weather to chance. Do as much research as possible and make all necessary reservations before the curtain goes up on your vacation.

If you want to be admitted to either gallery when the Senate or House is in session, eat lunch in the members' dining room, or if you desire VIP tours of the Capitol, White House, and FBI, contact your congressional representatives. Passes are limited, and six months prior to your visit is not too soon to write. Send your request, with the dates of your trip, to your senator, c/o U.S. Senate, Washington, DC 20510, or your representative, c/o U.S. House of Representatives, Washington, DC 20515.

Besides combing the travel shelves of your local library and bookstores, order brochures from the following sources: **Washington, D.C., Convention and Visitors Association,** 1212 New York Ave. NW, Washington, DC 20005 (tel. 202/789-7000); **Hotel Association of Washington, D.C.,** 1201 New York Ave. NW, Suite 601, Washington, DC 20005 (tel. 202/289-3141); **Capitol Reservations** (tel. toll free, 800/847-4832); **Bed 'n' Breakfast of Washington, D.C.,** P.O. Box 12011, Washington, DC 20002 (tel. 202/328-3510); **DC Committee to Promote Washington,** P.O. Box 27489, Washington, DC 20038-7489 (tel. 202/724-4091). For information on Metro rail service, write to the **Washington Metropolitan Area Transit Authority,** 600 5th St. NW, Washington, DC 20001 (tel. 202/637-7000), and request the "All About Metro" booklet or the "Metro Pocket Ride Guide," which is smaller but contains the same information. Both are free.

WHAT THINGS COST IN WASHINGTON	U.S. $
Taxi from National Airport to a downtown hotel	10.00–12.00
Taxi from Dulles Airport (Va.) to downtown	35.00
Local telephone call	.20
Double room at the Omni Shoreham Hotel (deluxe)	225.00
Double room at the Carlyle Suites (moderate)	109.00
Double room at the University Inn (inexpensive)	62.00
Lunch for one at Hard Rock Café (moderate)	16.00
Lunch for one at Flight Line cafeteria (budget)	7.00
Lunch (hot dog, soda, ice cream) from street vendor	2.75
Dinner for one at America (moderate)	20.00
Dinner for one at Hogs on the Hill (budget)	13.00
Coca-Cola in a restaurant	.95
Ice-cream cone	1.25
Roll of Kodak 100 film, 36 exposures	5.55
Admission to National Zoological Park	Free
Movie ticket	
Adult	6.50
Child	3.50

2. WHEN TO GO

THE CLIMATE   For obvious reasons, you'll probably plan your visit for spring or summer—when the kids are out of school. That's fine, but understand that the warm-weather months are when Washington is most crowded. Summer is the best time to take advantage of numerous free outdoor events and reduced hotel rates. However, the heat and humidity can wilt a cactus. But if you dress appropriately and sightsee early or late in the day, you'll fare well.

July and August are the warmest months, with average highs in the mid-80s. This is not to say it won't heat up to the mid-90s, which it does with disturbing regularity and oppressively high humidity. But help is always nearby. Nearly all the public buildings, restaurants, and hotels in Washington are air-conditioned, making a summer visit tolerable.

If your kids are pre-schoolers or budding geniuses who can afford to miss school, fall is a lovely time to visit. The weather is usually pleasant and mild and the rest of the world is at home. In winter, hotel prices are lowest and lines are shortest. So if it's crowds you detest and bargains you seek, pack your galoshes and come see Washington when she is decked out for the holidays.

Highs in December, January, and February are in the mid-40s, with lows around 30 degrees. Again, these are averages. The rainfall is evenly distributed throughout the year, so don't leave home without a raincoat. There's a lesson here: When it comes time to pack, take a tip from the Boy Scouts and "Be prepared."

Whichever season you choose, it will be the right one, as Washington overflows with excitement and charm year-round, even during the dog days of summer.

Average Monthly Temperatures

	Jan	Feb	Mar	Apr	May	June	July	Aug	Sept	Oct	Nov	Dec
Avg. High (F)	45	44	53	64	75	83	87	84	78	68	55	45
Avg. Low (F)	27	28	35	44	55	63	68	66	60	48	38	30

HOLIDAYS On the following legal national holidays, banks, government offices, and post offices are closed. Subways (Metrorail) and buses (Metrobus) operate less frequently, usually on a Saturday or Sunday schedule (tel. 637-7000 for information). Museums, stores, and restaurants vary widely in their open/closed policy. To avoid disappointment, call before you go.

January 1 (New Year's Day), Third Monday in January (Martin Luther King Jr. Day), Last Monday in May (Memorial Day), July 4 (Independence Day), First Monday in September (Labor Day), Second Monday in October (Columbus Day), November 11 (Veteran's Day/Armistice Day), Last Thursday in November (Thanksgiving Day), and December 25 (Christmas Day).

The Tuesday following the first Monday in November is Election Day. It is a legal holiday in presidential election years (1992, 1996, etc.).

KIDS' FAVORITE EVENTS

Whether you decide to visit Washington in June or January, or any time in between, you'll find a wide range of special events to enhance your sightseeing. Most are free.

For the latest information before you leave home, contact the **Washington, D.C., Convention and Visitors Association,** 1212 New York Ave., NW, Washington, DC 20005 (tel. 202/789-7000), and request the quarterly "Calendar of Events" brochure, or stop by the **Visitor Information Center** at 1455 Pennsylvania Ave. NW (tel. 202/789-7038) for a copy. It's open from 9am to 5pm, Monday through Saturday. Also consult the "Weekend" section of the *Washington Post* every Friday. Before you attend a special event, it's wise to call and verify the time and location. Some changes and cancellations are inevitable.

JANUARY

○ *Martin Luther King Jr.'s Birthday* *This national holiday is celebrated the third Monday in January with speeches, dance performances, and choral presentations. Check local newspapers for free commemorative events (tel. 202/755-1005).*

○ *Washington Boat Show* *Kids love boats—in or out of the water. Consider the experience a healthy exercise in fantasizing for the entire family. The weeklong show is held midmonth at the Washington Convention Center, 900 9th St. NW (tel. 202/789-1600). Admission.*

□ **Robert E. Lee's Birthday Bash,** at the Custis-Lee Mansion in Arlington Cemetery, features 19th-century music, food, and memorabilia (tel. 703/557-0613). Free. Visit Lee's boyhood home at 607 Oronoco St. and the Lee-Fendall House at 614 Oronoco St. in Old Town Alexandria (tel. 703/548-1789). Admission.

○ *Inauguration Day* *This is held on January 20 of every fourth year when the President is sworn in at the West Front of the Capitol. The next presidential inauguration will be January 20, 1993. A colorful—and very lengthy—parade follows the ceremony from the Capitol to the White House along Pennsylvania Avenue.*

FEBRUARY

○ *Black History Month* *This is observed by museums, libraries, and recreation centers with special exhibits, events, and performances to celebrate African-American contributions to American life. Check the local newspapers and magazines for events (tel. 202/357-2700).*

○ *Abraham Lincoln's Birthday* *A moving wreath-laying ceremony and reading of the Gettysburg Address at the Lincoln Memorial on February 12 commemorate the birthday of the 16th U.S. president. It's truly inspiring (tel. 202/619-7222).*

○ *Chinese New Year Parade* *Although younger kids may be frightened by the firecrackers announcing the Chinese lunar new year, the colorful street parade of lions and dragons, dancers and music-makers through*

Chinatown (H Street NW, between 5th and 8th streets) is great family fun. After the parade, fill up on dumplings and duck (Peking, of course) at one of Chinatown's many restaurants. Note: Sometimes the Chinese New Year is in early March. Blame it on the moon.

✪ ***George Washington's Birthday*** *The father of our country's natal day is celebrated with a parade through Old Town Alexandria's historic district. Wear your cleanest white stockings and powdered wig (tel. 703/838-4200). Free. On February 22 a ceremony is held at the Washington Monument co-sponsored by the National Park Service and Washington National Monument Society (tel. 202/426-6700). Free. George Washington's Mount Vernon estate features a family celebration on Presidents' Day, on the third Monday of the month (tel. 703/780-2000). Free.*

☐ **Washington Flower & Garden Show** gives you the opportunity to get a jump on spring at the Washington Convention Center, 900 9th St. NW (tel. 202/789-1600). Admission.

MARCH

☐ **U.S. Botanic Garden's Easter Flower Show** A different floral theme is featured every year at this dazzling rite of spring. You'll see more colors than the kids have in their Crayola boxes at home (tel. 202/225-8333). Free.

☐ **St. Patrick's Day Parades** On the Sunday closest to St. Patty's Day, it's top o' the mornin' at the festive afternoon parade down Constitution Avenue, from 7th to 17th streets, NW, with floats, bagpipes, bands, and dancers (tel. 202/424-2200). Old Town Alexandria also celebrates the wearin' of the green with a procession down King Street (tel. 703/549-4535).

✪ ***Ringling Bros. and Barnum & Bailey Circus*** *The world's only three-ring circus pitches its tent at the D.C. Armory for two weeks of thrills and chills that extend into April. Treat your loved ones if they've never been. It's still the greatest show on earth (tel. 703/448-4000).*

✪ ***Smithsonian Kite Festival*** *Breeze on down to the Washington Monument grounds for this annual event that draws kite makers from all over the country. Prizes and trophies are awarded for homemade kites (tel. 202/357-3244).*

✪ ***National Cherry Blossom Festival*** *In late March or early April if you hit this right—no snow, no gale winds, no August-in-spring weather—the breathtaking vision of thousands of cherry trees blooming around the Tidal Basin will take your breath away. There's a parade of floats with sweet young cherry-blossom princesses, free concerts, a marathon, a Japanese-lantern-lighting ceremony, and fireworks (tel. 202/737-2599 or 202/789-7000 for general information; 202/728-1135 for parade ticket* *information; 202/485-9666 for a blossom update). See Chapter 4, "Parks and Gardens," for more about the famed trees.*

APRIL

❂ **White House Easter Egg Roll** *Children 8 and under, accompanied by an adult, are invited on Easter Monday to the South Lawn of the White House, where free eggs (hard-boiled or wooden, depending on the activity) and entertainment are offered out. Although there's a crunch of people—and eggshells—your kids may find the event exciting. Line up early at the Southeast gate of the White House on East Executive Avenue (tel. 202/456-2200). Free.*

☐ **Imagination Celebration** The John F. Kennedy Center for the Performing Arts plays host to several top national children's theater companies. Free or modestly priced (tel. 202/416-8000).

☐ **Arbor Day** This one-day celebration at Bon Air Park in Arlington, VA, features hay rides, forestry games, and nature programs for the whole family. Small trees are given as souvenirs (tel. 703/358-6400). Free.

☐ **Thomas Jefferson's Birthday** On April 13, gather at the Jefferson Memorial to honor the birthday of this renaissance man and third U.S. president with military drills and a wreath-laying ceremony (tel. 202/619-7222). Free.

❂ **White House Spring Garden Tour** *On one weekend only you can see the Children's Garden with its bronze impressions of the hands and feet of White House children and grandchildren among the tulips and azaleas. Line up at least an hour early. (tel. 202/456-2200). Free.*

☐ **Smithsonian's Washington Craft Show** For four glorious days at the Departmental Auditorium, 1301 Constitution Ave. NW (tel. 202/357-2700), this show of fine crafts features one-of-a-kind works from more than 100 exhibitors from all over the country. Strollers are not allowed, but backpacks are available. Watch little hands. You break, you pay! Admission.

☐ **William Shakespeare's Birthday** is celebrated April 20 at the Folger Shakespeare Library with music, theater, children's events, and food (tel. 202/544-7077). Free.

☐ **Trolley Car Spectacular.** Take a trip down memory lane and ride an antique trolley at the National Capital Trolley Museum in Wheaton, MD. Bring your camera (tel. 301/384-6088). Free.

❂ **"Wings & Things" Open House** *One weekend a year, the public is invited to visit the Air & Space Museum's Paul E. Garber Facility in Silver Hill, MD. Wait till you see the airplanes and spacecraft that didn't make it into the Air & Space Museum downtown (tel. 202/357-2700). Free.*

❂ **Gross National Parade** *You'll want to arrive early for this zany parade, sponsored annually by WMAL Radio to benefit the Police Boys and Girls*

Clubs of D.C. The parade begins at 2pm at 18th Street and M Street NW and moves west on M to Wisconsin Avenue (tel. 202/686-3215). It's a scream! Free.

MAY

☐ **Market Day Street Festival** On the first Sunday in May, the streets around Eastern Market, 7th and C Streets SE, are filled with vendors selling clothes, jewelry, and artifacts to benefit Friendship House. Enjoy carnival rides, crafts, music, and food while you browse (tel. 202/546-7600). Free.

☐ **National Cathedral Flower Mart** Children's games, flower booths, entertainment, and food spring up everywhere on the grounds of the majestic National Cathedral, Wisconsin Avenue & Woodley Road NW. There's an extensive selection of herbs for sale (tel. 202/537-6200). Free.

✪ *Air Show at Andrews AFB   Oooh and aah over the Army's Golden Knights parachute team and aerial show by the Air Force Thunderbirds in their F-16s at this weekend open house at Andrews Air Force Base in Camp Springs, MD. Kids can climb aboard aircraft and tanks. Go early, allow plenty of driving time, and bring earplugs (tel. 301/981-1110).*

☐ **Greek Spring Festival** Gorge on Greek souvlaki and baklava while enjoying music, games, clowns, and arts and crafts at Saints Constantine and Helen Greek Orthodox Church, 4115 16 St. NW (tel. 202/829-2910). Free.

☐ **Memorial Day Weekend Concert** The Sunday of Memorial Day weekend Washington's own National Symphony Orchestra will serenade you on the West Lawn of the Capitol (tel. 202/619-7222 or 202/416-8100). Bring a blanket. Free.

☐ **Arlington Cemetery Memorial Day Ceremonies** Witness wreath-laying ceremonies at the Kennedy gravesite and Tomb of the Unknowns and services at the Memorial Amphitheater accompanied by military bands (tel. 703/697-5187). Free.

☐ **American Sailor** From the last Wednesday in May, and every Wednesday thereafter through early September, a multimedia presentation showcases the history of the U.S. Navy at the Washington Navy Yard waterfront at 9pm (tel. 202/433-2218). Free, but reservations are required.

JUNE

✪ *Dupont–Kalorama Museum Walk Day   Textile demonstrations, video programs, house tours, hands-on art, music, and street food provide fun for the whole family at this neighborhood happening (tel. 202/387-2151). Shuttle service is provided. Free.*

☐ **Alexandria Red Cross Waterfront Festival** Tall ships berth at Alexandria's historical waterfront during this family-oriented weekend featuring ethnic foods, entertainment, arts and crafts, and the blessing of the fleet (tel. 703/549-8300). Free.

⊗ *Festival of American Folklife* *One of the most popular annual events in the nation's capital, the folklife festival on the Mall is filled with music, crafts, ethnic foods, and America's rich folk heritage (tel. 202/357-2700). Free. Note: The festival usually spills over into July.*

JULY

⊗ *Independence Day Celebration* *The nation celebrates its birthday in grand style, beginning with a 12:30pm parade along Constitution Avenue (tel. 202/619-7222). Visit the Declaration of Independence at the National Archives, then enjoy entertainment all afternoon at the Sylvan Theatre on the Washington Monument grounds (tel. 202/426-6841). At 8pm the National Symphony plays on the Capitol West Lawn (tel. 202/426-0268), and a fantastic fireworks display starts at 9:30pm (tel. 202/426-6841). Bring something soft and dry to sit on (tel. 202/619-7222). Check newspapers July 3 and 4 for details. Free.*

☐ **Bastille Day Waiters Race** Behold the waiters scurrying down Pennsylvania Avenue with trays of champagne glasses on July 14. The race for a grand prize trip to Paree begins at 20th Street & Pennsylvania Avenue NW at noon (tel. 202/452-1132). Free.

☐ **Civil War Living History Day** Take a torchlight tour of Union and Confederate camps and watch "soldiers" in Civil War uniforms reenact a battle and perform drill competitions at Fort Ward Museum and Park, 4301 W. Braddock Rd., Alexandria, VA (tel. 703/838-4848). Free.

☐ **Virginia Scottish Games** One of the largest Scottish festivals in the United States features Highland dancing, fiddling competitions, a heptathlon, animal events, and plenty of puffed-cheeked bagpipers. It's held at Episcopal High School, 3901 W. Braddock Rd., Alexandria, VA (tel. 703/838-4200). Free.

AUGUST

⊗ *Navy Band Lollipop Concert* *Kids of all ages are invited to the Sylvan Theatre on the Washington Monument grounds for lollipops and a special kid-pleasing evening sweetened by the U.S. Navy Band (tel. 202/433-2394). Free.*

☐ **U. S. Army Band's "1812 Overture"** The Salute Gun Platoon of the 3rd U.S. Infantry provides the noisy finale to this patriotic concert by the U.S. Army Band at the Sylvan Theatre, Washington Monument grounds (tel. 202/693-3399). Free.

☐ **National Frisbee Festival** Over Labor Day weekend (late August or early September), disc-catching dogs are but one highlight of this annual noncompetitive Frisbee festival that's also well attended by world-class champions of the two-legged variety. It's held on the Mall near the Air & Space Museum (tel. 301/645-5043). Heads up! Free.

⊗ *International Children's Festival* *The three-day family arts celebration at Wolf Trap Park for the Performing Arts in Vienna, VA., has an exciting assortment of workshops and performances (tel. 703/255-1900). Admission.*

✪ **Renaissance Festival** *Crownsville, MD (about 30 miles from downtown), is the site for a 16th-century fair with jousting matches, magicians, wandering minstrels, and crafts. A special children's area has pony rides, a zoo, and Tudor-era amusements. Armor up on weekends from late August to mid-October (tel. 202/970-2188). Admission.*

SEPTEMBER

☐ **Labor Day Weekend Concert** The National Symphony bids adieu to summer, even though it's usually still hot as blazes, with a concert on the West Lawn of the Capitol (tel. 202/619-7222 or 202/416-8100). Free.

☐ **College Park Airport Open House and Air Fair** Fly over here with your crew for airplane and helicopter rides, an air show, and exhibits at the area's oldest airport, at 6709 Cpl. Frank Scott Dr., College, Park, MD (tel. 301/864-5844). Free.

☐ **Adams Morgan Day** Visit Washington's most culturally diverse neighborhood and enjoy crafts, music, and cuisine from all points of the globe (tel. 202/332-3292). Free.

☐ **National Capital Trolley Museum Fall Open House** See the April listing.

☐ **Constitution Day Commemoration** On September 17 at the National Archives, Constitution Avenue at 8th Street NW, visit the Constitution on the anniversary of its signing. A naturalization program and honor guard ceremonies are part of the day's events (tel. 202/501-5215). Free.

✪ **Rock Creek Park Day** *Children's activities, environmental and recreational exhibits, foods, crafts, and music highlight the celebration of Washington's largest park, which reached the ripe old age of 100 in 1990 (tel. 202/426-6832). Free.*

OCTOBER

✪ **Kinderfest** *A fall festival for the 6-and-under set at Watkins Regional Park in Upper Marlboro, MD, features games, rides, pumpkin painting, and scarecrow making (tel. 301/249-9220). Free admission, but bring money for rides and food.*

☐ **Greek Fall Festival and Christmas Bazaar.** Games for kids, a Greek buffet, arts and crafts, jewelry, and oriental rugs are featured at this lively bazaar at Saint Sophia Cathedral, 36th Street and Massachusetts Avenue NW (tel. 202/333-4730). Music and dancing after 5pm. Free.

☐ **U.S. Navy Birthday Concert** Wear your dress blues to this U.S. Navy Band concert celebrating the Navy's 217th birthday (tel. 202/433-6090). Free, but tickets must be picked up prior to the concert.

☐ **White House Fall Garden Tour** See the Rose Garden, South Lawn, and beautiful beds of multi-hued chrysanthemums, while enjoying the upbeat sounds of a military band (tel. 202/456-2200). Free.

✪ *Halloween Monster Bash* *Come to a costume party October 31 at the Capital Children's Museum, 3rd and H streets NE (tel. 202/638-5437). Admission.*

NOVEMBER

☐ **Veterans' Day Ceremonies** Military band music accompanies a solemn ceremony honoring the nation's war dead. The Memorial Amphitheater at Arlington National Cemetery is the service site, where the President or another high-ranking official lays a wreath at the Tomb of the Unknown Soldier (tel. 202/475-0843). Free.

✪ *Sugarloaf's Autumn Crafts Festival* *Puppet shows and storytelling will keep the youngsters happy while grownups shop for holiday gifts and souvenirs sold by 400 artists and craftspeople at the Montgomery County Fairgrounds in Gaithersburg, MD (tel. 301/540-0900). Admission.*

DECEMBER

✪ *Festival of Music and Lights* *More than 200,000 twinkling bulbs sparkle and gleam on the greenery at the Washington Mormon Temple in Kensington, MD, through Twelfth Night. Concerts are held nightly until New Year's Eve (tel. 301/587-0144, or 202/662-7480). Free.*

✪ *Woodlawn Plantation Christmas* *Get a taste of Christmas, old Virginia style, as musicians and carolers serenade you at this historic estate, which was a wedding gift from George Washington to his foster daughter Nelly Custis and her husband (who was Washington's nephew), Lawrence Lewis. Wagon rides and refreshments are part of the holiday fun (tel. 703/780-4000). Admission.*

✪ *Scottish Christmas Walk* *A parade through historic Old Town Alexandria, VA, includes special activities for children, tartan-clad bagpipers and Highland dancers, and house tours (tel. 703/549-0111). Free.*

☐ **"A Soldier's Gift"** This holiday offering of seasonal music from the U.S. Army Band is held at D.A.R. Constitution Hall (tel. 202/696-3647). Free, but tickets are required. Write to: "A Soldier's Gift," P.O. Box 24074, Washington, DC 20024.

☐ **Old Town Christmas Candlelight Tours** Several historic homes, dressed up with period decorations, open their doors to visitors. Music, colonial dancing, and refreshments add to the festive atmosphere (tel. 703/838-4200). Admission.

☐ **Holiday Celebration** Holiday crafts, ethnic food, stories, and music at the Smithsonian's National Museum of American History demonstrate how Americans celebrate Christmas, Hanukkah, Kwanzaa, and the New Year. The display of theme-decorated Christmas trees was curtailed in 1990 due to "budget cuts." If you'd like to see "The Trees of Christmas" return, write to your representative in Congress. Join the holiday fun at the Smithsonian (tel. 202/357-2700). Free.

✪ *People's Christmas Tree Lighting* *The People's Christmas Tree, towering some 60 feet, is lighted each year on the west side of the Capitol to herald the holiday season. There's music, too (tel. 202/224-3069). Free.*

✪ *National Christmas Tree Lighting and Pageant of Peace* *Every year on the Ellipse (between the White House and Constitution Avenue) one or more members of the First Family throws the switch that lights the nation's blue spruce Christmas tree and 57 Scotch Pine siblings, representing the 50 states, the District of Columbia, and the six U.S. territories. Musical and choral performances take place every evening except Christmas through December 30. (tel. 202/619-7222). Free.*

☐ **U.S. Navy Band Holiday Concert** A free concert awaits all holiday revelers at D.A.R. Constitution Hall, 1776 D St. NW (tel. 202/433-6090). Free, but reservations are required.

☐ **U.S. Botanic Garden's Christmas Poinsettia Show** See more than 3,000 poinsettias in red, white, pink, and peppermint nestled in a holiday wonderland of wreaths and trees (tel. 202/225-7099). Free.

✪ *Children's Hanukkah Festival* *Games, music, entertainment, and food light up the B'nai B'rith Klutznick Museum, 1640 Rhode Island Ave. NW (tel. 202/857-6583). Admission.*

✪ *Kennedy Center Holiday Celebrations* *Since its opening in 1971, the Kennedy Center has been celebrating the holidays in grand style. The festivities include a "Messiah" Sing-A-Long, Hanukkah Festival, Christmas Eve and New Year's Eve programs, and concerts by local children's choruses (tel. 202/467-4600). Many events are free.*

✪ *White House Christmas Candlelight Tours* *See the White House all dressed up in mistletoe and holly. Maybe you'll catch First Dog Millie leaving a note for Santa. Show up early at the East Gate on East Executive Avenue NW or you'll be left out in the cold (tel. 202/456-2200). Free.*

3. WHAT TO PACK

FOR YOU Washingtonians are less formal than they used to be, thank heavens, but since this *is* the nation's capital, a bit of decorum is prescribed when it comes to dress. You needn't run out and buy a new wardrobe, however, unless you're a nudist. Any time of the year casual clothes—jeans, sweatsuits, and your most comfortable walking shoes—are acceptable for sightseeing. If you're planning on dining in an elegant restaurant, include something dressier. A few of the fancier places require men to wear jackets. (But why in the world would you be taking your kids to a place like that?)

It's easy to pack for summer. Bring the lightest clothing you own—cotton is infinitely preferable to polyester—and double the number of T-shirts, sport shirts, or blouses you normally wear on a summer day. Washingtonians measure the heat by the number of shirts they soak, as in: "Yesterday was a real scorcher, a three-shirter!" Leave short-shorts and tube tops at home where they belong, unless you are planning a side trip to the beach.

Fall, winter, and spring frequently blur, so prudent packing means bringing clothing that can be layered. In fall, warm weather is the rule, often lingering well into October or November. But every rule has an exception, so don't forget a jacket. In the winter, you'll need a heavy topcoat, even though a mild day occasionally surfaces, to everyone's pleasure. Some years spring sneaks by while everyone is asleep: sometimes it lasts several weeks. May 1991, a record-breaker, had about 15 days with temperatures over 90 degrees. Be prepared and bring a mix of winter and summer things.

Be sure to include a sweater or sweatshirt, no matter what the season. In summer, the overly air-conditioned public buildings and restaurants can deliver a cruel shock to your overheated system.

Since precipitation is spread fairly evenly throughout the year, follow my mother's advice and always take a raincoat. Mother knows best.

FOR THE KIDS Layering is the name of the game when it comes to packing for children. Unless you're traveling with an infant or toddler, packing for them is the same as packing for you, except their stuff takes up less space. Remind teenagers, who often insist on taking enough weekend gear to outfit an entire Third World country for a decade, that nobody in Washington has seen their clothes before, so they don't have to pack every stitch they own.

A raincoat and rain hat make sense in any season, but I suggest leaving umbrellas at home. They're a hazard and too easy to lose. Waterproof boots, warm gloves, and a hat with ear flaps are wintertime necessities.

As every parent knows: The younger the child, the more clothes he or she will mess up. Since a washer and dryer may not be handy, plan two or three outfits per day for kids under 5 and throw in a few extra shirts for good measure. Take at least one extra outfit for little ones in a carry-on bag. If all their gear is stowed in the cargo hold, overhead rack, or trunk you won't be a happy parent if you have to change a wet, smelly outfit in a hurry. Include enough diapers—and then some—to keep the baby's bottom dry until you can get to your suitcase or a store.

When traveling by plane, make sure everyone has a sweatshirt or sweater. It can get downright chilly once you're airborne, and airline blankets disappear quickly. Ask your pediatrician about oral decongestants and nasal sprays, especially if your kids have colds. Changes in cabin pressure, especially during takeoffs and landings, can cause excruciating inner-ear pain in some ultrasensitive kids.

Don't forget two laundry bags or a couple of pillowcases for dirties. Most hotels have laundry and/or dry cleaning services, but they can be costly. There are a few laundromats in D.C., but they may not be convenient to where you're staying, and watching the family wash tumble dry is probably a low-priority item on your list of things to do in Washington. Pack Woolite or fill a couple of small plastic sandwich bags with powdered laundry soap so you can do emergency wash in the sink.

4. HEALTH & OTHER PRECAUTIONS

HEALTH   If you or your children require **medication,** pack plenty, preferably in a carry-on bag. Be prepared for **motion sickness.** Make sure you have a bottle of liquid Dramamine close at hand. Kids who are fine in a car may get sick on a boat, plane, or train, and vice versa.

You'll want a **first-aid kit.** A small, basic kit is available at most pharmacies. For a more comprehensive kit, contact the American Red Cross (tel. 201/568-8787) and ask how to obtain a Top Gun EMS Kit, which is endorsed by the Red Cross. It comes in a compact easy-to-pack size, but is filled with all you'll need in most emergencies.

In addition, remember grownup- and children's-strength aspirin or Tylenol, a thermometer, cough syrup, a plastic cup, flexible straws, baby wipes, a plastic spoon, nightlight, and pacifiers.

If you or the kids wear **eyeglasses,** by all means bring backups. If extra pairs are unavailable, bring the prescriptions. You can't sightsee if you can't see!

Before you leave, get a list of your **kids' inoculations** and the dates they were administered from your pediatrician. In an emergency, you're not apt to remember this information, and your hometown doctor might be out on the golf course without a beeper.

If possible, before you leave home obtain the name of a **Washington, D.C., pediatrician** from your hometown physician or relatives or friends in the Washington area. If your child spikes a fever of 102 in the middle of the night, you won't feel like flipping through a couple of hundred unfamiliar names in the Yellow Pages.

If you are caring for someone else's child, make sure the child's parent or guardian has filled out and signed a **notarized letter** giving you the legal right to authorize medical and surgical treatment. Basically, it should say, "So-and-So has the right to authorize medical/surgical treatment after all attempts to reach parents fail." Although, according to one hospital spokesman, "No invasive treatment will be done unless a parent can be notified. In case of a life-threatening emergency, doctors will take responsibility until the parent can be notified." According to doctors and lawyers these forms will "facilitate treatment" even though they may not be legally binding. If you have custodial care of a child with divorced parents, it's wise to get forms from both parents.

If you've never taken a first-aid course or earned a Boy Scout or Girl Scout first-aid badge, pick up a copy of *A Sigh of Relief,* by Martin I. Green (Bantam Books, $14.95 in paperback). It'll tell you everything you need to know about the most common childhood emergencies and how to treat them.

SAFETY   There are a few general safety precautions that should be discussed ahead of time, and one that especially applies to sightseeing jaunts.

If You Become Separated   Discuss with your kids what they should do if they get separated from you during the trip. Some parents dress their kids in bright colors when they're sightseeing. Probably because I put the fear of God in them every time we entered a crowded museum, my kids rarely wandered off—for long. The few times they strayed, I heard them before I saw them. You may want to take a tip from preschool groups on field trips and have your very young ones wear a nametag that includes the name and phone number of your hotel.

Fire   When you check into your room, give the kids a little time to settle in before rushing off to an activity. Find the nearest fire exits and discuss the dos and don'ts of fire safety. If there isn't a card in the room describing emergency procedures, ask for one at the front desk.

5. GETTING THE KIDS INTERESTED

Successful family vacations don't just happen by serendipity. If you follow these simple guidelines, your family will have a good time and fill several scrapbooks with happy memories: (1) Help your kids gather information about the nation's capital; (2) Plan ahead and allow them input in organizing your sightseeing schedule; and (3) Think small. Prioritize your sightseeing objectives, leaving time for recreational and spontaneous activities such as chasing squirrels and eating ice cream. More about this in Chapter 4, "What Kids Like to See & Do."

Preschoolers have probably learned something about Washington, D.C., from watching TV. Supplement their sketchy knowledge by purchasing a basic book about the city and reading it with them nightly. Those old enough to read and write will know it's the home of the president of the United States and they may have heard about the giant pandas in the National Zoo, but they might badger you with, "Why can't we go to Walt Disney World again instead of dumb old Washington?"

SPECIAL PROJECTS

Of course, as a family vacation destination, Washington is *anything* but boring and yucky. Your mission, should you decide to accept it, is to get your kids so fired up about the impending trip that they probably won't sleep the night before you leave home.

Here are some suggestions for accomplishing this end. First, ask them to jot down every time they see or hear something about Washington, D.C., or its residents. If they listen to the radio, watch TV, or pick up a newspaper occasionally for something other than the comics and sports scores, this will be a snap. You can discuss their lists at mealtime and "fill in the blanks." They may shock you and learn the details of the latest government scandal completely on their own.

Borrow from your local library or purchase one or more of the many books on Washington to help familiarize them with the city. Then they'll be better able to participate in planning the family's sightseeing activities. If they have a say in what they see and do, everyone will have a more enjoyable vacation.

Encourage them to write to the **Washington, D.C., Convention and Visitors' Association,** 1212 New York Ave. NW, Washington, DC 20052, for free brochures and maps. They should also read Chapter 4 "What Kids Like to See and Do" and write down the attractions that most interest them. They can request information about any of the Smithsonian's museums by writing: **Public Affairs Office, Smithsonian Institution,** Washington, DC 20560. Attention: *Name of specific museum.*

Under your supervision, the kids can also send away for maps and guidebooks. The widest selection I've ever seen is available at **Travel Books Unlimited,** 4931 Cordell

Ave., Bethesda, MD 20814 (tel. 301/951-8533). Request their catalogue, which comes with an order form. They ship worldwide and accept major credit cards. Kids love getting mail and, like adults, enjoy the excitement of anticipating and planning a vacation.

"Washington, D.C.: A Capital Adventure," part of the Video Visits series, is a marvelous 50-minute tape with drop-dead photography and well-paced, informative narration. The tape gives a wonderful overview of the city's history and major sightseeing highlights while painlessly delivering a mini-lesson in American government. It's available for rent at some video stores or by mail order for $24.95 plus shipping from Travel Books Unlimited (see above). If this doesn't whet their little travel appetites, nothing will.

6. GETTING THERE

BY PLANE

AIRPORTS The Washington, D.C., area is served by three major airports. **Washington National Airport** (National), just across the Potomac River in Virginia, is about 15–30 minutes from downtown in non-rush-hour traffic. It is the most convenient airport to downtown, but also the most congested and most difficult to get in and out of. A $775 million renovation plan is currently underway at National. New approach roads are being built, old ones are being rehabilitated, and a new main terminal with 35 gates is scheduled to open in 1995. Personally I would rather walk or fly into Dulles or Baltimore-Washington International until the construction is completed. As a spokesperson for the airport recently said, "It's going to get worse before it gets better."

Washington Dulles International Airport (Dulles), also in Virginia, and **Baltimore-Washington International** (BWI), a few miles south of Baltimore, Maryland, are each about a 45-minute ride from downtown.

AIRLINES Scheduled domestic airlines flying into Washington's three airports include: **America West** (tel. toll free 800/247-5962), **American** (tel. toll free 800/433-7300), **Continental** (tel. toll free 800/525-0280), **Delta** (tel. toll free 800/221-1212), **Midwest Express** (tel. toll free 800/452-2022), **Northwest** (tel. toll free 800/225-2525), **TransWorld Airways—TWA** (tel. toll free 800/438-2929), **USAir** (tel. toll free 800/428-4322), **United** (tel. toll free 800/241-6522), and **USAir** (tel. toll free 800/428-4322).

For a quarterly guide to flights in and out of National and Dulles, write to: **Metropolitan Washington Airports Authority,** P.O. Box 17045, Washington Dulles International Airport, Washington, DC 20041. To receive a similar guide for BWI, write to: **Maryland Aviation Administration,** Marketing and Development, P.O. Box 8766, BWI Airport, MD 21240-0766.

Typical Fares If you've flown recently, you know there is no such thing as a "typical" or "normal" fare. For every flight there are usually several fares available

FROMMER'S SMART FAMILY TRAVELER:
AIRFARES

VALUE-CONSCIOUS TRAVELERS SHOULD TAKE ADVANTAGE OF
THE FOLLOWING:

1. Shop all the airlines that fly to Washington, D.C., from your area and inquire about charters.
2. Ask for the lowest-priced fare, not just for a promotional fare. Ask about special family fares.
3. Keep calling the airline of your choice. As the departure date nears, additional low-cost seats may become available.
4. Be flexible. Getting the best price usually means flying midweek, sometimes at off-peak hours.
5. Avoid holidays and other high-traffic periods when fares are at their highest.
6. Ask airlines about their family tour packages. Land arrangements are often cheaper when booked with an air ticket.

under three main categories: first class, coach, and discount. Although visitors to Washington benefit from a wide choice of flights, they grow dizzy deciphering the ever-changing fare structure.

Generally, midweek fares ticketed a month or more in advance are the lowest. Holidays are often subject to blackout restrictions, as in "no bargains spoken here." Winter fares are usually lowest and summer fares highest. Watch for newspaper ads announcing special promotions. They pop up unexpectedly throughout the year and can save you big bucks. If you don't qualify for a promotional or other reduced fare, you could end up paying substantially more for your ticket. To get the most for your travel dollar, plan well in advance and do a bit of comparison shopping by calling the airlines or consulting an accredited travel agent.

Just what kind of savings are we talking about with advance-purchase fares? At this writing, if you flew on American, regular round-trip coach fares and lowest advance-purchase fares are as follows between Washington's National Airport and these cities:

	Regular Fare	**Advance-Purchase**
N.Y.–D.C.	$360	$138
Chicago–D.C.	$802	$178
Atlanta–D.C.	$718	$178
L.A.–D.C.	$1,434	$318
Boston–D.C.	$450	$138

By the time you read this, fares will no doubt have changed, but the vast savings for advance-purchase tickets will still hold.

Do also inquire about money-saving packages that include hotel accommodations, car rentals, tours, etc., with your airfare.

The airlines frequently offer special family fares as well. Children under 2 who do not occupy a seat usually travel free and, depending on the airline, various discounts apply to kids between the ages of 2 and 12. If you will be traveling with an infant, toddler, or active preschooler, request the seats behind the bulkhead, where you'll have more leg room and they'll have more play room, when you make your reservation. Many planes have special fittings for bassinets, and some will allow you to use your child's car seat. To find out if your particular brand of car seat is approved by the Federal Aviation Administration, request "Child/Infant Safety Seats Acceptable for Use in Aircraft" from the Community and Consumer Liaison Division, APA-400 Federal Aviation Administration, Washington, DC 20591 (tel. 202/267-3479). Also ask about special meals for the kids. The worst hamburger or hot dog should taste better than rubbery chicken.

The Shuttles To and From New York The shuttles are convenient because you can just show up, buy a ticket, and hop on the next plane out.

The **Shuttle,** which flies out of La Guardia's Marine Terminal in New York and Washington National Airport, has hourly flights leaving on the half-hour every day from 8:30am to 9:30pm, except Saturday when the last departure is at 8:30pm. The one-way fare is $142, except all day on Saturday and Sunday until 2:30pm when the fare is reduced to $92.

The **Trump Shuttle,** which runs from its own terminal at La Guardia Airport in New York to Washington National Airport, has flights leaving on the hour Monday through Friday from 7am to 9pm, and Sunday from 4 to 9pm when the one-way fare is $142; flights leave every *odd* hour on Saturday from 7am to 9pm and Sunday from 9am to 3pm when one-way fares are $92.

Check with them when you're planning your trip, however, as they sometimes have advance-purchase round-trip discount fares.

BY TRAIN

Amtrak offers daily service to Washington from several East Coast, Midwest, and West Coast cities. Travelers from the Far West change trains in Chicago. The lowest fares are usually available in winter and spring. Disabled passengers are entitled to a 25% reduction on regular one-way coach fares. Disabled children between the ages of 2 and 11 can travel for 50% of the disabled adult fare. The discount does not apply to the Metroliner. In spring 1991 the cheapest round-trip fare between New York and Washington was $89 (every day but holidays) for an unreserved seat at off-peak times. At peak times, a round-trip ticket was $124. On the faster, more streamlined Metroliner, with reserve seating, the fare was $79 each way.

Between Boston and Washington the regular round-trip excursion fare was $115; between Chicago and Washington, $156. Kids up to the age of 15 pay half the lowest available coach fare when accompanied by a passenger 18 or older, and every adult passenger is allowed two children's fare tickets.

For information and reservations, call Amtrak (tel. toll free 800/872-7245). Amtrak also offers a plan whereby travelers arrive by rail and return by air. Savings are about 30% off the regular one-way fares for each leg. Recently renovated **Union Station,** at Massachusetts Avenue and North Capitol Street, a stone's throw from the Capitol, connects Amtrak with Metro's rapid rail service to other areas of the District and the Maryland and Virginia suburbs.

Many Amtrak trains also stop at the New Carrollton Station in Lanham, Maryland, about 10 minutes by rail and 20 minutes by car from Union Station. Long-term parking is available at New Carrollton. If you're staying in the Maryland suburbs, this may be more convenient than Union Station.

Maryland Rural Commuter System (MARC) operates trains between Union Station in Washington, BWI Airport, and downtown Baltimore Monday through Friday (tel. toll free 800/325-RAIL).

Between New York and Washington, Amtrak (which has stations in New Jersey, Pennsylvania, Delaware, and Maryland) is still the most efficient means of transportation, despite some disappointments.

Kids enjoy train travel because it is less confining than a car or plane, and it's fun visiting the snack bar. You may want to consider giving your children a food allowance to last the entire trip, so they don't bug you every few minutes.

BY BUS

Greyhound/Trailways buses connect just about the entire country with Washington, D.C. They pull in at a terminal at 1st and L streets NE (tel. 202/565-2662). The closest Metro station is Union Station, four blocks away. The bus terminal area is not what you'd call a showplace neighborhood, so a taxi is advisable.

Fare structure on these buses is a little more complex, not always based on distance traveled. For instance, the regular round-trip fare at this writing between Washington and Chicago ($98.70) is less than the discounted seven-day advance purchase fare ($125.10) between Washington and Atlanta. The good news is that when you call Greyhound/Trailways to make a reservation, they'll always give you the lowest fare options. Do call in advance, once again, since some discount fares require advance purchase. Others, such as the current round-trip fare between New York and Washington ($47.50), restrict departure times in both cities. (Regular N.Y.-D.C. round-trip fare is $77.) The "Moneysaver" ticket allows travel between any two cities for $68 one way or $136 round trip with a 30-day advance purchase.

BY CAR

Most visitors arrive in Washington by car. Although a car is necessary if you wish to take excursions to many points outside the city, it can be a real liability in the downtown area. Washington's streets are congested and its drivers—many of whom learned to drive elsewhere or not at all—follow many different rules of the road. The result can be less than pleasant. In addition, parking in most sectors is expensive and/or nonexistent. If your sightseeing plans are restricted to the city and close-in environs, consider leaving the family buggy at home. You'll have a far better time. The District's efficient subway system will transport your brood to within a short walk of all the major attractions.

If you have to drive, arm yourself with a decent map, highlight the route with a yellow marking pen, and familiarize yourself with the major arteries before you leave home. Lesson I: The **Capital Beltway** (hereinafter known as the Beltway) encircles Washington and has 56 interchanges that intersect with all the major approach routes to the city. The eastern segment of the Beltway is part of **I-95**, which joins Baltimore, Maryland, to the north and Richmond, Virginia, to the south. The rest of the Beltway is designated **I-495**. Fortunately, legislation is being pushed through to set up dual I-95/I-495 signs along the I-95 portion. People have been known to drive the entire 66 miles of the Beltway before realizing their mistake. Don't be one of them. Study your map!

North of the city, **I-270** links the Maryland suburbs with **I-70** at Frederick. To the southwest, **I-66** and **U.S. 50** connect with the Virginia segment of I-495. If you're a member of **AAA**, request a Trip-Tik and other pertinent information (tel. 800/763-6600 or 703/222-6000) before you depart.

To help you plan your car trip, here are some approximate driving distances (in miles) from several cities:

Atlanta	634	Montréal	544
Boston	471	Miami	1,070
Chicago	712	New York	236
Los Angeles	2,727	Pittsburgh	251

Be sure to stop at least every hour or two so everyone can stretch, grab a few deep breaths of fresh air, have a snack, and make a pit stop. You know how hard it is for you to be cooped up in one position for a long time? Well, it's twice as hard for them.

KEEPING THE KIDS ENTERTAINED

Keeping kids entertained while traveling can be a challenge, especially if the trip is long and they are cold, hot, hungry, tired, restless, or just plain ornery. So pack a few age-appropriate toys, games, artsy-craftsy items, and books. If you're traveling with toddlers, be sure to bring their favorite stuffed animal or security blanket. Between naps and feedings, a couple of small dolls or toys without sharp edges *should* amuse a wee one—that and climbing all over everything within a six-mile radius. I've heard that the motion of riding in a car, train, or plane lulls little children to sleep. Unfortunately, my kids didn't know this until they were about three years old. I hope you are luckier. If not, try bribing them with a snack or toy, then turn up the volume on your Walkman and tough it out.

Most school-age kids are easier to deal with and are content with a bag of crayons, colored pencils, or non-permanent markers, and plenty of paper. Depending on the child's age, supplement the art supplies with some of the following: books, magnetic games, Colorforms, write-and-wipe boards, cassette tapes, travel-size board games, and a deck of cards. Forget jigsaw puzzles and games with lots of little pieces. If they're really bored, you can always regale them with a story about your youth. Guaranteed they'll fall asleep in two minutes.

Interest older kids in starting a travel diary. All it takes is a blank notebook and pen. Traveling with teenagers? You don't have to entertain them. You're not even supposed to act like you know them. They'll probably be hooked up to some kind of offensive noise before you've backed out of the driveway.

Let kids pack their very own entertainment bag or backpack. They'll learn to be selective if you limit what they can bring, either by the number of items or tonnage. Parents may want to tuck something new in a carry-on case for when the kids tire of what they've brought from home.

Even if you forget the crayons, books, and video games, you'll be forgiven *if* you have food. Don't travel *anywhere* without food, even if you're just driving from Baltimore. Easily stowable snacks such as nuts, fruit, pretzels or chips, and juice will keep a hungry or irritable crew from mutiny. Eating en route gives everyone something to do and helps pass the time. This is no time to count calories. You're on vacation. If there's a chance you'll miss a meal en route (and who among us has traveled and not missed a meal?), take sandwiches. They don't have to be fancy but, believe me, your family will think you're Mother Teresa for remembering. Pack perishables in a small plastic cooler and toss in some of those cute little artificial ice cubes.

CHAPTER 2

GETTING TO KNOW WASHINGTON, D.C.

1. **ORIENTATION**
- **NEIGHBORHOODS IN BRIEF**
2. **GETTING AROUND**
- **FAST FACTS: WASHINGTON, D.C.**

Welcome! You and your family are about to embark on an adventure in one of the most exciting and scenic cities in the world. No matter what your hailing port is, sometime during your stay you will no doubt want to adopt Washington as a second home. And what a home it is, with decor inspired by the likes of Washington, Jefferson, and Lincoln. The city's style is clearly eclectic as Old South mixes with high-tech; marble and granite blend with cherry blossoms and magnolias; ethnic festivals mix with presidential inaugurals; and the nation's history bumps noses with tomorrow's headlines. Have fun discovering with your children the many facets of the captivating, inspiring, and enchanting city that is Washington, D.C.

1. ORIENTATION

ARRIVING

BY PLANE If you're arriving by commercial airline, you will land at one of Washington's three major airports.

From Washington National Airport (National) in Virginia. Be fore-warned that a massive renovation is ongoing until at least 1995. During construction in and around National, the "normal" 15-minute ride into town in non–rush-hour traffic could take a half hour or more.

Taxi service fares are based on a zone system within the District and on mileage when you cross into Maryland or Virginia, so fares will vary according to distance. For example, if you are staying at the White House (lucky you!), the fare is $6.80 for the first passenger, $1 for each additional person, plus a $1 gate fee (charged to all taxi drivers at National). One child under 5 rides free with a person 16 or older. The fare for two adults and two kids (over 5) would be $10.80. There is rarely a shortage of cabs, but the lines of people waiting to get into them sometimes stretch to the end of the main runway.

Note: Moe Harmon, supervisor for taxi rates at the Washington Metropolitan Area Transit Commission warns visitors that many unlicensed drivers hustle and rip off passengers at National. For this reason, he suggests you take a D.C.- or Virginia-licensed cab. To protect yourself, before you pull away from the curb: (1) Look for the driver's photo identification card; if it's not visible and the driver hesitates to provide it, get out and try another cab. (2) State your destination and request a receipt *with mileage* and other pertinent information. When exiting the cab, check the information on the receipt and note the cab number on the door. You'll need this information should you wish to lodge a complaint against a fraudulent driver. "Don't trust anyone!" Moe advises. Call 331-1671 to report any problems.

Some hotels provide **shuttle service.** Check to see if yours is one of them. Trains on **Metro's Blue and Yellow lines** stop at National. The station is a 5- to 10-minute walk from the main terminal, a little less from the North Terminal. If you're bogged down with baggage and babies, take the **courtesy van** from the Main Terminal to the Metro station. Despite the fact that the station is on the wrong side of a congested road, Metro is the quickest way to get to many locations in the District and beyond. Count on a 30- to 40-minute ride into D.C. To help you, maps, fares, and traveling times are posted at every stop. Trains run Monday through Friday from 5:30am to midnight; Saturday from 8am to midnight, Sunday from 10am to midnight (tel. 202/637-7000, from 6am to 11:30pm).

From Washington Dulles International Airport (Dulles) in Chantilly, Virginia, Dulles is a 45-minute ride to D.C. in optimum conditions and $35 **taxi** fare to downtown Washington. **The Washington Flyer Shuttle** provides door-to-door bus service from Dulles to the Airport Terminal Building, 1517 K St. NW, as well as to Bethesda, Maryland, the West Falls Church, Virginia Metro stop; and Washington National Airport (tel. 703/685-1400). Buses leave Dulles for downtown Washington seven days a week, every 30 minutes from 5:20am to 9:50pm. At 1517 K St. NW, passengers transfer to vans going to several hotels throughout the city. The all-inclusive price (which may be higher by the time you read this) is $14 one way, $22 round trip. Children 6 and under ride free. For late arrivals, there is an 11pm **Inter-Airport Express bus,** with an intermediary stop at Washington National Airport.

From Baltimore-Washington International Airport (BWI) Located due south of Baltimore, Maryland, BWI is about 35 miles from downtown Washington. **Taxi** fare is about $40 per family. The **Airport Connection** (tel. 301/261-1091 or 301/441-2345), operating daily (call for exact times), will whisk you to the Airport Terminal Building at 1517 K St. NW. The one-way fare is $13, round-trip is $23, free for kids 6 and under. Door-to-door service is also available from BWI to Prince George's County and Montgomery County, Maryland. Train service is available daily on **Amtrak** (tel. toll free 800/USA-RAIL) and weekdays on **MARC** (tel. toll free 800/325-RAIL) at the BWI Rail Station, 5 minutes from the airport. A **courtesy shuttle** runs weekdays between 5:20am and 11:30pm. Weekend service may be less regular.

BY TRAIN If you arrive by Amtrak, your first glimpse of Washington will be recently refurbished **Union Station,** at Massachusetts Avenue NE and North Capitol Street. The kids may want to spend their entire vacation in the station. No doubt they'd have a swell time at the food court, movies, shops, and restaurants,

Union Station is well located near the U.S. Capitol, there's Metro service right in the building, and taxis are plentiful. The grand scale of the station, so beautifully restored, does much to heighten the excitement of arrival.

BY BUS The terminal for **Greyhound/Trailways** is at First and L streets NE (tel. 202/289-5155; 301/565-2662 for schedules and fares). The Union Station Metro is four blocks away. Call me timid, but I love life and the neighborhood leaves something to be desired, so I wouldn't go strolling around here. In fact, to play it safe, consider taking a taxi to your hotel.

BY CAR Have a decent map and a preplanned route to your hotel if you're planning to arrive by car. You may find the usually warm and helpful natives less than hospitable if you're crawling along in the left lane while trying to figure out whether you're in Maryland, Virginia, or Iowa. If you're lost, take the nearest exit and pull into a shopping center, gas station, or fast-food restaurant and ask for assistance. A spokesperson at AAA advises against pulling off the road, except in an emergency. On many of the area's highways—especially the Capital Beltway (Beltway)—the shoulders are often dangerously narrow, so take a few extra minutes and arrive safely.

Whether you are arriving from the north (I-270, I-95, I-295); south (I-95, Route 1, Route 301); east (Route 50/301, Route 450), or west (Route 7, Route 50, I-66, Route 29/211), you will run into the Beltway, whether you like it or not. The 66-mile road encircles Washington, D.C. The eastern segment of the Beltway is part of I-95. To confuse you, the rest is known as I-495, but, mercifully, plans are afoot to change the signs to I-495/I-95. Before you leave home, make sure you have directions from the intersection of the Beltway and whichever interstate or road you will be traveling to your destination. You don't want to spend your vacation riding the Beltway. There's no room service and not much of a view.

At some hotels parking is included in the room rate. Find out ahead, or you may be unpleasantly surprised by having to shell out up to $15 a day. Also ask if there is a reparking charge every time you use the car.

TOURIST INFORMATION

PRINT INFORMATION

In downtown Washington, the **Visitor Information Center,** 1455 Pennsylvania Ave. NW (tel. 202/789-7038), has a wide selection of maps and brochures listing restaurants, attractions, activities, and accommodations. Hours are Monday through Saturday, 9am to 5pm. Also check the front section of the C & P Telephone book *Yellow Pages;* its more than 30 pages of valuable information and maps will help you get your bearings.

If you need help sorting out mixed-up tickets, retrieving lost baggage, or locating lost family members, the **Travelers Aid Society** will come to the rescue. Besides maintaining desks at all the airports and Union Station, a central office at 512 C St. NE is open weekdays from 9am to 5pm. An emergency phone line operates 24 hours a day (tel. 202/546-3120).

To find out what's going on day by day, see Washington's two daily newspapers, *The Washington Post* (the Thursday "Weekly" section and Friday "Weekend" section are especially helpful) and *The Washington Times. City Paper,* a spirited weekly, is published every Thursday and is available at downtown shops and restaurants. *Jewish Week* comes out every Thursday. If you're staying in the suburbs, the Friday *Journal Newspapers* (no relation to the *Wall Street Journal),* is full of things to do and see.

The *Washingtonian,* a popular monthly magazine, lists area events, previews major happenings, and reviews restaurants, besides providing the lowdown on "inside" Washington.

A calendar of Smithsonian exhibits and activities for the coming month appears during the third week of each month in *The Washington Post.*

TELEPHONE RECORDINGS & INFORMATION (*Note:* Washington's 202 area code is not needed if you are in D.C.)

> Convention & Visitors Association (tel. 789-7000)
> Dial-a-Museum (tel. 357-2020)
> Dial-a-Phenomenon (tel. 357-2000)
> National Archives (tel. 523-3000)
> Recreation and Parks (tel. 673-7660)
> Tourist Information (tel. 737-8866)

CITY LAYOUT

Depending on their ages and interests, kids will easily recognize the shape of the District of Columbia as resembling a marquise diamond, a kite, or a baseball diamond with a big chunk missing between third base and home.

The District was originally laid out on a grid, and if you pay attention to a few general rules, you should have little difficulty finding your way around. It will help enormously if you consult a map while digesting the following.

The U.S. Capitol marks the center of the city, which is divided into quadrants: **Northeast (NE), Northwest (NW), Southeast (SE),** and **Southwest (SW).** All addresses are followed by one of the four designations. Pay attention to them, as the same address can (and often does) appear in all four quadrants of the city. Most tourist attractions are either in NW or SW.

MAIN ARTERIES & STREETS **North Capitol Street** and **South Capitol Street** run north and south, respectively, from the Capitol. **East Capitol Street**—you guessed it—divides the city north and south. Here the plot thickens. Instead of West Capitol Street lies the area known as the **National Mall.** The north side of the Mall is Constitution Avenue, the south side is Independence Avenue.

Lettered Streets above and below (north and south if you prefer) East Capitol Street run east and west and are named **alphabetically,** beginning with A Street. Just to keep things interesting, there is no B or J Street, although Constitution Avenue on the north side of the Mall and Independence Avenue on the south side are the equivalent of B Street. After W Street, one-syllable, two-syllable, and three-syllable street names come into play. There are many exceptions, however, but don't lose sleep over them. Chances are your travels won't take you into three-syllable territory very often.

Numbered streets run north and south, so, theoretically at least, there's a 1st Street (NE and SE; NW and SW) on either side of the Capitol. Here comes the fun part. Radiating from the Capitol, like so many wheel spokes, are a bunch of **avenues**

bearing state names. They slice diagonally through the numbered and lettered streets, creating a host of circles and sometimes havoc. If you're new in town, it is possible to drive several times around these circles before finding the continuation of the street you were on.

The primary artery is **Pennsylvania Avenue,** scene of parades, inaugurations, and other splashy events. Pennsylvania runs northwest between the Capitol and the White House. In the original plan, the president was supposed to have an uninterrupted view of the Capitol Building from the White House. But Andrew Jackson placed the Treasury Building between the White House and the Capitol, blocking off the presidential vista. Pennsylvania Avenue continues on a northwest angle to Georgetown from the White House.

Constitution Avenue, paralleled to the south most of the way by **Independence Avenue,** runs east-west flanking the U.S. Capitol and the Mall with its many major museums (and important government buildings to the north and south), the Washington Monument, the Ellipse and the White House to the north, on past the Reflecting Pool to the Lincoln Memorial and the Potomac River.

Washington's longest avenue, **Massachusetts Avenue,** runs north of and parallel to Pennsylvania. Along the way you'll find Union Station and Dupont Circle, central to the area known as Embassy Row. Farther out are the Naval Observatory (the vice president's residence is on the premises), Washington National Cathedral, and American University. Then Massachusetts Avenue just keeps going, right into Maryland.

Connecticut Avenue, running more directly north, starts at Lafayette Square directly facing the White House. It's the city's Fifth Avenue, the boulevard with elegant eateries, posh boutiques, and expensive hotels.

Wisconsin Avenue, from the point where it crosses M Street, is downtown Georgetown. Antique shops, trendy boutiques, discos, restaurants, and pubs all vie for attention. Yet somehow Georgetown manages to keep its almost-European charm.

FINDING AN ADDRESS Finding an address in Washington, D.C., is easy. In any four-digit address, the first two digits indicate the nearest lower-numbered cross street. For example, 1750 K Street, NW is between 17th and 18th streets in the northwest quadrant of the city. In a three-digit address, look at the first digit. A restaurant at 620 H Street, NW would be between 6th and 7th streets.

Finding an address on a numbered street is a little stickier. Your kids may want to remove their socks when they run out of fingers in this exercise. Suppose you're looking for 808 17th Street NW. First, you must assume that the addresses between A and B streets are numbered in the 100s, between B and C in the 200s, C and D in the 300s, and so on. Following this line of reasoning, the first digit in 808 signifies eight letters or blocks away from A Street. I am not making this up, so start counting! If you come up with H, you're a winner, as 808 17th Street is between H and I streets. This will become a game to your kids, who will find your destination while you're still deciding which part of the city you're in. My own kids think I fabricated this entire section. They have been finding their way around D.C. for years with two magic words "Where is . . . ?"

NEIGHBORHOODS IN BRIEF

To help you get acquainted with the city, the following alphabetical rundown will give you a fix on Washington's major sightseeing areas.

Adams-Morgan Centered around 18th Street and Columbia Road NW, colorful, vibrant, multiethnic Adams-Morgan is host to many international shops and restaurants. Whether you hunger for Ethiopian, Italian, Latin American, or practically any other cuisine, family appetites will be well satisfied. You'll encounter fewer briefcases and button-down shirts and minds than in any other sector of the city. Parking, however, is a problem.

Capitol Hill Known affectionately as "the Hill," this area encompasses more than the awe-inspiring U.S. Capitol. Bounded by the western side of the Capitol to the west, H Street NE to the north, RFK Stadium to the east, and the Southwest Freeway to the south, it is home to the Library of Congress, the Folger Shakespeare Library, Union Station, the Botanic Garden, and, especially for the kids, the Capital Children's Museum. The restaurants are especially kid-friendly.

Downtown Critics like to argue that Washington has no downtown. See for yourself the area centered around Connecticut and K streets NW that extends east to about 7th Street, west to 22nd Street, north to P Street, and south to Pennsylvania Avenue. The heart of the business community beats here, and you'll find such diverse attractions as the White House, downtown department stores and boutiques, Chinatown, the Convention Center, street vendors hawking everything from soft pretzels to designer knock-offs, and many of the city's finest restaurants.

Dupont Circle Surrounding the Dupont Circle Park, known for its fountain, pigeons, and ongoing chess games, at the intersection of Connecticut and Massachusetts avenues NW, lies an area colored by the many artists and free spirits who reside there. Several of the city's best known art galleries, diverse restaurants, interesting shops, and bookstores abound. It's a great place for browsing and people watching.

Foggy Bottom Once an industrial center, Foggy Bottom lies west of the White House, stretching about 10 blocks to the foot of Georgetown. Pennsylvania Avenue and Constitution Avenue are its northern and southern perimeters, and the area features beautifully restored historic homes on quiet tree-lined streets. Foggy Bottom derives much of its panache and cosmopolitan flavor from the Kennedy Center for the Performing Arts and George Washington University.

Georgetown Long a favorite tourist draw, this bustling area that was once a prosperous tobacco port centers around Wisconsin and M streets NW. Visitors are drawn to Georgetown's historic homes, fine stores and restaurants, C & O Canal, pre-Revolutionary Old Stone House, and magnificent Dumbarton Oaks Gardens and Museum. One of the reasons for all the bustling here is the presence of the Georgetown University campus. Walk, bike, or take a boat ride on the canal—all popular warm-weather respites.

The Mall Your kids will think you're crazy when you tell them they can't buy anything at this "Mall." They can, however, visit several of the Smithsonian museums, the Hirshhorn, the Lincoln Memorial, Washington Monument, Vietnam Veterans' Memorial, and take a ride on an antique carousel. This lush parklike parcel between the Capitol and Lincoln Memorial attracts kite fliers, joggers, frisbee-tossers, polo players, and picnickers.

2. GETTING AROUND

BY PUBLIC TRANSPORTATION

Getting around Washington is child's play—with one exception. Unless you absolutely have to, don't drive to D.C., because you're apt to waste precious time crawling through Washington's heavily trafficked downtown streets. There is little commercial parking in the Smithsonian/Mall area and, when it's available, it's very expensive. Washington's Metrorail subway system is so reliable, efficient, clean, and quiet—it's even carpeted!—your kids may want to spend their whole visit riding underground. With many of the major sightseeing attractions close to one another, your own two feet are often the best means of transportation. Besides, walking is the one sure way to savor small, unexpected sights that you might otherwise miss.

DISCOUNT PASSES

For $6 Metro offers a **Family Tourist Pass,** a package of four passes good for bus or rail travel all day on Saturday, Sunday, or holidays (but not July 4). The Family Tourist Pass, sold up to one month in advance of its use, is available at Metro Center, 13th and G Streets NW, at selected hotels, and at several Metro stations from the Quick Fares 'N Stamps vendors (tel. 202/637-7000). Kids 4 and under always ride free on Metro. Senior citizens (65 and older) and handicapped persons with valid proof ride Metrorail and Metrobus for a reduced fare.

FOR DISABLED VISITORS

Washington welcomes with open arms and relatively few obstacles visitors with physical disabilities. Most of the museums, monuments, and public buildings—as well as many theaters and restaurants—are accessible to the disabled. Metro, the public transportation system, is rated among the nation's best for accommodating the disabled. Call for information (tel. 202/962-1245). For a copy of *A Capital City!*, which includes accessibility information for 100 attractions in the metropolitan area, write to the **Washington, D.C., Convention and Visitors Association,** 1212 New York Ave. NW, Washington, DC 20005 (tel. 202/789-7000). For additional information and a copy of *Access Washington,* call the **Information Center for Handicapped Individuals** (tel. 202/347-4986).

BY SUBWAY Metrorail (Metro) is Washington's subway system. Washingtonians will tell you that the quality of life has vastly improved since Metro began operating in 1976. Nearly completed, the system's 100 miles of track blanket the metropolitan area, reaching deeply into the Maryland and Virginia suburbs. The cars, surprisingly graffiti-free, are streamlined and attractive with air-conditioning and comfortable upholstered seats. You can forget the shrill, grinding noises you may have endured in other cities' subways. Metro is quiet. With stations just two or three minutes apart, you're never more than a short walk from all the major attractions. Metro was designed with safety in mind. There are no dark nooks and crannies in the stations to shelter criminals, and Metro Transit Police (MTP) constantly monitor and patrol the trains and stations. Even if you have no reason to ride Metro during your visit, invent one for the kids' sake. It's definitely one of life's kinder, gentler rides. For

NEIGHBORHOODS IN BRIEF

CAPITOL HILL

Logan Circle

Rhode Island Ave.

DOWNTOWN

THE MALL

P St.

ADAMS-MORGAN

DUPONT CIRCLE

13th St.

13th St.

P St.

P St.

FOGGY BOTTOM

GEORGETOWN

Potomac River

Arlington

WASHINGTON, D.C.

Neighborhoods
in Brief

Adams-Morgan 3
Capitol Hill (Northeast, Southeast) 7
Downtown 6
Dupont Circle 4
Foggy Bottom (West End) 2
Georgetown 1
The Mall (Southwest) 5

All About Metro and a pocket guide write to Washington Metropolitan Area Transit Authority, 600 5th St. NW, Washington, DC 20001 (tel. 202/637-7000).

The five lines—**Red, Blue, Orange, Yellow,** and **Green**—operate Monday through Friday from 5:30am to midnight, Saturday from 8am to midnight, and Sunday from 10am to 6pm. A Saturday or Sunday schedule is usually adopted on holidays, and evening hours are sometimes extended for special events such as the Fourth of July fireworks. Trains run about every 10 minutes, more frequently during rush hour. Marking the entrance to every Metro station is a narrow brown column inscribed with the letter M. Below the M is a colored stripe or stripes that tell you which line or lines operate there. If you don't have a copy of *All About Metro*, request one from the kiosk attendant, who will answer any routing or farecard questions you may have.

Your ticket to ride is a computerized farecard from the intimidating-looking machines near the entrance. Under the distance-based fare system, you pay the minimum during non-rush hours (9:30am to 3pm weekdays and all day Saturday and Sunday) and the maximum during rush hours (5:30 to 9:30am and 3 to 7pm weekdays). The minimum fare is $1, the maximum is $3.15. Save by riding between 9:30am and 3pm and again after 7pm. Fares are posted beneath the large colored map, and the machines take nickels, dimes, quarters, $1 bills, $5 bills, $10 bills, and $20 bills. On farecards valued at $10 or more, you'll receive a 5% discount. If you arrive at a destination and your farecard comes up short, add what's necessary at an Addfare machine near the exit gate. *Warning:* Change is returned in coins. If you feed the machine a $10 bill for a $1 fare, you'll be walking around with mighty heavy pockets the rest of the day.

Because you need a farecard to enter *and* exit each station, keep it handy for reinsertion at your destination. If you will be transferring to Metrobus, pick up a transfer—good for full fare within the city and a discount on Maryland and Virginia fares—on the mezzanine level when you enter the system (*not* your destination station).

Purchase a round-trip farecard when possible to save time. On your last day in D.C., plan carefully. There are no cash refunds on amounts showing on your farecard.

The **Bike-on-Rail program** permits riders to take their bikes on Metro after 7pm Monday through Friday and all day Saturday, Sunday, and holidays (but never on July 4). You must first pass a written test to get the required $15 permit (tel. 202/962-1116).

BY BUS   You don't have to be a genius to figure out the **Metrobus** system, but it helps. The 13,000 stops on the 1,500-square-mile route (it operates on all major D.C. arteries and in the Virginia and Maryland suburbs) are indicated by red, white, and blue signs. However, the signs just tell you what buses pull into a given stop (if that), not where they go. For routing information, call 637-7000. Using a computer, a transit information agent can tell you the most efficient route from where you are to where you want to go (using bus and/or subway) almost instantly. Calls are taken daily between 6am and 11:30pm, but the line is often busy, so don't wait until the last minute to call.

If you travel the same route frequently and would like a free map and time schedule, ask the bus driver or call 637-7000 and request one. Information about free parking in Metrobus fringe lots is also available from this number.

THE METRORAIL SYSTEM

LEGEND

RED LINE: Glenmont/Shady Grove

ORANGE LINE: New Carrollton/Vienna

BLUE LINE: Addison Road/Franconia-Springfield

GREEN LINE: Branch Avenue/Greenbelt (should be completed by 1994)

YELLOW LINE: Huntington/U Street-Cardozo

Base fare in the District is $1, and transfers are free. There are additional charges for travel into Maryland and Virginia suburbs. Bus drivers are not equipped to make change, so be sure to *carry exact change or tokens.* The latter are available at 250 ticket outlets (call the above number for locations and hours of operation). If you're going to be in Washington for a while, and plan to use the buses a lot, consider a 2-week pass such as the $19 **D.C. Only Pass** good for unlimited Metrobus rides within the District and $4 worth of Metrorail rides. These are also available at ticket outlets. Others include zones in Virginia or Maryland.

Most buses operate daily just about around the clock. Service is very frequent on weekdays, especially during rush hours. On weekends, and late at night, your wait will be a bit longer.

There's a full bus information center (the Metro Sales Facility) at Metro Center Station (12th and F streets) where tokens, special bus tickets, and all else is available.

Up to two children under 5 ride free with a paying passenger on both the Metrorail and the Metrobus, and there are reduced fares for senior citizens (tel. 962-1179) and the disabled (tel. 962-1245). Finally, should you leave something on a bus, on a train, or in a station, call Lost and Found at 962-1195.

BY CAR

Within the District a car is a luxury, as public transportation is so comprehensive. It can even be an inconvenience, especially during spring and summer when traffic jams are frequent, parking spaces almost nonexistent, and parking lots ruinously expensive. But there's a great deal to see in the D.C. vicinity, and for most attractions in Virginia and Maryland you will want a car.

All the major car-rental companies are represented here. Some handy phone numbers: **Budget** (tel. 800/527-0700); **Hertz** (tel. 800/654-3131); **Thrifty** (tel. 800/367-2277); **Avis** (tel. 800/331-1212); **Alamo** (tel. 800/327-9633).

BY TAXI

Surprise! You can take taxis in Washington without busting your budget—at least in some cases. District cabs work on a zone system. If you take a trip from one point to another in the same zone, you pay just $2.60 to $3, regardless of the distance traveled. So it would cost you $3 to travel a few blocks from the U.S. Botanic Garden to the Museum of American History, the same $3 from the Botanic Garden all the way to Dupont Circle. They're both in Zone 1. Also in Zone 1 are most other tourist attractions: the Capitol, the White House, most of the Smithsonian, the Washington Monument, the FBI, the National Archives, the Supreme Court, the Library of Congress, the Bureau of Engraving and Printing, the Old Post Office, and Ford's Theatre. If your trip takes you into a second zone, the price is $4.20, $5.20 for a third zone, $6.20 for a fourth, and so on. But you're unlikely to travel more than three zones unless you're staying in some remote section of town.

So far fares are pretty low. Here's how they can add up. There's a $1.25 charge for each additional passenger after the first, so a $3 Zone 1 fare becomes $6.75 for a family of four (though one child under 6 can ride free). There's also a rush-hour surcharge of $1 per trip between 4 and 6:30pm weekdays. And there are surcharges as well for large pieces of luggage (15¢ each), for fuel (50¢ per trip), and for calling a taxi ($1.50). Tipping is up to you, but the going rate is 10% to 15% of the fare.

TAXICAB ZONES

N

LEGEND:

Zone Fares

Single Passenger and Shared Riding Rate Per Passenger

Subzone	
1 Zone	$2.60
2 Zones	3.00
3 Zones	4.20
4 Zones	5.20
5 Zones	6.20
6 Zones	7.20
7 Zones	8.20
8 Zones	9.20
	10.20

Group Rates:
$1.25 extra for each additional passenger after first passenger in group

P.M.:
Rush-hour (4:00–6:30 P.M.) Surcharge—$1.00 per trip

Radio Dispatch:
Surcharge—$1.50

NOTE: Fares are doubled during periods of snow emergency as Declared by the District of Columbia Taxicab Commission.

———— MAJOR ZONE BOUNDARIES

- - - - SUBZONE BOUNDARIES

The zone system is not used when your destination is an out-of-district address (like the airport); the fare is then based on mileage covered—$2 for the first mile or part of a mile and 60¢ for each additional half mile or part. You can call 331-1671 to find out what the rate should be between any point in D.C. and an address in Virginia or Maryland. Call 767-8370 for inquiries about fares within the District.

It's generally easy to hail a taxi; there are about 9,000 cabs, and drivers are allowed to pick up as many passengers as they can comfortably fit in (provided the new passenger doesn't take the first passenger more than five blocks out of the way). If your group is small, you can count on sharing the taxi. You can also call a taxi, though there is a charge for doing so of $1.50. Try **Diamond Cab Company** (tel. 387-6200), **Yellow Cab** (tel. 544-1212), or **Capitol Cab** (tel. 546-2400). They're three of the oldest and most reputable companies.

For a copy of "The Consumer Guide to Taxicabs," write to the **D.C. Taxicab Commission,** 2041 Martin Luther King Jr. Ave. SE, Washington, DC 20020 (tel. 767-8380). If you have a complaint, note the driver's name and cab number and call the **Taxicab Complaint Office** (tel. 727-5401).

BY TOURMOBILE

If you're visiting Washington for the first time, consider the Tourmobiles—open-air blue-and-white sightseeing trams that run on routes along the Mall and as far out as Arlington Cemetery and even (with coach service) Mount Vernon.

You may take the Washington and Arlington Cemetery tour or tour Arlington Cemetery only. The former visits 15 different sights on or near the Mall and three sights at Arlington Cemetery: the gravesites of the Kennedy brothers, the Tomb of the Unknowns, and Arlington House.

Here's how the Tourmobile system works. You may board vehicles at 15 different locations:

The White House
The Washington Monument
The Arts & Industries Building
The National Air and Space Museum
Union Station
The Capitol
The National Gallery of Art
The Museum of Natural History
The Museum of American History
The Bureau of Engraving and Printing
The Jefferson Memorial
West Potomac Park (free parking here)
The Kennedy Center
The Lincoln Memorial
Arlington National Cemetery (including the Tomb of the Unknowns, the Kennedy gravesites, and Arlington House)

You pay the driver when you first board the trams. Along the route, you may get off at any stop to visit monuments or buildings. When you finish exploring each area, you

step aboard the next Tourmobile that comes along without extra charge. The trams travel in a loop, serving each stop every 20 to 30 minutes. One **fare** allows you to use the trams for a full day. The cost is $8.50 for adults, $4 for children 3 to 11. For Arlington only, adults pay $2.75; children, $1.25. Trams follow "figure-8" circuits from the Capitol to Arlington and back. Children under 3 ride free always. Between June 15 and Labor Day you can also buy a ticket after 4pm good for the rest of the afternoon and the following day ($10.50 for adults, $5 for children); the rest of the year the same offer pertains after 2pm. Well-trained narrators give commentaries about sights along the route and will answer your questions. It's an ideal way to cover a lot of ground comfortably, especially with kids in tow.

Tourmobiles operate year round on the following schedules. From June 15 through Labor Day, they ply the Mall between 9am and 6:30pm. After Labor Day, hours are 9:30am to 4:30pm. From Arlington, between October and March, they start at 8am and end at 5pm. April through September, the hours are 8am to 7pm.

For further Tourmobile information, call 554-7950.

Tourmobile also runs round-trip tours to Mount Vernon from April to October. Coaches depart from the Arlington National Cemetery Visitors Center at 10am, noon, and 2pm, and from the Washington Monument at 10:15am, 12:15pm, and 2:15pm. The price is $16.50 for adults, $8 for children, including admission to Mount Vernon. A combination tour of Washington, Arlington Cemetery, and Mount Vernon is $25.50 for adults, $12.50 for children—much cheaper than the Gray Line equivalent. Another offering is the **Frederick Douglass National Historic Site Tour,** including a guided tour of Douglass's home, Cedar Hill. Departures are from the same points as the Mount Vernon tour, at 10am. Adults pay $5; children, $2.50. A 2-day **Combination Frederick Douglass Tour and Washington-Arlington Cemetery Tour** is also available at $16.50 for adults, $8 for children. For both the Mount Vernon and Frederick Douglass tours you must reserve at least an hour in advance.

OLD TOWN TROLLEY TOURS

A service similar to Tourmobile's is Old Town Trolleys, in operation since 1986. For a fixed price, you can get on and off these green and orange open-air vehicles as many times as you like at 12 locations (listed below) in the District. Most of the stops are at or near major sightseeing attractions, including Georgetown. The trolleys operate 7 days a week between 9am and 4pm. Cost is $14 for adults, $5 for ages 5 to 12, under 5 free. The full tour, which is narrated, takes 90 minutes, and trolleys come by every 15 to 30 minutes. The following stops are made:

Union Station
Hyatt Regency Hotel (near U.S. Capitol and Mall)
Pavilion at the Old Post Office
Grand Hyatt (near Ford's Theatre)
J. W. Marriott (near the White House)
Capital Hilton (near the National Geographic Society)
Washington Hilton (near Phillips Collection)
Sheraton Washington (near National Zoo)
Georgetown Park Mall

Lincoln Memorial
Holiday Inn Capitol Hill (near Air and Space)
U.S. Capitol

Tickets can be purchased at all stops except the Lincoln Memorial. For details, call 269-3020.

FAST WASHINGTON, D.C.

American Express There is an **American Express Travel Service** office downtown at 1150 Connecticut Ave. NW (tel. 457-1300), one uptown near Chevy Chase, Md., at 5300 Wisconsin Ave. NW (tel. 362-4000), and several in the Maryland/Virginia suburbs.

Area Codes If you are calling a D.C. number from somewhere else, dial 202. If you are in D.C. and calling D.C., no area code is needed. In D.C., dial 301 for the close-in Maryland suburbs; 410 for Baltimore, Annapolis, and the Eastern Shore of Maryland; and 703 for suburban Virginia.

Babysitters Many hotels will secure a bonded sitter for your brood. If not, call **Sitters Unlimited** (tel. 703/250-5250), Georgetown University (tel. 687-4187), American University (tel. 885-1800), or George Washington University (tel. 994-6495). Their rates are $8 per hour, 50¢ for each additional sibling, $4 per hour for other children, plus $5 for round-trip transportation or parking fee at the hotel. There's a 4-hour minimum.

Business Hours Most **business offices** are open from 8:30 or 9am to 5 or 5:30pm. Federal government office hours are staggered, with some agencies beginning work before sun-up. **Banks** are usually open Monday through Friday, from 9am to 2pm. Some are also open Saturday from 9am until noon. Most **shops** open at 9:30 or 10am and close at 6pm. A large number, especially those in malls, remain open until 9pm or later, and some extend their hours during the Christmas holidays and in the summer.

Congresspersons To locate your senator or congressional representative, call the Capitol switchboard (tel. 224-3121).

Deaf Emergency Call 727-9334.

Dentist Call 1-800/DOCTORS or 723-5323. You can also call the **Dental Referral Service** at 547-7615, Mon–Fri 8am–4pm. Several dentists specializing in pedodontics (kids' dentistry) are listed in the *Yellow Pages* under "Dentists, Grouped by Practice."

Doctor **Physicians Home Services,** 2440 M St. NW (tel. 202/331-3888), makes house calls 24 hours a day and will come to your hotel if you are staying in the District. Kids who are not too sick are seen in the downtown office during regular hours. PHS accepts credit cards, travelers' checks, personal checks with adequate identification, and cash.

Drugstores For free, same-day delivery, call **Maxwell & Tennyson Pharmacy,** 916 19th St. NW (tel. 223-9797), before 10am. The **Peoples Drug Store**

chain has two 24-hour locations: 7 Dupont Circle NW (tel. 785-1466) and 14th Street and Thomas Circle, NW (tel. 628-0720). Two of Peoples' suburban all-night stores are at Bradley Boulevard and Arlington Road, Bethesda, MD (tel. 301/656-2522), and Lyon Village Shopping Center, 3133 Lee Highway, Arlington, VA (tel. 703/522-0260).

Emergencies Call **911** for fire, police, or ambulance. For poison control, call 625-3333. Also see Chapter 1, "Health and Other Precautions."

Eyeglasses For same-day service on most prescriptions, call **Atlantic Optical,** 1747 Pennsylvania Ave. NW (tel. 466-2050) or **Sterling Optical,** 520 10th St. NW (tel. 783-8310) or 1900 M St. NW (tel. 728-1041).

Hairdressers/Barbers If you want a new look and can't wait until you go home, ask your concierge to recommend a hair stylist (there are 16 pages of beauty salons in the District *Yellow Pages*). For a quick cut, wash, and blow dry that's reasonable, and no appointment is necessary, the whole family can try the **Hair Cuttery** at 1645 Connecticut Ave. NW near Dupont Circle (tel. 232-9685), 1342 G St. NW (tel. 638-8032), and four other area locations.

Hospitals In case of a life-threatening emergency, call 911. For those emergencies not requiring immediate ambulance transportation but requiring emergency-room treatment, call one of the following hospitals. To save time and aggravation, call first and get directions. You or your taxi driver may need them.

Children's Hospital National Medical Center, 111 Michigan Ave. NW (tel. 202/745-5203 for emergency room; 202/745-5000 for general information).

George Washington University Hospital, 901 23rd St. NW (tel. 202/994-3211 for emergency room; 202/994-1000 for general information).

Georgetown University Hospital, 3800 Reservoir Rd. NW (tel. 202/784-2118 for emergency room; 202/687-5050 for general information).

Howard University Hospital, 2041 Georgia Ave. NW (tel. 202/865-6100).

Providence Hospital, 1150 Varnum St. NE (tel. 202/269-7001 for emergency room; 202/269-7000 for general information).

Sibley Memorial Hospital, 5255 Loughboro Rd. NW (tel. 202/537-4080 for emergency room; 202/537-4685 for physician referral).

Washington Hospital Center, 110 Irving St. NW (tel. 202/877-6701 for emergency room; 202/877-7000 for general information).

Laundry/Dry Cleaning **Washtub Laundromat,** 1511 17th St. NW (tel. 332-9455), is a self-service coin-operated laundry. For complete laundry and dry cleaning services with pickup and delivery, contact **Bergmann's** (tel. 703/247-7600). For same-day dry cleaning service, try **MacDee Quality Cleaners** at 1639 L St. NW (tel. 296-6100) or 1822½ N St. NW (tel. 457-0555), open Monday through Saturday. Most hotels provide laundry and dry-cleaning services and/or have coin-operated laundry facilities.

Libraries The **Martin Luther King Memorial Library** at 901 G St. NW is open Sunday from 1 to 5pm., Monday through Thursday, from 9am to 9pm, Friday and Saturday from 9am to 5:30pm (tel. 727-1111). See the *Blue Pages* of the C & P Telephone book for branch library locations.

Liquor Laws Minimum drinking age is 21. Establishments can serve alcoholic beverages Mon–Thurs 8am–2am, Fri–Sat until 2:30am, and Sun 10am–2am. Liquor stores are closed on Sun.

Lost Property If you lose something on an **Amtrak** train, call Union Station (tel. 202/383-3109); on **Metro** (rail or bus), go to 1600 5th St. NW, 5th floor, room 5C (tel. 962-1195); on a **Greyhound/Trailways** bus, 1005 First St. NE (tel. 202/565-2662). If you leave something in a **taxicab,** call the individual company and give the taxi driver's name or I.D. number. Each airport and airline maintains a lost-and-found department (See Chapter 1, "Getting There," "By Plane"). If you left something in a hotel room, check with the front desk or concierge.

Newspapers and Magazines See "Tourist Information" in this chapter.

Police In an emergency, dial **911.** For a non-emergency, call 727-4326. For the location of the nearest district headquarters, call 727-1000.

Post Office The National Capital Post Office, at North Capitol Street and Massachusetts Avenue NE (tel. 523-2337), is open Monday through Saturday from 7am to midnight, Sunday from 7am to 8pm. During renovation, the entrance is at North Capitol Street and G St. NE. For the location of the post office nearest your hotel, ask at the front desk. For ZIP code information, call 682-9295.

Safety I wish I could tell you that there is no crime in Washington, but I don't want my nose to grow like Pinocchio's. Despite adverse media hype, the areas in which you'll be spending most, if not all, of your time are relatively safe. To help ensure that your family has a safe visit, stay out of dark and deserted areas and don't wander aimlessly. Always have a destination in mind. Criminals are known to prey on those who appear defenseless, so be alert to what's going on around you and walk purposefully. If your kids are very young, hold their hands. Make sure you have a plan if you are separated. Kids old enough to understand should know the name and address of their hotel.

Always lock your hotel room, car doors, and trunk. Wear a moneybelt and keep a close eye on your pocketbook, camera, and wallet. Hold onto your purse in a restaurant; don't drape it over a chair back or put it on an empty seat. When you buy something, put your money and credit cards away and secure your wallet before you go out on the street. Leave the family jewels at home, and what you do bring, don't flash.

Taxes The sales tax on merchandise is 6% in D.C., 5% in Maryland, and 4.5% in Virginia. The restaurant tax is 8% in D.C., 5% in Maryland, and 4.5% in Virginia. The hotel sales tax is 11% in D.C. plus a $1.50-per-night occupancy tax, 10% in Maryland, and 9.5% in Virginia.

Time Washington, D.C., is on Eastern Standard Time, except when Daylight Savings Time is in effect from the first Sunday in April (clocks are moved ahead one hour) to the last Sunday in October (clocks are moved back one hour). When it's noon in Washington, it's 11am in Chicago, 10am in Denver, and 9am in Los Angeles. To find out the local time, dial 844-2525.

Weather For the local weather forecast, call 936-1212. If you want the extended outlook for the area, call 899-3240.

Useful Telephone Numbers You might find the following telephone numbers useful during your stay.

Deafpride, Inc. (Voice/TTY), 675-6700
Dial-a-Museum, 357-2020
Dial-a-Park, 619-7275
Dial-a-Story, 638-5717
D.C. Rape Crisis Center, 333-7273

Metro Information, 637-7000
Smithsonian Information Center, 357-2700
Public School Information, 724-4044
Time of Day, 844-2525
Travelers' Aid, 546-3120
Visitor Information Center, 789-7038

CHAPTER 3

FOR FOREIGN VISITORS

1. PREPARING FOR YOUR U.S. TRIP

2. GETTING TO & AROUND THE U.S.

- **FAST FACTS: FOR THE FOREIGN TRAVELER**

Entering a foreign country for the first time can be bewildering at best, especially if you don't speak the language. If you're traveling with kids, your difficulties multiply. Not only do you have to deal with your own uncertainties and frustrations, but you must reassure your little ones, who may be overwhelmed by the baffling strangeness of new sights, sounds, and smells. This chapter is designed to ease your transition by answering your most immediate questions. For help in planning your visit, read Chapters 1 and 2 and share the information with your children. Knowing something about the city will help them to feel involved, lessen their anxieties, and stimulate their curiosity.

Although you're bound to feel strange at first, you won't be alone. In 1990 more than 19 million tourists from around the world visited Washington, D.C., and many who now call the nation's capital home began or spent portions of their lives elsewhere. If you have any doubt, wait until you hear all the foreign languages and accents spoken on Washington's streets. Regardless of their origins, the residents of the nation's capital are friendly and eager to help visitors. Don't be shy. Ask lots of questions, even if your English is less than perfect. You and your children are in for a real treat. Remember to put film in your camera and take a tip from the natives—"Go with the flow!"

1. PREPARING FOR YOUR U.S. TRIP

The **International Visitors Information Service (IVIS),** 733 15th Street NW, at H Street, Suite 300 (tel. 202/783-6540), is a nonprofit, community volunteer organization that provides special services to D.C.'s many visitors from abroad. Here you can talk to staff members in your own language and obtain foreign-language publications and brochures. IVIS has a language bank of volunteers who speak dozens of languages on call. They'll provide assistance with accommodations, sightseeing, dining, and other traditional tourist needs. IVIS is open weekdays from 9am to 5pm, but phones are manned 7 days a week from about 6am to 11pm.

ENTRY REQUIREMENTS

DOCUMENT REGULATIONS

Canadian citizens may enter the U.S. without visas; they need only proof of residence.

British, Dutch, French, German, Italian, Japanese, Swedish, and Swiss citizens traveling on valid national (or EC) passports do not need a visa for holiday or business travel in the U.S. of 90 days or less if they hold round-trip or return tickets and if they enter the U.S. on an airline or cruise line that participates in the no-visa travel program.

(Note that citizens of these visa-exempt countries who first enter the U.S. may then visit Mexico, Canada, Bermuda, and/or the Caribbean islands and then reenter the U.S., by any mode of transportation, without needing a visa. Further information is available from any U.S. embassy or consulate.)

Citizens of countries other than those above require:

- a valid **passport,** with an expiration date at least 6 months later than the scheduled end of the visit to the U.S.; and
- a **tourist visa,** available without charge from the nearest U.S. consulate; the traveler must submit a completed application form (either in person or by mail) with a passport photograph attached.

Usually you will be given your visa at once, or within 24 hours at most; try to avoid the summer rush from June to August. If applying by mail, enclose a large stamped, self-addressed envelope, and expect an average wait of 2 weeks. Visa application forms are also available at airline offices or from leading travel agents as well as from U.S. consulates. The U.S. tourist visa (visa B-2) is theoretically valid for a year, and for any number of entries, but the U.S. consulate that gives you the tourist visa will determine the length of stay for a multiple- or single-entry visa. However, there is some latitude here, and if you are of good appearance and can give the address of a relative, friend, or business connection living in the U.S. (useful, too, for car rental, passage through Customs, etc.), you have an excellent chance of getting a longer permit if you want one.

MEDICAL REQUIREMENTS

No inoculations are needed to enter the U.S. unless you are coming from areas known to be suffering from epidemics, especially of cholera or yellow fever.

If you or your children have a medical condition that requires treatment with a syringe or medications containing controlled substances, carry a valid signed prescription from your (or their) physician to allay any suspicions that you are smuggling drugs.

TRAVEL INSURANCE

All such insurance is voluntary in the U.S.; however, given the very high cost of medical care, I cannot too strongly advise every traveler to arrange for appropriate coverage before setting out. There are specialized insurance companies that will, for a relatively low premium, cover:

- loss or theft of your baggage;
- trip-cancellation costs;

- guarantee of bail in case you are sued;
- sickness or injury costs (medical, surgical, and hospital);
- costs of an accident, repatriation, or death.

Such packages (for example, "Europe Assistance" in Europe) are sold by automobile clubs at attractive rates, as well as by banks and travel agencies.

2. GETTING TO & AROUND THE U.S.

Travelers from overseas can take advantage of the **APEX (Advance-Purchase Excursion) fares** offered by all the major U.S. and European carriers. Aside from these, attractive values are offered by **Icelandair** on flights from Luxembourg to New York or Orlando; and by **Virgin Atlantic** from London to New York/Newark or Miami.

Some large airlines (for example, TWA, American, Northwest, United, and Delta) offer travelers on their transatlantic or transpacific flights special discount tickets under the name **Visit USA,** allowing travel between any U.S. destinations at minimum rates. They are not on sale in the U.S., and must therefore be purchased before you leave your foreign point of departure. This system is the best way of seeing the U.S. at low cost. You should obtain information well in advance from your travel agent or the office of the airline concerned, since the conditions attached to these discount tickets can be changed without advance notice.

For more information on getting to or around Washington, D.C., read "Getting There" in Chapter 1 and "Getting Around" in Chapter 2.

 FOR THE FOREIGN TRAVELER

Accommodations   See Chapter 8.

Automobile Organizations   Auto clubs will supply maps, recommended routes, guidebooks, accident and bail-bond insurance, and, most important of all, emergency road service. The leader, with 850 offices and 28 million members, is the **American Automobile Association (AAA),** with national headquarters at 1000 AAA Drive, Heathrow, FL 32745 (tel. 407/444-7000). Check telephone book for local offices. Membership for both U.S. citizens and foreign visitors ranges from $17 to $56, depending on which particular local office you join. AAA also has a 24-hour emergency toll-free number: 800/336-4357. The AAA can provide you with a "Touring Permit" validating your driving license. Members of some foreign auto clubs that have reciprocal arrangements with AAA enjoy AAA's services at no charge.

Auto Rentals   To rent a car you need a major credit card or you'll have to leave a sizable cash deposit ($100 or more for each day). Minimum driver age is usually 21, and you'll need a valid driver's license.

Shop around—rates vary from company to company, from location to location (airport vs. downtown, Florida vs. New York City). In addition, companies offer unlimited-mileage options vs. per-mile charges and also special discounts on weekends, for example. So it pays to shop around. Use the major companies' toll-free 800 numbers to do this. Other variable costs to check include drop-off charges if you're picking up the car in one city and leaving it in another, the cost of daily collision damage and personal accident insurance. And always return your car with a full tank—the rental companies charge excessive prices for gasoline.

The major companies are: **Hertz** (toll free 800/654-3131), **Avis** (toll free 800/331-1212), **National** (toll free 800/227-7368), **Budget** (toll free 800/527-0700), and **Dollar** (toll free 800/421-6868). Also check the smaller local companies and **Rent a Wreck** (toll free 800/535-1391), if there is one in a particular city.

Business Hours Public and private **offices** are usually open Mon–Fri 9am–5pm.

Banking hours are generally Mon–Fri 9am–2pm, but in some cases till 6pm on Fri, and sometimes also on Sat morning.

Post offices are open Mon–Fri 8am–5:30 or 6pm and Sat 8am–noon.

Store hours are Mon–Sat 9:30 or 10am–5:30 or 6pm, though often till 9pm one or two evenings a week. Shopping centers, drugstores, and supermarkets are open 9am–9pm 6 days a week (sometimes 7 days, and in some cases even 24 hours).

Museum hours vary widely. The norm is 10am–5:30pm 7 days a week (a few close on Mon). See Chapter 4 for details about days and hours of individual museums.

Climate See "Climate" in Chapter 1.

Currency & Exchange The U.S. monetary system has a decimal base: one **dollar** ($1) = 100 **cents** (100¢).

The commonest **bills** (all green) are the $1 ("a buck"), $5, $10, and $20 denominations. There are also $2 (seldom encountered), $50, and $100 bills (the two latter are not welcome when paying for small purchases).

There are six denominations of **coins:** 1¢(1 cent, or "penny"); 5¢ (5 cents, or "nickel"); 10¢ (10 cents, or "dime"); 25¢ (25 cents, or "quarter"); 50¢ (50 cents, or "half dollar"); and rare—and prized by collectors—the $1 piece (both the older, large silver dollars and the newer, small Susan B. Anthony coin).

Traveler's checks denominated in *dollars* are accepted without demur at hotels, motels, restaurants, and large stores. But as any experienced traveler knows, the best place to change traveler's checks is at a bank.

However, the method of payment most widely used is the **credit card:** VISA (BarclayCard in Britain, Chargex in Canada), MasterCard (EuroCard in Europe, Access in Britain, Diamond in Japan, etc.), American Express, Diners Club, and Carte Blanche, in descending order of acceptance. You can save yourself trouble by using "plastic money," rather than cash or traveler's checks, in 95% of all hotels, motels, restaurants, and retail stores. A credit card can serve as a deposit when renting a car, as proof of identity (often carrying more weight than a passport), or as a "cash card," enabling you to draw money from banks that accept them.

Note: The "foreign-exchange bureaus" so common in Europe are rare even at airports in the U.S., and nonexistent outside major cities. Try to avoid having to change foreign money, or traveler's checks denominated other than in U.S. dollars, at a small-town bank, or even a branch bank in a big city; in fact, leave any currency other than U.S. dollars at home—it may prove more nuisance to you than it's worth.

Customs & Immigration   Every adult visitor may bring in, free of duty: 1 liter of wine or hard liquor, 200 cigarettes or 100 cigars (but *no* cigars from Cuba) or 3 pounds (1.35kg) of smoking tobacco; $400 worth of gifts. These exemptions are offered to travelers who spend at least 72 hours in the U.S. and who have not claimed them within the preceding 6 months. It is altogether forbidden to bring into the country foodstuffs (particularly cheese, fruit, cooked meats, and canned goods) and plants (vegetables, seeds, tropical plants, etc.). Foreign tourists may bring in or take out up to $10,000 in U.S. or foreign currency with no formalities; larger sums must be declared to Customs on entering or leaving.

The visitor arriving by air, no matter what the port of entry—New York, Boston, Washington, D.C., Miami, Honolulu, Los Angeles, or the rest—should cultivate patience and resignation before setting foot on U.S. soil. The U.S. Customs and Immigration Services are among the slowest and most suspicious on earth. On some days, especially summer weekends, you may wait to have your passport stamped at Miami or New York's John F. Kennedy Airport for nearly 2, sometimes 3 hours. The situation is just as bad at other major international airports. Add the time it takes to clear Customs and you will see that you should make very generous allowance for delay in planning connections between international and domestic flights—an average of 2 to 3 hours at least. Make sure the kids have some small games, toys, or amusements to pass the time. Who knows, a Customs official may take pity on you for traveling with children, and whisk your family through in a jiffy.

In contrast, for the traveler arriving by car or by rail from Canada, the border-crossing formalities have been streamlined to the vanishing point. And for the traveler by air from Canada, Bermuda, and some points in the Caribbean, you can go through Customs and Immigration at the point of *departure,* which is much quicker and less painful.

Drinking Laws   As with marriage and divorce, every state, and sometimes every county and community, has its own laws governing the sale of liquor. The only federal regulation (based on a judgment of the U.S. Supreme Court on June 23, 1987) restricts the consumption of liquor in public places anywhere in the country to persons aged 21 or over (states not respecting this rule may be penalized by a withdrawal of federal highway funds). In D.C., establishments can serve alcoholic beverages Mon–Thurs 8am–2am, Fri–Sat until 2:30am, and Sun 10am–2am. Liquor stores are closed on Sun.

Electric Current   U.S. wall outlets give power at 110–115 volts, 60 cycles, compared to 220 volts, 50 cycles, in most of Europe. Besides a 110-volt converter, small appliances of non-American manufacture, such as hairdryers or shavers, will require a plug adapter with two flat, parallel pins.

Embassies & Consulates   All embassies are located in Washington, D.C., as it's the nation's capital, and many consulates are located here as well. Among the embassies here are those for **Australia,** 1601 Massachusetts Ave. NW, Washington, D.C. 20036 (tel. 202/797-3000); **Canada,** 1746 Massachusetts Ave. NW, Washington, D.C. 20036 (tel. 202/785-1400); **Ireland,** 2234 Massachusetts Ave. NW, Washington, D.C. 20008 (tel. 202/462-3939); **New Zealand,** 37 Observatory Circle NW, Washington, D.C. 20008 (tel. 202/328-4800); **United Kingdom,** 3100 Massachusetts Ave. NW, Washington, D.C. 20008 (tel. 202/462-1340). You can get the telephone numbers of other embassies and consulates by calling "Information" in Washington, D.C. (dial 411 within D.C.'s 202 area code; elsewhere, dial 1/202/555-1212). Or consult the phone book you'll find in your hotel room.

Emergencies In Washington, D.C., as in all major cities you can call the police, an ambulance, or the fire brigade through the single emergency telephone number **911.** For a deaf emergency, dial 727-9334; for a non-emergency situation, dial the police at 727-4326. Another useful way of reporting an emergency is to call the telephone-company operator by dialing **0** (zero, *not* the letter "O"). Outside major cities, call the local police department or the fire brigade at the number you will find in the local telephone book.

If you encounter such travelers' problems as sickness, accident, or lost or stolen baggage, it will pay you to call **Travelers' Aid,** 1015 12th St. NW (tel. 347-0101), an organization that specializes in helping distressed travelers, whether American or foreign.

Gasoline [Petrol] One U.S. gallon equals 3.75 liters, while 1.2 U.S. gallons equals one imperial gallon. You'll notice there are several grades (and price levels) of gasoline available at most gas stations. And you'll also notice that their names change from company to company. The unleaded ones with the highest octane are the most expensive (most rental cars take the least expensive "regular" unleaded) and leaded gas is the least expensive, but only older cars can take this any more, so check if you're not sure.

Holidays On the following legal national holidays, banks, government offices, post offices, and many stores, restaurants, and museums are closed:

January 1 (New Year's Day)
Third Monday in January (Martin Luther King Day)
Third Monday in February (Presidents Day, Washington's Birthday)
Last Monday in May (Memorial Day)
July 4 (Independence Day)
First Monday in September (Labor Day)
Second Monday in October (Columbus Day)
November 11 (Veterans' Day/Armistice Day)
Last Thursday in November (Thanksgiving Day)
December 25 (Christmas Day)

Finally, the Tuesday following the first Monday in November is Election Day, and is a legal holiday in presidential-election years.

Individual listings in the appropriate chapters will tell you when an establishment is closed.

Legal Aid The foreign tourist, unless positively identified as a member of the Mafia or of a drug ring, will probably never become involved with the American legal system. If you are pulled over for a minor infraction (for example, of the highway code, such as speeding), never attempt to pay the fine directly to a police officer; you may wind up arrested on the much more serious charge of attempted bribery. Pay fines by mail, or directly into the hands of the clerk of the court. If accused of a more serious offense, it is wise to say and do nothing before consulting a lawyer. Under U.S. law, an arrested person is allowed one telephone call to a party of his choice. Call your embassy or consulate.

Mail If you want your mail to follow you on your vacation, you need only fill out a change-of-address card at any post office. The post office will also hold your mail for up to 1 month. If you aren't sure of your address, your mail can be sent to you, in your name, **c/o General Delivery** at the main post office of the city or region where you expect to be. The addressee must pick it up in person, and produce proof of identity (driver's license, credit card, passport, etc.). In D.C., mail can be sent to you for up to a 30-day period c/o General Delivery, Washington, DC Post Office, 900 Brentwood Rd. NE, Washington, DC 20066-9998, USA (tel. 682-9595).

Generally to be found at intersections, mailboxes are blue with a red-and-white stripe, and carry the inscription "U.S. MAIL." If your mail is addressed to a U.S. destination, don't forget to add the five-figure postal code or ZIP (Zone Improvement Plan) code, after the two-letter abbreviation of the state to which the mail is addressed (CA for California, MA for Massachusetts, NY for New York, and so on).

D.C.'s main post office (tel. 523-2628) is located opposite Union Station at Massachusetts Ave. and N. Capitol St. It's open weekdays 7am–midnight, Sat–Sun until 8pm.

Newspapers/Magazines National newspapers include the *New York Times, USA Today,* the *Wall Street Journal* and the *Christian Science Monitor.* There are also innumerable national news weeklies including *Newsweek, Time, U.S. News & World Report.* **Newsroom,** 1753 Connecticut Ave. NW.

Foreign newspapers and magazines are available at **Periodicals,** 3109 M St. NW.

Radio & Television Audiovisual media, with three coast-to-coast networks—ABC, CBS, and NBC—joined in recent years by the Public Broadcasting System (PBS) and the cable network CNN, play a major part in American life. In big cities like Washington, D.C., televiewers have a choice of about a dozen channels (including the UHF channels), most of them transmitting 24 hours a day, without counting the pay-TV channels showing recent movies or sports events. All options are usually indicated on your hotel TV set. You'll also find a wide choice of local radio stations, each broadcasting talk shows and/or a particular kind of music—classical, country, jazz, pop, gospel—punctuated by news broadcasts and frequent commercials.

Safety Whenever you're traveling in an unfamiliar city, stay alert. Be aware of your immediate surroundings. Wear a moneybelt—or better yet, check valuables in a safe-deposit box at your hotel. Keep a close eye on your possessions and be sure to keep them in sight when you're seated in a restaurant, theater, or other public place. Don't leave valuables in your car—even in the trunk. Every city has its criminals. It's your responsibility to be aware and be alert even in the most heavily touristed areas.

Taxes In the U.S. there is no VAT (Value-Added Tax), or other indirect tax at a national level. Every state, and each city in it, has the right to levy its own local tax on all purchases, including hotel and restaurant checks, airline tickets, etc. It is automatically added to the price of certain services such as public transportation, cab fares, phone calls, and gasoline. It varies from 4% to 10% depending on the state and city, so when you are making major purchases such as photographic equipment, clothing, or high-fidelity components, it can be a significant part of the cost.

Each locality also has the right to levy its own separate tax on hotel occupancy. Since this tax is in addition to any general sales tax, taken together these two taxes can add a considerable amount to the basic cost of your accommodations.

In the District, in addition to your hotel rate, you pay 11% sales tax and $1.50 per room per night in hotel tax. In Virginia, sales tax is 4.5%, while hotel tax varies throughout the state. In Maryland, sales tax is 5%, hotel tax 9.5%.

Foreign visitors must also pay a $10 Customs tax on entry to the U.S., and a $6 departure tax.

Telephone, Telegraph & Telex **Pay phones** are an integral part of the American landscape. You will find them everywhere: at street corners; in bars, restaurants, public buildings, stores, service stations; along highways; and elsewhere. Outside the metropolitan areas public telephones are more difficult to find. Stores and gas stations are your best bet.

Unlike the mail and the railroads, the telephone is not a public-service system. It is run by private corporations, which perhaps explains its high standard of service. In the District local calls cost 20¢.

For **long-distance or international calls,** stock up with a supply of quarters; the pay phone will instruct you when, and in what quantity, you should put them into the slot. For direct overseas calls, first dial 011, followed by the country code (Australia, 61; New Zealand, 64; United Kingdom, 44; and so on), and then by the city code and the number of the person you wish to call. For Canada and long-distance calls in the U.S., dial 1 followed by the area code and number you want.

Before calling from a hotel room, always ask the hotel phone operator if there are any telephone surcharges. These are best avoided by using a public phone, calling collect, or using a telephone charge card.

For **reversed-charge or collect calls,** and for **person-to-person calls,** dial 0 (zero, *not* the letter "O") followed by the area code and number you want; an operator will then come on the line, and you should specify that you are calling collect, or person-to-person, or both. If your operator-assisted call is international, ask for the overseas operator.

For local **directory assistance** ("information"), dial 411; for **long-distance information,** dial 1, then the appropriate area code and 555-1212.

Like the telephone system, **telegraph and telex** services are provided by private corporations like ITT, MCI, and above all, Western Union, the most important. You can bring your telegram in to the nearest Western Union office (there are hundreds across the country), or dictate it over the phone (a toll-free call, 800/325-6000). You can also telegraph money, or have it telegraphed to you, very quickly over the Western Union system.

Telephone Directory See "Yellow Pages," below.

Time The U.S. is divided into four **time zones** (six, if Alaska and Hawaii are included). From east to west, these are: eastern standard time (EST), central standard time (CST), mountain standard time (MST), Pacific standard time (PST), Alaska standard time (AST), and Hawaii standard time (HST). Always keep changing time zones in mind if you are traveling (or even telephoning) long distances in the U.S. For example, noon in New York City (EST) is 11am in Chicago (CST), 10am in Denver (MST), 9am in Los Angeles (PST), 8am in Anchorage (AST), and 7am in Honolulu (HST). Washington, D.C. is EST.

Daylight saving time is in effect from the first Sun in April until the last Sun in Oct (actually, the change is made at 2am on Sun) except in Arizona, Hawaii, part of Indiana, and Puerto Rico. Daylight saving time moves the clock 1 hour ahead of standard time.

Tipping This is part of the American way of life, on the principle that you must expect to pay for any service you get. Here are some rules of thumb:

Bartenders: 10%–15%.

Bellhops: at least 50¢ per piece; $2–$3 for a lot of baggage.

Cab drivers: 15% of the fare.

Cafeterias, fast-food restaurants: no tip.

Chambermaids: $1 a day.

Cinemas, movies, theaters: no tip.

Checkroom attendants (restaurants, theaters): $1 per garment.

Doormen (hotels or restaurants): not obligatory.

Gas-station attendants: no tip.

Hairdressers: 15%–20%.

Parking-lot attendant: 50¢ ($1 in hotels).

Redcaps (airport and railroad station): at least 50¢ per piece; $2–$3 for a lot of baggage.

Restaurants, nightclubs: 15%–20% of the check.

Sleeping-car porters: $2–$3 per night to your attendant.

Toilets Washington reminds many visitors of Paris, but with one striking exception: You won't find a public facility on every street corner. Fortunately, you won't see as many men relieving themselves publicly either. Museums, hotels, and department stores have clean, well-lighted bathrooms, some with tables for changing babies. Depending on what you're used to, you may be overjoyed when you discover our soft toilet tissue. While restaurant restrooms are *supposed to be* for patrons only, those in hotel lobbies, shopping malls, and department stores are fair game. If you or your child has an emergency, and you're near a restaurant, ask the maître d' if you can use the pay phone. Usually there's a restroom a few feet away. If there's an attendant, it is proper to leave 25¢ or 50¢.

Yellow Pages There are two kinds of telephone directory available to you. The general directory is the so-called **White Pages,** in which private and business subscribers are listed in alphabetical order. The inside front cover lists the emergency number for police, fire, and ambulance, and other vital numbers (like the Coast Guard, poison-control center, crime-victims hotline). The first few pages are devoted to community service numbers, including a guide to long-distance and international calling, complete with country codes and area codes.

The second directory, printed on yellow paper (whence its name, *Yellow Pages*), lists all local services, businesses, and industries by type of activity, with an index at the back. The listings cover not only such obvious items as automobile repairs by make of car, or drugstores (pharmacies), often by geographical location, but also restaurants by type of cuisine and geographical location, bookstores by special subject and/or language, places of worship by religious denomination, and other information that the tourist might otherwise not readily find. The *Yellow Pages* also include city plans or detailed area maps, often showing postal ZIP codes and public transportation routes.

THE AMERICAN SYSTEM OF MEASUREMENTS

Length

```
1 inch (in.)  =  2.54cm
1 foot (ft.)  =  12 in.      =  30.48cm  =  .305m
1 yard        =  3 ft.       =  .915m
1 mile (mi.)  =  5,280 ft.   =  1.609km
```

To convert miles to kilometers, multiply the number of miles by 1.61 (for example, 50 miles × 1.61 = 80.5km). Note that this conversion can be used to convert speeds from miles per hour (m.p.h.) to kilometers per hour (km/h).

To convert kilometers to miles, multiply the number of kilometers by .62 (example, 25km × .62 = 15.5 mi.). Note that this same conversion can be used to convert speeds from kilometers per hour to miles per hour.

CAPACITY

```
1 fluid ounce (fl. oz.)  =  .03 liter
1 pint                   =  16 fl. oz.  =  .47 liter
1 quart                  =  2 pints     =  .94 liter
1 gallon (gal.)          =  4 quarts    =  3.79 liter  =  .83 imperial gal.
```

To convert U.S. gallons to liters, multiply the number of gallons by 3.79 (example, 12 gal. × 3.79 = 45.48 liters).

To convert U.S. gallons to imperial gallons, multiply the number of U.S. gallons by .83 (example, 12 U.S. gal × .83 = 9.95 imperial gal.).

To convert liters to U.S. gallons, multiply the number of liters by .26 (example, 50 liters × .26 = 13 U.S. gal.).

To convert imperial gallons to U.S. gallons, multiply the number of imperial gallons by 1.2 (example, 8 imperial gal. × 1.2 = 9.6 U.S. gal.).

WEIGHT

```
1 ounce (oz.)  =  28.35 grams
1 pound (lb.)  =  16 oz.     =  453.6 grams   =  .45 kilograms
1 ton          =  2,000 lb.  =  907 kilograms =  .91 metric ton
```

To convert pounds to kilograms, multiply the number of pounds by .45 (example, 90 lb × .45 = 40.5kg).

To convert kilograms to pounds, multiply the number of kilos by 2.2 (example, 75kg × 2.2 = 165 lb.).

AREA

```
1 acre                  =  .41 hectare
1 square mile (sq. mi.) =  640 acres  =  2.59 hectares  =  2.6km
```

To convert acres to hectares, multiply the number of acres by .41 (example, 40 acres × .41 = 16.4ha).

To convert square miles to square kilometers, multiply the number of square miles by 2.6 (example, 80 sq. mi. × 2.6 = 208km).

To convert hectares to acres, multiply the number of hectares by 2.47 (example, 20ha × 2.47 = 49.4 acres).

To convert square kilometers to square miles, multiply the number of square kilometers by .39 (example, 150km × .39 = 58.5 sq. mi.).

TEMPERATURE

To convert degrees Fahrenheit to degrees Celsius, subtract 32 from °F, multiply by 5, and then divide by 9 (for example, 85°F − 32 × 5/9 = 29°C).

To convert degrees Celsius to degrees Fahrenheit, multiply °C by 9, divide by 5, and add 32 (example, 20°C × 9/5 + 32 = 68°F).

CLOTHING SIZES

WOMEN'S DRESSES, COATS, AND SKIRTS

American	3	5	7	9	11	12	13	14	15	16	18
Continental	36	38	38	40	40	42	42	44	44	46	48
British	8	10	11	12	13	14	15	16	17	18	20

WOMEN'S BLOUSES AND SWEATERS

American	10	12	14	16	18	20
Continental	38	40	42	44	46	48
British	32	34	36	38	40	42

WOMEN'S STOCKINGS

American	8	8½	9	9½	10	10½
Continental	1	2	3	4	5	6
British	8	8½	9	9½	10	10½

WOMEN'S SHOES

American	5	6	7	8	9	10
Continental	36	37	38	39	40	41
British	3½	4½	5½	6½	7½	8½

CHILDREN'S CLOTHING

American	3	4	5	6	6X
Continental	98	104	110	116	122
British	18	20	22	24	26

CHILDREN'S SHOES

American	8	9	10	11	12	13	1	2	3
Continental	24	25	27	28	29	30	32	33	34
British	7	8	9	10	11	12	13	1	2

MEN'S SUITS

American	34	36	38	40	42	44	46	48
Continental	44	46	48	50	52	54	56	58
British	34	36	38	40	42	44	46	48

MEN'S SHIRTS

American	14½	15	15½	16	16½	17	17½	18
Continental	37	38	39	41	42	43	44	45
British	14½	15	15½	16	16½	17	17½	18

Note: Shirts are sized on a combination of the collar and sleeve length.

MEN'S SHOES

American	7	8	9	10	11	12	13
Continental	39½	41	42	43	44½	46	47
British	6	7	8	9	10	11	12

Note: Foot width should also be taken into account.

MEN'S HATS

American	6⅞	7⅛	7¼	7⅜	7½	7⅝
Continental	55	56	58	59	60	61
British	6¼	6⅞	7⅛	7¼	7⅜	7½

WHAT KIDS LIKE TO SEE & DO

You could spend an entire childhood—make that lifetime—discovering the wonders of Washington. So be realistic and scale down your expectations. It's better to spend ample time on a few attractions than to dash through a multitude. You want pleasant memories when you return home—not ulcers.

Look to your children when planning your itinerary. Be sure to factor in time for relaxing. Visit a few well-chosen sites and then let off steam in one of the city's many parks and recreational areas. Dunk in the hotel pool or browse in one of the glitzy indoor malls if shopping is your favorite sport. Remember, this is a vacation, not an endurance contest!

If you're on a tight schedule, concentrate your sightseeing around the downtown area known as the National Mall. Here you will find the presidential monuments, many of the Smithsonian museums, the U.S. Capitol, White House, and numerous other attractions—all free.

On the Mall, stop first at the "Castle," 1000 Jefferson Drive SW (tel. 357-2700), open every day but December 25 from 9:30am to 5:30pm. The flagship of the Smithsonian Institution recently underwent a massive renovation to the tune of $2.7 million. Press a button on one of the 13 video-display monitors to dispense information on the Smithsonian and more than 100 other attractions. Eleven pages alone are devoted to kid-pleasing things to do and see. You may have trouble prying your progeny away from the monitors—the highly imaginative and colorful graphics rival Nintendo.

A 20-minute video is shown throughout the day giving a Smithsonian overview, and electronic wall maps put you in touch with all the popular attractions. Knowledgeable staff are on hand to give directions and answer questions, and guides printed in seven languages are available for foreign visitors. While you're at the Castle, inquire about the Smithsonian Young Associate Program, which offers workshops, films, and live performances for children throughout the year (tel. 357-3030).

P.S.: Before you leave the Castle, visit the Children's Room, open daily from 10 am to 5:30 pm. The original *trompe l'oeil* fantasy garden and skylights have been restored to their original state in the cozy, light-filled room. From here you can exit to the Mall's enchanting Enid A. Haupt Victorian Garden.

A little inside information: Washingtonians chuckle when tourists ask for directions to *the* Smithsonian, which actually comprises 14 museums and the National

Zoological Park. When asking directions, be specific or you could end up at Air & Space when you want Natural History.

In 1846, when English scientist James Smithson willed to the United States funds to establish an institution "for the increase and diffusion of knowledge among men" he probably never imagined that today, the Smithsonian conglomerate would house some 137 million artifacts, encompass numerous buildings, and become a major tourist attraction. In 1990, one-third of the 14 million people who visited the Smithsonian did so in June, July, and August.

Several museums extend summer hours, so check with the individual museums, and bear in mind that Mondays are quietest, Saturdays and Sundays busiest; early morning and late afternoon are the least crowded. Tuck these Smithsonian phone numbers in your wallet or commit them to memory: Information (tel. 357-2700) and Dial-A-Museum (tel. 357-2020).

If you're traveling with very young children, be sure to allow a half-day or more to meet the residents of the National Zoo, about a 15-minute Metro ride from downtown. Also, toddlers to pre-teens enjoy the many hands-on experiences awaiting them at the Capital Children's Museum near Union Station. There are enough attractions in Washington to keep your children's days filled from nursery school to college. Here are a few suggested itineraries, tailored for different age groups.

SUGGESTED ITINERARIES

IF YOU HAVE 3 DAYS

For Toddlers

Day 1: Run, do not walk, to the Zoo. Go early, especially in the summer and on weekends. There's plenty to keep everyone occupied for several hours. Pack a picnic or buy lunch at one of the snack bars or the cafeteria/restaurant on the premises.

Day 2: Visit the animal exhibits, coral reef, and insect zoo in the National Museum of Natural History. Don't forget to say hello to Uncle Beazely, a 25-foot triceratops who holds court on the Mall. Grab lunch in the cafeteria or from a vendor, and eat outside, weather permitting. A pleasant alternative is the Food Court at the Old Post Office Pavilion, where there's usually family entertainment. In the afternoon, visit the Aquarium in the Commerce Department. If you're not too tired, cross the street to the National Museum of American History and single out one or two exhibits.

Day 3: See one of the movies in the Air and Space Museum, but don't sit too close to the screen. The larger-than-life images and booming soundtrack may frighten the kids. Afterward, spend a half-hour or so looking around; that's about all kids this age can take. Have lunch in the Flight Line, then play tag or fly a kite on the Mall, or ride Metro to Union Station for lunch and browsing—maybe they'll doze while you shop. If they still have energy on tap, go to the Capital Children's Museum.

For 6- to 8-year-olds

Do as the toddlers do—it's not babyish!—or . . .

Day 1: Hop on a Tourmobile tram and, after you've passed everything once and listened to the narrator's spiel, spend the afternoon visiting one or two sights that interest you most.

Day 2: Visit the Air & Space Museum in the morning, then have lunch on the Mall. After lunch, take a look at the Hirshhorn, especially the outdoor sculpture garden. Ride the carousel. Cross the Mall to the Museum of Natural History and/or the Museum of American History, or cast an eye (but not a fishing line) into the tanks of the Commerce Department's Aquarium. Have dessert at The Shops at National Place or the Old Post Office Pavilion, or go back to your room and rest. You deserve it.

Day 3: See more currency than you ever dreamed of at the Bureau of Engraving and Printing. Energize with lunch on the go, then return to the past at the DAR Museum's Children's Attic. If time and energy permit, see the Washington Monument and Lincoln Memorial. Parents and older kids will want to take a slight detour to the Vietnam Veterans Memorial. In the warm weather months, rent a boat or bicycle and paddle or pedal away the afternoon. In winter, ice skate or build a snowman on the Mall. Take a bus tour or taxi to see the monuments after dark.

For 8- to 10-year-olds

Day 1: Start early and spend the morning at the FBI. Have lunch at the Hard Rock Café. Visit Ford's Theatre and, across the street, the Petersen House, where Lincoln died. Then hop on Metro and choose one of the following: explore National Geographic Society's Explorers Hall; stroll around Dupont Circle or Adams Morgan, stopping for dessert along the way; or see the Phillips Collection.

Day 2: Divide the day into thirds for a Mall crawl. Start at the Air & Space Museum (be sure to buy movie tickets *first*). Have lunch on the Mall, then hit the Natural History and American History museums. Pick up a map at each information desk and concentrate on a few exhibits. Between thirds, play catch or touch football, or fly a kite (you can buy one in the Air & Space Museum's gift shop) on the Mall. If you're still upright after dinner, see Washington at night.

Day 3: Spend the day on "the Hill." See the Capitol, then say hello to your Senator or Representative. Eat at one of the many kid-friendly places on the Hill or at Union Station. (See Chapter 7, "Where Kids Like to Eat"). As time permits, see one or more of the following: Supreme Court, Library of Congress, Folger Shakespeare Theatre, Eastern Market, Union Station, or the Capital Children's Museum. Wind down with a visit to the exotic world of the U.S. Botanic Garden at the foot of Capitol Hill.

For Preteens

Day 1: Same as Day 1 for 8-to-10-year-olds. Walk around Georgetown after dinner, see a movie, or go to a comedy club.

Day 2: Same as Day 2 for 8-to-10-year-olds. You may want to skip a museum or two and substitute the U.S. Archives or Arlington National Cemetery. Or maybe your idea of a good time is to shop till you drop in Georgetown or an indoor mall. Take a nighttime tour of the major sights. Go out for late dessert.

Day 3: Same as Day 3 for 8-to-10-year-olds, omitting the Capital Children's Museum. Ride a bike, take a hike, or pick out something else you like. A visit to

Arlington National Cemetery, Mt. Vernon (by boat in nice weather), or Alexandria's Old Town is in order. See a show, sporting event, or concert at night.

1. KIDS' TOP 10 ATTRACTIONS

Picking Washington's top 10 attractions for kids is like naming the top 10 restaurants in New York—next to impossible. Depending on your kids' ages and interests, your family's top 10 will probably include a mix of some of the following along with suggestions from "More Attractions" and "For Kids with Special Interests."

THE NATIONAL MUSEUM OF AMERICAN HISTORY, 14th Street and Constitution Avenue NW, entrances on Constitution Avenue and Madison Drive. Tel. 357-2700.

RAINY-DAY SUGGESTIONS

If rainy days and Mondays get you down, skip the monuments, zoo, and anywhere else you'll be unprotected from the elements.

Best bets in foul weather are museums, galleries, movies, or a shopping mall. Pick two museums close together and practice sprinting between them while dodging the raindrops. I used to wrap my kids in plastic yard-and-leaf bags and drag them downtown on rainy days because everything was less crowded. If you're museumed out, head for Union Station, the Old Post Office Pavilion, The Shops at National Place, or Georgetown Park to eat and browse. Is there a better way to pass a nasty afternoon than eating good food and spending money?

Catch a movie you were too busy to see at home. Tickets at many D.C. theaters are $3.25 or less before 6pm. At Union Station's nine-screen theater complex, you can duck in and out of features until the weather improves.

If it's drizzling halfheartedly, take Metro's Yellow Line to King Street, and hop a bus or walk to Old Town, Alexandria. Kids and grownups alike get fired up in the Torpedo Factory, where 150 artists and craftspeople work and sell their creations in full view of spectators Tuesday through Sunday. There are plenty of historic sights, shops, and restaurants in the neighborhood to keep everyone satisfied (see Chapter 9, "Easy Excursions, Old Town, Alexandria" section).

Another great place to ride out a storm is the U.S. Botanic Garden at the foot of Capitol Hill.

If your hotel has an enclosed pool, enjoy getting wet indoors. Write postcards, catch up on reading, or plan tomorrow's activities. When the crew grows restless, order a pizza and watch TV, or indulge in the ultimate midday luxury—a nap.

KIDS' TOP 10 ATTRACTIONS

Bureau of Engraving & Printing ❶
Capital Children's Museum ❷
The Capitol ❸
Federal Bureau of Investigation ❹
Jefferson Memorial ❺
Lincoln Memorial ❺ᴬ
National Air & Space Museum ❻
National Geographic Society's Explorers Hall ❼
National Museum of American History ❽
National Museum of Natural History ❾
National Zoological Park ❿
Washington Monument ❺ᴮ

★ Major aspects of America's cultural, scientific, and technological life come alive here, creating intrigue for kids of all ages. Three floors, packed with exhibits that bridge 200 years—from the country's early days (the original Star-Spangled Banner that inspired our national anthem) to the present (Archie and Edith Bunker's well-worn chairs and the Fonz's leather jacket)—give an overview of social history American style.

Preschoolers enjoy the first-floor exhibits devoted to farm and power machinery and transportation, especially the 280-ton steam locomotive in the railroad gallery and early automobiles. **"The Information Age,"** a $10-million exhibition that opened in 1990, demonstrating the many ways technology has affected the gathering and dissemination of information, draws kids 8 and up with its touch-screen interaction stations. Don't pass up the chance to visit the **Palm Court,** an authentic reconstruction of a Victorian ice-cream parlor, and sample one of the tempting confections (see Chapter 7, "Where Kids Like to Eat").

Witness the museum's version of a garage sale. **"A Material World"** salutes many of the brand-name products that helped shape this country. If you buy the theory that items such as a G.E. toaster, Eames chair, and Electrolux vacuum cleaner are barometers of our changing cultural values, you could be right. Kids may not get the message, but they'll definitely go for the '86 Swamp Rat XXX, the first top-fuel dragster to cruise at 270 m.p.h.

No doubt, you will run to see the **First Ladies' gowns,** because that's what you're supposed to do when in Washington. Many think this is the best exhibit in the museum; others disagree. Anyway, it's worth a few minutes of your time.

"After the Revolution" is an exhibit of late-18th-century Americana, where kids can peer into a log house and typical New England and Southern interiors to see what family and community life was like for America's first generation. Afterward, head for the Hands-on History Room, a must for all family members; it is scheduled to reopen in April 1992 after extensive renovation and expansion. Explore at your own pace precise reproductions of museum artifacts, and touch four centuries of American history. Try ginning cotton, weaving Indian-style baskets, decoding telegraph messages, and a host of other activities.

Take a peek at the colossal Horatio Greenough **statue of George Washington** out of uniform. The public was outraged when toga-clad George was first placed in the Capitol rotunda in 1841, and the 20-ton statue was moved a couple of times before finding a permanent home at this museum. Looks like he's not budging.

For anyone out of a stroller, **"A Nation of Nations"** could be the most interesting exhibition of all. It focuses on common experiences, like sports, entertainment, and military service, that have joined diverse ethnic groups to create a distinctively American culture. Everyone gets a kick out of **"Men and Women: A History of Costume, Gender, and Power"** (and to think women suffered in some of those contraptions masquerading as underwear!).

Swing by the **Foucault Pendulum** on the second floor. This may be your golden opportunity to witness the earth's rotation. It's easy to become hypnotized as the pendulum swings slowly back and forth, knocking over the encircling pegs one by one. Tell your kids the pendulum's arc stays the same, but the earth is moving underneath it. When you're done explaining it to them, come explain it to me.

The third floor is of special interest to those whose hobbies include **music, stamps, photography, ceramics, the graphic arts, medals, ship models,** and, last but not least, **money**—a hobby they all seem to share. Don't miss *Old Glory* or the *Philadelphia,* a gunboat built and sunk in 1776 that was raised in 1935. In the **"Lingering Shadows"** area, kids can try their hands at shadow art on a table lighted from below, a megahit with the small fry.

Admission: Free.

Open: Daily 10am–5:30pm. **Closed:** Dec 25. **Metro:** Smithsonian or Federal Triangle.

THE NATIONAL MUSEUM OF NATURAL HISTORY, 10th Street and Constitution Avenue NW (second entrance on Madison Drive). Tel. 357-2700.

I'm partial to this museum, and so are most kids. If you're entering from the Mall, you'll be welcomed by Uncle Beazley, a lifesize triceratops. Start your tour on the ground floor, where you'll see about 300 **birds** native to the eastern United States. Next, go to the four-story, marble-pillared rotunda on the first floor. The kid hasn't been born who won't ooh and aah over the **8-ton African bush elephant** who is over 13 feet tall!

Why save the best until last? Head for the **Insect Zoo** upstairs, where you'll meet the only living residents outside of the aquariums. Leave your arachnophobia at the door before meeting the tarantulas. Inspect the cockroaches, residents of a beehive and ant colony, leaf-cutting ants, millipedes as big as Buicks, and the amazing Amazon walking stick (a dead ringer for Tommy Tune). The insects live behind Plexiglas—until mealtime. If you're interested in observing a tarantula's table manners, be here for chow call, weekdays at 10:30 and 11:30am and 1:30pm. Weekend meals are served at 12:30 and 1:30pm (they like to sleep late). Guides circulate to answer questions and dispell myths. I held up well on my last visit until a volunteer invited an adorable 3-year-old to wrap his fingers around a repulsive-looking tobacco horn worm in the pupa stage. Good luck!

The **fossil collection** has specimens of creatures that swam in the seas 600 million years ago and a 70-million-year-old dinosaur egg. Skeletons of dinosaurs who lived more than 100 million years ago are always big hits, and kids who grew up with *Jaws* go nuts over the partial jaw of a huge prehistoric shark with 6-inch teeth. Be sure to explore the adjacent Life in the Ancient Seas exhibit.

In the hall off the rotunda featuring **Native Cultures of the Americas,** the diorama that depicts an Eskimo boy fishing is especially pleasing to younger children. Preschoolers also feel at home in the **Discovery Room,** where they can touch everything but a few very fragile items. Among the room's treasures are large, labeled boxes of bones, reptile skins, and sea urchins. There's even a preserved rattlesnake in a jar. The Discovery Room is open September through May, Monday through Thursday from noon to 2:30pm, and Friday through Sunday from 10:30am to 3:30pm. From Memorial Day to Labor Day the hours are 10:30am to 3:30pm. Free passes are given out at the door.

Mammals, especially those shown in their natural habitats, engross young visitors. President Theodore Roosevelt, the old Rough Rider himself, shot many of the big game animals displayed here during an African safari. ("Walk softly, but carry a big gun.") The penguins in the **"Birds of the World"** exhibit are particularly appealing.

Wait till they get their first glimpse of the 92-foot blue whale suspended from the ceiling in the **"Life in the Sea"** hall undergoing renovation piecemeal as we go to press. The most exciting sights are contained in two 3,000-gallon aquariums. One demonstrates a tropical Caribbean reef ecosystem; the other, the subarctic waters off

Maine. Wave-generating machines and other devices simulate actual conditions in each distinctive ecosystem. Older kids should catch the video that shows Smithsonian scientists researching the ecosystems. You don't have to understand what's going on to enjoy the underwater scene.

The **minerals, crystals, and gems** on the second floor cause young eyes to sparkle plenty, but the most dazzling sight of all is the 45.5-carat Hope diamond, valued at $100 million. This, the most visited object in all the Smithsonian museums, was once owned by Washington socialite Evalyn Walsh McLean, who wore the stone frequently despite its supposed curse. (We should all be so cursed.) Just between us, the 330-carat Star of Asia, a cabochon-cut star sapphire, is no slouch. Maybe your kids will get some good ideas for your next birthday present.

Moon rocks brought back by the Apollo astronauts and a 1,371-pound meteorite are on display in the **"Earth, Moon, and Meteorites"** hall. If your kids are into rocks, volcanoes, or earthquakes, they'll like it here. Show them the working seismograph. Sometime in 1992, the hall housing the gems, minerals, and fossils will close for renovation and expansion.

For school-aged kids with an interest in such matters, murals, dioramas, and films help explain the origins and legacies of ancient civilizations in **"Western Civilization: Origins and Traditions."**

Children over 12 may want to visit the **Naturalist Center** in Room C-119, where they can examine specimens, do research, and utilize the library, microscopes, and small audiovisual lab to identify objects they've found. The center is open Monday through Saturday from 10:30am to 4pm and Sunday from noon to 5pm (tel. 357-2804).

Admission: Free.

Open: 10am–5:30pm. **Closed:** Dec 25. **Metro:** Smithsonian or Federal Triangle.

THE NATIONAL ZOOLOGICAL PARK, opposite 3000 Connecticut Avenue NW. Tel. 673-4800 or 673-4717.

More than 5,000 animals call the National Zoo home, and your kids will probably want to see each and every one. Occupying more than 160 verdant acres, the zoo boasts many rare and endangered species and is a front-runner in the breeding, care, and exhibition of its residents. Part of the Smithsonian Institution, the zoo is the premier attraction for kids in D.C. When the **"nursery"** fills in May and June, it's an especially appealing time to bring your little ones. Go early on weekends, during school vacations, and in the summer, not only because it's less crowded, but because the animals are spunkier.

Olmsted Walk is the main drag, and more than 3 miles of trails crisscross the park. If you follow the numbers and helpful signs along the way, you won't get lost. The terrain is hilly, so leave your flipflops under the bed and wear your most comfortable nonskid shoes. Be sure to lift up your kids in strollers so they can see everything. If they nap along the way, you could easily spend half a day or longer. Older kids, of course, can go on forever, and you'll probably be the one shouting "Uncle."

Stop first at the **Education Building** near the zoo's entrance to pick up a map and see one of three zoo-related movies shown from 10:30am to 3pm. In the **ZOOlab,** youngsters from 3 to 7 are encouraged to handle animal bones and skins, nests, and feathers. Volunteers are on hand to answer questions. Listen to the tape recordings of animal sounds. How many can your kids identify?

Everyone has heard of the prize pair, Ling-Ling and Hsing-Hsing, a 1972 gift to the children of the United States from the People's Republic of China. The giant pandas, whose reproductive problems continue to make front-page news, love to sleep. Your best chance of catching them up and about is to arrive at feeding times, 11am and 3pm. The pandas are off Olmsted Walk near the park's entrance.

Nearby are the large land mammals—rhinos, hippos, giraffes, and elephants. The elephants give a demonstration at 10:30am that's a real crowd pleaser, and they're usually fed around 3pm. You'll be happy to know that the renovated **Elephant House** looks and smells much better than it used to. Follow Olmsted Walk to the large and small cats, monkeys, apes, and reptiles.

The **HERPlab**, in the **Reptile House,** is geared to kids 6 and up. A milksnake, leopard gecko, and other live animals encased in clear boxes, can be viewed up close and personal. Kids can touch turtle bones and test their knowledge of reptiles and amphibians with question-and-answer cards that relate to each specimen. Visitors are encouraged to utilize the activity boxes, library, and displays to increase their appreciation of these frequently maligned creatures.

Kids are always entertained by the antics of the **otters, seals,** and **sea lions,** so childlike in their playfulness and spontaneity. Try to catch the sea lions' training demonstration at 11:30am (check first at the information desk), and don't miss peering through the window in the otter pool for a closeup of these endearing animals' high jinks.

A recently opened **invertebrate exhibit,** the only one of its kind in the United States, features tanks of starfish and sponges (the crabs didn't make it), as well as spiders displayed very much out in the open. While you may be turned off, your kids will, no doubt, want to inspect the dirt-filled sandbox inhabited by a bunch of creepy-crawlers.

The **Great Outdoor Flight Cage** is a sky-high, mesh-enclosed hemisphere 130 feet in diameter your little chickadees can enjoy. Older kids and adults may carry their featherweight concerns to the Bird Resource Center (formerly BIRDlab) at the rear of the **Bird House** and take a guided tour of a room in which eggs incubate and zoo workers examine some of our ailing fine feathered friends.

Smokey the Bear, for many years one of the zoo's biggest attractions, now resides in that great forest in the sky. A statue pays tribute to the brown bear who immortalized the phrase "Only you can prevent forest fires."

As we go to press, the **Amazon Rain Forest exhibit** is due to open. The eagerly awaited addition will feature completely natural vegetation to support a broad array of plants and animals, and the emphasis will be on invertebrates.

Snackbars and ice-cream stands are scattered throughout the park. At the **Panda Café,** enjoy a fast-food break at umbrellaed tables. The **Mane Restaurant/ Cafeteria** is at the bottom of the hill if you started at Connecticut Avenue. The hot dogs, pizza, and tuna sandwiches aren't bad. Many visitors prefer to bring sandwiches, buy drinks and ice cream, and dine al fresco at one of the zoo's grassy picnic areas.

The gift shop in the Education Building carries a wonderful selection of zoo-related books on several reading levels, plush animals, and animal puzzles.

Admission: Free. Limited paid parking; free handicapped parking in Lots A and B; some street parking. Strollers rent for $3 plus a $35 deposit or your driver's license. Pets are not allowed in the park and may perish in the unshaded parking lots.

Open: Daily, weather permitting, Apr 15–Oct 15, grounds 8am–8pm, animal buildings 9am–6pm; Oct 16–Apr 14, grounds 8am–6pm, animal buildings 9am–4:30pm. **Closed:** Dec 25. The ZOOlab, HERPlab, and Bird Resource Center are open Apr–Oct Fri 10am–1pm, Sat–Sun 10am–2pm; Nov–Mar weekends only. **Metro:** Cleveland Park (an easier walk) or Woodley Park-Zoo (an uphill climb).

NATIONAL AIR AND SPACE MUSEUM, Sixth Street and Independence Avenue SW (enter at Independence Avenue or Jefferson Drive). Tel. 357-2700.

Longer than two football fields, the most visited museum in the *world* is a huge pinkish-marble monolith, which opened July 1, 1976, in time for the U.S. Bicentennial. Not much to look at from the outside, the magic begins when you enter. Inside, major historical and technological feats of air and space flight are documented in 23 exhibit areas.

Almost every specimen in the Air & Space Museum was flown or used to back-up the craft, and this creates excitement and a sense of immediacy in kids of all ages. The planes suspended from the ceiling appear to be in flight, and younger kids (young enough not to be embarrassed) may want to lie down and look straight up for the maximum effect. Before your family flies off in different directions, line up at the **Langley Theater** and buy tickets ($2.75 adults; $1.75 kids) for one or more of the special flight-related movies shown several times a day on the five-story Imax screen. If you have time for only one, make it *To Fly*. You won't ever forget it. (See the "Cinema" section in Chapter 6 for details.)

Next, if you're interested in catching a heavenly show suitable for kids 10 and up at the **Albert Einstein Planetarium,** buy your tickets ($2.75 adults; $1.75 kids) before you begin circling the exhibits. Don't let your little jet-setters slip into different orbits on the way to the ticket booth.

Stop at the information desk for a floor plan and free guide for young children, "5-4-3-2-1." To avoid wasting time and energy—this place is *huge*—note the exhibits that interest your crew most. If you have kids over 8 or 10, decide if you want to take the 1½-hour free guided tour (daily at 10:15am and 1pm) or rent a taped tour, with narration by astronauts. Call ahead for information on group tours. With kids under 6, it's best to see the highlights on your own.

Now you may begin your tour. Start with **"Milestones of Flight,"** in the two-level gallery at the museum's entrance. Highlights include the Wright brothers' 1903 Flyer, Charles Lindbergh's *Spirit of St. Louis,* John Glenn's Friendship 7, Gemini 4, the Apollo 11 command module *Columbia,* Pioneer 10, and Chuck (The Right Stuff) Yeager's Bell X-1. Don't leave without touching the moon rock (excuse me, "Lunar Sample").

If the line isn't too long, school-aged kids love to walk through the **Skylab orbital workshop,** a backup for America's first space station. Check out the Apollo lunar module on the first floor's east end.

The Surveyor, Lunar Orbiter, and Ranger are hangared in the hall devoted to **"Lunar Exploration Vehicles."** In **"Rocketry and Space Flight,"** the evolution of the spacesuit is traced. Those interested in aviation history will want to see the *Vega* flown by Amelia Earhart on the first transatlantic flight by a woman, and the *Chicago,* which took nearly six months (with no food or beverage service) to complete the first around-the-world flight.

Tomorrow's astronauts will learn more about the early years of manned space flight in **"Apollo to the Moon,"** and most everyone is curious about the Soviet SS-20 that landed in the NASM in 1990 in exchange for a Pershing II on display in St. Petersburg.

Younger children enjoy peering up at the mildly menacing Curtiss P40E Warhawk with the shark smile and boarding a replica of an airplane carrier hangar deck in **"Sea-Air Operations."** A new gallery devoted to World War I aviation opened in November 1991. Kids may board the nose section of an American Airlines DC-7.

Computer whizzes will appreciate **"Beyond the Limits: Flight Enters the Computer Age,"** which shows, with the aid of interactive computers, how computer technology is applied to aerospace in such areas as aerodynamics, design, flight testing, and flight simulation. The model of the X-29 aircraft, Cray-1 supercomputer, and the radio-controlled HIMAT aircraft are but a few of the must-sees for kids who are smart enough to understand the right stuff.

Be sure to touch down in the **Shuttle Shop** and **Museum Gift Shop** to pick up some freeze-dried ice cream for snackin'. The selection of books, kites, models, and souvenir posters and T-shirts is one of the best in the city.

The **Flight Line Cafeteria,** with views of the Mall and Capitol, and more formal **Wright Place restaurant** are ideal refueling spots. (See the "Mall/ Museum" section of Chapter 7, "Where Kids Like to Eat").

Currently, the NASM overflow is housed in the Paul E. Garber Facility in Suitland, Maryland (tel. 202/357-1400). Free tours for kids over 12 of the unheated, un-air-conditioned warehouse are given by appointment only. Call Monday through Friday between 9am and 3pm to make reservations. The facility usually holds an open house in late April. If your family is really spacey and your kids are old enough, breeze over to Garber.

Parents of babies will appreciate the clean and well-equipped unisex **Baby Service Station** across from the gift shop.

Admission: Free.

Open: Daily 10am–5:30pm; extended summer hours. **Closed:** Dec 25. **Metro:** L'Enfant Plaza (Smithsonian Museums exit).

Three U.S. presidents have been honored with monuments in the nation's capital: George Washington, Abraham Lincoln, and Thomas Jefferson. Try to see all three. I could wax poetic on the feelings elicited by each, but you should find out for yourself. *P.S.:* I have counted the three monuments as one "Top 10" selection.

THE WASHINGTON MONUMENT, 15th Street and Constitution Avenue NW. Tel. 426-6839 (Monument #1).

If you flew into National Airport at night, you were treated to the supreme view of the monument. Standing 555 feet, the marble and granite obelisk with walls that taper from 15 feet at the base to 18 inches at the top is an engineering marvel. Nearly a century passed from its conception to the actual construction between 1848 and 1884—a story and a half if you have the time and interest to research it. One interesting sidelight: It is not positioned exactly according to L'Enfant's plan, but had to be shifted eastward a tad because the original site was too marshy.

To avoid very long lines, come on a weekday if at all possible. Arrive before 8am or after 8pm during extended summer hours.

Since tourists are no longer allowed to climb the 897 steps, you'll have to take the elevator—faster than in most apartment buildings—and you'll be at the top in little over a minute. The view is spectacular, especially after dark. If you're fortunate enough to be on the Mall for the Fourth of July festivities, the sight of the fireworks over the monument is thrilling.

Designed by Robert Mills, architect of the Treasury and Old Patent Office buildings, the monument is two-tone, but not by original design. Notice how the stones darken about 150 feet from the base. Because the Civil War and other matters caused significant construction delays, when the government resumed the project in the 1870s the "new" marble, mined from another part of the quarry, was darker. If you've ever tried to match paint, you'll understand the problem.

When enough Park Service staff is on hand, you may take a **"Down the Steps" tour** to see the carved stones incorporated in the interior (one is from the Parthenon) and learn more about the monument's construction. Be forewarned, once you begin your descent down the *eight hundred and ninety-seven* stairs, you can't change your mind. This is no place for the claustrophobic, because there are no windows and quarters are tight near the top. The tour is usually given at 10am, 2 and 7pm in the summer—it's air-conditioned inside—but it's best to call ahead. The rest of the year, tours are scheduled according to supply (of guides) and demand (of tourists).

On summer evenings, the U.S. Army, Navy, Marine, and Air Force bands play on a rotating basis at the Sylvan Theater, on the monument grounds. See Chapter 6, "Their Kind of Entertainment)

Admission: Free.

Open: Daily first Sun in Apr–Labor Day, 8am–midnight; rest of the year 9am–5pm. **Closed:** July 4 and Dec 25. **Metro:** Smithsonian.

THE LINCOLN MEMORIAL, west of the Mall at 23rd Street NW, between Constitution and Independence avenues NW. Tel. 426-6895 (Monument #2).

★ I had an English professor who said if you weren't moved by the Lincoln Memorial, your heart had probably stopped.

If the only image you hold of the 16th U.S. president is on a penny, toss it aside and come see this one. The 19-by-19-foot statue of a seated, contemplative Abraham Lincoln, was designed by Daniel French. It took 28 blocks of marble and four years of carving to complete, and is the focal point in the classically inspired monument by Henry Bacon.

A gleam in some politician's eye shortly after Lincoln's death in 1865, this Parthenon lookalike was not completed until 1922. The Doric columns number 36, one for each state in the Union at the time of Lincoln's death. The names are inscribed on the frieze over the colonnade. The names of the 48 states at the time of the memorial's dedication appear near the top of the monument, and a plaque for Alaska and Hawaii was added later.

The stirring words of Lincoln's Gettysburg Address and Second Inaugural Address are carved into the limestone walls and, above them, allegorical murals by Jules Guerin represent North-South unity and the freeing of the slaves.

If you can come here at night, when the crowds thin out, do so. From the rear of the memorial look across the Potomac to Arlington National Cemetery and the eternal flame at John F. Kennedy's grave. From the steps, take in the Reflecting Pool, a nighttime mirror of the memorial, and past it to the Washington Monument, Mall, and Capitol. If the sight doesn't grab you, well, my English professor spoke the truth.

Unfortunately, visitors can no longer tour the cavern under the monument's foundation to see the stalagmites and stalacites, due to the presence of asbestos.

Admission: Free.

Open: Daily 24 hours a day. Park staff on duty 8am–midnight. **Metro:** Foggy Bottom.

THOMAS JEFFERSON MEMORIAL, south shore of Tidal Basin, West Potomac Park. Tel. 426-6821 (Monument #3).

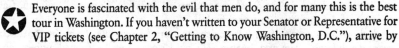 Some students of history think Jefferson was the Rodney Dangerfield of his time, that he "got no respect." While the memorials to Washington and Lincoln enjoyed prestigious downtown addresses for quite a spell in accordance with L'Enfant's plan, Mr. Jefferson wasn't appropriately honored until April 13 (his birthday) in 1943, when the Jefferson Memorial was dedicated.

Well, good things come to those who wait. On a parcel reclaimed from the Potomac, on line with the south axis of the White House, a memorial was erected similar to Rome's Pantheon. This architectural model was so favored by Jefferson, he utilized its columned rotunda design at the Virginia State Capitol, University of Virginia, and Monticello.

Above the entrance, he is seen standing before Benjamin Franklin, John Adams, Roger Sherman, and Robert Livingston, members of the committee appointed to write the Declaration of Independence. Engraved on the interior walls are inscriptions from Jefferson's writings that sum up his philosophies on freedom and government. History buffs will note that certain "liberties" were taken with the Declaration of Independence. There are 11 mistakes that can't be blamed on the typing pool. Can your kids find them?

The Capitol, White House, Washington Monument, and Lincoln Memorial are visible from the steps, and it's a front-row seat for the Cherry Blossom festival. See if your kids can connect the Jefferson and Lincoln Memorials and Washington Monument to form a triangle. After a visit to the memorial, you'll probably agree that Jefferson finally received the respect that he deserved. For high drama, come at night. If the kids don't think it's awesome, leave them home next time.

Admission: Free.

Open: Daily, 8am–midnight. **Closed:** Dec 25. Accessible by car, cab, or Tourmobile; **Metro** (Smithsonian) is a hike.

FEDERAL BUREAU OF INVESTIGATION (FBI), J. Edgar Hoover FBI Building, Pennsylvania Avenue & 10th Street NW (tour entrance, E Street between 9th and 10th Streets). Tel. 324-3447.

Everyone is fascinated with the evil that men do, and for many this is the best tour in Washington. If you haven't written to your Senator or Representative for VIP tickets (see Chapter 2, "Getting to Know Washington, D.C."), arrive by

8:30am, especially in spring and summer, for the hour-long tour conducted every 15 minutes, Monday through Friday, 8:45am to 4:15pm.

Don't let your first impression of the hideous $126-million concrete bunker—dubbed "Fort Hoover" by locals—put you off. It took only four years to design and eight years to build, so what do you expect? Once inside, well-versed, uniformed guides will take you past a series of exhibits detailing past and current FBI work. Let your kids stand close to the guide, so they don't miss a thing.

A brief introductory film gives a historical overview of the bureau's activities. With any luck your kids won't recognize a relative among the Ten Most Wanted, the famous list begun in 1950. According to FBI gospel, two fugitives whose pictures were recognized here by tourists were later apprehended. The late Yippie/radical Abbie Hoffman claimed that he took the FBI tour several times while on the lam.

Although they may not recognize Al Capone or Ma Barker in the rogues' gallery, your kids will snap to attention when they see the gangsters' weapons, U.S. Crime Clock as it ticks off the numbers and frequency of violent crimes in this country, devices used by spies for transporting microfilm, and an actual surveillance tape. Along the way, you'll be shown more than 5,000 confiscated firearms, as well as a roomful of furs, jewelry, silverware, and art objects seized in narcotics and tax evasion cases. Sorry, no sample souvenirs.

If you happen to see a white-coated technician examining a bloody fabric sample in the Serology Lab, be assured, it's the real thing. They don't use props here. Drug samples and related paraphernalia, and a world map showing the routes taken by carriers of illicit substances into this country, are part of the Drug Enforcement Agency's (DEA) exhibit. You'll also learn how the bureau is waging the battle against illegal drugs.

The Instrumental Analysis Unit, where a car's make and model can be determined from a paint chip, the Firearms Identification Unit, and hairs and fibers lab are of special interest to older children.

What leaves kids gasping, however, is the tour's bang-up finish. In a small auditorium facing a firing range, you'll hear and see a sharp-eyed agent pump several rounds from a 9mm automatic pistol and submachine gun (successor to the notorious Tommy Gun) into several defenseless paper targets, which end up like so many slices of swiss cheese. What a show! The experience may keep your youngsters on the straight and narrow more than anything else they encounter. Don't miss it.

Admission: Free.

Open: Mon–Fri 8:45am–4:15pm. Closed weekends and federal holidays.
Metro: Metro Center, Federal Triangle, or Gallery Place.

THE CAPITOL, east end of the Mall, entrance on East Capitol Street and 1st Street NE. Tel. 225-6827.

Not to acquaint your family with the Capitol would be un-American; and even if your home is outside the U.S.A., go. The Capitol will give you a sense, more than any other federal building, of what this country is all about. As you face the Capitol's East Front, the Senate side is north (right) and the House side is south. Flags fly over the respective sides when either is in session, and night sessions are indicated by a light burning in the dome. Information on committee meetings is published weekdays in the *Washington Post*'s "Today in Congress" column. Call ahead if you're interested in a specific bill.

A short-but-sweet half-hour tour departs every few minutes from the **Rotunda** every day between 9am and 3:45pm. The guides are so well-scrubbed, upbeat, and knowledgeable, they must be running for office. Encourage older kids to ask questions during the tour, then allow time for wandering around and attending a hearing or committee meeting, usually held in the morning or other times when Congress is not in session. If you have toddlers, quit while you're ahead after the introductory tour.

The guides do a marvelous job describing the history of Statuary Hall, where the House met from 1807 to 1857. Note the bronze plaque on the floor where John Quincy Adams collapsed on February 21, 1848. He died in an adjoining room soon thereafter. Due to an acoustical anomaly, whispers can be heard across the room, and your guide will demonstrate this phenomenon to your kids' delight.

The Rotunda's cast-iron dome (which replaced the original one of copper and wood) was begun in 1855 and finished in 1863 during Lincoln's presidency. It has a diameter of nearly 100 feet and weighs 9 million pounds. Don't get nervous. You're safe standing on the Rotunda floor, 180 feet beneath it, as more than 5,000 tons of ironwork provide the girding.

Constantino Brumidi's allegorical fresco, the *Apotheosis of Washington,* lines the very top of the dome and depicts Washington accompanied by Liberty, Victory, and Fame. The 13 figures crowned with stars represent the 13 original states. If your neck stiffens looking up at the masterpiece, pity poor Brumidi who spent 11 months on his back to complete the glorification of Washington. More than 25 years of Brumidi's handiwork is also evidenced elsewhere in the Capitol—in the frieze encircling the rotunda, the Senate reception room, the President's Room, and first-floor Senate corridors.

The **Crypt** was originally intended as Washington's final resting place, but his relatives *insisted* on Mt. Vernon. So, instead of Washington, the Crypt holds changing exhibits that tell about the history and construction of the Capitol.

If you visit the **House gallery,** the Democrats will be seated to the right of the presiding officer and Republicans to the left. Senators have assigned seats, according to seniority, but representatives do not, and a system of bells informs those not in attendance what is going on. Wouldn't the kids love this when they're absent from school?

The Supreme Court met in the **Old Supreme Court Chamber** from 1800 to 1860. Thomas Jefferson was sworn in as president here in 1801, and in 1844 Samuel F.B. Morse sent the first telegraph message, "What hath God wrought," to Baltimore.

If you visit the handsome **Old Senate Chamber,** imagine for a moment the highly charged pre-Civil War atmosphere as rich oratory and heated debate filled the air. No wonder this was considered the hottest show in town for many years. When crowds overflowed the galleries, it is said some senators politely gave their seats to ladies. Today, they lose their seats to ladies.

Before you leave, do two things: (1) Take your kids down to the basement for a ride on the **mini-railway** connecting the Capitol with the Senate and House office buildings; (2) Stroll around to the West Front for an unbroken **view** of the Mall, Washington Monument, and Lincoln Memorial.

A *parting crumb of trivia:* The 19½-foot statue of *Freedom,* perched atop the dome since 1863, was supposed to be nude. You can imagine what a furor that caused in the mid-1800s, so sculptor Thomas Crawford draped the figure in a flowing robe. Despite the feathers flowing from the eagle-topped helmet, Freedom is not a Native American.

Morning VIP tours, appropriate for kids 10 and up, include admission to the House and Senate galleries. Usually, the House and Senate convene from noon until late afternoon, but exceptions are almost a rule. Whether you want the special tour, or just passes to the galleries, you must write your representative or senator far in advance (see "Tourist Information" in Chapter 1, "Planning a Trip to Washington, D.C."). Last-minute passes are sometimes available if you stop at your senator's office. Call if you don't know the location (tel. 224-3121). Passes are given to noncitizens who show their passports to the Sergeant of Arms of the Senate or the Doorkeeper of the House.

Admission: Free.

Open: Daily 9am–4:30pm (last tour at 3:45pm). Closed Thanksgiving, Dec 25 and Jan 1. **Metro:** Capitol South.

THE CAPITAL CHILDREN'S MUSEUM, 800 3rd St. NW (at H Street). Tel. 543-8600 or 638-5437 (recorded information).

⭐ How refreshing after filing through museums and shops filled with signs warning, "Please Do Not Touch" or "You Break, You Pay," to visit this facility where you can tell your kids, "Go ahead, touch!" Learning is strictly a hands-on affair for toddlers to teens at the Capital Children's Museum. In the **International Hall,** kids can head south-of-the-border by donning Mexican clothes, making tortillas, grinding Mexican chocolate beans, or doing the Mexican hat dance. Don't forget to pet Rosie the goat.

Younger children experience things here well out of their reach in the real world, like exploring beneath a city street, driving a bus, visiting an automated factory, or wandering through a maze in the **Changing Environments exhibit.**

Little hands can hunt and peck on a Braille typewriter, tap a communique in Morse code, or send a message on a ship's blinker. A highlight of the exhibits tracing the history of communication, from Ice Age cave drawing to satellite-delivered data, is the highly interactive **U-TV studio,** where aspiring anchors and producers can utilize the same state-of-the-art special effects equipment used by the pros. After learning some behind-the-scenes secrets, kids will have fewer illusions about what they see on the tube. For this contribution alone, CCM deserves an award.

Special weekend activities are open to all, and performances (frequently with audience participation) in the **Storyteller Theater** are ongoing throughout the year (tel. 298-0575). Workshops and classes on radio/TV, video production, photography, and animation are held in the **MediaWorks center** (tel. 675-4178). In late October, CCM hosts a **Halloween party** that culminates in a parade—by costumed visitors only. If you take Metro, pick up lunch at Union Station and enjoy the museum's picnic area.

Admission: $5 for adults and children 2 and older, $2 for senior citizens (60 and above), free for kids under 2.

Open: Daily 10am–5pm. **Closed:** Thanksgiving, Dec 25, Jan 1, and Easter. **Metro:** Union Station (the museum is only a few blocks away, but this is not the best neighborhood, so take a taxi).

NATIONAL GEOGRAPHIC SOCIETY'S EXPLORERS HALL, 17th Street & M Street NW. Tel. 857-7588.

⭐ Before entering Explorers Hall, watch the short introductory videotape to familiarize young trailblazers with the National Geographic Society's mission of "increasing and diffusing geographic knowledge." Permanent and temporary exhibits focus on ancient civilizations, human evolution, and global and space expeditions. Most exhibits are too sophisticated for kids under 8, but older children enjoy **Explorers Hall** for its relatively intimate size. Here, complex geographic information is explained at a level they can readily understand and appreciate by using the many interactive exhibits and videos.

Of special interest to toddler tagalongs is a replica of **Jacques Cousteau's undersea diving bell,** a huge globe with a waistline bigger than Daddy's (*this* equator measures a whopping 34 feet around!), and the **Mammals kiosk,** where the touchscreen reveals pictures of 700 animals and 155 vocalizations. **Henry the macaw** (hopefully, still drawing breath as you read this) is the aging mascot of a massive 2,000-year-old stone head from La Venta, Mexico. If Henry is in a particularly good mood, he may introduce himself or wow you with his paper-shredding act.

Test your trivial pursuit of geophysical knowledge in **Geographica,** feel a tornado, walk beneath a flying dinosaur, or experience orbital flight in **Earth Station One.** Your kids may have to drag you away from Global Access, an educational, fun-to-play video game. After picking a country you'd like to know more about, choose specific topics (history, culture, flora and fauna, etc.) from the menu. *Voilà!* Press a button and the living atlas knows all, sees all, and tells all.

Kids discover the remote-controlled video microscope reveals a much sharper image than the one in biology class, and seeing the flag and paraphernalia from Admiral Robert E. Peary's 1909 expedition to the North Pole drives home one history lesson in a hurry. Lower elementary school groups get a lesson in geography and map studies in **The Young Geographers Show.**

Take the same International Gallup Poll Survey of geographic knowledge that was administered worldwide in 1988. The U.S. fared poorly compared with other industrialized nations, and 75% of the U.S. adults polled couldn't find the Persian Gulf on a map.

In the **Television Room,** scenes from the Society's enormously popular and instructive TV series are aired. Peruse the Washington sky overhead in the small planetarium, then take a gander at a nearly 4-billion-year-old moon rock. Pick up past and current copies of the *National Geographic* magazine, a wide and interesting selection of beautifully photographed books for the whole family, intricately detailed maps, globes, and souvenirs in the **Explorers Den.**

Admission: Free.

Open: Mon–Sat 9am–5pm, Sun and hols 10am–5pm. **Closed:** Dec 25. **Metro:** Farragut North (Connecticut Ave. and L St. exit) or Farragut West.

THE BUREAU OF ENGRAVING AND PRINTING, 14th and C Streets SW. (enter on 14th Street) Tel. 447-9709 or 447-0193.

You can bet your bottom dollar that the buck *starts* here. Kids old enough to appreciate money will go gaga over the green stuff. My son has never recovered from being denied a souvenir $5 bill after touring the bureau for the first time when he was 6. He still can't understand why, with all that moolah, the bureau couldn't spare a bill.

Get here early (by 8:30am in spring and summer) for the short film and 25-minute self-guided tour. The bureau prints Treasury bonds, nearly 40 billion postage stamps a year, and White House invitations. Workers in round-the-clock shifts print about 22 million notes per day; that's about $77 billion annually.

Intaglio is not some new pasta shape, but the process by which the bills are printed. Each sheet (plain old paper at the start) picks up color from ink-filled lines engraved in the heavy steel plates. The backs are printed first; the faces the next day. At the FBI, you'll learn that counterfeiting at this level is very difficult.

If you think pieces of eight were invented by Robert Louis Stevenson for *Treasure Island,* stop between 8:30am and 3:30pm at the **Visitors Center,** where you'll find the real thing as well as electronic games and video displays related to the "root of all evil." You may also purchase a souvenir bag of shredded green. (Incidentally, the life expectancy of a $1 bill is 18 months. Easy come, easy go.)

Admission: Free.

Open: Mon–Fri, 9am–2pm. **Closed:** Federal holidays and the week between Dec 25 and Jan 1. **Metro:** Smithsonian.

2. MORE ATTRACTIONS

ANACOSTIA NEIGHBORHOOD MUSEUM, 1901 Fort Place SE in Fort Stanton Park. Tel. 357-2700.

You have to cross Washington's lesser known river, the Anacostia, to get to this Smithsonian facility that focuses on black art, culture, and history. To supplement its permanent collection and changing exhibits, the Anacostia offers free family workshops and shows throughout the year. Call the museum's education department (tel. 287-3369) to find out about upcoming children's activities.

Admission: Free.

Open: Daily 10am–5pm. **Closed:** Dec 25. **Metro:** Federal Triangle; walk to 10th St. and Pennsylvania Ave. NW and take any "A" bus.

ARLINGTON NATIONAL CEMETERY, Arlington, VA (west side of Memorial Bridge). Tel. 703/692-0931.

More than 216,000 of our war dead are buried in the hallowed hills overlooking the nation's capital from the Virginia side of the Potomac River.

Try to include this in your itinerary, especially if you have school-age children in tow—there is much to feed the mind and the spirit.

Specially trained members of the 3rd Infantry Regiment from adjacent Fort Myer guard the simple but inspiring white marble **Tomb of the Unknown Soldier** day and night. The soldiers are part of the nation's oldest military unit known as the Old Guard, which dates back to colonial times. The changing of the guard takes place every half hour from April through September, and every hour on the hour from October through March.

The **Memorial Amphitheatre** is the setting for Memorial and Veterans' Day services. Junior historians interested in the Spanish-American War will want to see the mast from the U.S.S. *Maine* ("Remember the *Maine*") on the other side of Memorial Drive.

The imposing Greek Revival mansion at the top of the hill, **Arlington House,** once belonged to Gen. Robert E. Lee and Mary Randolph Custis, who just happened to be Martha Washington's great-granddaughter. Although the estate became Union property during the Civil War, the government ultimately bought the property, and since 1933 the National Park Service has been cutting the grass and taking care of the

ARLINGTON NATIONAL CEMETERY

400 m
444 yd
0

Netherlands Carillon

To Marine Corps War Memorial

Jackson Ave.

Lincoln Dr.

Sherman Dr.

FORT MYER

Arlington House (Custis-Lee Mansion)

Meigs Dr.

Garfield Dr.

Iran Memorial/ Challenger Memorial

U.S.S. Maine Memorial

Farragut Dr.

Jackson Circle

Confederate Memorial

Rough Riders Monument

McPherson Dr.

Memorial Dr.

Wilson Dr.

Memorial Amphitheatre/ Tomb of the Unknowns

Nurses Memorial

Porter Dr.

Grant Dr.

Pershing Dr.

Jesup Dr.

U.S. Coast Guard Memorial

Sheridan Dr.

Roosevelt Dr.

Memorial Gate

ARLINGTON CEMETERY

Visitor Center

Arlington Memorial Bridge

Lady Bird Johnson Park

Memorial Dr.

McClellan Dr.

York Dr.

Eisenhower Dr.

Arnold Dr.

Porter Dr.

Marshall Dr.

Patton Dr.

Jefferson Davis Hwy.

Boundary Dr.

Washington Blvd.

Pentagon

110

27

244

Abrams, Gen. Creighton 27
Barrow, T. Sgt. Joe L. 18
Bonesteel, Gen. Chas. III 28
Boyington, Col. "Pappy" 17
Bradley, Gen. Omar 1
Brown, Gen. George S. 24
Bryan, Col. William Jennings 33
Byrd, R. Adm. Richard E. 15
Chaffee, Lt. Comdr. Roger 29
Chennault, Lt. Gen. Claire Lee 13
Decker, Gen. George H. 21
Douglas, Justice William O. 6
Grissom, Lt. Col. Virgil I. 30
Halsey, Ft. Adm. William Jr. 14
Holmes, Capt. Oliver Wendell 5
James, Gen. Daniel 11
Kennedy, Pres. John F. 8

Kennedy, Robert F. 9
L'Enfant, Pierre Charles 16
Leahy, Ft. Adm. W.D. 12
Lincoln, Capt. Robert Todd 3
Louis, Joe: see Barrow, Joe Louis
Marshall, Gen. George C. 20
Murphy, Audie 26
Peary, R. Adm. Robert E. 34
Pershing, Gen. George 32
Reed, Maj. Walter 31
Rickover, Adm. Hyman 7
Scobee, Comdr. Francis 23
Sheridan, Gen. Philip H. 10
Smith, Capt. Michael 19
Taft, Pres. William H. 2
Wainwright, Gen. Jonathan 4
Warren, Chief Justice Earl 25

furnishings. Check out the servants' quarters during the free self-guided tour (9:30am to 4:30pm October through March; until 6pm April through September).

The marble, slate, and Cape Cod fieldstone **gravesite of John F. Kennedy,** 35th U.S. president, and two of his infant children, lies off Sheridan Drive on the sloping lawn below Arlington House. At night the Eternal Flame can be seen from the Rooftop Terrace of the Kennedy Center and several other D.C. vantage points. **Senator Robert Kennedy's grave** lies close by, marked by a simple cross. The site is best visited early in the morning before the masses arrive.

Pierre L'Enfant was moved from a pauper's grave to his final resting place near Arlington House when it finally dawned on those in power that, despite his supposedly cantankerous disposition, L'Enfant did a bang-up job designing Washington.

The **Marine Corps Memorial** and statue of the marines raising the flag over Iwo Jima are near the Orde-Weitzel Gate at the north end of the cemetery. The U.S. Marine Drum and Bugle Corps and Silent Drill team perform at the Iwo Jima Memorial Tuesday evenings at 7pm in the summertime (late May through August). Free shuttle buses whisk visitors from the Visitors Center to the parade site (tel. 433-4173). Nearby is the 49-bell **Netherlands Carillon** (tel. 703/285-2598), where you can climb the tower (kids under 12 must be with an adult), and every spring visitors tiptoe through 15,000 blooming tulips. Enjoy a concert by guest carillonneurs on Saturdays and holidays during April, May, and September from 2 to 4pm. In June, July, and August, the concerts are from 6:30 to 8:30pm.

Just north of Arlington Cemetery at **Fort Myer,** visit the caisson platoon stables of the Old Guard, which counted George Washington as one of its members. The horses, used in processions and presidential funerals, can be viewed Monday through Friday from noon to 4pm. Drive here or take a taxi from the Arlington Cemetery Metro or Visitors Center. Nearby, the Old Guard Museum contains displays dating from the Revolutionary War era. The museum is open Monday through Saturday from 9am to 4pm, Sunday from 1 to 4pm.

Admission: Free.

Open: Apr–Sept 8am–7pm, until 5pm the rest of year. **Metro:** Arlington Cemetery on the Blue Line. You can also walk across Arlington Memorial Bridge (from near the Lincoln Memorial), or board a Tourmobile downtown or at the Visitor Center.

ARTS AND INDUSTRIES BUILDING, 900 Jefferson Dr. SW, on the south side of the Mall. Tel. 357-2700.

The contents of this brick and sandstone edifice, the first National Museum, constitute a time capsule of Victoriana. The 1876 Philadelphia International Exposition was re-created here for the nation's 1976 Bicentennial and celebrates the first 100 years of American technology. Have a look at everyday objects found in a Victorian home, samples of 19th-century clothing, and a copies of *Uncle Tom's Cabin* and cookbooks of the day in the North Hall. Older kids enjoy wandering through the West Hall exhibits of items from a bygone era—an ice cream machine, telegraph, and printing press.

A 45-foot model of the cruiser U.S.S. *Antietam* and the restored 1876 Santa Cruz Railroad locomotive engine are real kid-pleasers. See actual pieces of Plymouth Rock and Lincoln memorabilia too.

Actors, dancers, mimes, musicians, and puppeteers grace the Discovery Theater stage in performances for children during the school year (tel. 357-1500). See Chapter 6 for details.

Admission: Free.

Open: Daily 10am–5:30pm. Closed Christmas. **Metro:** Smithsonian.

B'NAI B'RITH KLUTZNICK MUSEUM, 1640 Rhode Island Ave. NW. Tel. 857-6583.

More than 20 centuries of Jewish history are documented in the first-floor museum of B'nai B'rith headquarters. Supplementing the permanent collection of religious books, Torahs, Judaic art, and ceremonial objects are special exhibits focusing on immigration, the Holocaust, and other aspects of Jewish history. Visit the sculpture garden and museum shop for books, ceremonial items, and crafts. A family Hanukkah celebration is held every December.

Admission: Free, but donations appreciated.

Open: Sun–Fri 10am–5pm. **Closed:** Sat and Jewish and legal hols. **Metro:** Farragut North.

THE CORCORAN GALLERY OF ART, 17th Street and Constitution Avenue NW. Tel. 638-3211.

Although Washington's first museum is best known for its permanent collections of American and French Impressionist art and special exhibitions of contemporary art and photography, the first-floor double atrium and imposing marble staircase may impress kids more than what's hanging on the walls. **Tours** are conducted daily at 12:30pm. The Corcoran School of Art offers a four-year program to students of the fine arts and photography and offers studio classes for children of all ages.

Before you look at a single work, stop in the gift shop and pick up a treasure hunt sheet and coloring/sticker book—*Presenting the Past: An American Journey*—to enhance your visit. The two-volume *American Paintings in the Corcoran Gallery of Art*, which discusses major pieces in the collection, is written at a level many school-age children can understand. The gift shop also carries a good selection of children's books and educational trinkets. For information on special events and group tours, call the education department (tel. 638-3211, ext. 320).

Admission: Free.

Open: Tues–Sun 10am–4:30pm; Thurs 10am–9pm. **Closed:** Mon, Dec 25 and Jan 1. **Metro:** Farragut West or Farragut North.

DAR MUSEUM, 1776 D St. NW. Tel. 879-3240.

⭐ Do not pass go, do not collect $200, just make a beeline for the Children's Attic on the second floor, where you'll find 18th- and 19th-century children's furniture, toys, and dolls. Dollhouse aficionados will delight in the miniature furniture and accessories. To introduce young ones to early American history, one-hour **Colonial Adventure tours** for 5- to 7-year-olds are held the first and third Sundays of every month from 2 to 3pm. Groups of 2 to 15 are welcome, as long as they've made reservations well in advance (tel. 879-3239). Kids don Colonial-style garb and visit a reproduction of a one-room house while imagining what it would be like to sleep in a trundle bed right beside their parents. The "Touch of Independence" area is filled with touchable kid-size period furniture and old-style toys and dolls. A rectangular piece of wood that looks like a cutting board bears the alphabet and Lord's Prayer on a small piece of paper. This horn book, so named because a thin sheet of animal horn protected the paper from the elements, was once a child's introduction to reading. Adults can tour the furnished state rooms while the kids are discovering history.

Admission: Free.
Open: Mon–Fri 8:30am–4pm; Sun 1–5pm. **Closed:** Sat. **Metro:** Farragut West; walk south on 17th Street.

DEPARTMENT OF INTERIOR MUSEUM, 1849 C St. NW. Tel. 208-4743.

If you thought the Interior Department was a government decorating firm, do pay a visit here to see what the National Park Service, Fish and Wildlife Service, Geological Survey, Office of Territorial and International Affairs, and Bureaus of Land Management, Reclamation, Mines, and Indian Affairs are all about. Many aspects of their activities are well-displayed in the museum's exhibits of Native American artifacts and crafts, mapping techniques, mineral specimens, and early land bounties (grants of land given in lieu of monetary payment for military service). Across the hall in Room 1023, the Indian Craft Shop sells quality Indian pottery, jewelry, and other crafts Monday through Friday from 8am to 5pm.

Admission: Free
Open: Mon–Fri 8am–4pm. **Closed:** federal hols. Adults must have a photo I.D. (driver's license will do). **Metro:** Farragut West.

DEPARTMENT OF STATE DIPLOMATIC RECEPTION ROOMS, 23rd and C streets NW. Tel. 647-3241.

Kids over the age of 12 who are interested in seeing a $30 million showcase of 18th-century American furniture and decorative arts can take a fine arts tour of the diplomatic reception rooms on the eighth floor of the State Department. Renovation has been ongoing since 1961, and the results are spectacular. The terrace view of the Lincoln Memorial and Potomac River aren't bad either.

Admission: Free.
Open: Tours Mon–Fri 9:30am, 10:30am, 3pm, by reservation only. **Metro:** Foggy Bottom.

FORD'S THEATRE AND LINCOLN MUSEUM, 511 10th St. NW between E and F streets. Tel. 347-4833 for box-office information, 426-6927 for museum.

On April 14, 1865, President Abraham Lincoln was shot by John Wilkes Booth while attending a performance of *Our American Cousin* at Ford's. Lincoln was carried to the house of William Petersen across the street, and the president died there the next morning. The incident was anything but good for business, and Ford's was not used again as a theater until 1968. In the interim, it was a records-processing site and Army Medical Museum before Congress coughed up the funds to fully restore the theater to its 1865 appearance.

Among the Lincoln memorabilia in the **basement museum** are the clothes Lincoln wore the night he was assassinated and the Derringer pistol used by Booth. Two of the more eerie items in the exhibit are the Lincoln life mask and plaster casts of his hands. Audiovisual displays describe Lincoln's early life, political experiences, and presidential years.

Several shows have gone on to Broadway after premiering at Ford's, and every December Dickens's *Christmas Carol* is revived. Catch a performance at this historic theater if time permits. Students with an ID get reduced-price tickets half an hour before curtain time.

Visit the **Petersen House ("The House Where Lincoln Died")** at 526 10th Street (tel. 426-6830) to round out your picture of Lincoln's assassination. It gives me the willies but kids love it. Because the bed in the ground-floor bedroom was too short, Lincoln was laid diagonally across it. The original blood-stained pillow makes a powerful impression on kids (and adults too). In the front parlor, the clock is stopped at 7:22am, the time of Lincoln's death. In 1896 the government bought the house for $30,000, and now it is maintained by the National Park Service.

Admission: Free.

Open: Daily 9am–5pm. **Closed:** Dec 25. **Metro:** Metro Center.

THE FREER GALLERY OF ART, Jefferson Drive at 12th Street SW on the south side of the Mall. Tel. 357-2104.

After extensive renovation, the Freer will reopen late in 1992 or early in 1993. Special family programs are planned. Detroit industrialist and art connoisseur Charles Lang Freer, who made a bundle in railroad cars, was James McNeill Whistler's chief patron. Assembled here is one of the world's largest Whistler collections (over 1,200 pieces), as well as Asian art and paintings by late-19th- and early-20th-century American artists. A new underground gallery joins the Freer to the Sackler Gallery.

The Peacock Room, moved piece by piece from London to Detroit to Washington, is reason enough to visit the Freer. Sophisticated kids over 10 enjoy the fascinating story behind this extraordinary dining room.

Admission: Free.

Open: Daily 10am–5:30pm. **Closed:** Dec 25 and through early 1993. **Metro:** Smithsonian (Mall or Independence Avenue exit).

HIRSHHORN MUSEUM AND SCULPTURE GARDEN, Independence Avenue and 8th Street SW on the south side of the Mall. Tel. 357-2700.

⭐ While other teenage boys were looking through art books for erotica, a young Latvian immigrant, Joseph Hirshhorn (1899–1981), was buying etchings in New York. The rest, as they say, is history. The museum bearing his name opened in 1974 with his little "gift" of mostly 20th-century art—2,000 pieces of sculpture and 4,000 paintings and drawings. When Hirshhorn died in 1981 at the age of 82, additional works were bequeathed from his estate. The collection continues to receive gifts from other donors, and in 1989 it was the seventh most visited museum in the United States.

Even kids who gag at the mention of going to an art museum find something to like at the Hirshhorn. Since preschoolers relate best to large tactile objects, take them outside to the sculpture garden. Your little ones will realize the sculptor had a boat in mind when he created *Isis* on the museum's plaza. Is there a kid alive who hasn't heard of Mickey Mouse? Witness the aluminum and steel *Geometric Mouse*. Examine *Needle Tower* from several angles, then imagine the size of the person who would sit in what could be Paul Bunyan's humongous oak chair. Even very young kids are awed by *The Burghers of Calais* and *The Miner*. Afterward, they can cool their intellectual heels while riding the carousel next to the garden.

Kindergarteners on up are intrigued by the museum's doughnut-like inner space. It's easy to become disoriented while traversing the concentric rings, but that's part of the fun. Paintings hang on windowless walls in the outer circle, while sculptures and plenty of comfortable seating fill the inner circle where light pours in through

WASHINGTON, D.C.

Arlington National Cemetery ❶
Arts & Industries Building ❷
B'nai B'rith Klutznick Museum ❸
Constitution Gardens ❹
Corcoran Gallery of Art ❺
DAR Museum ❻
Department of Interior Museum ❼
Department of State Diplomatic
    Reception Rooms ❽
Dumbarton Oaks Gardens ❾
Dupont Circle Park ❿
Ford's Theatre & Lincoln Museum ⓫

Freer Gallery of Art ⓬
Hirshhorn Museum & Sculpture
    Garden ⓭
John F. Kennedy Center ⓮
Lady Bird Johnson Park ⓯
Library of Congress ⓰
Marine Corps Museum ⓱
National Aquarium ⓲
National Arboretum ⓳
National Archives ⓴
National Building Museum ㉑
National Gallery of Art ㉒

MORE ATTRACTIONS

National Museum of African Art 23
National Museum of American Art 24
National Museum of Women in the
    Arts 25
Navy Memorial Museum 26
Octagon House 27
Old Post Office Pavilion 28
Old Stone House 29
Phillips Collection 30
Renwick Gallery 31
Rock Creek Park 32
Sackler (Arthur M.) Gallery 33

Shakespeare Theatre 34
Smithsonian Building 35
Theodore Roosevelt Island 36
U.S. Botanic Garden 37
Vietnam Veterans Memorial 38
Washington Dolls' House
    & Toy Museum 39
Washington National Cathedral 40
West Potomac Park 41
White House 42
Woodrow Wilson House Museum 43

floor-to-ceiling windows. There is a museum shop and an auditorium on the first floor (lower level). On the second floor, look for *Guardian Angel* and works by Rodin and Degas. Ask your kids which of Matisse's "Heads of Jeanette" looks like you in the morning. Upstairs, introduce them to Henry Moore's work.

Kids 10 and older can explore on their own (if it's okay with you) after viewing a short orientation film. They may like the portraits by Eakins and Sargent, before moving on to Bellows's *Ringside Seats,* Sloane's *Carmine Street,* and works by O'Keeffe, de Kooning, Dali, Pollock, and others. Many young people find the more abstract works appealing, even though "they don't look like anything." For a sweeping panorama of the Mall area, peer out the windows of the Abram Lerner Lounge, and don't miss Calder's *Fish* mobile. It used to dangle in the Hirshhorns' Connecticut hallway.

At the information desk, pick up a calendar of events and ask about the Saturday films for kids. **Tours** are given Monday through Saturday at 10:30am, noon, and 1:30pm; on Sunday at 12:30, 1:30, 2:30, and 3:30pm. In the museum shop you'll find posters, art books, and prints.

Admission: Free.

Open: Daily 10am–5:30pm; sculpture garden 7:30am–dusk (closed now—call for reopening dates). **Closed:** Dec 25. (Strollers are not allowed inside and have to be left at the checkroom where infant backpacks are available.) **Metro:** L'Enfant Plaza (Smithsonian Museums exit).

THE JOHN F. KENNEDY CENTER FOR THE PERFORMING ARTS, 2700 F St. NW. Tel. 467-4600.

The best part of visiting the Kennedy Center, as far as kids under 12 are concerned, is throwing coins in the River Terrace fountains and taking in the sights from the Roof Terrace. The beauty of the surrounding scene—the Potomac waterfront, Georgetown, Rosslyn, part of Arlington Cemetery—is further enhanced at night.

See the 15-minute **movie** in Motor Lobby A, then decide if your kids are sufficiently interested to take the 50-minute **guided tour.** If not, pick up brochures at the Friends Information Center (Plaza Entrance, Hall of States) and walk them through the Grand Foyer, Hall of Nations, and Hall of States, blanketed with 4,150 yards of red carpet. They'll like the flags, high ceilings, and bust of JFK. Between 10am and 1pm, you can peek in the theaters. Wouldn't the crystal chandelier (a gift from Austria) in the Opera House make a nice diamond brooch?

Except for a handful of theaters and performing groups, Washington was culturally desolate before the Kennedy Center opened its doors in 1971. Although the center's architecture (by Edward Durell Stone), artistic policies, and internal politics continue to arouse controversy, one thing's for sure: Any day you can come here you'll see a handful of performances by the best and brightest. To find out about Kennedy Center events, see Chapter 6, "Their Kind of Entertainment."

Admission: Free.

Open: Daily 10am–9pm; continuous free tours 10am–1pm. **Metro:** Foggy Bottom. **Bus:** No. 46 down New Hampshire Avenue from Dupont Circle or No. 18 from Metro Center.

LIBRARY OF CONGRESS, Capitol Hill, 1st Street SE between Independence Avenue and East Capitol Street. Tel. 707-5458.

The nation's library is also the world's largest. Established as a research center for Congress in 1800, the library's first collection, then housed in the Capitol, was burned during the War of 1812. The cornerstone for the **Thomas Jefferson Building** section, a formidable example of Italian Renaissance architecture, was laid in 1890, and construction lasted 11 years until it was complete. (When you're on the Hill stop to see the exterior and Great Hall of the Thomas Jefferson Building, and enjoy the view of the Capitol from the west steps.)

Anyone over high-school age may do research here but, unlike your public library at home, you may not borrow the books. More than 500 miles of shelves fill the Thomas Jefferson, James Madison, and John Adams buildings. The **Main Reading Room,** located in the Jefferson Building, reopened in June 1991 after a 3-year shutdown for restoration, part of an $81.5 million facelift to be completed in 1995. The only way for nonresearchers to gain entry into the Main Reading Room is during the hour-long **guided tour,** which leaves from the Visitor Services Center in the ground-floor lobby Monday through Friday at 10am, 1 and 3pm. Kids 12 and older should find the tour interesting; anyone younger, *bor*-ing. *America's Library,* a 20-minute film, is shown every half hour (on the hour and half hour) Monday through Friday from 9am to 9pm, Saturday from 9am to 5pm, Sunday from 1 to 5pm. Among the special collections housed in 20 reading rooms are children's literature and genealogy.

The Gutenberg Bible and Giant Bible of Mainz are displayed on the main floor, along with rotating exhibits of photographs, music manuscripts, prints, and posters. Skip the Jefferson Building tour with young children and head for the **Madison Building** next door on 1st Street, between Independence Avenue and C Street SE. The Copyright Office, one of the library's departments, is located here. On the fourth floor the copyright exhibit features one of the original Maltese falcons, masks from *Star Wars,* Bert and Ernie puppets, Barbie dolls, posters, and more! Visit anytime between 8:30am and 9:30pm.

Admission: Free.

Open: Mon–Fri 8:30am–9:30pm; Sat–Sun 8:30am–6pm. **Closed:** Dec 25 and other major hols.

Metro: Capitol South.

MARINE CORPS MUSEUM, Washington Navy Yard, Building 58, 9th and M streets SE. Tel. 433-3354.

With the exception of former Marines, many visitors don't know this museum exists. The history of the Corps is traced, from the John Hancock–signed commissioning papers of the first officer in 1775 to a skull-and-crossbones Sandinista flag from Nicaragua. Kids gravitate to the Vietnamese exhibit, which evokes images of Vietcong guerillas and steamy rice paddies. Not just a repository for battle memorabilia, the small museum provides an overview of American history from our country's earliest days to the present.

Admission: Free.

Open: Mon–Sat 10am–4pm; Sun noon–5pm. **Metro:** Eastern Market.

NATIONAL AQUARIUM, Department of Commerce, 14th Street and Constitution Avenue NW. Tel. 377-2826.

More than 250 species are contained in 50 tanks at the oldest public aquarium in the nation. Assorted salt- and freshwater fish, including sharks, eel, and Japanese carp, get along swimmingly. The piranhas—you'll be happy to learn—have their own tank.

The sharks are fed Monday, Wednesday, and Saturday at 2pm; the piranhas Tuesday, Thursday, and Sunday at 2pm. In the "touch tank" kids can get their hands wet examining horseshoe crabs and other noncarnivorous beach-dwellers. **Admission:** $2 adults, 75¢ kids 3–12 and seniors. **Open:** Daily 9am–5pm. **Closed:** Dec 25. **Metro:** Federal Triangle.

NATIONAL ARCHIVES, Constitution Avenue and 8th Street NW. Tel. 501-5000 for information on exhibits and films, 501-5402 for research information.

If you have any doubts about the inscription on the statue out front—"What is past is prologue"—step inside the rotunda. The building is a classical structure with 72—count 'em—Corinthian columns designed by John Russell Pope, architect of the National Gallery and Jefferson Memorial. Trivia fact No. 479: Because the building was built on a creek that ran through the city, more than 8,500 pilings had to be driven into the ground before construction could begin. Take a gander first at the 1297 version of the Magna Carta, then at the Declaration of Independence, two pages of the Constitution, and the Bill of Rights. Every night our country's three "Charters of Freedom," already sealed in helium-filled bronze and glass cases, are lowered into a bomb- and fireproof 55-ton steel and concrete vault. During the day armed guards keep an eye on things, so kids will have to look elsewhere for show-and-tell souvenirs.

The National Archives is also the storehouse for 5 million photos (including Mathew Brady's Civil War snapshots), nearly 12 million maps, charts, and aerial photographs, and 91 million feet of motion-picture film. And talk about odd couples, the Archives has a photo of Elvis Presley and Richard Nixon at the White House in 1970.

Thousands of old newsreels can be screened in the motion picture, sound, and video branch on the ground floor, but you have to make an appointment first. Be sure to pick up an events schedule listing films, lectures, and workshops. I strongly recommend the free behind-the-scenes **docent tours,** appropriate for school-age kids and adults, weekdays at 10:15am and 1:15pm. Call the tour office between 9am and 4pm and reserve well in advance (tel. 501-5205).

Alex Haley began searching for his *Roots* here. So can you!

Children under 16 must be accompanied by an adult. Researchers 16 and older must have a valid photo ID. Call first for details. Research rooms are open from 8:45am to 10pm Monday through Friday and 9am to 5pm Saturday, except for federal holidays. Use the Pennsylvania Avenue entrance and stop in Room 400 for advice before you begin your quest. **Admission:** Free.

Open: Daily after Labor Day–Mar 31 10am–5:30pm; 10am–9pm Apr–Labor Day. **Closed:** Dec 25. **Metro:** Archives.

NATIONAL BUILDING MUSEUM, Judiciary Square, at F and G streets between 4th and 5th streets NW. Tel. 272-2448.

Once you visit the former Pension Building, which somewhat resembles Rahway Prison on the outside, part Roman bath and Renaissance palace on the inside, you'll know why this museum is dedicated to the building arts. The magnificence of the setting far surpassed the entertainment and starring players at an inaugural ball I attended here some years ago.

Several government agencies have occupied the space between 1926, when the

Pension Bureau vacated, and 1981, when Congress appropriated funds for restoration. The Great Hall measures 316 feet by 116 feet, and the ceiling is 159 feet high. That's about 15 stories. Take your kids without any fanfare; perhaps blindfold them first. If they're not impressed, give them mouth-to-mouth.

A permanent exhibition, "An Architectural Wonder: The U.S. Pension Building," details the building's history and construction, while other nonpermanent exhibits deal with architecture and the building arts.

Admission: Free.

Open: Mon–Fri 10am–4pm; Sat–Sun noon–4pm. Closed major holidays.

Metro: Judiciary Square.

NATIONAL GALLERY OF ART, on the north side of the Mall between 3rd and 7th Streets NW (entrances at 6th Street and Constitution Avenue or Madison Drive). Tel. 737-4215.

Those of you old enough to remember Ed Sullivan will recall his fondness for telling audiences, "This is a really big show." Well, the National Gallery is a really big show. Let's dispense with how to get in and out first. The East and West Buildings are connected by an underground concourse with a moving walkway. You can enter the West Building from the Mall (Madison Drive) or Constitution Avenue at 6th Street; also at 4th or 7th streets between Constitution Avenue and Madison Drive. The only above-ground entrance to the East Building is on 4th Street.

Baby strollers are available at each entrance. Information on special exhibitions, tours, lectures, films, and concerts are available on the main floor of the Rotunda or ground floor of the East Wing. When there's a *"really* big show," go Monday or Tuesday before noon. Children's and family guides and programs complement the special exhibitions (tel. 842-6249).

In 1989, the National Gallery topped the list of the 10 most popular art museums in the United States, attracting more than 6.2 million visitors. The classically inspired **West Building,** another Pope creation, houses 12th- to 20th-century sculpture and paintings within its 500,000-square-foot interior. Industrialist Andrew Mellon's collection formed the nucleus, augmented by the sizable collections of Samuel H. Kress, Joseph Widener, Chester Dale, and numerous individual donors.

Given its size and the breadth of its exhibitions, the West Building can be overpowering and bewildering to an adult. It'd be better to show the kids a few things here and then hightail it over to the **East Building,** where contemporary art reigns supreme.

Here are a few suggestions in the West Wing that may appeal to them: The Byzantine *Madonna and Child,* Giotto's *Madonna and Child,* Filippino Lippi's or Botticelli's *Portrait of a Youth,* Raphael's *St. George and the Dragon,* anything by El Greco (kids think he's "weird"), Holbein's *Portrait of Edward VI as a Child,* Fragonard's *Young Girl Reading,* and Renoir's *A Girl with a Watering Can.* They may like Winslow Homer, too, but you can definitely skip the Renaissance tapestries and furniture.

Do show them the bronze statue of *Mercury* on top of the fountain in the rotunda, then head for either of the lovely colonnaded **Garden Courts.** Under arched skylights, with comfortable upholstered chairs overlooking putti fountains, these courts are sublime settings to rest museum-weary feet (and children).

The **East Building** is like a breath of fresh air, and if your kids see nothing more than the soaring ground-level central court with its three-story-high Calder mobile and vibrant (much-too-large-for-the-living room) Miró tapestry, you will have accomplished something. Ask them if they recognize the shape of the building. It's a trapezoid, which architect I. M. Pei ingeniously divided into two interconnected triangles.

Usually, kids are drawn either to the neatness of Mondrian's grids or the sloppiness of Motherwell's splotches. See what they make of the latter's inkblot, *Reconciliation Elegy*. Their answers should make for interesting conversation. Roy Lichtenstein's *Look Mickey* will strike a familiar chord, while Matisse's *Large Composition with Masks* enchants all ages.

Don't leave without inspecting the Concourse level. Kids love the moving walkway and the waterfall next to the Concourse Buffet, good for a snack or meal from 10am to 4pm, Monday through Saturday, and 11am to 5pm on Sunday.

Admission: Free.

Open: Mon–Sat 10am–5pm, Sun 11am–6pm; extended summer hours. Closed Dec 25 and Jan 1. **Metro:** Archives or Judiciary Square.

THE NATIONAL MUSEUM OF AFRICAN ART, 950 Independence Avenue SW. Tel. 357-2700 or 357-4600.

Most kids over 5 find the carved wooden masks, fertility dolls, and somewhat menacing Cameroon court figure of particular interest in here, the only museum in the United States dedicated solely to African art. The collection of mostly 19th- and 20th-century traditional arts and artifacts, formerly housed in cramped Capitol Hill quarters, relocated in 1987 to its spacious new underground home. The tomblike setting is shared with the Sackler Gallery of Asian and Near Eastern Art. More than 6,000 objects in the permanent collection are displayed in rotating exhibits. One or two weekends a month (more often in summer) there's storytelling for kids, focused on an individual country or special subject. Inquire at the information desk.

Admission: Free.

Open: Daily 10am–5:30pm. **Closed:** Dec 25. **Metro:** Smithsonian.

NATIONAL MUSEUM OF AMERICAN ART, 8th and G streets NW. Tel. 357-3176.

The evolution of American art can be traced from colonial times to today in the nation's oldest federal art collection. Often confused with the National Museum of American History, the NMAA has been at the same address for more than two decades and shares quarters with the National Portrait Gallery in the former Old Patent Office Building. Even if you haven't a prayer of arousing their interest in American art this trip, come see the building, a replica of the Parthenon in Athens. At various times it was a Civil War barracks and hospital, site of Lincoln's second inaugural ball, and temporary quarters for the Department of Interior and Civil Service Commission before reopening in 1968 after extensive renovation.

For the most part, works are chronologically arranged. Those most likely to light a spark are the art of the West Gallery; the paintings by Albert Pinkham Ryder (dark and creepy) and Winslow Homer (bright and upbeat); and James Hampton's glittering and shimmering *The Throne of the Third Heaven*, which is a great ad for aluminum foil. Take a look at the Lincoln Gallery, with its 32 marble pillars and 28-foot-high ceiling.

Admission: Free. Tours are given weekdays at noon and weekends at 2pm.

Open: Daily 10am–5:30pm. **Closed:** Dec 25. **Metro:** Gallery Place or Metro Center.

NATIONAL MUSEUM OF WOMEN IN THE ARTS, 801 13th St. NW at New York Avenue NW. Tel. 783-5000.

Opened in 1987 after $8 million worth of restoration to the former Masonic Grand Lodge, the museum has over 1,200 paintings, prints, and sculpture by 400 women spanning five centuries. Come for Mary Cassatt, Georgia O'Keeffe, Helen Frankenthaler, Elaine de Kooning, Käthe Kollwitz, and Judy Chicago.

Admission: Suggested contribution $3 for adults, $2 for children.

Open: Mon–Sat 10am–5pm, Sun noon–5pm. **Metro:** Metro Center.

NAVY MEMORIAL MUSEUM, Building 76, Washington Navy Yard, 9th and M Streets SE. Tel. 433-2651.

The history of the U.S. Navy is chronicled from the Revolutionary War to the present. Kids especially love the model ships and weaponry. They can turn a sub periscope, climb on cannons, and work the barrels of anti-aircraft weapons. When they tire of war games they can board the destroyer U.S.S. *Barry* berthed outside.

Admission: Free.

Open: Mon–Fri 9am–4pm, Sat–Sun 10am–5pm. **Metro:** Eastern Market, then a 15-minute walk—I'd take a taxi.

OCTAGON HOUSE, 1799 New York Ave. NW. Tel. 638-3105.

Built in 1800 as a summer retreat for a family of wealthy Virginia planters, the Federal-style townhouse (not really a perfect octagon) was a temporary home for President Madison and the missus after the British burned the White House during the War of 1812. Madison signed the Treaty of Ghent here in 1815. Today it's the headquarters of the American Institute of Architects, who built offices behind the house. The building is undergoing a major restoration that includes archeological examination, and finds from the dig will be on display. Tours are of interest to kids 12 and older.

Admission: $2 donation appreciated.

Open: Tues–Fri 10am–4pm, Sat–Sun noon–4pm. **Metro:** Farragut West.

OLD POST OFFICE PAVILION, 1100 Pennsylvania Ave. NW between 11th and 12th streets. Tel. 289-4224.

⭐ Families love to come here to eat, shop, and enjoy the family entertainment. Do take a few minutes from your chicken wings and peanut butter fudge to inspect a most impressive building. Built in 1899 as quarters for the federal postal department, it suffered years of neglect. The three-level renovated complex reopened in May 1984, thanks largely to the efforts of Nancy Hanks. The stage was once a dirt basement, and you may get dizzy, but look up 196 feet to the skylight roof. Not bad, huh?

If you do nothing else, tour the clock tower. The vista, from the equivalent of a high rise's 12th floor, is astounding. Check out the 10 Congress Bells, replicas of those at Westminster Abbey. They range from 600 to 3,000 pounds, and each one is about 5 feet in diameter. In change ringing, the order in which the bells are struck changes continuously, and it takes nearly 4 hours to go through all the permutations. A full peal honors the opening and closing of Congress, State occasions, and national holidays. You may attend a practice session Thursdays between 6:30 and 9:30pm.

Admission: Free.

Open: Stores: Mon–Sat 10am–8pm, Sun noon–6pm; Restaurants: Mon–Sat 10am–9:30pm, Sun noon–8pm. **Metro:** Federal Triangle.

THE OLD STONE HOUSE, 3051 M St. NW. Tel. 426-6851.

Stop here when you're in Georgetown. Kids feel comfortable in this modest pre-Revolutionary house, probably because it's small like they are. During the summer, concerts are held in the garden, where you can picnic. A candlelight tour is held around Christmas. See "Gardens and Parks" in this chapter for more information.

Admission: Free.

Open: Wed–Sun 8am–4:30pm. House closed Thanksgiving, Dec 25 and Jan 1. Gardens open daily. **Metro:** Foggy Bottom, then a 15-minute walk or take any no. 30 bus from Pennsylvania Avenue.

THE PHILLIPS COLLECTION, 1600 21st St. NW at Q Street Tel. 387-0961.

✪ The Phillips is a rich repository of Impressionist, Post-Impressionist, and contemporary American paintings. Kids take to the intimate museum off Dupont Circle because it is homey (maybe not like *your* home, but homey nonetheless), with furniture, polished floors, and Asian rugs. Most kids react favorably to the playfulness of Klee's works, the sunny colors and good feeling of Renoir's *The Luncheon of the Boating Party,* and the large color canvases of Mark Rothko. When you enter pick up *A Child's Adventure Into The Artist's World of Color,* a guide for adults and kids 6 to 12 to use together. The Phillips also sponsors **Family Saturdays** and **parent/child workshops.** Call to be put on a mailing list (tel. 387-2151). You can grab a light bite at Suzanne's Café, Tuesday through Saturday, 10am to 4pm, and Sunday 2 to 4:30pm. The museum shop has a nice selection of posters, postcards, and art books.

Admission: Free, but contributions appreciated.

Open: Tues–Sat 10am–5pm; Sun 2–7pm. **Closed:** July 4, Thanksgiving, Dec 25 and Jan 1. Free tours Wed and Sat at 2pm. **Metro:** Dupont Circle, Q Street exit.

THE RENWICK GALLERY, Pennsylvania Avenue at 17th Street NW. Tel. 357-2700.

Washington's first private art museum was the original home of the Corcoran collection. Some of the exhibits showcasing contemporary crafts and decorative arts appeal to kids over 10 or 12; some don't. Most kids over 6 have at least a momentary appreciation of the interior space, especially the 90-foot Victorian Grand Salon with its wainscotted plum walls and 38-foot skylight ceiling, reached by a broad, carpeted staircase. You almost expect the trumpets to announce your arrival.

The same mathematical wizard who counted the walls in the Octagon House must have been at work here too. The so-called Octagon Room—with six, not eight sides—was designed for Hiram Powers's nude, *The Greek Slave,* now in the Corcoran. Because of its prurient nature (for the Victorian era), viewing times were once different for men and women.

Admission: Free.

Open: Daily 10am–5:30pm. **Closed:** Dec 25. **Metro:** Farragut North or Farragut West.

THE ARTHUR M. SACKLER GALLERY [OF ASIAN AND NEAR EASTERN ART], 1050 Independence Ave. SW. Tel. 357-2700.

⭐ The Sackler shares half of a subterranean double-pavilion complex with the National Museum of African Art. Plants, skylights, and fountains remind you from time to time that you haven't been buried alive. Chinese bronzes, Southeast Asian sculpture, and Persian manuscripts may not appeal to your kids, and the folks at the Sackler know this. They have ongoing programs—such as shadow-puppet performances to enhance the Indonesian exhibits—that make art less remote. After a visit, kids come away with a better understanding of the cultures represented at the Sackler. For information about museum programs and temporary exhibits, call 357-3200, or inquire at the information desk.

When you ascend to daylight, visit the Victorian-style **Enid A. Haupt Garden,** with its geometric parterre. On one side of the garden you can enter a moongate to an Asian garden; on the other, a waterfall cascades into a small pond. The garden is open Memorial Day to Labor Day 7am–8pm, 7am–5:45pm the rest of the year.

Admission: Free.

Open: Daily 10am–5:30pm. **Closed:** Dec 25. Tours Mon–Fri 11:30am and 2:30pm; Sun 11:30am. **Metro:** Smithsonian.

THE SHAKESPEARE THEATRE, 450 Seventh St. NE. Tel. 547-3230.

⭐ Although it would take a major bribe to get most kids to visit the Folger Shakespeare Library's rare collection of manuscripts and books by the Bard and his contemporaries at the Folger Library (201 E. Capitol St. SE), the same youngsters are turned on by first-rate productions in the Shakespeare Theatre's new 447-seat residence in the Lansburgh Building on Seventh Street NE. A resident acting company presents several classical productions every year. The majority are by Will, often updated with contemporary sets and costumes and actors such Kelly McGillis and Stacy Keach. The theater is a magnet for school groups who find brushing up on Shakespeare far more palatable here than in the classroom. The Shakespeare Theater at the Folger Library is a faithful replica of an Elizabethan theater and presents lesser-known and repertory works.

Admission: Free to visit; admission for performances.

Open: Daily Apr 15–Labor Day; closed Sun Labor Day–Apr 15. **Metro:** Archives or Gallery Place.

THE SMITHSONIAN BUILDING [THE "CASTLE"], 1000 Jefferson Dr. SW. Tel. 357-2700.

As I mentioned earlier, the flagship of the Smithsonian Institution recently underwent a massive renovation to the tune of $2.7 million. Press a button on one of the 13 video-display monitors to dispense information on the Smithsonian and more than 100 other attractions. Eleven pages alone are devoted to kid-pleasing things to do and see. You may have trouble prying your progeny away from the monitors—the highly imaginative and colorful graphics rival Nintendo.

For more information and suggestions, see the introductory material at the beginning of this chapter.

Admission: Free.

Open: Daily 9:30am–5:30pm. **Closed:** Dec 25. **Metro:** Smithsonian.

THE SUPREME COURT, 1st Street NE, between East Capitol Street and Maryland Avenue Tel. 479-3000.

About 150 cases are heard annually by the highest court in the nation, empowered by Article III of the Constitution to ensure congressional, presidential, and state actions comply with the Constitution.

In the imposing structure of classic Greek design, once thought too grandiose for its intention, the Supreme Court hears cases during about half the weeks from the first Monday in October through April. Only about 100 seats are reserved for the public, so arrive by 9am. Cases are heard Mondays through Wednesdays from 10am to 3pm, with a lunch-hour recess from noon to 1pm. While children are welcome in the courtroom, no disruptions are tolerated. This is serious stuff! Phone the information office or consult the *Washington Post*'s "Supreme Court Calendar" for the schedule.

From mid-May to early July, you may attend half-hour sessions on Mondays at 10am, when the justices release orders and opinions. Older children are fascinated by the many rituals attendant with the justices' entrance. You can tell them that "Oyez! Oyez!" is French legalese for "Hear ye, hear ye."

When the court is not in session, you may attend a free **lecture** (9:30am–3:30pm, every hour on the half hour) about Court procedure and the building's architecture. Follow up the lecture with a walk through the Great Hall and see the 20-minute film on the workings of the Court.

On the ground floor, take a look at the imposing spiral staircases and Court-related exhibits. There's also a gift shop on this level, and good meals are served at the adjoining cafeteria (see Chapter 7, "Where Kids Like to Eat"). From the top of the entrance steps, there's a wonderful view of the Capitol.

Admission: Free.

Open: Mon–Fri 9am–4:30pm. **Metro:** Capitol South or Union Station.

VIETNAM VETERANS MEMORIAL, just across from the Lincoln Memorial at 21st Street and Constitution Avenue NW, east of Henry Bacon Drive. Tel. 634-1568.

The Wall, 140 panels of polished black granite stretching almost 500 feet, honors the nearly 60,000 men and women who died or remain missing as a result of the Vietnam War. The wall's two segments meet at an angle; one end takes aim at the Washington Monument, the other, the Lincoln Memorial. Names are listed chronologically, from the first casualty in 1959 to the last in 1975. Although many leave the site misty-eyed, children too young to know anything of the Vietnam War will probably be bored. Vietnam veteran Jan Scruggs initiated the project in 1979 and, since opening on November 13, 1982, the memorial has been one of the most visited sites in Washington.

Admission: Free.

Open: Daily 24 hours, with rangers on duty 8am–midnight. **Metro:** Foggy Bottom (walk east on H or I Street, turn right at 21st Street and walk for 6–7 blocks).

WASHINGTON DOLLS' HOUSE & TOY MUSEUM, 5236 44th St. NW. Tel. 244-0024.

What a treasure house this is! I can't imagine any youngster from 18 months to 80 years not finding pleasure in this wonderland of exquisite dollhouses and antique toys. Founded by writer and avid dollhouse and toy collector Flora Gill

Jacobs in 1975 with *half* of her personal collection, the museum has acquired additional space and numerous gifts from Jacobs and other donors over the years.

If learning were this much fun in school, kids would get all As. The Dibb House is pure Victorian fantasy. The 1920s mansion by Tynietoy (the Rolls of dollhouses) sports an old radio and female figure with a "bob"; (see how the playing cards are fanned out just-so on the parlor table). Viewing "A Shop Windowful of Shops" is like walking down a 19th-century Main Street. Lest boys think this is sissy stuff, show them the early Lionel electric train, shoe-box size dentist's office, Humpty Dumpty circus, and "The Ultimate Ark." They may not admit it, but they'll like the dollhouses too.

In the second-floor shops, collectors will find books and magazines on dolls and dollhouses, furniture and accessories—even miniature quiltables—and cases full of consignment items.

A small Edwardian tearoom with potted palms, glass-topped tables, and an old scale that promises to deliver "honest weight one cent," is available for birthday parties by reservation. Young ladies and gentlemen are served sandwiches and sweets by staff in period dress.

Admission: $3 adults, $1 children under 14.

Open: Tues–Sat 10am–5pm, Sun noon–5pm. **Closed:** Mon. **Metro:** Friendship Heights.

WASHINGTON NATIONAL CATHEDRAL (Cathedral Church of St. Peter and St. Paul), Massachusetts and Wisconsin avenues NW. Tel. 537-6200.

⭐ The sixth largest religious structure in the world sits atop Mount St. Alban, and the top of the tower is 676 feet above sea level—that's high, given Washington's zero elevation. The Gothic-inspired cathedral was begun in 1907, but not until 1990, with the completion of the twin west towers, was the cathedral officially consecrated. Pick up an illustrated guide in the Cathedral Museum Shop detailing the history and architecture before touring on your own, or take the 45-minute guided tour.

Seeing the **Rose Window** in the North Transept at dusk is a religious experience in itself. The vaulted ceiling above the 518-foot-long nave is 102 feet high. This should elicit a "Wow" from blasé you-know-whos. Everything is scaled down to their size in the charming **Children's Chapel,** and the **Pilgrim Observation Gallery** has a fantastic view of Washington beyond the flying buttresses and gargoyles. The Gallery is open Monday through Saturday from 10am to 3:15pm, Sunday from 12:30 to 2:45pm.

Meander through nearly 60 magnificent acres of heavily treed and beautifully landscaped prime real estate. Stop in at the **Bishop's Garden** (open daily during daylight hours) and the **Herb Cottage,** where you can purchase herbs not readily available at most supermarkets Monday through Saturday from 9am to 5pm, Sunday from 10am to 5pm.

The **Flower Mart,** held the first Friday and Saturday in May, features rides, puppet shows, and other activities for kids. In the **Cathedral Medieval Workshop,** kids get a taste of medieval life through arts and crafts projects overseen by guides. They'll learn the purpose of gargoyles (to carry rainwater) while modeling their own out of clay, and they can also try their hand at carving limestone, or, perhaps, make a mini–stained-glass window. The Workshop (tel. 537-2930) is held Saturdays, from 11am to 2pm on a first-come, first-served basis.

Admission: Free.

Open: Mon–Sat 10am–4:30pm, Sun 12:30–2:45pm. **Metro:** Cleveland Park, then on Calvert Street take bus no. 96 "McLean Gardens" to the cathedral. **Bus:** N up Massachusetts Avenue from Dupont Circle.

WHITE HOUSE, 1600 Pennsylvania Ave. NW (visitor entrance at East Gate on East Executive Avenue). Tel. 456-7041.

⭐ *Plan I:* Get up with the birds so you can line up by 8am for free tickets, available at the booths on the Ellipse behind the White House (15th Street and Constitution Avenue NW). If you do get tickets, you're apt to wait an hour or more (except in the winter), before you are herded quickly (without a guide) through part of the First Family's residence. You will see little, and your kids will see less. The tour—not counting time in line—takes less than 20 minutes. Sound like fun?

Plan II: Write to your Senator or Representative at least one month (six would be better) in advance of your visit and request tickets for the special early-morning guided VIP tour, which takes about 45 minutes. The tour is appropriate for kids over 12, says a White House spokesperson. Much history, sure to bore the pants off small fry, is included. Tickets are limited, so don't expect miracles. If tickets are sold out, buy some picture postcards as a souvenir and tell the folks back home the White House was lovely.

If you can't even get a VIP tour, visit this magnificent residence/museum on your own another time. Most kids don't give a hoot about watered-silk walls, Turkish Herede carpets, or Bellange chairs anyway.

Kids do enjoy the annual Easter egg roll, and the spring and fall garden tours (see Chapter 1, "Kids' Favorite Events" section, for details). A word of caution: Friends waited more than 2 hours in line with their two young sons to get into the 1991 egg roll. Their advice: Take plenty of snacks.

Admission: Free.

Open: Tues–Sat 10am–noon Closed: During presidential functions. **Metro:** McPherson Square or Farragut North or West.

WOODROW WILSON HOUSE MUSEUM, 2340 S St. NW. Tel. 387-4062.

The handsome mansion just off Embassy Row in Kalorama is the only former president's residence in the District open to the public (the White House doesn't count). Wilson lived in this stately residence for three years after his second term, and his widow, Edith, resided here until her death in 1961. Since then, it's been maintained by the National Trust.

Visitors are surprised to learn that despite his stern appearance and demeanor, the former scholar and university president was just a regular guy—a movie buff who was a fan of Tom Mix and subscribed to *Photoplay* magazine. On a more sublime level, you can see Wilson's inaugural bible, the casing of the first shell fired in World War I, White House Cabinet chair, and a vintage 1915 elevator. The 45-minute guided tour gives insight into the private life of the man behind the wire-rimmed spectacles. Programs for school groups are available during the school year.

Admission: $4 for adults, $2.50 for students and senior citizens, free for children under 7.

Open: Tues–Sun 10am–4pm. Closed Mon and major holidays.

3. FOR KIDS WITH SPECIAL INTERESTS

AIRPORTS

DULLES AIRPORT, Chantilly, VA. Tel. 703/471-7838.

★ Kids 5 and over can tour Eero Saarinen's soaring masterpiece and ride on a mobile lounge to the midfield terminal, where they will see the tower and learn about different planes. Those over 8 (in groups of five or more) are allowed to visit the airport fire department too, by appointment. The drive alone is worthwhile, especially at dawn or dusk, but never during rush hour, to view this stunning example of avian architecture.

Admission: Free.
Open: 24 hours, tours Mon–Fri.
Directions: Constitution Avenue to Theodore Roosevelt Bridge, Route 66 west, bear left and follow signs to Dulles Airport *only*. From Key Bridge, take Route 29 to Route 66 and follow the signs.

NATIONAL AIRPORT, Alexandria, VA. Tel. 703/557-2045.

The best place to see the action is not in the airport itself. Drive *through* the airport and onto the G.W. Parkway toward D.C. Immediately after exiting the airport, make the first right into the large parking area adjacent to the Potomac River known as Gravelly Point. It's a stone's throw from the end of the runway. While the noise may scare tiny tots, most school-age kids love to come here. Bring earplugs.

Admission: Free
Open: 24 hours.

MONTGOMERY COUNTY AIRPARK, 7940 Airpark Rd., Gaithersburg, MD. Tel. 301/977-0124.

Kids don't feel intimidated at this pint-sized suburban airport where they can watch small private and charter planes take off and land. Weather permitting, tours are held daily April through September by appointment.

Admission: Free.
Open: Year round. **Metro:** Shady Grove, then taxi to the airport.

COLLEGE PARK AIRPORT, 6709 Cpl. Frank Scott Dr., College Park, MD. Tel. 301/864-5844.

★ The *world's* oldest continuously operating airport opened its doors—make that field—in 1909. Wing it on your own and visit the recently upgraded museum (tel. 301/864-1530), then get something to eat in the 94th Aerosquadron (tel. 301/699-9400). Kids love this restaurant. It's decorated like a World War I squadron and faces the runway! They may be too excited to eat. Every September, the airport hosts a weekend Air Fair with airplane, helicopter, and hot-air balloon rides, displays, and children's entertainment.

Admission: Free.
Open: Wed–Sun 11am–4pm. **Metro:** New Carrollton, then a 5-minute taxi ride. (An airport Metro stop is due in 1993.)

FACTORIES

MASH'S HAM FACTORY, 5801 Columbia Park Rd., Landover, MD. Tel. 301/773-3322.

Even though this is not a slaughterhouse, the tour is not for the squeamish. Visitors 15 and older are shown the entire process of how a pig's hind leg ends up as a ham sandwich. You may switch to tuna fish after this one.

For information on the GM factory, see Chapter 9, "Easy Excursions," Section 6—Baltimore.

Admission: Free.

Open: Weekdays, by appointment. **Metro:** Landover.

FARMS

CLAUDE MOORE COLONIAL FARM AT TURKEY RUN, 6310 Old George-town Pike, McLean, VA. Tel. 703/442-7557.

If they think they have it rough, take the kids here to see how their colonial forebears lived. Watch a poor colonial family (Park Service staff) in period dress split logs, make clothes, and tend livestock. The one-room cabin is a real eye-opener. Go on a weekday if possible. Special events are ongoing throughout the year.

Admission: $1 for kids 3–12 and seniors, $2 for adults. Large groups should call ahead.

Open: Apr–mid-Dec Wed–Sun 10am–4:30pm. **Closed:** Late Dec–March, Thanksgiving, rainy days.

Directions: Beltway to Exit 13 (Rte 193 east), go 2½ miles to the marked access road on the left to the farm, or take the G.W. Parkway to Rte 123 south, go 1 mile, turn right to Rte 193, then right into the marked access road to the farm.

OXON HILL FARM, 6411 Oxon Hill Rd., Oxon Hill, MD. Tel. 301/839-1177.

★ This is a working farm from around 1900 operated by the Park Service, and activities abound for visiting farmhands. Little ones can pet the animals while older siblings learn about farm life by watching seasonal demonstrations of cider pressing, corn harvesting, and sheep shearing. A cow-milking demonstration is at 10:30am and 4pm. The chicken feeding and egg gathering take place at 10am and 2pm. A highlight of the self-guided nature walk is the stunning panorama of the Potomac River, Washington, and Virginia. For group reservations, call weekdays between 2:30 and 4pm (tel. 301/839-1176).

Admission: Free.

Open: 8:30am–5pm daily.

Directions: Beltway to Exit 3A (Indian Head Highway south), turn right at first intersection, right onto Oxon Hill Road and follow it to the farm on the right.

FARMERS' MARKETS

Kids enjoy wandering through the many markets that sell seasonal produce, plants and flowers, homemade foodstuffs, and baked goods. Some are magnets for garage sale junkies. Here are a few of the larger markets.

ADAMS-MORGAN, Columbia Road and 18th Street NW (Perpetual Bank). Tel. 678-2800.

Organically grown produce, homemade baked goods and foods, and crafts are featured. The same goods are sold at the D.C. Market.
Open: Every Sat. **Metro:** Dupont Circle.

D.C. OPEN AIR MARKET, Oklahoma Avenue and Benning Road NE (parking lot 6 near RFK Stadium). Tel. 678-2800.
The same basic stuff as the Adams-Morgan market is sold here, but inside much larger quarters. Regulars tell me the produce is particularly fresh, and Saturday is the best and busiest day.
Open: Tues and Thurs 7am–6pm, Sat 6am–4pm. **Metro:** Stadium/Armory.

EASTERN MARKET, 7th Street SE, between North Carolina Avenue and C Street Tel. 543-7293.
This is more like a bazaar. The market jumps on Saturday with music and other entertainment. You'll find everything from hog jowls and oxtails to fresh produce and seafood. Teens love the secondhand clothes, knickknacks, and funky jewelry. On summer weekends farmers' stalls line the street.
Admission: Free.
Open: Tues–Sat 7am–5pm, later in summer. **Metro:** Eastern Market.

HOLOGRAPHY

HOLOGRAPHY WORLD COLLECTION, 800 K St. NW (Tech World Plaza, South Lobby). Tel. 408-1833.
Holy holography! Kids eat this up, although the guide lost me after explaining all you need is "a laser, mirror, and photosensitive plate" to produce these wild-looking three-dimensional fine-art holograms. There's much fragile stuff here, so kids under 8 are less welcome than kids over 8. Wait till you see "Microchip," and "Moon Moth"—positively otherworldly. My favorite is a hologram of Mike Ditka with his mouth closed for a change. Call ahead (two to three weeks in spring and summer) to make reservations for the 20-minute tour. For those who want more, visit the **Art, Science and Technology Institute,** 2018 R St. NW (tel. 667-6322). It's open Tuesday through Sunday from 11am to 6pm.
Admission: $5 per person (includes tour); $4 each for groups of four or more.
Open: Mon–Fri 11am–6pm. **Metro:** Gallery Place (7th and H streets exit).

MEDICAL STUFF

NATIONAL MUSEUM OF HEALTH AND MEDICINE, Walter Reed Army Medical Center, Building 54, Georgia Avenue and Elder Street NW. Tel. 576-2348.
Older kids with a strong stomach and interest in medicine and/or pathology won't want to miss this. The museum has numerous exhibits of diseased, injured, and defective body parts, which I prefer not to go into. Of particular interest are Lincoln's skull bone and President Garfield's spine. Don't bring young children. They won't sleep a wink.
Admission: Free.
Open: Mon–Fri 9:30am–4:30pm; Sat, Sun, hols 11:30am–4:30pm. **Metro:**

Takoma Park. Take a taxi or walk two blocks (pass the elementary school) to the Delafield St. entrance.

NATURE CENTERS

AUDUBON NATURALIST SOCIETY (WOODEND), 8940 Jones Mill Rd. Chevy Chase, MD. Tel. 301/652-9188.

Kids can explore self-guided nature trails in this 40-acre wildlife sanctuary and learn about conservation and the environment in special programs. Activities are geared to children 4 and up, with day and weekend family programs.
Admission: Free.
Open: Grounds open daily, dawn to dusk; building open Mon–Fri 9am–5pm.
Closed: Holidays. **Metro:** Silver Spring; then take a taxi.
Directions: Drive north on Connecticut Avenue, turn right onto Jones Bridge Road, then left at Jones Mill Road.

ROCK CREEK NATURE CENTER, Rock Creek Park, 5200 Glover Rd. NW. Tel. 426-6829.

Plenty of self-guided nature trails and hands-on activities distinguish this facility in the District's largest park. Guided nature walks, films, planetarium shows, and live animal presentations are scheduled throughout the year. Call ahead for specifics and see the section on "Gardens and Parks" in this Chapter.
Admission: Free.
Open: Wed–Sun 9am–5pm, closed Mon and Tues. **Directions:** North on Connecticut Ave., turn right onto Military Rd., then turn right onto Glover Rd.

NEWSPAPERS

THE WASHINGTON POST, 1150 15th St. NW. Tel. 334-7969.

Aspiring journalists who are at least 11 years old or in fifth grade can tour the newsroom, composing room, and pressroom of this Washington daily. Walking tours are given Monday and Thursday at 10 and 11am and at 1, 2, and 3pm by reservation. Don't expect to see the presses running. Because the *Post* is a morning paper, the action takes place while you're fast asleep.
Admission: Free.
Open: Mon and Thurs tours. **Metro:** McPherson Square.

POLICE STATION

DISTRICT OF COLUMBIA METROPOLITAN POLICE STATION, 300 Indiana Ave. NW. Tel. 939-8721.

Tours of the communication division, gun control section, and line-up room are given weekdays for families and large groups by reservation.
Admission: Free.
Open: Mon–Fri tours by appointment only. Call a week or more in advance.
Metro: Archives.

POST OFFICE

MAIN POST OFFICE, 900 Brentwood Rd. NE (between Rhode Island and New York avenues). Tel. 636-1208.

Kids who are at least 5 years old or in kindergarten are encouraged to put their stamp of approval on the facility where up to 5 million pieces of mail are processed every day. They'll be dazzled by the OCRs (optical character readers) that scan nine addresses per second to make sure the ZIP codes and cities match.

Admission: Free.

Open: Tues–Sat tours 9:30am–6pm; reserve at least 24 hours ahead. **Metro:** Rhode Island Avenue.

PRINTING

GOVERNMENT PRINTING OFFICE, H and North Capitol streets NW. Tel. 275-3541.

In the shadow of Union Station, GPO prints reams and reams of paper for government bureaucrats to shuffle, file, and shred, including the Congressional Record, the Federal Register, forms, brochures, documents, and even congressional stationery. Because the tours are for "specialized groups only," if you're traveling solo, hook up with one or more families and adopt an important-sounding name. (P.S. There's more action early in the morning.)

Admission: Free.

Open: Mon–Fri 9am–1pm for group tours by reservation. **Metro:** Union Station.

RADIO

VOICE OF AMERICA, 330 Independence Ave. SW (enter on C Street only). Tel. 619-3919.

Not far from the Air and Space Museum, the world's largest radio station welcomes those in the eighth grade or above to visit the downtown facility where programs are broadcast worldwide on 26 channels in 42 languages! During the 45-minute tour you will see the control room, hear part of a feature show and, perhaps, catch the evening news in Russian. Foreign visitors, who outnumber Americans by a wide margin, are excited when they recognize broadcasters they listen to at home.

Admission: Free.

Open: Tours Mon–Fri at 8:40, 9:40, and 10:40am and 1:40 and 2:40pm. Call for reservations. **Metro:** Federal Center.

SATELLITES

INTELSAT, Connecticut Avenue and Van Ness Street NW. Tel. 944-7841.

Let's have a show of hands. How many have heard of Intelsat (International Telecommunications Satellite Organization)? Well, the satellites of this large international cooperative carry most TV signals in and out of the United States and about 50% of the world's telephone, fax, and telex services. Twice a week, kids over 12 (or in the sixth grade) can tour the visitors center to watch technicians monitoring launches, view scale models of satellites, and admire the futuristic operations center. The most stunning sight of all is a huge map peppered with lots of tiny colored lights that mark the locations of Intelsat earth and tracking stations.

Admission: Free.

Open: Tours by appointment only (call at least a week in advance) on Tues at 10am and Thurs at 3pm. **Metro:** Van Ness/UDC.

SCULPTURE

If it hasn't already been done, someone should write a book on Washington's outdoor sculpture (please don't look at *me*). Here are a handful with special appeal for kids.

ALBERT EINSTEIN Nestled in the gardens of the National Academy of Sciences at 2101 Constitution Avenue NW, his comfortable-looking lap invites little ones to climb up and rest awhile.

THE AWAKENING Located at Hains Point in East Potomac Park, this is a sort of scary giant struggling to free himself from the ground. Don't worry, he can't hurt you.

THE LONE SAILOR He stands windblown at the U.S. Navy Memorial outside Market Square, Pennsylvania Avenue and 7th Street NW, where military bands give concerts on summer evenings.

LUNCHBREAK Located at Washington Harbour, 30th and K streets NW in Georgetown, is an overalled workman enjoying lunch on a park bench, and he looks like he's for real.

UNCLE BEAZLEY Located on the Mall side of the Museum of Natural History, 10th Street and Constitution Avenue NW, is the world's friendliest triceratops. He's standing guard to make sure none of his friends escape from the museum.

GIANT COOTIE BUG The cootie welcomes visitors to the Capital Children's Museum, 800 3rd Street NE. Be careful it doesn't catch you!

SPACE FLIGHT

GODDARD SPACE FLIGHT CENTER, Greenbelt, MD. Tel. 301/286-8981.

About a half-hour from downtown, you can reach the stars in beautiful downtown Greenbelt. Kids over 4 are fascinated by the hands-on interactive displays. On the first and third Sunday of every month, bring your own or be an observer at the model rocket launch, an activity suitable for all ages. Tours for kids in sixth grade and above are given Wednesday, Thursday, and Friday afternoons at 2:30pm and three weekends a month. The longer Sunday tour includes stops at the testing and evaluation center, where they check and double-check satellites and payloads. On Goddard Community Day, usually held in the fall, visitors are allowed to tour NASA facilities normally closed to the public. Bring lunch to enjoy in the picnic area, and pick up space-age souvenirs in the gift shop.

Admission: Free.

Open: Sept–May Wed–Sun 10am–4pm; June–Aug daily 10am–4pm. **Closed:** Major holidays. Call for specific tour information. **Directions:** Take New York Ave. to I-295 North (Baltimore-Washington Parkway), turn left on Greenbelt Road (Route 193), turn left at Soil Conservation Road, then left at the first gate.

STARGAZING

ALBERT EINSTEIN PLANETARIUM, National Air and Space Museum, 7th Street and Independence Avenue SW. Tel. 357-2700.

✪ Several times a day, there's a half-hour show related to the stars. The special effects are neat, and kids over 8 or 10 should find the show interesting. If they want more, they can also listen to a brief taped message about current stargazing conditions (tel. 357-2000).

Admission: $2.50 adults, $1.50 kids 12 and under.

Open: Daily 10am–5:30pm. **Closed:** Dec 25. Call for show times.

NAVAL OBSERVATORY, Massachusetts Avenue at 34th Street NW (enter the South Gate). Tel. 653-1507 or 653-1543 (recording).

✪ On a clear night, you can see forever at the Naval Observatory. You'll have stars in your eyes after peering through the huge telescope at celestial bodies 25,000 light-years away. Line up at least 30 minutes before tour time. The 1½-hour tour is first-come, first-served on Monday evenings. Call before 5:30pm to see if it will be a "star-light, star-bright" night.

Admission: Free.

Open: Nov–Mar Mon 7:30pm; Apr–Oct Mon 8:30pm. Closed: Holidays.

ROCK CREEK NATURE CENTER, 5200 Glover Rd. NW. Tel. 426-6829.

Free planetarium shows are given weekend afternoons for kids 4 and older. A show for kids and adults that changes monthly is given weekends and Wednesday afternoons at 3:45pm. See "Nature Centers" above.

TV

WRC-TV CHANNEL 4, 4001 Nebraska Ave. NW (between Wisconsin and Massachusetts avenues). Tel. 885-4037.

Boob-tube fans at least 6 years old or in first grade can take a 40-minute behind-the-scenes tour of the newsroom, studios, control room, and weather center of WRC-TV.

Admission: Free.

Open: Tours weekly by reservation. Call at least two weeks in advance. **Metro:** Tenleytown.

WEATHER

NATIONAL WEATHER SERVICE, Sterling, VA (near Dulles Airport). Tel. 703/260-0107.

Pint-sized weather prognosticators who are at least in the third grade can tour this facility by appointment. Groups of two or more are welcome. It may not be around the corner, but it's surely worth the ride if you can find out why they have so much trouble forecasting the D.C. weather.

Admission: Free.

Tours: By appointment only. **Directions:** Theodore Roosevelt Bridge to Route 66 west to Dulles Toll Road to Route 28 north to Route 606 west 3½ miles.

NATIONAL WEATHER SERVICE SCIENCE AND HISTORY CENTER, Metro II Building, 1325 East-West Hwy., Silver Spring, Md. Tel. 301/427-7622.

Inspect the latest meteorological instrumentation used by NOAA (the National Atmospheric and Oceanic Administration), see models of a hurricane-hunter airplane, and listen to the weather message phone banks. There's also an exhibit of actual

weather instruments as they appeared in a Midwest weather observation office a century ago. Press a button, and you will be showered with a history of the weather service and a sprinkling of weather trivia.
Admission: Free.
Open: Mon–Fri 8:30am–5pm. **Metro:** Silver Spring.

4. LETTING OFF STEAM

Museums are marvelous mind expanders, but little people (and big people too) grow restless after too much hard-core enrichment. To avoid fatigue and brain strain, temper periods of sightseeing with visits to places where kids can romp, roam, and let off steam. (We all know what happens to steam when it isn't allowed to escape.) You won't have far to look for a patch of park or grassy green, because downtown and the environs are chock full of open space, playgrounds, and recreational areas. And the largest front lawn in the neighborhood—the National Mall—is a Frisbee toss away from many downtown attractions.

GARDENS & PARKS

AZTEC GARDEN, OAS Building, 17th St. and Constitution Ave. NW. Tel. 458-3000.
Kids enjoy the exotic banana, coffee, palm, and rubber trees growing on the Tropical Patio at the headquarters of the world's oldest organization of nations. Epitomizing the mission of the OAS is the Peace Tree, planted by President William Howard Taft in 1910. Walk to the back of the building for a display of seasonal plants around the dazzling blue-tiled pool. The fellow overseeing this lush scene is the Aztec god of flowers, Xochipilli.
Admission: Free.
Open: Mon–Fri 9:30am–5pm. **Metro:** Farragut West.

BATTERY-KEMBLE PARK, Chain Bridge Road, between Nebraska Avenue and MacArthur Boulevard NW. Tel. 426-6833.
In a residential area not far from the C & O Canal, this mile-long park boasts flowering dogwood trees in spring, a beautiful fall display of autumn leaves, and good sledding and cross-country skiing in winter. You can fly a kite, play football, baseball, or soccer on one of the fields, picnic, and take a nature walk.
Open: Daily dawn to dusk.
Directions: Take Canal Road, turn right onto MacArthur Boulevard, then turn right onto Chain Bridge Road.

BROOKSIDE GARDENS, 1500 Glenallan Ave., Wheaton, MD. Tel. 301/949-8230.
A visit here is like a month in the country. Besides formal and natural-style landscaping on 50 acres (part of Maryland's park system), Brookside is known for its azaleas, rose gardens, and other seasonal displays. Little kids like the aquatic garden and conservatory filled with exotic plants, a wooden bridge, and waterfall that ends in a tiny stream they can tiptoe across. Many of the 2,000 volumes in the horticultural library are geared to young people and may be used on-site.

Admission: Free.
Open: Daily 9am–dusk. Conservatory 9am–5pm. **Closed:** Dec 25. **Directions:** Take Georgia Ave. north from the Beltway, turn right on Randolph Rd; after 2 blocks, turn right at Glenallan Avenue.

CONSTITUTION GARDENS, West Potomac Park, Constitution Avenue, between the Washington Monument and Lincoln Memorial. Tel. 485-9880.

✪ Feed the ducks, turtles, fish, and an occasional frog, in the six-acre lake of this park, which has walks, bike paths, and a landscaped island reached by a footbridge. Kids can sail small boats near the water's edge, but they are not allowed to go in the water. Have a picnic—there's plenty of room on the 14 acres—and see the monument memorializing the 56 signers of the Declaration of Independence. The Vietnam Veterans Memorial is in the western corner of the park.

DUMBARTON OAKS GARDENS, 1703 32nd St. NW (entrance on R Street between 31st and 32nd streets). Tel. 342-3200.

✪ Restless feet love to explore every inch of the 16-acre formally designed gardens that lie in the center of Georgetown. The winding brick paths lend themselves to spirited games of hide and seek. Spring is glorious when forsythia, narcissus, tulips, daffodils, and flowering trees bloom in profusion. The roses and wisteria flower in late spring and summer, and fall brings forth a showy display of foliage and chrysanthemums. Strollers are allowed, but may be more of a hindrance because of the gardens' many steps and levels. No visitor to Washington should leave the city without stopping here.

Admission: $2 for adults, $1 for seniors and kids 12 and under.
Open: Apr–Oct 2–6pm; Nov–Mar 2–5pm.
Directions: Take a taxi; or walk from anywhere in Georgetown; Foggy Bottom Metro is a mile away; and parking is almost nonexistent.

DUPONT CIRCLE PARK, Dupont Circle (intersection of Connecticut, Massachusetts, and New Hampshire avenues NW).

Sit, sun, or stalk the pigeons at Washington's largest circle park. There's plenty of entertainment—intended and unintended—particularly on weekends. Some mighty serious chess games are played here, and you and yours are welcome to watch as long as you don't kibbitz.

EAST POTOMAC PARK, Ohio Drive SW (south of Independence Avenue and east of the Tidal Basin). Tel. 426-6765.

✪ A one-way road outlines the 300-plus acres of human-made peninsula between the Potomac River and Washington Channel. Depending on who's counting, 1,200 to 1,800 cherry trees bloom in late March or early April. You can stroll, bike, or fish. A well-equipped playground at Hains Point attracts kids with its colorful climbing apparatus. Most are fascinated by the off-putting statue of a half-buried figure known as *The Awakening*. The park has picnic grounds; a public swimming pool (tel. 863-1309), 24 tennis courts (tel. 554-5962), and one 18-hole and two 9-hole golf courses (tel. 863-9007). Call for information on the permit you'll need to use the tennis courts.

Admission: Free.
Open: Dawn to dark.

FARRAGUT SQUARE, Connecticut Avenue and K Street NW.

Noontime concerts are held in the summer in this pretty park in the heart of D.C.'s business district. Brown-bag it on a nice day and watch the power bunch lunch.

GLOVER ARCHBOLD PARK, MacArthur Boulevard and Canal Road to Van Ness Street and Wisconsin Avenue. Tel. 426-6833.

★ The mix of towering trees, a bird sanctuary, and colorful wild flowers make this long, narrow 100-acre park, which stretches south from Massachusetts Avenue to Canal Road, a popular destination for families. At 44th Street and Reservoir Road, a two-mile nature trail begins. There are plenty of picnic areas too.

Open: Daily dawn to dusk.

KAHLIL GIBRAN MEMORIAL GARDEN, 3100 Massachusetts Ave. NW (opposite the British Embassy).

The quiet, reflective garden, steps away from busy Massachusetts Avenue, opened in May 1991 to honor the Lebanese-born mystical poet who spent much of his life in the United States writing thoughtful phrases that have been devoured for several decades by college kids in search of themselves. Some of Gibran's pithier musings are inscribed in the benches near the main fountain. The bronze bust of Gibran is by Washington sculptor Gordon Kray. Make your pilgrimage on foot; neighborhood parking is sparse.

Admission: Free.

Open: Dawn to dusk.

HILLWOOD GARDENS, 4155 Linnean Ave. NW. Tel. 686-5807.

The gardens of Marjorie Merriweather Post's estate include a formal French garden, rose garden, and Japanese garden with a waterfall, lanterns, and bridges. More than 5,000 orchids grow in the greenhouse, and there's a café on the premises. Kids under 12 are not admitted.

Admission: $2.

Open: Tues–Sat 10:30am–3:30pm.

Directions: Take Connecticut Avenue north, turn right onto Tilden Street, then left on Linnean Avenue.

KENILWORTH AQUATIC GARDENS, Kenilworth Avenue and Douglas Street NE. Tel. 426-6905.

See the Egyptian lotus (said to be Cleopatra's favorite), just one of the more than 100,000 water plants growing on 11 acres of ponds in this sanctuary. About 70 varieties of water lilies bloom in May and June. Except in the dead of winter, kids will see turtles, frogs, and small fish. Bring binoculars in spring; migrating waterfowl and songbirds are frequent visitors. If you come in the morning, you won't miss the night-blooming tropicals, which close by late morning. There are picnic tables and a playground.

Admission: Free.

Open: Daily 7am–3pm. **Metro:** Minnesota Avenue or Deanwood. Take the V-2 bus to Kenilworth Avenue and Polk Street and walk one block to gardens. (This is not a good neighborhood to walk through, so you may want to take a taxi.)

LADY BIRD JOHNSON PARK, adjacent to G.W. Memorial Parkway, VA.

Although considered part of D.C., the former Columbia Island is accessible only by footbridge from the Virginia side of the Potomac River. I don't suggest it. The best way to enjoy the sight—a must in spring—is to drive or be driven. The park was dedicated to Mrs. Johnson in 1968 to recognize her efforts at beautifying the city and the nation. More than 2,500 dogwoods and *one million* daffodils (I did not make this up) create a gorgeous blanket of gold in the spring. At the south end is a 15-acre grove of white pines, azaleas, and rhododendrons, designated as the Lyndon Baines Johnson Memorial Grove.

Directions: From D.C., drive over the Arlington Memorial Bridge, take the G.W. Memorial Parkway south to and through National Airport, continue north on the parkway to Memorial Bridge and D.C.

LAFAYETTE PARK, between Pennsylvania Avenue and H Street NW, across from the White House.

Check out the statues of Andrew Jackson and Lafayette, whose heads are favorite roosting spots. Protesters, pigeon lovers and haters, bureaucrats, and people watchers fill the benches and sprawl on the grass at all hours of the day and night. Depending on their ages, your kids might enjoy talking to the protestors or feeding some of the tamest squirrels in the area.

Metro: McPherson Square or Farragut West.

MONTROSE PARK, R Street at Avon Place NW, Georgetown. Tel. 426-6833.

What a honey of a spot this is! Come here to picnic, commune with nature, or ramble through the heavily wooded terrain. Lover's Lane, which forms the western boundary, is a cobblestoned path that led to Baltimore in the 18th century.

Admission: Free.

Open: Daily dawn to dusk. **Directions:** From M Street, go north on 29th Street, turn left on R Street.

NATIONAL ARBORETUM, 3501 New York Ave. NE. Tel. 475-4815.

⭐ Visitors are tree-ted to one breathtaking sensory experience after another at this 444-acre haven in northeast D.C., established by an act of Congress in 1927 to educate the public and do research on trees and shrubs. The arboretum is a special place and the staff is excellent, so most children, regardless of age, enjoy a visit here. The **koi** (Japanese carp) outside the Information Center approach Brobdingnagian proportions, reaching nearly 3 feet in length and weighing in at 30 pounds. If possible, be here for noon feedings. The lily pads are said to be sturdy enough to support a small child, but please don't try it—those koi have big appetites.

Worth a visit any time of the year, the arboretum is most popular from late March through October. In late April and May, the **azalea display** (about 70,000 last count) draws crowds. Kids can sniff the contents of the **Herb Garden** or become intoxicated in June and July when 100 fragrant varieties of roses perfume the air in the Herb Garden. The medicinal, dye, Native American, beverage, and fragrance gardens are of special interest to young people, as well as the knot garden with its dwarf evergreens. Some of the specimens in the **National Bonsai Collection**—a gift from Japan to mark our Bicentennial—are over 300 years old! Don't leave without seeing the national Capitol columns, the only things salvaged from the Capitol's original facade after renovation of the central portion in 1959. You'll think you've wandered onto an American Stonehenge.

Admission: Free.

Open: Mon–Fri 8am–5pm, weekends and holidays 10am–5pm; Bonsai collection and Japanese garden daily 10am–2:30pm. **Metro:** Stadium-Armory; then take a B-2, B-4, or B-5 bus to Bladensburg Road and R Street. Walk east 300 yards to the R Street gate; or take New York Avenue (east) and enter the service road immediately after crossing Bladensburg Road.

RAWLINS PARK, E Street between 18th and 19th streets NW.

This urban park gets passing grades most of the year, but when the magnolias bloom, it rates an A-plus.
Admission: Free.
Open: Dawn to dusk. **Metro:** McPherson Square or Farragut North or West.

ROCK CREEK PARK, 5000 Glover Rd. NW (Visitor Information Center). Tel. 426-6832.

The leader of Washington parks, which celebrated its centennial in 1990, is a 4-mile-long, 1,800-acre parcel that fills the center of northwest D.C. like cream cheese in a bagel. The park, 85% of which is natural, is nothing short of fantastic, and you should introduce your kids to some of its many wonders during your stay. But not after dark.

If time allows only one stop, make it the **Nature Center and Planetarium,** at 5200 Glover Road NW (tel. 426-6829), where kids will find exhibits pertaining to the park's natural history and wildlife, and meet a few of the latter. **Guided nature walks** and **self-guided trails** begin and end here. The center is open year round, Wednesday through Sunday, from 9am to 5pm; closed Mondays, Tuesdays, and holidays. Special **hikes, activities,** and **talks** geared to young trailblazers take place every month. To receive the upcoming month's activity calendar, call 426-6829. The Park Service does a dynamite job with this program.

Here are a handful of the park's other attractions (call or write for more information and an indispensable map). A **1.5-mile exercise course** for fitness freaks and joggers begins near Calvert Street and Connecticut Avenue NW. You can rent a horse or take riding lessons at the **Rock Creek Horse Center** (tel. 362-0117), or blaze 11 miles of bridle trails. Fulfill your day's exercise quota and hike or **bike** your way through the park. Much of the sign-posted bike route running from the Lincoln Memorial through the park and into Maryland is paved and separate from traffic. On Saturdays, Sundays, and holidays Beach Drive is closed to traffic between Military and Broad Branch roads. **Picnic** areas abound—some can be reserved; all require permits (tel. 673-7646). **Tennis courts** at 16th and Kennedy streets NW must be reserved from April to November (tel. 673-7646). Kids into war games should see **Fort deRussey, Fort Reno,** or **Fort Bayard,** among the 68 forts built to protect Washington during the Civil War.

Kids over 6 can get a taste of early-19th-century life and watch millstones (powered by a water wheel) grind corn and wheat into flour at **Pierce Mill,** near the intersection of Beach Drive and Tilden Street NW (tel. 426-6908). Although the mill is open from 8am to 4:30pm Wednesday through Sunday, most of the action takes place on weekends from noon to 2pm. You can buy the stone-ground flour/meal after your tour. The corn makes wonderful bread! Weekday group tours are given by reservation. A short walk from the mill is the **Art Barn,** where local artists display their works.

At **Thompson's Boat House,** near the Kennedy Center and Watergate, you can rent a boat and meander up the Potomac; or hop on a bike and explore nearby Theodore Roosevelt Island.

and summer hours. Call first, because hours change seasonally. Arrive early on weekends.

Fletcher's Boat House, 4940 Canal Road NW (tel. 244-0461), rents canoes, rowing shells, small sailboats, and rowboats. **Jack's Boats,** 3500 K Street NW in Georgetown (tel. 337-9642), rents canoes and rowboats. **Thompson's Boat Center,** Rock Creek Parkway and Virginia Avenue NW (tel. 333-4861), rents canoes, rowboats, shells, double shells, and Sunfish. **Tidal Basin,** 15th Street and Maine Avenue SW (tel. 484-0206), rents pedalboats.

FISHING

Every Friday's "Weekend" section of the *Washington Post* lists what fish are running and where. My fishing friends tell me mid-March until July is prime fishing time. Nonetheless you'll catch *something* (maybe an old tire?) from late February through October. Cast your line for catfish, bass, and stripers from the wall along the Washington Channel at Haines Point; anywhere near Chain Bridge; or the seawall north of the Wilson Bridge in Alexandria, Virginia. If you want to fish with the big boys, try a half- or full-day charter. Call the **Rod 'N Reel** in Chesapeake Beach, Maryland (tel. 301/855-8351). It's about a 45-minute drive from D.C., and kids of all ages are welcome as long as someone is watching them.

Please be careful when you fish the Potomac. Every year several people drown in its unforgiving waters, especially treacherous and turbulent after heavy rains. Heed warning signs. They're posted for a reason. Be particularly cautious of slippery rocks along the shoreline.

HIKING

Many city and suburban parks have hiking trails (see the "Gardens and Parks" section in this chapter), and the Blue Ridge Mountains and Appalachian Trail are well within reach for a day trip. Some of the best local hiking for families is along the **C&O Canal** (184 miles!); **Theodore Roosevelt Island, Rock Creek Park,** and the **U.S. National Arboretum** (see "Gardens and Parks" in this chapter). On the Maryland side of Great Falls Park, 11710 MacArthur Boulevard, Potomac (tel. 301/299-3613), the four-mile **Billy Goat Trail** is a favorite of older kids. The trail's entrance is off a towpath less than 2 miles south of the park's entrance. Nobody said you have to do the entire trail on your first try.

ICE SKATING

About once every five years, Washington endures a severely cold winter. One of the few pleasant aspects of this phenomenon is that the C & O Canal and Reflecting Pool (between the Lincoln Memorial and Washington Monument) freeze over for skating. It's a scene straight from Currier & Ives, and one that your kids won't want to miss. Call the U.S. Park Service (tel. 619-7222) to find out if the ice is thick—and safe—enough.

Even in temperate weather, you won't be left out in the cold. At the **National Sculpture Garden Ice Rink,** on the Mall in front of the Archives, 7th Street and Constitution Avenue NW (tel. 371-5340) and **Pershing Park Rink,** 14th Street and Pennsylvania Avenue NW (tel. 737-6938), you can skate from December through March. Skate rentals are about $4.

In the suburbs, The **Fairfax Ice Arena,** 3779 Pickett Rd., Fairfax, Virginia (tel. 703/323-1132), is open year round and offers skate rentals, lessons, and a pro shop. Don't be surprised if you run into a few Olympic hopefuls in training. In Maryland, there's an outdoor skating rink at **Bethesda Metro Center,** outside the Hyatt Regency Hotel (tel. 301/636-0588). Two covered outdoor rinks, **Cabin John Ice Skating Rink,** 10610 Westlake Dr., Bethesda (tel. 301/365-0585), and **Wheaton Ice Rink,** at Arcola and Orebaugh avenues, Wheaton (tel. 301/649-2703), attract families from October through March. Both offer skate rentals and lessons. Cabin John has lockers and a snack bar too.

KITE FLYING

The best kite flying is in spring and fall. During most of the summer, a breeze attracts media attention, and in winter, well, it's too chilly most days. Look no further than the Mall for the optimum kite-flying space with no overhead impediments. Otherwise, head for the nearest school or playground. If you forgot to pack a kite, go to the **Air and Space Museum's gift shop** at 6th Street and Independence Avenue SW, or the **Kite Loft,** The Shops at National Place, 1331 Pennsylvania Ave. NW (tel. 737-1505)—if it flies, they have it.

Every year in late March, the Smithsonian sponsors a **kite festival** on the west side of the Washington Monument (tel. 357-2700). There are two hitches—the kite has to be homemade and it's supposed to remain airborne for at least one minute at an altitude of 100 feet or more. Ribbons are awarded to winners in different age groups, and trophies are given in several categories. If you're in town, don't miss it.

SAILING

The **Mariner Sailing School,** Belle Haven Marina, south of Alexandria, Virginia (tel. 703/768-0018), rents windsurfers, sunfish, and larger sailboats to experienced sailers. During the summer months, kids 8 to 15 can take a five-day sailing course or windsurfing lessons. The **Washington Sailing Marina,** Dangerfield Island off the George Washington Memorial Parkway, Alexandria, Virginia (tel. 703/548-9027), runs a one-week Red Cross sailing program for kids 10 to 16 during the summer. For information on sailing instruction on the Chesapeake Bay in Annapolis, Maryland (about 35 miles from downtown), see the Annapolis entry in Chapter 9, "Easy Excursions."

SWIMMING

In the good old summertime you're not completely out of luck if your hotel lacks a swimming pool. For the location of the public pool nearest you, call the D.C. **Department of Recreation Aquatic Program** (tel. 576-6346). Most pools are open from mid-June through Labor Day. The nicest **pools** are located at 34th Street and Volta Place NW in Georgetown; 25th and N streets NW; and East Potomac Park.

ORGANIZED TOURS

An easy way to see D.C.'s major attractions without wearing out the troops is by guided tour. Ride one of the National Park Service's **Tourmobile's** (tel. 554-7950) trams and get on and off as often as you like. This is the area's largest sightseeing operation and the only one licensed to make stops at attractions on the Mall. The **Washington/Arlington Cemetery tour,** which takes in 15 downtown attractions and the Kennedy gravesites, Tomb of the Unknown Soldier, and Arlington House at Arlington Cemetery, is $8 for adults, $4 for children 3 to 11, free for kids 2 and under. Between Labor Day and mid-June, a ticket purchased after 2pm ($10 adults, $5 kids) is good for the rest of the day *and* the following day. In summer, the same rule applies to tickets purchased after 4pm. The combined tour makes for a grueling day, and I wouldn't recommend it for kids under 10. Opt instead for the Washington *or* the Arlington Cemetery tour and, perhaps, do Mount Vernon another day.

You can also make tracks for an **Old Town Trolley Tour** (tel. 269-3020), which has the advantage of pick-up and drop-off service at many D.C. hotels, but the disadvantage of not stopping along the Mall. The 90-minute tour stops at 12 major attractions and, like the Tourmobile, you may get on and off the trolley as many times as you like. The cost is $14 for adults, $5 for kids 5 to 12, and free for kids 4 and under.

Gray Line Sightseeing Tours (tel. 289-1995) offers several tours—from three hours to two days—in and around D.C. and to destinations as far as Williamsburg, Virginia. **Gray Line** departs from convenient Union Station, and picks up passengers at some hotels. My kids still get nauseated or fall asleep after 20 minutes on a bus. Hopefully, yours are different. I wouldn't try an all-day trip with pre-schoolers, who may view the confinement as an invitation to riot. The **Washington After Dark tour,** for my money, is the best of all. Lap-sitters will probably go to sleep, which is fine, while older kids will enjoy seeing the nightlit monuments, federal buildings, and Georgetown.

Tour de Force (tel. 703/525-2948) creates motorcoach and walking tours mainly for incoming groups, but also arranges individual guides for families who prefer a private tour. Call for rates.

If you're considering a small, lesser-known tour company, make sure the tour guides are licensed. A friend once signed up for a Monday tour of the White House with a fly-by-night operation. The White House is closed on Monday. Be cautious. You don't want to hear about Washington from some kid recently arrived from Minnesota who makes up commentary along the way.

CRUISES

Since two sides of the Washington "diamond" front rivers—the Potomac and Anacostia—at least once during your stay you should cast off from terra firma and see the city from the water. The luxurious, 600-passenger *Spirit of Washington* (tel. 554-8000) offers lunch, brunch, dinner, moonlight, and Mount Vernon cruises from Pier 4, 6th and Water streets SW. Forget the dinner and moonlight cruises with kids—too long, too expensive, and too boring for them. The two-hour lunch and brunch cruises in the Washington Channel aboard the carpeted, climate-controlled ship are fine if your kids will do justice to the copious seafood buffet and dessert. Tuesday through Friday lunch is $17.95 (no kiddie discounts), Saturday lunch is $21.45, Sunday brunch is $21.45. Reservations are a must.

If you want to spend a fun-filled half day and visit a major sight, and food is secondary, board the *Spirit of Mount Vernon* (same telephone number as above) and cruise down the Potomac to George Washington's beautiful estate. Cruises depart Tuesday through Sunday at 9am and 2pm every month but November and December.

Tickets are $18 for adults, $16.25 senior citizens, $10.75 kids 6 through 11, $7.75 kids 2 through 5. You'll have ample time to look around Mount Vernon before the return voyage. You may not bring food aboard, but rest assured there's a concession stand selling all the drinks and fast food their little tummies can hold. There's also a restaurant at Mount Vernon. Arrive at the dock one hour before departure time.

In the tradition of the Parisian *bâteau mouche* on the Seine, the riverboat-restaurant **Dandy** (tel. 703/683-6090) plies the waters of the Potomac several times a week. Luncheon and dinner cruises depart Old Town, Alexandria, for a leisurely run up the Potomac past historic monuments and memorials, the Kennedy Center, Watergate, Rosslyn (Virginia), and Georgetown before heading back to port. Kids 10 and older with the palate and patience for a 3-course lunch or 5-course dinner with mostly adults will enjoy this cruise. But the magnificent scene, particularly at night, doesn't come cheap. Prices range from $25 for the weekday lunch cruise to $55 for the Saturday dinner cruise. Reservations are a must (tel. 703/683-6076).

5. PERFECT FOR STROLLING

Walking is the best way to see Washington, which was carefully planned and laid out on a grid. It's easy to find your way around (see Chapter 2, "Getting to Know Washington, D.C."), and once you get the hang of subdividing the District, you'll blaze your own trails. Although the shortest distance between two points may be a Metrorail ride, you'll shortchange your kids and yourselves, missing some of D.C.'s charm and beauty, if you fail to explore what can only be discovered on foot.

GEORGETOWN

Georgetown is the ideal neighborhood for a strolling. Kids of all ages take to the unique hodgepodge of old and new. Reminders of the past remain and invite exploration—the C&O Canal, historic buildings and homes, and lush parks. On the flip side, scores of up-to-date shops and restaurants line Wisconsin Avenue and M Street and fill Georgetown Park. Take a map and wear comfortable shoes; the area is hilly and some sections are paved with brick or cobblestone. Your kids will be so tired at the end of the walk, they'll sleep for 48 hours.

If you begin at the Foggy Bottom Metro at 23rd and I streets NW, walk north on 23rd Street to Washington Circle and go left around the circle to Pennsylvania Avenue. Continue on Pennsylvania to the end and make a left at M Street. The Old Stone House is at 3051 M Street. Or if you prefer, take *any* 30 bus on Pennsylvania Avenue [near Foggy Bottom Metro] to Georgetown.

The **Old Stone House,** the only pre-Revolutionary building still standing in D.C., was built in 1765, and the five rooms are furnished with items typical of the late 18th and early 19th centuries. It is open Wednesday through Sunday from 8am to 4:30pm. The real treasure on this site is the typical cottage garden behind the house. It is open daily, but closed on Christmas. Kids can run up and down the hilly lawn (no pesticides are used on the grass) and everyone can enjoy the magnificent flowers that bloom from early spring into October. The garden spills over with picnickers in nice weather.

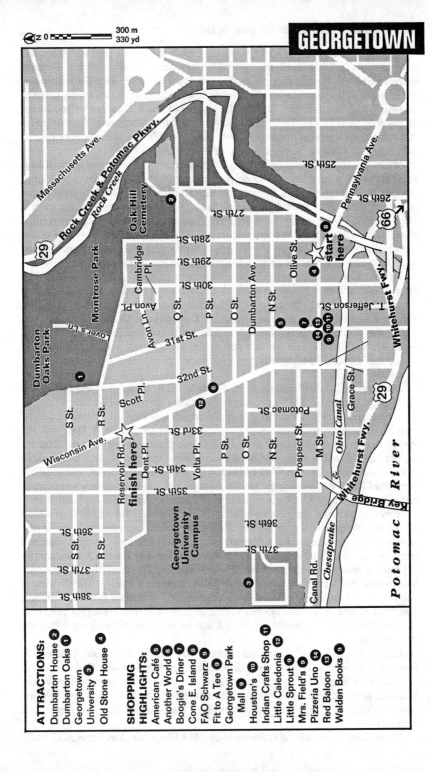

GEORGETOWN

ATTRACTIONS:
Dumbarton House ❷
Dumbarton Oaks ❶
Georgetown
University ❸
Old Stone House ❹

**SHOPPING
HIGHLIGHTS:**
American Café ❺
Another World ❻
Boogie's Diner ❼
Cone E. Island ❽
FAO Schwarz ❾
Fit to A Tee ❾
Georgetown Park
Mall ❾
Houston's ❿
Indian Crafts Shop ⓫
Little Caledonia ⓬
Little Sprout ❾
Mrs. Field's ⓮
Pizzeria Uno ⓮
Red Baloon ⓭
Walden Books ❾

When you leave, cross M Street (watch the traffic!) to Thomas Jefferson Street, and head down the hill toward the river. The kids may want to stop at **Animal Sensations,** which sells cartoon art. Farther down you'll see **The Georgetown,** the only canal boat, on your left. One-hour cruises depart several times a day between mid-April and late October. Stop at the **National Park Service office** in the Foundry Mall, 1055 Thomas Jefferson St., for tickets and information. You may prefer to detour along the canal towpath, a lovely place to stroll. The water's odor can get a mite strong in summer, but most of the time it's tolerable.

When you reach the end of Thomas Jefferson Street, you've arrived at **Washington Harbour,** a large complex of offices, private residences, restaurants, and shops fronting the Potomac River. Don't trip over the two painters slapping blue paint on the pale brick (sculptor J. Seward Johnson strikes again!). At the bottom of the stairs is "Lunchbreak." Walk along the promenade. Theodore Roosevelt Island is straight ahead. Watergate and the Kennedy Center are to the left. The planes in and out of National need no introduction. Key Bridge, to the right, connects Arlington, Virginia, and Georgetown. At the far right of the promenade is a lovely park.

Exit the area on K Street (under the Whitehurst Freeway) and walk west to 31st Street. Make a right at 31st, go one short block and left at South Street. Measure your fitness level as you climb the steep hill with attached homes banked on the right. Turn right at Wisconsin Avenue, the southern end of **Georgetown's shopping district.** The Indian Craft Shop sells Native American crafts, art, and jewelry. Closer to M Street are the Red Balloon for toys and games; Georgetown Tees, selling souvenir shirts; and Nature Food, where you can stock up on healthy stuff before your ice-cream break.

Houston's (1065 Wisconsin Ave.), **Clyde's** (3236 M St.), and **Pizzeria Uno** (3211 M St.) are all within two blocks of Wisconsin Avenue and M Street.

Serious shoppers will want to inspect **Georgetown Park** at Wisconsin and M Streets. Among the 100 shops on the multi-level mall are **Fit To A Tee,** with the zaniest collection of shirts ever assembled in one place; **Georgetowne Zoo** for stuffed animal aficionados; **Little Sprout,** with specialized and personalized clothing for young children; **FAO Schwarz** for toys, **Waldenbooks,** and good old **Mrs. Field's.** If it's been more than 20 minutes since you ate, there are a number of restaurants and cafes. Get back on track and continue your uphill exploration of:

Wisconsin Avenue along the west (left) side of the street. Movie buffs should head for **Movie Madness** next to the Key Theater for posters and post cards, while teen girls can make a necessary stop at **Benetton.** Jocks will find their favorite college and pro teams' tee-shirts and souvenirs in **The National Locker Room.** A few doors up are **Kemp Mill Records** and **Mrs. Field's** cookies. The inimitable Commander Salamander has leatherware, way-out fashions, tees, and jewelry. They'll spray a colored streak in your hair or make you up for free. At P Street and Wisconsin Avenue, **Another World** sells comic books and related games and tees. Have your palm read by Mrs. Natalie before crossing at Volta Place for the downhill walk on Wisconsin Avenue's east side.

Detour: If you have the time and strength, continue up Wisconsin Avenue to R Street, and go right to Dumbarton Oaks Gardens between 31st and 32nd Streets. All ages enjoy the formal gardens and grassy expanses on the 10-acre parcel. It's especially beautiful in spring and fall. There are reflecting pools, broad terraces, and twisting paths to hold the attention of little ones. See "Gardens and Parks" earlier in this chapter.)

Thank heavens for **Little Caledonia** at 1419 Wisconsin Ave. between O and P streets. With so many Georgetown businesses changing hands faster than the weather, this mainstay is still doing things right after 50 years. The shop's intimate toy nook specializes in stuffed animals and miniatures.

Stop and smell the flowers at **Peter's Flowerland** before you "weave on down the road" to **The Wiz,** which has records, tapes, and CDs. Teenage girls and their moms go for the attractive, casual clothes at **Britches Great Outdoors for Women,** 1357 Wisconsin between Dumbarton and O streets. The ecological-minded Nature Company, one of the best browsing stores in the city, sells everything from bird feeders, minerals, and nature tapes to books, T-shirts, and compasses. There's another **Georgetown Tees,** followed in quick succession by **The Gap** (for teens and adults), **Olsson's Books and Records, Hats in the Belfry,** and **Britches Great Outdoors,** with good-looking stuff for teenage boys and men.

Stop for a meal, slice of mile-high chocolate cake, or fountain treat at the 50's-style **Boogie's Diner,** at 1229 Wisconsin Avenue between M and Prospect streets. Break bread at the **American Cafe** (1211 Wisconsin Avenue between M and N streets), or have them pack you a movable feast to be eaten by the canal or in the Old Stone House garden.

When you've had enough, you can catch a no. 30 bus anywhere along Wisconsin Avenue or M Street back to Foggy Bottom Metro. Or, retrace your steps east across M Street—check out **Benetton 0-12** for children's fashions. **Cone E. Island** dishes out walkaway sundaes in a cone at 2816 Pennsylvania Ave. Continue to Washington Circle, and bear right around the circle to 23rd Street and the Metro.

CHAPTER 5

THEIR SHOPPING LIST

Once upon a time—not that long ago—D.C. residents flocked to New York and other "big" cities to find what they wanted. Now, however, it's easy to shop till you drop in Washington. Flashy multilevel malls, dependable department stores, and trendy boutiques are as much a part of the D.C. landscape as cherry blossoms and government red tape. Shopping has become an increasingly competitive sport over the last few years as more discount stores have moved into the area, giving the full-price standbys a run for their money.

Garfinckel's, once the grand dame of F Street, bit the dust in 1990, leaving Woodward & Lothrop and Hecht's to stand guard over Washington's old downtown shopping area bordered by F, 7th, G, and 14th streets NW. Around the Connecticut Avenue and K Street business corridor, vendors and specialty shops nudge each other for elbow room and your business. About six blocks north, Dupont Circle attracts browsers and buyers alike with its many galleries and one-of-a-kind, sometimes funky, retail establishments. Georgetown, long a haven (and heaven) for shopping mavens, fans out from Wisconsin Avenue and M Street NW. It's best known for fashionable clothing and housewares boutiques, antique shops, and the ever-so-voguish Georgetown Park mall. In recent years, many of the oldtime establishments have been eclipsed by record, souvenir, and beauty shops. Some things haven't changed, however, since I was a college student in D.C. during the Middle Ages. Georgetown is still a numero uno draw for area teenagers, especially on weekends.

Store Hours   Although most stores in the D.C. area are open Monday through Saturday from 9:30 or 10am to 5 or 6pm, many are also open on Sunday and have extended hours one or more evenings, so you should always call ahead.

Sales Tax   The sales tax in D.C. is 6%.

ARTS & CRAFTS

CRAFT KIT & CABOODLE, 827-A Wintergreen Plaza, Rockville, MD. Tel. 301/294-1314.

Crafty kids will have a field day choosing a project from among the paints, woodworking, découpage, beads, miniatures, stenciling, and needlework kits at this emporium. Call for hours and directions.

INDIAN CRAFTS SHOP, Department of the Interior, 18th and C streets NW. Tel. 208-4056.

★ This is an excellent source for top-quality Native American crafts, from inexpensive weavings and sand paintings to elaborate squash-blossom necklaces. To gain entrance to the building, you need photo ID—a passport, government I.D., or driver's license. Open Monday through Friday from 8:30am to 4:30pm. **Metro:** Farragut West.

PEARL ART & CRAFT SUPPLIES, 5695 Telegraph Rd., Alexandria, VA. Tel. 703/960-3900.

One of the world's largest arts and crafts discount centers, Pearl has everything you need for any craft you can name, as well as a large selection of art materials. When it comes to craft supplies, Pearl is a gem. Open Monday through Saturday from 9am to 7:45pm and on Sunday from 10am to 6pm. **Metro:** Huntington.

SULLIVAN'S ART SUPPLIES, 3412 Wisconsin Ave. NW. Tel. 362-1343.

Sullivan's draws dabblers and professionals alike. The well-stocked space adjacent to Sullivan's Toy Store has all the basic oils, acrylics, watercolors, canvas, and brushes that a mini-Picasso or Cassatt could desire. Open Monday through Friday from 10am to 6pm (to 8pm on Thursday), Saturday from 9:30am to 5:30pm, and on Sunday from noon to 4pm. **Metro:** Tenleytown, then take any 30 bus 1 mile south.

TORPEDO FACTORY ART CENTER, 105 N. Union St., Alexandria, VA. Tel. 703/838-4565.

Kids love watching the potters, sculptors, stained-glass artisans, and other craftspeople do their thing in this renovated World War I munitions plant. Most items are for sale. Open daily from 10am to 5pm. **Metro:** King Street.

VISUAL SYSTEMS, 1019 19th St. NW, at K Street NW. Tel. 331-7090.

Visual Systems has "everything your art desires," with a mind-boggling array of fine art, drawing, and drafting supplies. This is doodlers' paradise—hundreds of marking pens in enough colors to make a rainbow blush. Open Monday through Friday from 8:30am to 6pm and on Saturday from 9am to 5pm. Branch stores in Bethesda and Rockville, Maryland, and Fairfax and Baileys Crossroads, Virginia. **Metro:** Farragut West or Farragut North.

BALLOONS

BALLOON BOUQUETS. Tel. 785-1290.

If you're celebrating a birthday or other special occasion during your visit, send a balloon bouquet of plain or imprinted latex or mylar balloons with or without a toy, stuffed animal, cake, or flowers. One call to Balloon Bouquets and you'll have the world on a string. Some same-day delivery service is available. Orders are taken Monday through Saturday from 9am to 5pm.

THE PAPER STORE, 613 Massachusetts Ave. NW. Tel. 789-1316; 1803 Wisconsin Ave. NW. Tel. 333-3200; also several suburban locations.

Select your own plain or stamped balloons to blow up, or save your breath and let The Paper Store fill them with helium. They also carry a variety of plain and decorated mylars and the biggest selection of party supplies and favors around. Call for specific hours; check the *Yellow Pages* for branch information.

BOOKS

A HAPPY THOUGHT, 4836 MacArthur Blvd. NW. Tel. 337-8300.
This cozy, well-stocked neighborhood bookstall has a wide selection for bookworms of all ages. It also hosts visiting children's authors who read from their works at informal gatherings. Open Tuesday through Saturday from 11am to 4pm. Take the D4 bus from Georgetown or call for directions.

A LIKELY STORY, 1555 King St., Alexandria, VA. Tel. 703/836-2498.
More than 20,000 titles are shelved in this 2,000-square-foot children's book store just two blocks from the King Street Metro stop. Special programs include Saturday storytimes, workshops, and author appearances. There's a play area for younger kids so older siblings can take their time making selections. Call to be placed on the mailing list for the store's newsletter showcasing new titles and upcoming events. It's published five times a year. Open Monday through Saturday from 10am to 6pm and Sunday from 1 to 5pm. **Metro:** King Street.

AUDUBON NATURALIST BOOK SHOP, 8940 Jones Mill Rd., Chevy Chase, MD. Tel. 301/652-3606.
Run by the Audubon Naturalist Society at the Woodend nature center, this shop carries a variety of nature books, beginner naturalist guides, and educational coloring books. Best of all, it's a wingbeat away from a nature preserve where youngsters can search for their favorite feathered friends. Open Monday through Friday from 10am to 5pm (Thursday until 8pm) and on Saturday from 9am to 5pm. Call for directions.

BORDERS BOOK SHOP FOR KIDS, 11520A Rockville Pike, Rockville, MD. Tel. 301/816-1067.
Leave it to Borders! In September 1991 they opened a Borders for Kids in a shopping center across the parking lot from the main bookstore. In the cozy uncrowded separate quarters, staff who are especially knowledgeable about young people's books will help your kids find what they are looking for. The new space contains more than 19,000 titles and a performing area with a small stage for readings and pint-size productions. Open Monday through Saturday from 9am to 9pm and Sunday from 11am to 8pm. **Metro:** White Flint.

CHESHIRE CAT, 5512 Connecticut Ave. NW. Tel. 244-3956.
One of the three oldest children's bookstores in the United States, it has been eliciting Chessycat grins from young people for 14 years in its homey setting on upper Connecticut Avenue. Besides an extensive collection of titles for kids of all ages, the Cheshire Cat features author visits and fills mail and phone orders promptly. Open Monday through Saturday from 9:30am to 5:30pm. **Metro:** Friendship Heights, then E2, E4, or E6 bus.

CROWN BOOKS, 1710 G St. NW. Tel. 789-2277.
Of Crown's many branches, the G Street location has the best selection of

children's books. With 40% off *New York Times* hardcover best sellers, 25% off paperbacks, and 10% to 20% discounts on everything else, how can you go wrong? **Metro:** Farragut West.

In addition to the above, centrally located branches are at 2020 K St. NW (tel. 659-2030), 3131 M Street NW (tel. 333-4493), New Hampshire Avenue and M Street NW (tel. 822-8331), and 1275 K Street NW (tel. 289-7170). All the above except G Street are open 7 days a week. Call for hours.

FAIRY GODMOTHER, 319 7th St. SE. Tel. 547-5474.

Most of the Fairy Godmother's space, half a block from the Eastern Market Metro stop, is devoted to children's books. The rest is filled with toys, stuffed animals, and tapes. Besides carrying one of the area's largest selection of children's books for toddlers to young adults, the store has a sizable stock of parenting books. If you've been having trouble in this department, let your Fairy Godmother help you. Open Monday from noon to 6pm and Tuesday through Saturday from 11am to 6pm. **Metro:** Eastern Market.

FRANCIS SCOTT KEY BOOK SHOP, 1400 28th St. NW, at O Street. Tel. 337-4144.

The juvenile section of this Georgetown fixture (since 1939!) features hardcover children's classics and contemporary works. If you can get your kids to put down their Spiderman comics for a few minutes, stop in here. Maybe they'll get hooked on classics. Open Monday through Saturday from 9:30am to 6pm. **Metro:** Dupont Circle (then G2 "Georgetown" bus) or Foggy Bottom (then 32, 34, or 36 bus).

GOVERNMENT PRINTING OFFICE, 710 N. Capitol St. NW, between G and H streets. Tel. 275-2091.

Perhaps you didn't know, but the world's largest printer is right in the heart of li'l ole D.C. No matter how weird or way out your kids' hobbies are, or if they're researching a term paper, or trying to decide which CD player to buy, they can probably find a book or pamphlet on the subject here. With more than 16,000 titles currently in print, the GPO is a browser's heaven and also sells photographs, prints, lithographs, and posters. **Metro:** Union Station.

The GPO has another location at 1510 H St. NW (tel. 653-5075). Call for days and hours.

KRAMERBOOKS & AFTERWORDS, 1517 Connecticut Ave. NW, between Q Street and Dupont Circle. Tel. 387-1462.

After making a purchase at this ever-popular Washington institution, you don't have to wait to get back to your hotel room to begin reading. Just step into the café-within-a bookstore ("Afterwords"—get it?) for a meal or snack and sink your teeth into a juicy new book. Owner David Tenney carries a very respectable selection of children's books ("but not *all* of them," he says), as well as quality paperbacks and major foreign works. Kids love this place. You will too. Open Monday through Thursday from 7am to 1am, round the clock Friday through Sunday. **Metro:** Dupont Circle.

LADO INSTITUTE BOOK STORE, 2233 Wisconsin Ave. NW. Tel. 338-3133.

Stock up here on foreign-language and English (as a second language) books. Children's classics are also available on tape. Open Monday through Friday from 9am to 7:30pm, Saturday from 9am to 2pm. **Metro:** Tenleytown; then take any bus 15 blocks down Wisconsin Avenue to the store.

LOWEN'S, 7201 Wisconsin Ave., Bethesda, MD. Tel. 301/652-1289.

Lowen's is known primarily as a toy store, but they also carry a fine selection of reading matter, from *Pat the Bunny* and colorful pop-ups to quality paperbacks for older siblings. They've been around forever, and they know what kids like. Call for hours and directions. **Metro:** Bethesda.

NATIONAL ZOO BOOKSTORE, Education Building, opposite 3000 Connecticut Ave. NW. Tel. 673-4967.

Before or after visiting their favorite beasties, toddlers and preschoolers can browse through a selection of picture books, while their older siblings peruse more sophisticated works on animal behavior, research, and conservation. Located near the zoo's main entrance, it's open every day but Christmas. Open daily from 9am to 6pm May to September, 9am to 5pm rest of year. **Metro:** Woodley Park-Zoo or Cleveland Park.

THE NATURE COMPANY, 1323 Wisconsin Ave. NW. Tel. 333-4100.

I double-dare you to walk out of one of these attractive, made-for-browsing stores (part of a national chain) without buying at least one beautifully photographed nature volume to be enjoyed by the entire family. Open Monday through Saturday from 10am to 10pm, Sunday till 6pm. **Metro:** Foggy Bottom or Rosslyn.

The other branches are located at Union Station, 50 Massachusetts Ave. NE (tel. 842-3700); Fashion Centre at Pentagon City, 1100 S. Hayes St., Arlington, VA (tel. 703/415-3700); Tysons Corner Center, McLean, VA (tel. 703/760-8930). Call for hours and days.

OLSSON'S BOOKS & RECORDS, 1307 19th St. NW, just off Dupont Circle. Tel. 785-2662 for records; 785-1133 for books.

Olsson's is a class act. The hushed tones, knowledgeable staff, and classical music contribute to the soothing, cocoonlike atmosphere. Olsson's has an excellent selection of kids' books, including several shelves of classics. All recommendations are tagged. **Metro:** Dupont Circle.

Additional locations include 1200 F Street at Metro Center (tel. 393-1853 for records, 347-3686 for books), and 1239 Wisconsin Avenue NW, between M and N Streets (tel. 338-6712 for records, 338-9544 for books). All locations are open daily; call for hours.

SECOND STORY BOOKS, 2000 P St. NW. Tel. 659-8884; 4836 Bethesda Ave., Bethesda, MD. Tel. 301/656-0170.

A little dust never hurt anyone. The Bethesda location has a separate children's room where little ones can choose from a large selection of well-priced books that are in better shape than you are. Call for hours and directions.

SMITHSONIAN MUSEUM SHOPS: National Museum of American History, 14th Street and Constitution Avenue NW. Tel. 337-2716; Air & Space Museum, 7th Street and Independence Avenue, SW. Tel. 357-1387; Museum of Natural History, 10th Street and Constitution Avenue NW. Tel. 357-1527.

The museum shops are prime sources for a vast assortment of educational books geared to different reading and comprehension levels. The titles relate to subjects embraced in the museums. If you're shopping for lasting souvenirs or gifts for the folks back home, look no further. Call for hours of operation and directions.

COMIC BOOKS

ANOTHER WORLD, 1504 Wisconsin Ave. NW, at P St. Tel. 333-8650, or 333-8651.

If comics are your kids' intellectual nourishment, step into Another World in Georgetown to feed their need. You'll also find comic T-shirts and games. A recorded message lists all the new comics stocked since the previous week. Open Monday through Thursday from 10:30am to 7pm, Friday and Saturday from 11am to 9pm, and on Sunday from noon to 7pm. **Metro:** Foggy Bottom, then take any 30 bus.

BIG PLANET COMICS, 4908 Fairmont Ave., Bethesda, MD. Tel. 301/ 654-6856.

Cowabunga! Big Planet carries the latest Teenage Mutant Ninja Turtles, Disney, and Archie comics, along with vintage Nancy and Sluggo and Popeye for Mom and Dad. Comic-related toys, posters, and T-shirts are also available in Big Planet's new quarters close to Bethesda Metro. Call for hours of operation and directions. **Metro:** Bethesda.

COMPUTERS, CAMERAS & ELECTRONICS

Prices for audio/video equipment, cameras, and computers are very competitive, and although Washington, D.C., is known for many things, electronics is not one of them. Check the *Yellow Pages* and watch for ads in the *Washington Post* and *Washington Times.* If you don't find what you want, call 47th Street Photo, Inc., in New York City (tel. toll free 800/221-7774), for audio/video equipment, cameras, computers, and darkroom accessories under one roof. Regarding computers: Because the three entries originally on this list have gone out of business in the past six months, I am gun-shy to recommend more. Ask around, and check the newspapers and the *Yellow Pages* at the time of your visit.

CIRCUIT CITY, 10490 Auto Park Dr., Bethesda, MD. Tel. 301/469-8028; 1905 Chain Bridge Rd., Tysons Corner, VA. Tel. 703/893-6112; also seven other suburban locations.

For TVs, radios, stereo equipment, CD players, and VCRs, Circuit City is highly competitive. Don't let the sometimes overzealous salespeople get to you. If they claim to be out of an advertised "special," ask for the manager. Call for directions and hours.

PENN CAMERA EXCHANGE, 915 E St. NW. Tel. 347-5777, or toll free 800/347-5770.

Those in the know swear by Penn Camera for its knowledgeable help, complete stock, and discounted prices on brand-name equipment. Penn not only sells new cameras, but buys, trades, rents, and repairs used equipment. Check the Friday *Washington Post* ("Weekend" section) for announcements of special sales. Open Monday through Friday from 9am to 6pm, Saturday from 10am to 5pm. **Metro:** Metro Center or Gallery Place.

WASHINGTON, D.C.

Washington, D.C.,
Shopping

Air & Space Museum Shop **1**
Al's Magic Shop **2**
Another World **3**
Beadazzled **4**
Benetton 0-12 **5**
Blockbuster's **6**
Crown Books **7**
Explorer's Den **8**
GapKids and babygap **9**
Georgetown Park Mall: **10**
   FAO Schwarz
   Fit To A Tee
   Georgetown Zoo
   Little Sprout
   Waldenbooks

Government Printing Office **11**
Hecht's **12**
Indian Crafts Shop **13**
Kids Closet **14**
Kids' Stuff **15**
Kramerbooks & Afterwords **16**
The Map Store **17**
Mazza Gallerie: **18**
   B. Dalton Bookstore
   Disc Shop
   Jane Wilner
Museum of Natural History Shop **19**
National Gallery of Art Shop **20**
National Map Gallery **21**

WASHINGTON, D.C., SHOPPING

Rhode Island Ave.
Vermont Ave.
P St.
O St.
N St.
13th St.
12th St.
11th St.
10th St.
M St.
New York Ave.
North Capitol St.
M St.

L St.
Mc Pherson Square
16th St.
15th St.
14th St.
Mt. Vernon Square
K St.
I St.
Franklin Park
1st St.
H St.
1st St.
Union Station

McPHERSON SQUARE
Lafayette Square
30
H St.
METRO CENTER
12
G St.
35
8th St.
9th St.
7th St.
6th St.
5th St.
GALLERY PLACE
Massachusetts Ave.
3rd St.
4th St.
2nd St.
1st St.
11
21
UNION STATION
23

Ellipse Rd.
29
F St.
E St. 27
26 Pennsylvania Ave.
FEDERAL TRIANGLE
50 22 1
D St.
C St.
395
Louisiana Ave.

Constitution Ave.
19
20
15th St.
THE MALL
1

SMITHSONIAN
14th St.
10th St.
Independence Ave.

L'ENFANT PLAZA
12th St.
6th St.
FEDERAL CENTER S.W.
CAPITOL SOUTH
1st St.

Tidal Basin
Francis Case Memorial Bridge
14th St. Bridge
395
SW Frwy.
4th St.

East Potomac Park
Washington Channel
7th St.
Richmond, Fredericksburg & Potomac Railroad

Metro Stop **M** Information **i**

National Museum of American History Gift Shop 22
National Zoo Bookstore 23
Newsroom 24
Olsson's Books & Records 25
The Pavilion at the Old Post Office 26
Penn Camera Exchange 27
Rand McNally Map & Travel Store 28
Shops at National Place: 29
  Barston's Child's Play
  Benetton
  Dallas Alice
  The Kite Loft
  Magic Masters
  Sharper Image

Sunny's Surplus 30
Tower Records 31
Tower Video 32
Union Station Shops: 33
  Brookstone
  Flights of Fancy
  The Great Train Store
  The Nature Company
  Sam Goody
  Time Flies
Urban Outfitters 34
Woodward & Lothrop 35

RENT-A-COMPUTER, 4853 Cordell Ave., Bethesda, MD. Tel. 301/951-0811.

Here's a clever concept. Rent a computer short-term or for the long haul while deciding if you want to buy. IBM equipment is a specialty, and Rent-A-Computer guarantees delivery service within four hours. Call for hours and directions.

RITZ CAMERA, 1740 Pennsylvania Ave. NW. Tel. 737-1740; nine other D.C. locations, including several in Maryland and Virginia.

This is a one-stop photo shop that sells and repairs equipment, and the salespeople know what they're talking about. Ritz offers one-hour photo finishing and instant passport photos, and sells frames, albums, and other cute, gimmicky photo holders. Check the *Yellow Pages* for other addresses and phone numbers.

SHARPER IMAGE, The Shops at National Place, 529 14th St. NW. Tel. 626-6340.

You can drop your kids at the Sharper Image in the morning, return several hours later, and they will not miss you. If it's electronic, high-tech, or digital; and it also lights up, hums, and/or performs many functions simultaneously, it's waiting to be discovered at the Sharper Image. Open Monday through Wednesday and Saturday from 10am to 7pm, Thursday and Friday from 10am to 8pm, Sunday from noon to 5pm. **Metro:** Metro Center.

There's another branch at 3276 M St. NW (tel. 337-9361).

DEPARTMENT STORES

HECHT'S, 12th and G streets NW, at Metro Center. Tel. 628-6661.

Running neck and neck with Woodie's, Hecht's has also been in business almost forever—for about a century, anyway. This new flagship store, which opened its doors in 1985, is a five-story temple of chrome, glass, and polished wood. Some of the old charm is gone, but the salespeople are still friendly and accommodating. The selection of children's clothing is abundant for all age groups and moderately priced. If you forgot to pack something, you will find it here and not get ripped off in the process. Hecht's also has a **Ticketron** outlet. Open Monday through Saturday from 10am to 8pm, Sunday from 11am to 6pm. **Metro:** Metro Center.

Besides the downtown store, Hecht's has 13 suburban stores.

LORD & TAYLOR, 5225 Western Ave. NW. Tel. 362-9600.

This smallish version of the famous Fifth Avenue store is located one block from the Friendship Heights Metro stop near Chevy Chase, MD. You'll find high-quality children's merchandise, and most is fairly priced. Lord & Taylor's frequent sales are legendary. Open Monday through Saturday from 10am to 8pm, Sunday from 11am to 6pm. **Metro:** Friendship Heights.

There are also two Virginia stores and one in Maryland—check the *Yellow Pages* for locations and telephone numbers.

NEIMAN-MARCUS, Mazza Gallerie, 5300 Wisconsin Ave. NW. Tel. 966-9700.

I know people who shop for their kids' clothes at Neiman's. They also feed them sirloin steak rather than hamburger. What can I say? The children's departments tend to be low on merchandise and high on prices, and the salespeople vary from friendly and charming to haughty—like they're doing you a favor to wait on you. Let Granny do the buying here. **Metro:** Friendship Heights.

There is a Neiman-Marcus branch at The Galleria at Tysons II in McLean, VA. Tel. 703/761-1600. Call for specific branch information about hours and days and directions.

WOODWARD & LOTHROP, 11th and F streets NW. Tel. 347-5300.

Woodie's, as it's affectionately known by the satisfied customers who shop regularly in the 10-story, full-service department store, is hardly the new kid on the block, having opened in 1880. Woodie's sells quality merchandise at reasonable prices, and the selection for kids strikes a healthy balance between the tried-and-true and whatever is "in" at the moment. It's easy to clothe a kid for life at Woodie's. Many have. The Terrace Restaurant has a special kids' menu and is known for its desserts, like Stephen's Brownie with ice cream, hot fudge, marshmallow sauce, and pecans. Better try clothes on first. Open Monday through Saturday from 10am to 8pm, Sunday from 11am to 6pm. **Metro:** Metro Center.

There are 15 other Woodward & Lothrop stores in the D.C. area; check your phone book for other locations.

IN THE SUBURBS

BLOOMINGDALE'S, White Flint Mall, North Bethesda (they can call it North Bethesda or Kensington, but it's still Rockville to me), MD. Tel. 301/984-4600; Tysons Corner, McLean, VA. Tel. 703/556-4600.

A Bloomie's is a Bloomie's is a Bloomie's. Taking a cue from their famous trendsetting mother in New York, these two suburban offspring do their best to satisfy the buying appetites of material girls and boys. If you're unfamiliar with the store, you'll be pleasantly surprised. Sure, there are plenty of overpriced imports, but most of the prices are competitive. The White Flint store lost me when they redecorated and moved departments here, there, and everywhere a few years ago. They should hand out maps. Call for open hours and directions.

I. MAGNIN, White Flint Mall, Rockville Pike, North Bethesda, MD. Tel. 301/468-2900.

A lovely store that's service-oriented, but its kids' departments need beefing up. It's an okay place to bring the grandparents when they're treating. This branch of the prestigious West Coast department store has dynamite sales in all departments.

SAKS FIFTH AVENUE, 5555 Wisconsin Ave., Chevy Chase, MD. Tel. 301/657-9000.

When my kids were very young, I loved shopping for them at Saks. But when their outfits began costing more than mine, I stopped shopping there—except when my mother came to town. Kids grow up so fast. If yours are still young enough to tolerate your picking out special clothing for them, head for Saks. **Metro:** Friendship Heights. Call for hours and directions.

Although not in D.C., or close in, two other department stores worth noting are **Macy's,** The Galleria, 2255 International Dr., McLean, VA (tel. 703/556-0000), or

Pentagon City, 1000 S. Hayes St., Arlington, VA (tel. 703/418-4488), and **Nordstrom,** The Galleria at Tysons II, 2255 International Dr., McLean, VA (tel. 703/761-1121), Pentagon City, 1400 S. Hayes St., Arlington, VA (tel. 703/415-1121), or Montgomery Mall, Bethesda, MD (tel. 301/365-4111). Call for hours and directions.

DRUGSTORES

Washington's major drugstore chain, carrying diversified merchandise that ranges from frozen foods to charcoal briquettes to items of interest to kids, is **Peoples** (with about 40 stores). Check your phone book for the most convenient locations. There's a 24-hour Peoples at 14th Street and Thomas Circle NW off Vermont Ave. (tel. 628-0720), another at Dupont Circle (tel. 785-1466), both with round-the-clock pharmacies.

FASHIONS

I went to college for what it costs to outfit a young child these days, and don't even talk to me about teenagers. Medical school is cheaper. You'll find everything from designer duds to awesome army surplus for kids from cradle to Corvette in the following listings.

BENETTON, The Shops at National Place, 1331 Pennsylvania Ave. NW. Tel. 737-5544; 1234 Wisconsin Ave. NW. Tel. 337-0632; Mazza Gallerie, 5300 Wisconsin Ave. NW Tel. 362-6970.
This Italian-based company sells comfortable, trendsetting clothing through its franchise stores all over the world. Chances are your teenage daughters are familiar with it already. A separate section in the above-listed stores is devoted to kids from 6 months to 12 years. Other area stores (tel. 333-9792) sell adult sizes only. Call for hours and directions.

BENETTON 0-12, 2001 M St. NW. Tel. 331-8880; 3108 M St. NW. Tel. 333-7839.
You'll find the same stylish merchandise here as in the big people's store, but scaled down to fit kids from infancy to age 12 (0–12). You can't argue with success; there are more than 150 Benetton children's stores across the United States. Call branches for open hours and directions.

CHOCOLATE SOUP, 10400 Old Georgetown Rd., Bethesda, MD. Tel. 301/564-1111.
The shop with the delectable name and equally delicious children's clothing carries familiar name brands and its own Chocolate Soup label. The reasonably priced, good-looking garb in girls' sizes infant to 14, boys' infant to 7, makes me wish I still had little ones to outfit. My kids don't even let me pick out their Kleenex anymore—I always choose the wrong color. Open Monday through Wednesday from 10am to 6pm, Thursday and Friday from 10am to 8pm, Saturday

from 10am to 6pm, and on Sunday from noon to 5pm. **Metro:** Medical Center, then take J2 bus "Montgomery Mall."

THE GAP, 1217 Connecticut Ave. NW. Tel. 638-4603; 2000 Pennsylvania Ave. NW. Tel. 429-6862; also about a dozen suburban stores.

To go with their large selection of jeans in many styles, colors, and weights for waists 28 inches and larger, the Gap carries color-coordinated shirts, sweaters, tees, and accessories. Merchandise is attractively displayed and prices are competitive. There are usually racks of amazingly low, sale-priced items in the back of the store. The sweatsuits and jeans wear like iron. Check the *Yellow Pages* and call the branch stores for hours and directions.

GAP KIDS AND BABY GAP, 2000 Pennsylvania Ave. NW. Tel. 429-8711.

Finally! The same classic, tough-wearing denim and casual wear made famous by the "senior" Gap has hit D.C. for babies (size newborn to 24 months) and kids (size 2 to 12). If your hometown doesn't have a Gap Kids, stock up. Open Monday through Friday from 10am to 8pm, Saturday from 10am to 6pm, and on Sunday from noon to 5pm. **Metro:** Foggy Bottom.

JANE WILNER, Mazza Gallerie, 5300 Wisconsin Ave. NW. Tel. 966-1484.

If you're looking for something special when Sir Stork arrives, tiptoe into Jane Wilner. Imported layettes and christening gowns are featured at this attractive uptown boutique, which also carries bassinets, cradles, and accessories for the new arrival. Open Monday through Friday from 10am to 8pm, Saturday from 10am to 6pm, and on Sunday from noon to 5pm. **Metro:** Friendship Heights.

JUST BOYS, JUST SHOES, JUST SO, 3301 New Mexico Ave. NW. Tel. 966-2697, 244-2224, 244-0500, respectively.

Start at Just So for quality coed clothing for infants and toddlers. A few steps away at Just Boys, you can dress your budding Beau Brummel in pricey but gentlemanly domestic and imported apparel, sizes 4 to 20. Girls can shop at Just So until they outgrow size 14. Just Shoes caters to boys and girls' growing feet from infant sizes to an adult 4. Open Monday through Saturday from 9:30am to 5:30pm. **Metro:** Tenleytown (a distance).

KIDS CLOSET, 1226 Connecticut Ave. NW. Tel. 429-9247; 1990 K St. NW. Tel. 466-5589.

For Absorba, Carters, Christian Dior, OshKosh By Gosh, and the like, stop at either downtown branch of Kids Closet. They have a plentiful selection of durable, attractive kidswear for boys and girls in sizes 3 months to size 14, and there are plenty of toys and accessories too! Call either branch for hours and directions. **Metro:** Farragut North or West.

KRAMER'S, Montgomery Mall, Bethesda, MD. Tel. 301/365-7988.

Kramer's is the kind of place that always seems to have what you can't find elsewhere, and the salespeople are exceedingly personable and helpful. More than once I've seen them display the patience of Job with kids who make no secret of the fact that they would rather be hanging by their thumbs than shopping.

Kramer's carries casual wear for girls sizes 7–14; sportswear and dress attire for boys 8–20 in slim, regular, huskies, and stouts (to size 24). They also have camp supplies, school uniforms, gifts, and accessories. Open Monday through Saturday from 10am to 9:30pm and on Sunday from noon to 6pm. **Metro:** Medical Center, then take J2 bus "Montgomery Mall."

LITTLE SPROUT OF GEORGETOWN, 3222 M St. NW. Tel. 342-2273.

Nestled on the second level of Georgetown Park, this exquisite little children's boutique carries unusual clothing and accessories mostly for infants, toddlers, and sizes 4–6x, with a few things for sizes 7–14. Don't miss the hand-painted tennis shoes (some with socks to match!) for newborn to size 8. You'll want a pair, even if your kids can't squeeze into them. T-shirt and pant sets can be personalized on the spot at no extra charge. Open Monday through Saturday from 10am to 9pm and on Sunday from 11am to 6pm. **Metro:** Foggy Bottom.

SEVENTH HEAVEN, Hechinger Mall, 16th Street and Benning Road NE. Tel. 388-5650.

No frills or gimmicks at Seventh Heaven, just a huge selection of discounted Gitano, Jordache, Guess, Levi's, and OshKosh at this popular shopping haunt of the young set. It's even more popular with value-conscious parents and grandparents. Seventh Heaven carries newborn to preteen sizes for girls; newborn to size 18 for boys; and has two branch stores in Maryland. Open Monday through Saturday from 10am to 6pm. **Metro:** Union Station, then take a taxi.

SUNNY'S SURPLUS, 1416 H St. NW. Tel. 347-2774.

For family shopping, give me a well-stocked Army-Navy store any day of the week. Sunny's sells boots, sneakers, work shoes, jeans, outerwear, socks (in larger sizes), and unisex T-shirts, sweatshirts, gloves, hats, and camping gear for creatures great and small. No wonder kids love to rummage through the goods and goodies here. They can pick up lots of colorful inexpensive items, like camouflage T-shirts, zany bandanas, backpacks, and maybe a canteen for those long hikes from the back door to the family car. Open Monday through Saturday—call for hours. **Metro:** McPherson Square.

There are two other branches: 917 F St. NW (tel. 737-2032) and 3342 M St. NW (tel. 333-8550), both open seven days a week—call for hours.

URBAN OUTFITTERS, 3111 M St. NW. Tel. 342-1012.

Attention all teens: If you like trendy, stylish clothing and funky but functional accessories for your room—all priced so they won't eat up next year's allowance—you'll love Urban Outfitters. They have a women's and men's department and carry some of the weird-looking shoes teens call fashionable. Don't overlook the large "renewal" section—a money-saving rather than a religious experience. Open Monday through Thursday from 10am to 10pm, on Friday and Saturday from 10am to 11pm, and on Sunday from noon to 8pm. **Metro:** Foggy Bottom.

WHY NOT? 200 King St., Alexandria, VA. Tel. 703/548-2080.

Why not, indeed! Be sure to include this cheery shop in your visit to Old Town. In business for more than 25 years, Why Not? stocks infant to preteen clothing for girls; infant through size 7 for boys. But it doesn't end there. A wide range of creatively displayed toys and books fill the two-story space and help to fashion a colorful and appealing environment. No wonder Why Not? continues to draw shoppers from around the Beltway. You'll feel good as soon as you walk in the door. Open Monday through Saturday from 10am to 9pm and on Sunday noon to 5pm. **Metro:** King Street (1½ miles).

RESALE SHOPS

KIDS' STUFF, 5615 39th St. NW, between McKinley and Northampton Sts., just off Connecticut Ave. Tel. 244-2221.

Big families may no longer be in fashion, but children still outgrow clothes at the alarming rate they did in hand-me-down days. That's why a store like this is such a find. This is no junk shop. The owners take on consignment only quality merchandise in excellent condition, and they display it attractively. You'll always find major brand and designer name clothing—OshKosh, Florence Eisman, Levi's, Laura Ashley, Cary, Mally, Polly Flinders, Ruth of Carolina—as well as toys, children's furniture, strollers, and even maternity clothes. And because Washington houses every foreign embassy, you'll also find wonderful European items. Open Monday through Saturday from 10am to 5pm. Closed the month of July and Saturdays in August. **Metro:** Friendship Heights.

T-SHIRTS

DALLAS ALICE, The Shops at National Place, 1331 Pennsylvania Ave. NW. Tel. 628-8686.

It's hard to choose from among the more than 300 entertaining styles, in kids' sizes from extra-small to extra-large, that fill this cozy corner shop. You'll find standard souvenir T-shirts, as well as many whimsical and humorous designs. Open Monday through Wednesday and Saturday from 10am to 7pm, Thursday and Friday from 10am to 8pm, and Sunday from noon to 5pm. **Metro:** Metro Center.

FIT TO A TEE, Georgetown Park Mall, 3222 M St. NW. Tel. 965-3650.

Every year I buy my little brother a birthday T-shirt at Fit To A Tee. My brother is 41, but who's counting. His favorite one is emblazoned with the skeletal structure of the torso, with all parts labeled. The shop is crammed with oodles of souvenir and message shirts for kids under and over 40, in sizes infant through XXX large. If you're in a bad mood, a visit here will cheer you up. Open Monday through Saturday from 10am to 9pm, Sunday from 11am to 7pm. **Metro:** Foggy Bottom.

FURNITURE

BELLINI JUVENILE DESIGNER FURNITURE, 12141 Rockville Pike, Rockville, MD. Tel. 301/770-3944; The Village at Shirlington, 4024 28th St. South, Arlington, VA. Tel. 703/379-1900.

They're not kidding about the designer part. Bellini sells top-of-the-line, European-crafted cribs, bunk beds, trundles, and bedding accessories to furnish little princes and princesses with beautiful beginnings. Call for branch hours and directions.

CARGO FURNITURE, 3222 M St. NW. Tel. 337-3106.

This stuff is built to last. Made of durable southern yellow pine, Cargo's bunk beds, dressers, desks, and bookcases have "indestructible" written on them and carry a lifetime guarantee. The bunk beds have built-in safety features, so whoever sleeps on top doesn't end up on the bottom. Open Monday through Friday from 10am to

9pm, Saturday from 10am to 7pm, and Sunday from noon to 6pm. **Metro:** Foggy Bottom, then take any 30 bus.

CONRAN'S, Georgetown Park Mall, Wisconsin and M streets NW. Tel. 298-8300.

Conran's sells attractive bed, desk, dresser units in white Melamine for growing youths. Kids will not outgrow the full-length bed or the clean, contemporary look of this furniture. Open Monday through Friday from 10am to 9pm, Saturday from 10am to 7pm, and on Sunday from noon to 6pm. **Metro:** Foggy Bottom, then take any 30 bus.

LEWIS OF LONDON, 12248 Rockville Pike, Rockville, MD. Tel. 301/468-2070; 7249 Arlington Blvd., Falls Church, VA. Tel. 703/876-9330.

Lewis knows a thing or two about creating stylish children's furniture. Besides several attractive lines of nursery furniture and accessories, the store sells juvenile furniture for older kids, plus strollers, highchairs, and infant clothing for tots up to 24 months. Call for branch hours and directions.

JEWELRY & BEADS

ACCENTS JEWELRY, 4919 Elm St., Bethesda, MD. Tel. 301/656-7307.

Come here for semi-precious beads (as little as 10 cents apiece), findings, and bead-stringing supplies. Accents also has jewelry-making classes. Call for open hours. **Metro:** Bethesda.

BEADAZZLED, 1522 Connecticut Ave. NW. Tel. 265-BEAD.

Cute name, eh? There are plenty of baubles, bangles, and beads, plus everything in bead-work supplies to keep you and yours from getting strung out. Open Monday through Saturday from 11am to 6pm and on Sunday from 1 to 5pm. **Metro:** Dupont Circle.

KITES

THE KITE LOFT, The Shops at National Place, 1331 Pennsylvania Ave. NW. Tel. 737-1505.

What a fun place! The Kite Loft has everything from flying discs, wind socks, and boomerangs to high flyers, box kites, and tetras. If you really want to get carried away, there's a $225 Phantom stunt kite. Earthbound? Try your hand at Yomega, the "yo yo with a brain." Open Monday through Wednesday and Saturday from 10am to 7pm, Thursday and Friday from 10am to 8pm, and on Sunday from noon to 5pm. **Metro:** Metro Center.

THE AIR & SPACE MUSEUM GIFT SHOP, 6th Street and Independence Avenue SW. Tel. 357-1387.

Your kids will be walking on air when they see the selection of kites (from $15 to $120) sold here. Kites are color coded according to degree of difficulty. Mine ("For 7-year-olds") is a breeze to fly. Launch your purchase on the Mall just outside the museum. Open daily from 10am to 5:30pm; extended summer hours. **Metro:** L'Enfant Plaza.

MAGIC SHOPS

AL'S MAGIC SHOP, 1012 Vermont Ave. NW. Tel. 789-2800.
If you're in the market for fake vomit, a squirt ring, or bug in an ice cube, you've come to the right place. A Washington landmark for more than half a century, Al's is loaded with sleight-of-hand paraphernalia. Exploding cigar, anyone? Open Monday through Friday from 9am to 6pm, Saturday from 9am to 4:30pm. **Metro:** McPherson Square.

MAGIC MASTERS, The Shops at National Place, 1331 Pennsylvania Ave. NW. Tel. 628-0779.
You have to see this place to believe it. In a tiny paneled alcove, impromptu shows throughout the day delight and lure shoppers. Meet Rocky the Raccoon, see three types of handcuffs used by Harry Houdini (plus a signed photograph), and let your kids trick you into buying something. You'll have a magical time. Open Monday through Saturday from 10am to 9pm and on Sunday from noon to 6pm. **Metro:** Metro Center.

MALLS

What did kids do before malls? I have *vague* recollections of hopscotch, marbles, and stick ball, but hanging out at malls has become an avocation for today's kids, who happily trade natural for fluorescent light and exercise for just hangin' out. You'll have no trouble keeping your little mall rats satisfied in Washington. Just bring lots of money. Besides these listings, there are countless malls in suburban Maryland and Virginia. (Maybe you'll want to keep this bit of information to yourself.)

GEORGETOWN PARK MALL, 3222 M St. NW., at Wisconsin Avenue. Tel. 342-8190.
This handsome multilevel complex with more than 100 upscale shops invites browsers and buyers with its warm brick Victorian interior, complemented by skylights, fountains, chandeliers, and beautiful plantings. Shopping at Georgetown Park is an event. FAO Schwarz, Mrs. Field's Cookies, Fit To A Tee, Georgetowne Zoo, Waldenbooks, and Little Sprout (a specialized children's clothing shop that personalizes on the spot) will please the kids most. Open Monday through Friday from 10am to 9pm, Saturday from 10am to 7pm, and on Sunday from noon to 6pm. **Metro:** Foggy Bottom.

MAZZA GALLERIE, 5300 Wisconsin Ave. NW., between Western Avenue and Jenifer Street. Tel. 966-6114, or 686-9515.
While Neiman-Marcus and most of the boutiquey shops at this très chic four-level mall will be out of reach for little people's tastes and allowances, there are some exceptions. The Disc Shop is a popular source for records, tapes, CD's, posters, and celebrity buttons, and there's a B. Dalton Bookseller branch and a Foot Locker store. Slip into McDonald's when a Big Mac attack hits, then dive into the divine "designer" chocolates at Kron Chocolatier. Open Monday through Friday from 10am to 8pm, Saturday from 10am to 6pm, and Sunday from noon to 5pm. **Metro:** Friendship Heights.

THE PAVILION AT THE OLD POST OFFICE, 1100 Pennsylvania Ave. NW. Tel. 289-4224.

It's nearly 200 feet straight up from the floor to the skylight canopy of this three-level complex of 30 retail shops and restaurants housed in a nearly 100-year-old edifice. Don't expect to do any major shopping here, but there are a few novelty shops, and The Candy Circus and Fudgery provide a sweet interlude. You can ride the glass elevator to the tower observation deck for a spectacular 360° view of downtown and the environs, then see the 10 massive bells (a Bicentennial gift from England) that are rung for state occasions. (By the way, the bellringers practice on Thursday evening between 6:30 and 9:30pm.) Kids always like eating in the Food Court. Free entertainment is presented daily in the atrium, but the third Saturday of every month it is geared especially to children. The mall itself is open from March to December, daily from 10am to 9:30pm and January and February on Monday through Saturday from 10am to 8pm and on Sunday from 10am to 6pm. **Metro:** Federal Triangle.

THE SHOPS AT NATIONAL PLACE, entrance on F St. NW, between 13th and 14th streets, or via the J.W. Marriott at 1331 Pennsylvania Ave. NW. Tel. 783-9090.

Get out your credit cards in preparation for shopping at this attractive four-tiered complex that opened in 1984 in the renovated National Press Building. Benetton 0-12, Dallas Alice (T-shirts), The Sharper Image, B. Dalton, Magic Masters, The Kite Loft, Barston's (toys), and Record Town beckon. Have a meal or a snack in the Food Hall on the top level, where American, Chinese, Italian, Japanese, and other varieties of fast food and desserts are available throughout the day. Open daily. Call for hours. **Metro:** Metro Center.

TYSONS CORNER CENTER, 1961 Chain Bridge Rd., at Rte. 7. Tel. 703/893-9400.

This well-known mall is about 30 minutes from town in McLean, Virginia (take the Beltway I-495 to Exit 11B and follow the signs). Among the 230 shops here are five major department stores—Bloomingdale's, Nordstrom, Lord & Taylor, Hecht's, and Woodward & Lothrop. Other notable emporia of interest to kids include the Nature Company, The Limited, Disney Store, Banana Republic, F.A.O. Schwarz, Waldenbooks, Britches of Georgetown, Woolworth's, and The Gap. Once again, and—very convenient—a U.S. Post Office. More than 30 restaurants run the gamut from Magic Pan to California Pizza Kitchen, and 8 movie theaters make this a good choice for an afternoon shopping spree followed by a relaxing family dinner and a film. There's free parking for 10,000 cars. Open Monday through Saturday from 10am to 9:30pm and Sunday from noon to 5pm. **Metro:** West Falls Church; from there you can catch a shuttle that runs every half hour in both directions.

UNION STATION, 40 Massachusetts Ave. NE. Tel. 371-9441.

Since reopening in 1988 after extensive renovation, Union Station has become a top tourist draw. All but the youngest children will marvel at the magnificent architecture and beautiful restoration before hunkering down for something good to eat at the lower-level Food Court, which can be entered via a majestic winding staircase. Nearly 100 shops are scattered among three levels. Of particular interest to kids: Time Flies (unusual clocks; East Hall); the Nature Company (environmentally themed items; West Hall); The Great Train Store (model trains, etc.;

Main Floor Level); Flights of Fancy (toys; Main Floor Level); Brookstone (gadgets; Main Floor Level); and Sam Goody (records). You can catch nine different movies in the cinema complex. Open Monday through Saturday from 10am to 9pm and on Sunday from noon to 6pm. **Metro:** Union Station.

MAPS

EXPLORER'S DEN, National Geographic Society, 17th and M streets NW. Tel. 857-7588.

The Den sells the Society's distinctive and finely detailed maps, as well as all National Geographic publications. You can also purchase back issues of *National Geographic* magazine, globes, games, and videos. Open Monday through Saturday from 10am to 9pm, and on Sunday from 10am to 5pm. **Metro:** Farragut North.

RAND MCNALLY MAP & TRAVEL STORE, 1201 Connecticut Ave. NW. Tel. 223-6751.

Expand your horizons at Rand McNally where they have maps of places you've never heard of, many attractively displayed like museum prints. There are also travel guides, travel-related gifts, and more than 30 globes, from a kid-size 6-incher to a special order 6-foot motorized sphere. Open Monday through Friday from 9am to 6:30pm (8:30pm on Thursday) and 10am to 6pm on Saturday. **Metro:** Farragut North.

THE MAP STORE, 1636 I St. NW. Tel. 628-2608.

The center of the local cartophiles' universe for 40 years, The Map Store has something for all age levels: wood puzzles of the continents and United States, inflatable and traditional globes, atlases, road and street maps, and even a world wastebasket for those who want to learn some geography while filing trash. Call for hours and days. **Metro:** Farragut West or Farragut North.

NATIONAL MAP GALLERY, Union Station, 50 Massachusetts Ave. NE. Tel. 789-0100.

If you arrive in D.C. by train, stop here for a choice selection of local maps. Babies and preschoolers can begin learning geography with Hugg-A-Planet's soft globe. The shop carries a large selection of foreign maps, and also stocks traditional globes, classroom aides, and gifts. Call for open hours. **Metro:** Union Station.

TRAVEL BOOKS UNLIMITED, 4931 Cordell Ave., Bethesda, MD. Tel. 301/951-8533.

Take your pick of more than 38,000 maps at this unique travel bookstore, and let your kids help plan your next vacation. Whether you pine for Essex, Estonia, or Ecuador—or any point in between—Travel Books Unlimited has it. This is a must for geography freaks. Open Tuesday through Saturday from 10am to 9pm and on Sunday from noon to 5pm. **Metro:** Bethesda.

NATURE TREASURES

THE NATURE COMPANY, Union Station, 50 Massachusetts Ave. NE. Tel. 842-3700; 1323 Wisconsin Ave. NW. Tel. 333-4100.

It's hard not to love this place. Luring kids *out* of here can be as difficult as getting them into bed at night. But it's worth it. Everything sold in these shops, part of a national chain, is nature-related: books, tapes, toys, prisms, bird feeders, posters, telescopes, and worlds more. The Wisconsin Avenue branch is open Monday through Saturday from 10am to 10pm, Sunday till 6pm. **Metro:** Foggy Bottom or Rosslyn for Wisconsin Avenue store. For information on the Union Station branch and the suburban stores, call the branches directly.

NATIONAL MUSEUM OF NATURAL HISTORY GIFT SHOP, 10th Street and Constitution Avenue NW. Tel. 357-2700.

Before or after your museum visit, stop at the gift shop. There's an interesting collection of books—many geared to kids—on natural history and anthropology, as well as fossil reproduction kits, shells, minerals, and much more. The Shop for Kids near the cafeteria on the first floor sells puppets, activity books, puzzles, and plush animals. The new Rotunda Shop on the second floor specializes in minerals. Open daily from 10am to 5:30pm, except December 25. Extended summer hours. **Metro:** Federal Triangle.

NEWSPAPERS & MAGAZINES

NEWSROOM, 1753 Connecticut Ave. NW. Tel. 332-1489.

Still going strong after 13 years, the Newsroom is a mainstay of the Dupont Circle area. The Newsroom carries more than 200 domestic and foreign newspapers and numerous magazines in 20 languages. The foreign-language department has books and tapes for kids who want to learn other languages. Open daily from 7am to 7pm. **Metro:** Dupont Circle.

PERFORMING ARTS SUPPLIES

BACKSTAGE, 2101 P St. NW. Tel. 775-1488.

Kids with an interest in the performing arts should take a cue from Washington thespians, musicians, and dancers and enter smiling at Backstage. Here is everything your kids will need to get their act together: an award-winning selection of scripts, costumes, dancewear, makeup, sheet music, and books. Open Monday through Saturday from 10am to 7pm, on Thursday till 8pm. **Metro:** Dupont Circle.

POSTERS

MOVIE MADNESS, 1222 Wisconsin Ave. NW. Tel. 337-7064.

Whether they're looking for a poster of their all-time favorite movie or new wave group to decorate a bedroom wall, kids will find it at Movie Madness. There's a large selection of movie and rock star postcards to sift through, and plenty of oldie-but-goodie posters to take Mom and Dad down Memory Lane. Open Monday through Thursday from 10am to 10pm, on Sunday from noon to 10pm. **Metro:** Foggy Bottom.

SPORTS TRADING CARDS

Every spring the Children's Baseball Trading Card Show is held at the Wakefield Recreation Center in Annandale, Virginia. Although vendors must be under 18, anyone may attend. For more information, call the Center (tel. 703/321-7081). The following D.C. shops (plus close to two dozen in Maryland and Virginia) sell trading cards and other sports-related memorabilia as well: **Scavengers of Georgetown,**

1210 31st St. NW (tel. 338-0077); **United Wholesalers,** corner of 4th Street and Florida avenue NE (tel. 546-7020).

TAPES, RECORDS & CDs

KEMP MILL RECORD SHOPS, 1518 Connecticut Ave. NW. Tel. 332-8247; 1260 Wisconsin Ave. NW (Georgetown). Tel. 333-1392. Also several other D.C. and suburban locations.

✪ The largest retail record chain in the D.C. area carries everything from Winnie the Pooh to 2 Live Crew. Kemp Mill carries an especially boss selection of whatever's hot, making it a popular gathering place for area preteens and teens. Call for directions and hours.

LOWEN'S, 7201 Wisconsin Ave., Bethesda, MD. Tel. 301/652-1289.

The popular suburban toy store also carries kids' tapes. Call for hours and directions.

OLSSON'S BOOKS & RECORDS, 1307 19th St. NW, off Dupont Circle. Tel. 785-2662 for records.

✪ It isn't called Olsson's Books & *Records* for nothing. Most kids head for the neon "Rock Room" sign, where there's always someone to give assistance. If your kids dig classical music, Olsson's has one of the best selections in the city; and if they don't have it, they'll order it. Open Monday through Saturday from 10am to 9pm and on Sunday from noon to 6pm. **Metro:** Dupont Circle.

SAM GOODY, 3111 M St. NW (Georgetown). Tel. 333-2248; Union Station. Tel. 289-1405; also numerous suburban locations.

An offshoot of the long-popular New York record store, Sam Goody has 17 stores in and around D.C. The M Street store is open Monday through Thursday from 10am to 10pm, Friday and Saturday from 10am to midnight and Sunday from noon to 7pm. Check the *Yellow Pages* for details.

TOWER RECORDS, 2000 Pennsylvania Ave. NW. Tel. 331-2400.

✪ "Awesome" was my son's succinct appraisal of Tower Records on his first visit. It's a two-story, 18,000-square-foot supermarket of records, tapes, and CD's in Foggy Bottom that has to be seen to be believed. Tower carries standard Sesame Street and Disney fare plus more than 200 kid-oriented selections for its discerning junior clientele. Everyone with kids should own a tape of Meryl Streep reading "The Tailor of Gloucester." Open daily from 9am to midnight. **Metro:** Foggy Bottom.

SHOES

ATHLETE'S FOOT, 942 F St. NW. Tel. 737-0125; Georgetown Park, 3222 M St. NW. Tel. 965-7262; and several other locations.

Who would have thought such a funny name would grow to become the area's largest seller of athletic-type shoes? Although some styles are available in infant's size 3, the selection runs wild in larger sizes. They also carry hiking boots for older kids. Call for hours and directions.

BOYCE & LEWIS, 439 7th St. NW. Tel. 638-5515.

In business for 63 years, Boyce & Lewis is a step ahead when it comes to fitting growing feet properly. They carry sizes 2 and up, in widths A-EEE for kids in regular and orthopedic shoes. They also sell shoes for Mom and Dad and stand by their logo—"no foot [is] too hard to fit." **Metro:** Gallery Place.

There are also branches in Bethesda, Maryland, and Fairfax, Virginia. Check the local phone book for details.

FLEET FEET, 1840 Columbia Rd. NW. Tel. 387-3888.

Adams-Morgan's total sports/fitness shop carries all the top names for fleet-footed kids and adults, beginning with size 2. **Metro:** Woodley Park or Dupont Circle.

FOOT LOCKER, 1850 M St. NW. Tel. 872-0458; 3221 M St. NW Tel. 333-7640; 529 14th St. NW. Tel. 783-2093; Mazza Gallerie, 5300 Wisconsin Ave. NW. Tel. 362-7427.

All the big-name brands of athletic type-shoes for both first-stringers and bench-warmers are carried by this national chain. There are also several Virginia and Maryland branches. Call whatever branch you plan to visit for hours and directions.

JUST SHOES, 3301 New Mexico Ave. NW. Tel. 244-2224.

From baby's first walker to size 4 adult, Just Shoes has everything—athletic and dress shoes, sandals, slippers, boots—to make little feet happy. Call for hours and directions.

RAMER'S SHOES, 3810 Northampton St. NW, off Connecticut Ave. Tel. 244-2288.

Hot-foot it to Ramer's, the friendly neighborhood shoe store one block below Chevy Chase Circle, for Stride Rite shoes, Keds, Sperry's, Sebago's, Little Capezio, and more in sizes 0–4½, widths AA to EEE. **Metro:** Friendship Heights, then take an E2, E4, or E6 bus. Call for hours and directions.

SPORTS GEAR

BICYCLE EXCHANGE, 4000 Wisconsin Ave. NW. Tel. 244-2800.

They carry a wide selection of recreational, touring, and racing children's bikes here, and free safety checks are given. Open Monday through Friday from 10am to 7pm (on Thursday till 9pm), Saturday from 10am to 5pm, and on Sunday from noon to 5pm. **Metro:** Tenleytown.

There are also several Virginia branches.

BIG WHEEL BIKES, 1034 33rd St. NW, at M Street. Tel. 337-0254; 315 7th St. SE. Tel. 543-1600.

If you're not interested in buying, Big Wheel rents kids' bikes (for adults too) at the 33rd Street location. Call for hours and details.

COUNTS' WESTERN STORE, 4905 Wisconsin Ave. NW. Tel. 362-1757.

Counts has hats and boots, riding apparel, English and Western saddles and everything else young riders need to feel at home on the range. Call for hours of operation. **Metro:** Friendship Heights.

DRILLING TENNIS SHOP, 1040 17th St. NW. Tel. 737-1100.

The shop is owned by Fred Drilling, Washington Tennis Patrons' Hall of Famer, and the staff will see that your youngster comes out swinging the right racquet from the store's selection for 2- to 12-year-olds. No kids' clothing here, but plenty of accessories. Open Monday through Friday from 9:30am to 6pm and on Saturday from 10am to 4pm. **Metro:** Farragut North or Farragut West.

HERMAN'S WORLD OF SPORTING GOODS, 4350 Jenifer St. NW. Tel. 537-1388.

Depending on the season, Herman's can outfit young athletes with equipment (and some clothing) for everything but sibling rivalry—skiing, soccer, baseball, football, lacrosse, tennis, golf, and volleyball. Herman's first opened its doors in 1917 in New York City and has been in the D.C. area for more than 20 years. Open Monday through Friday from 10am to 9pm, Saturday from 10am to 8pm, and on Sunday from 11am to 5pm. **Metro:** Friendship Heights. Also several suburban locations.

HUDSON TRAIL OUTFITTERS, 4437 Wisconsin Ave. NW. Tel. 363-9810.

Hudson Trail is a magnet for teens who are into hiking, biking, camping, and other outdoor activities. Quality gear, clothing, and accessories fill the rustic shop, and the youthful, healthy-looking salespeople are helpful and laid-back. Open Monday through Friday from 10am to 9pm, Saturday from 10am to 6pm, and on Sunday from noon to 5pm. **Metro:** Tenleytown.

Locations in Maryland and Virginia too.

ISLAND WATER SPORTS, 3005 M St. NW. Tel. 337-7420.

This is skateboard headquarters in the District. You can buy new or used boards or have your old one fixed. They also carry some beachwear—but no surfboards. Open Monday through Saturday from 11am to 8pm and on Sunday from noon to 6pm. **Metro:** Foggy Bottom.

IRVING'S, 1111 20th St., at L Street Tel. 466-8830.

An old-timer in the sporting goods business, Irving's is primarily an adult store, but they carry some seasonal gear and accessories for young people. Irving's suburban stores have more merchandise. Check the phone book and call before visiting. **Metro:** Farragut North or Farragut West.

NATIONAL DIVING CENTER, 4932 Wisconsin Ave. NW. Tel. 363-6123.

Glub, glub, glub . . . The youngest snorkeler can be outfitted here, but potential scuba divers must be 12. Besides stocking snorkeling and diving gear, they offer lessons (with open-water checkouts in Pennsylvania rock quarries) and diving trips off the Atlantic Coast and Caribbean. Call for specific details and schedules. **Metro:** Friendship Heights or Tenleytown.

NATIONAL LOCKER ROOM, 1331 Pennsylvania Ave. NW. Tel. 737-0001; 1240 Wisconsin Ave. NW. Tel. 333-9212.

Your kids' favorite college and pro team clothing is carried in adult sizes only; but there's lots of posters, mugs, and accessories to delight fans of all ages. Call for hours and directions.

SKI CENTER, Massachusetts Avenue and 49th Street NW. Tel. 966-5413.

Schuss down to the oldest ski shop in the South. The Ski Center has had an edge on ski stuff in the D.C. area for more than 30 years and can outfit all the younger members of your ski team with equipment and clothing. Call for seasonal details.

WASHINGTON GOLF CENTER, 1722 I St. NW. Tel. 728-0088.

Swing over here for kids-size clubs, bags, and practice equipment (but no clothes). Call for hours and days of operation. **Metro:** Farragut West.
There are also several branch stores in Maryland and Virginia.

TOYS

BARSTONS CHILD'S PLAY, The Shops at National Place, 1331 Pennsylvania Ave. NW. Tel. 393-2382.

Barstons attracts young customers by displaying unusual toys that can be played with. There's an excellent selection of Playmobil (W. Germany), Lego, Lundby dollhouse furniture, and Gund stuffed animals. This place is fun to visit, and you don't have to be under 3 feet tall to appreciate it. Open Monday through Wednesday and Saturday from 10am to 7pm, Thursday and Friday from 10am to 8pm, and on Sunday from noon to 5pm. **Metro:** Metro Center.

DAPY, Georgetown Park Mall, 3222 M St. NW. Tel. 333-5247.

Not your typical toy store, Dapy's is more of a variety store for kids with a sense of humor. There's lots of way-out stuff—wacky neon clocks, stress dolls that can be ripped apart, gumball machines, phony feet and hands, and my favorite—gorilla slippers. You have to see it to believe it. Open Monday through Friday from 10am to 9pm, Saturday from 10am to 7pm, and on Sunday from noon to 6pm. **Metro:** Foggy Bottom.

FAO SCHWARZ, Georgetown Park Mall, 3222 M St. NW. Tel. 342-2285.

The Tiffany's of toys, FAO Schwarz (no "t") is the offshoot of the famous New York City store featured in the movie "Big." Only top-quality playthings are sold here, with prices to match. They have a very large Nintendo selection and more than 100 Madame Alexander dolls. Although it may be scarfed up by the time you read this, for serious collectors there's a Bob Mackie–designed Barbie Doll wearing a dress stitched to her body à la Cher. Where are the tattoos? For the mall hours, see the Dapy entry above.

GEORGETOWNE ZOO, Georgetown Park Mall, 3222 M St. NW. Tel. 338-4182.

★ Create your own personal zoo from among the many occupants of this whimsical menagerie. You'll find stuffed animals by Steiff, Dakin, Gund, and others, along with your favorite storybook characters. Georgetowne Zoo also has activity books, hand puppets, and 99-cent items, and ships anywhere in the world. Cages are extra, of course. For mall hours, see the Dapy entry above.

GRANNY'S PLACE, 303 Cameron St., Alexandria, VA. Tel. 703/549-0119.

With a name like Granny's, you know the place will be cute and inviting before you walk in the door. Wooden playground equipment, unusual games, toys, puppets, and dolls are featured, along with clothing for infants to size 14. Granny's always had a way with kids. Call for hours and directions. **Metro:** King Street.

THE KITE LOFT: see listing under "KITES"

LOWEN'S, 7201 Wisconsin Ave., Bethesda, MD. Tel. 301/652-1289.

If Lowen's doesn't have it, try Santa's Workshop at the North Pole. Lowen's has been pleasing area kids for more than 30 years with a wonderful selection—now on three floors—of toys, books, hobbies, crafts, games, and dolls. The annual fall sale draws customers from several nearby states. Kids are bowled over by the Lego exhibits. Don't forget to grab a soft ice cream on the way out. Call for hours and directions. **Metro:** Bethesda.

RED BALLOON, 1073 Wisconsin Ave. NW. Tel. 965-1200, or 965-9397.

Children feel at home in this pint-size Georgetown shop crammed with intriguing handmade items, kaleidoscopes, imported toys and games, marionettes, and stuffed animals. There are plenty of small-price items too. Ask for the whimsically illustrated catalogue. Open Monday through Wednesday from 10am to 9pm, Thursday from 10am to 10pm, Friday and Saturday from 10am to 11pm, and on Sunday from noon to 7pm. **Metro:** Foggy Bottom, then walk.

SULLIVAN'S, 3412 Wisconsin Ave. NW. Tel. 362-1343.

If a film crew were scouting for a typical neighborhood toy store, Sullivan's would be the ideal. A feeling of comfortable disarray pervades the Cleveland Park shop. Kids of all ages will find plenty to toy with on the well-stocked shelves. There's a huge selection of art supplies, too. The most fun can be had up front, where 60 glass jars are filled with 99-cent toys. Open Monday, Tuesday, Wednesday and Friday from 10am to 6pm, Thursday until 8pm, Saturday from 9:30am to 5:30pm and Sunday from noon to 4pm. **Metro:** Tenleytown, then take any 30 bus.

THE GREAT TRAIN STORE, Union Station, 40 Massachusetts Ave. NE. Tel. 371-2881.

All aboard! Bachmann, Lionel, Mantua, and Marklin are but some of the model choo-choos carried at this unique shop on the main floor of the Concourse at—where else—Union Station. The store also sells books, videos, and railroad novelty items. It's a fascinating place to browse and take an imaginary railroad journey. Open Monday through Saturday from 10am to 9pm and Sunday from noon to 6pm. **Metro:** Union Station.

TOYS 'Я US, 11800 Rockville Pike, at Old Georgetown Road, Rockville, MD. Tel. 301/770-3376.

Santa's Workshop doesn't hold a candle to this warehouse of discount-priced toys, games, seasonal sports gear and outdoor equipment, juvenile furniture, and party supplies. Shop early or late unless you have nerves of steel and can withstand hundreds of tiny voices whining "I want . . ." à capella. Open Monday through Saturday from 9:30am to 9:30pm and Sunday from 11am to 6pm.

There are several other branches in suburban Maryland and Virginia; check the phone book for details.

TREE TOP TOYS, 3301 New Mexico Ave. NW. Tel. 244-3500.

This charming toy store near the campus of American University is known for its large selection of imported French dolls and baby toys. It's downright intimate, and not an inch of precious space is wasted. You'll find everything from infants' crib toys to big kids' games and models. Open Monday through Saturday from 9:30am to 5:30pm.

WASHINGTON DOLLS HOUSE AND TOY MUSEUM, 5236 44th St. NW. Tel. 244-0024.

This magical museum (see Chapter 4, "What Kids Like to See and Do") also sells a wonderful assortment of doll- and dollhouse-related books and magazines, furniture and accessories, and consignment items in the second-floor shops. For the avid collector, there are even miniature quilt kits. The women who work here obviously love what they're doing. Open Tuesday through Saturday from 10am to 5pm and on Sunday from noon to 5pm. **Metro:** Friendship Heights.

VIDEOS

Videotapes may be the next best thing to a baby-sitter—an ideal way to calm the kids after a frenetic day of sightseeing and buy a bit of quiet time for yourself. A lot of the neighborhood mom-and-pop stores are going under because of fierce competition from the national chains. Erol's, number one for several years, was purchased in 1991 by Blockbuster's. It hasn't been decided when the name change will occur. Stay tuned.

BLOCKBUSTER'S, 2332 Wisconsin Ave. NW (Georgetown). Tel. 625-6200; 2000 S St. NW (Dupont Circle). Tel. 319-0900; 2301 Georgia Ave. NW (Howard University). Tel. 234-6100; 4221 Connecticut Ave. NW (Van Ness). Tel. 686-2001.

⭐ This chain has come on like, well, blockbusters in the last few years, and there seems to be no stopping 'em. All the branches have a special kids' section, and rent VCRs that attach easily to a TV for around $12 for three nights. Call the desired branch for hours and directions.

TOWER VIDEO, 2000 Pennsylvania Ave. NW, 20th Street entrance. Tel. 223-3900.

In the heart of Foggy Bottom just four blocks from the White House, Tower Video has beefed up its selection of children's videos, now one of the largest in the city. On the opposite end of this mini-mall is Tower Records. Open daily from 9am to midnight. **Metro:** Foggy Bottom.

CHAPTER 6

THEIR KIND OF ENTERTAINMENT

1. **THEATER &
   PERFORMING ARTS**
2. **DANCE**
3. **CONCERT VENUES**
4. **COMEDY CLUBS**
5. **CINEMA**
6. **PUPPET SHOWS**
7. **STORY HOURS**
8. **CIRCUSES & RIDES
   FOR CHILDREN**
9. **SPECTATOR SPORTS**

Children's tastes in entertainment are as varied as their parents. Some kids like watching the pros shoot hoops; others enjoy seeing lions and tigers jump through them. Some junior culture-vultures are transported by "Swan Lake," while their middle-brow siblings think it's ducky to yuck it up with some odd birds in a comedy club. Whether your children's appetites run to Beethoven, blue-grass, or Bon Jovi, they won't go away hungry after sampling Washington's musical smorgasbord.

Once a sleepy southern town that died at 9pm (on a good night!), D.C. now hosts so many events simultaneously that you'll be hard pressed to choose from among them. D.C. is second only to New York in the quality and quantity of its theatrical productions, musical offerings, and dance performances. That's why we try harder!

If you have tickets to an evening event, consider ending your sightseeing mid-afternoon and enforce a rest period—with extra points for napping—so everyone will be "up" for a night on the town.

Check the *Washington Post* "Style" section Monday through Saturday, "Week-end" magazine on Friday, and "Show" section on Sunday to find out what's doin'. *Washingtonian* magazine and *The City Paper* are other good sources.

TICKETS

Depending on availability, you can pick up half-price tickets to most events the day of the performance *only* at **TICKETplace** on the F Street Plaza, between 12th and 13th streets NW near Metro Center (tel. TICKETS). It's cash only for half-price tickets, plus a 10% service charge, but credit cards are accepted for full-price tickets to future events. TICKETplace is open Tuesday through Friday from noon to 4pm, Saturday from 11am to 5pm; closed Sunday and Monday. Tickets for Sunday and Monday events are sold on Saturday.

Full-price tickets to most performances are also sold through **Ticketron** outlets (tel. 432-0200, or toll free 800/448-9009), including **Hecht's,** 12th and G streets NW, and **Woodward & Lothrop,** 11th and F streets NW. If you know before you leave home there's something special you want to see, call ahead. When you can't get what you want through ordinary channels, there are several ticket brokers in town. They're very defensive about being called "brokers," but that's what they are. Brokers buy blocks of premium seats and resell them with a sometimes hefty service charge tacked on. If you're desperate for an excellent seat to something special, try **Top Centre Ticket Service,** 2000 Pennsylvania Ave. NW. (tel. 775-4068).

1. THEATER & PERFORMING ARTS

The John F. Kennedy Center for the Performing Arts, the National Theatre, and Smithsonian Institution's Discovery Theater have the highest visibility as presenters of children's events, but numerous independent producers excel at delivering high-caliber entertainment for young people. Don't overlook them! The Kennedy Center, Arena Stage, National Theatre, and Shakespeare Theatre offer student discounts. (It wouldn't hurt to ask the other presenters about student tickets when you call.)

ADVENTURE THEATRE, Glen Echo Park, MacArthur Blvd. at Goldsboro Rd., Glen Echo, MD. Tel. 301/320-5331.

A mix of original and familiar children's plays for 4- to 10-year-olds is presented year round on Saturdays and Sundays at 1:30 and 3:30pm. The distinctive theater was once a penny arcade on the grounds of the former amusement park. Cap the afternoon with a ride on the Dentzel carousel, across from the theater.

Prices: All seats $4.50.

ALDEN THEATRE, McLean Community Center, 1234 Ingleside Ave., McLean, VA. Tel. 703/790-9223.

The "McLean Kids" series is a potpourri of kid-pleasing productions presented in the state-of-the-art Alden Theatre. Plays, puppet shows, music, and dance are performed weekends during the school year, and the theater is only a 20-minute ride from downtown. Call for show times and directions.

Prices: $4.50.

THE ARENA STAGE, Maine Avenue & 6th Street SW. Tel. 488-3300.

Many hit plays make it big at Arena, before moving to Broadway, and a roster of Arena "graduates" reads like a Who's Who in American Theater. If you want to introduce older children to drama at its finest, look no further. Since some productions are not suitable for young people, call the theater for an educated opinion and check the reviews in local papers.

Prices: $19–$34; 35% discount for full-time students except Saturday evening.

BETHESDA ACADEMY OF PERFORMING ARTS, 7300 Whittier Blvd., Bethesda, MD. Tel. 301/320-2550.

BAPA presents a handful of performances by academy students plus four or five performances by outside companies every year. The academy also offers classes and summer programs in the performing arts.

Prices: $4–$6.

CHILDREN'S DAY AT THE PAVILION, Old Post Office, 1100 Pennsylvania Ave. NW. Tel. 289-4224.

There's family entertainment daily, but it's geared especially to kids the third Saturday of every month when, throughout the afternoon, clowns, jugglers, musicians, and dancers do their thing.

Price: Free.

THE MAJOR CONCERT & PERFORMANCE HALL BOX OFFICES

Adventure Theatre tel. 301/320-5331
The **Arena Stage** tel. 488-3300
D.A.R. Constitution Hall tel. 638-2661
Discovery Theatre tel. 357-1500
Ford's Theatre tel. 347-4833
John F. Kennedy Center for the Performing Arts tel. 416-8000, or toll free 800/444-1324 for information, 467-4600 to charge tickets, 416-8340 for student tickets
National Theatre tel. 628-6161
Shakespeare Theatre tel. 546-4000
Wolf Trap Farm Park for the Performing Arts tel. 703/255-1868

CHILDREN'S THEATRE OF ARLINGTON, Gunston Arts Center, 2700 S. Lang St., Arlington, VA. Tel. 703/548–1154.
Three plays *for* and *by* children are staged annually by this community theater group. CTA also offers summer workshops for kids of all ages and classes during the school year.
Prices: $12 per season ticket (for 3 performances); $5 at the door.

DISCOVERY THEATER, Smithsonian's Arts and Industries Building, 900 Jefferson Dr. SW. Tel. 357-1500.
After several successful seasons, Discovery Theater is still packing them in with a varied selection of plays, storytelling, puppetry, and mime Tuesdays through Saturdays from October 'til late spring. Performances are most appreciated by kids 12 and under.
Prices: Tickets $3.50 for adults; $3 for ages 12 and under.

FORD'S THEATRE, 511 10th St. NW., between E and F streets. Tel. 347-4833.
Every December historic Ford's is the site of Dickens's *A Christmas Carol*. Many of the musical productions staged throughout the rest of the year are also suitable for families. **Metro:** Metro Center.
Prices: Tickets $23–$30; ask about student and senior discounts.

IMAGINATION CELEBRATION, Kennedy Center for the Performing Arts, at the southern end of New Hampshire Avenue NW and Rock Creek Parkway. Tel. 467-4600, or toll free 800/444-1234.
At this month-long arts festival every spring, more than 60 hour-long performances are given for kids 12 and under. In '91 one of the hands-on activities was street painting on the parking area in front of the building. **Metro:** Foggy Bottom, then no. 48 or 81 bus, or walk.
Prices: Tickets $3.50 adults; $3 kids 12 and under.

THE MARQUEE CABARET, Omni Shoreham Hotel, 2500 Calvert St. NW. Tel. 745-1023.
On Saturday from 12:30 to 1:45pm, enjoy lunch with a show especially geared to

kids by a musical comedy improvisation group. The kids help to produce the shows on the spot. **Metro:** Woodley Park-Zoo.
Prices: Tickets $5 for kids 4-12, $7 adults.

MARYLAND CHILDREN'S THEATRE, 7649 Old Georgetown Rd., Bethesda, MD. Tel. 301/652-7999.
The actors perform a variety of adaptations in this cozy little theater and frequently include glimpses of life behind the scenes.
Prices: Vary with the performance.

MOUNT VERNON CHILDREN'S THEATRE, Heritage Presbyterian Church, 8503 Fort Hunt Rd. Alexandria, VA. Tel. 703/768-0703.
Two major performances are presented annually, in November and March, by this noted ensemble group in Virginia's Mount Vernon area. Reservations are advised a week or two in advance (tel. 703/783-7212).
Prices: Vary with the performance.

SCANDAL TOURS. By telephone only. Tel. 783-7212.
This tour is squeals on wheels that will leave all but your youngest rolling in the aisles. Board a bus for an irreverent tour of the Vista International, Tidal Basin, the Capitol steps, and many other sites of notorious happenings. The tour operates Saturdays and Sundays only, and is suitable for older kids who are used to the type of humor dished out on "Saturday Night Live."
Prices: Tickets $27.

SATURDAY MORNING AT THE NATIONAL, National Theatre, 1321 E St. NW. at Pennsylvania Ave. NW. Tel. 783-3372.
October through April, two free shows are given Saturdays at 9:30 and 11am. The well-attended weekend series is as good as kids' entertainment gets, so arrive early. It's strictly first-come, first-seated. **Metro:** Federal Triangle.
Price: Free.

SHAKESPEARE THEATRE, 450 Seventh St. NW. Tel. 546-4000.
Introduce your kids over 10 to one of the well-produced plays by Shakespeare and his contemporaries in the new 447-seat venue that opened in November '91. In recent years, Stacy Keach, Kelly McGillis, and Superman himself (Christopher Reeve) have starred. Every September at an open house kids can see what goes on behind the scenes. The Shakespeare Free for All production of *Merry Wives of Windsor* was a big hit in June 1991 at the Carter Barron Amphitheatre, and the theater hopes to present more free Shakespeare in Rock Creek Park in future summers (tel. 426-0486). Your kids may end up liking English class after a visit here. The intimate, Elizabethan-style theater at the Folger Library, 201 E. Capitol St. SE, presents lesser-known and repertory works. **Metro:** Archives.
Prices: Tickets $19–$42; 50% discount on student and senior tickets one hour before curtain.

THEATER FOR YOUNG PEOPLE, Kennedy Center for the Performing Arts, at the southern end of New Hampshire Avenue NW and Rock Creek Parkway. Tel. 416-8830.
Hour-long programs include puppet shows, storytelling, and plays for kids 3 and

up. More than 250 performances are held on Friday, Saturday, and Sunday during the school year in the Terrace Theater and Theater Lab. A special Pre-school Series is designed for families with children 3 to 6. Call for a current brochure. **Metro:** Foggy Bottom.

Prices: Tickets $5–$12.

WOLF TRAP FARM PARK FOR THE PERFORMING ARTS, 1624 Trap Rd., Vienna, VA. Tel. 703/255-1868.

The best in music, opera, and dance play on the stage of the rustically beautiful 6,900-seat **Filene Center II** during the summer. At least one production per season is especially for children. Many families pack a picnic and blanket and opt for less expensive lawn seats.

The **International Children's Festival,** usually held over Labor Day weekend, features oodles of performances and workshops for kids of all ages (tel. 703/642-0862). Weekends October through May, the **Barnstorm series** for kids is a potpourri of story theater, folk music, puppetry, mime, ethnic dance, and storytelling in the pre-Revolutionary 350-seat German barn. Call 703/938-2404 for information. For nearly 20 summers, the National Park Service has sponsored Children's Theater in the Woods at Wolf Trap. Call for information (tel. 703/255-1827).

If you don't have wheels, take Metro to the West Falls Church (VA) station. In summer the Wolf Trap Express Shuttle bus ($3 round-trip) runs from the Metro every 20 minutes starting at 6:20pm to the Filene Center. Be advised that the last bus leaves Wolf Trap at 11pm. If you come by car, take I-495 to exit 12W (Dulles Toll Road); stay on the local exit road (you'll see a sign) until you come to Wolf Trap.

Prices: Vary with the performance.

2. DANCE

Washington draws the top professional ballet, modern, folk, and ethnic dance companies from all over the world. The Kennedy Center and Washington Performing Arts Society are leading presenters. In addition, the acclaimed Washington Ballet, numerous modern dance groups, and several student companies—many of which are springboards for tomorrow's professionals—are headquartered here. All perform regularly in the area. Tickets are usually nominally priced, often below $10. Most of the performing groups are affiliated with schools that offer a wide range of children's dance classes and workshops.

AMERICAN YOUTH BALLET, 1011 Colesville Rd., Silver Spring, MD. Tel. 301/593-5060.

This ensemble of young dancers performs several times a year in the Maryland suburbs.

Prices: Vary with the performance.

CAPITOL BALLET COMPANY, 1200 Delafield Place, NW. Tel. 882-4039.

The performing group of the Jones-Haywood School of Ballet dances in D.C. at different locations.

Prices: Vary with the performance.

0   500 y
    454 m

N

To
Marquee Cabaret
(Omni Shoreham) **"11"**
(up Conn. Ave. to Calvert St.)

P St.

22nd St.

N St.

M St.

Connecticut Ave.

FARRAGUT NORTH
M

Farragut Square

Pennsylvania

21st St.
20th St.
19th St.

29

FOGGY BOTTOM - GWU

Ave.

I St.
M

FARRAGUT WEST
M

66

18th St.

H St.

G St.

F St.

E St.

Virginia Ave.

D St.
6

C St.

32nd St.
Wisconsin Ave.
31st St.
30th St.
29th St.
28th St.
27th St.
26th St.
25th St.
24th St.
23rd St.

Rock Creek and Potomac Pkwy
Rock Creek

36th St.
35th St.
34th St.
33rd St.
Q St.
O St.

3

Whitehurst Freeway

Key Bridge

FORT MYER
M

ROSSLYN

DISTRICT OF COLUMBIA
ARLINGTON COUNTY, VIRGINIA

Georgetown Channel

Theodore Roosevelt Island

10

50

Constitution Ave.

17th St.

14

66

Theodore Roosevelt Memorial Bridge

Arlington Memorial Bridge

Arlington National Cemetery

i

Independence Ave.

West Potomac Park

Kutz Bridge

Tidal Basin

West Basin D.
Ohio Dr.

Potomac River

George Mason Memorial Bridge

WASHINGTON, D.C.

ENTERTAINMENT HIGHLIGHTS:
Air & Space Museum, Langley Theatre ❶
The Arena Stage ❷
Blues Alley ❸
Children's Day at the Pavilion,
  Old Post Office ❹
The Comedy Cafe ❺
DAR Constitution Hall ❻
Discovery Theatre, Arts & Industries Bldg. ❼
Ford's Theatre ❽
Hirshorn Museum Films ❾

Kennedy (John F.) Center
  for the Performing Arts: ❿
  American Film Institute
  Imagination Celebration
  National Symphony Orchestra
  The Opera House
  Theatre for Young People
  Young Performers Series
Marquee Cabaret ⓫
Martin Luther King
  Memorial Library ⓭

WASHINGTON, D.C., ENTERTAINMENT

National Theatre 12
The Patriot Center 14
Robert F. Kennedy Memorial Stadium 15
Shakespeare Theatre 16
Sylvan Theatre: 17
   Big Band Concert Series
   Military Ban Summer Concerts
Twilight Tattoo, The Ellipse 18
U.S. Marine Corps Evening Parades 19
U.S. Navy Concerts on the Avenue 20

CLASSICAL BALLET THEATER, 3501 Second St., Arlington, VA. Tel. 703/506-8911.

The Classical Ballet Theater presents *The Nutcracker* every December at the Thomas Jefferson Community Center in Arlington and performs at other times in suburban Virginia.

Prices: Vary with the performance.

DANCE PLACE, 3225 8th St. NE. Tel. 269-1600.

Under Carla Perlo's guiding light, Dance Place has been D.C.'s leading presenter of modern, jazz, and Afro dance for 11 years. Dance Place pulsates year-round with performances, classes, and workshops. Kids like the informal atmosphere of the performance space and are admitted free to the Sunday Fun for the Family Series. Located near the Brookland Metro stop (close to Catholic University), Dance Place is fun for all members of dance-lovin' families.

Prices: Tickets $5–$10; kids free sometimes.

MARYLAND YOUTH BALLET, 7702 Woodmont Ave., Bethesda, MD. Tel. 301/652-2232.

The MYB, under the direction of Hortensia Fonseca and Michelle Lees, presents a polished family concert series every spring featuring advanced ballet students. In 1990 MYB's premiere production of the *Nutcracker*—now a holiday fixture—sold out, and Jane Vorburger, the Sugar Plum Fairy, danced her way into American Ballet Theatre. Several of the country's finest classical dancers trained at MYB's academy and performed with the company before joining professional companies.

Prices: Tickets $6.50–$13.

METROPOLITAN BALLET THEATRE, 10076 Darnestown Rd., Rockville, MD. Tel. 301/762-1757.

Former New York City Ballet ballerina Suzanne Erlon established the MBT with local teacher Deborah Bailay. Many of the dancers are students at Erlon's North Potomac Ballet Academy and appear in the *Nutcracker* and other seasonal performances throughout the year.

Prices: Vary with the performance.

THE PRIMARY MOVERS, 4201 16th St. NW. Tel. 829-3300.

Besides teaching students "from 3 to 103," Rima Faber (who trained with Anna Sokolow and Martha Graham) directs this unique company of 6-to-12-year-olds who dance with infectious enthusiasm and abandon.

Prices: Vary with the performance.

THE WASHINGTON BALLET, 3515 Wisconsin Ave. NW. Tel. 362-3606.

D.C.'s only resident professional ballet company is directed by Mary Day and performs *The Nutcracker* several times every December at Lisner Auditorium, 21st and H streets NW. The fall, winter, and spring series at the Kennedy Center are suitable for kids over 8 who may find the program of short, varied works easier to digest than a full-length ballet. Guest artists (often noted alums) sometimes appear with, or choreograph for, the company. Once a year "Ballets From Within" features works by student choreographers.

Prices: Vary with the performance.

3. CONCERT VENUES

CLASSICAL MUSIC

Washington is home to the National Symphony Orchestra, the Washington Opera, and numerous first-rate chamber orchestras and choral groups, which give family and children's performances throughout the area. Guest artists also appear year round at many sites in and around the city. Consult the *Washington Post* and *Washington Times* or call the individual presenters for performance dates, times, and ticket prices, which vary widely. Family performances, especially around holidays, are often free.

D.C. YOUTH CHORALE, Duke Ellington School of the Arts, 35th and R streets NW. Tel. 282-0123.

Concerts by this citywide student chorus are held at various locations. Although most of the repertoire is classical, a healthy sprinkling of popular and folk selections is included.

D.C. YOUTH ORCHESTRA, Coolidge High School, Fifth and Sheridan streets NW. Tel. 723-1612.

Close your eyes and this youth orchestra sounds more harmonious than some professional ensembles. The spirited and impressive group of young people 5 to 19 years old has toured 15 countries and played for four U.S. presidents since its founding in 1960.

FAIRFAX CHORAL SOCIETY, 4028 Hummer Rd., Annandale, VA. Tel. 703/642-0862.

Concerts in the metropolitan area by the children's 65-voice chorus, as well as the "parent" groups—an 80-voice chorus and 25-voice chorale—always draw an admiring crowd.

NATIONAL SYMPHONY ORCHESTRA, John F. Kennedy Center for the Performing Arts, at the southern end of New Hampshire Avenue NW and Rock Creek Parkway. Tel. 416-8100.

Young People's and Family Concerts are important ingredients in the NSO's schedule of about 200 concerts annually. During the summer NSO treats families to free concerts on Memorial Day and Labor Day weekend and on the Fourth of July on the West Lawn of the U.S. Capitol. You can also catch them at Wolf Trap's Filene Center in Virginia.

WASHINGTON PERFORMING ARTS SOCIETY, 2000 L St. NW. Tel. 833-9800.

Besides a full schedule of concerts by internationally acclaimed orchestras, soloists, chamber groups, and dance companies, Washington's first presenter of cultural events, WPAS, sponsors the Parade of the Arts Family Series, designed for families with children 6 to 10.

YOUNG PERFORMERS SERIES, Kennedy Center for the Performing Arts. Tel. 467-4600.

Free musical performances by talented young people from the D.C. area are featured on alternate Wednesdays in the Grand Foyer. You may hear a Peabody Conservatory pianist, classical guitarist, or university voice students performing operatic excerpts.

BAND CONCERTS

One of the perks of visiting Washington in the summer is enjoying the free band concerts held at several downtown venues. Call first to double-check times, as scheduling varies from year to year. Watch local newspapers for information on military band concerts the rest of the year.

BIG BAND CONCERT SERIES, Sylvan Theatre (Washington Monument grounds). Tel. 619-7222.
Stomp your feet to the beat of the big band sound at the Sylvan Theatre every Wednesday from mid-June through August at 7pm.

MARINE CORPS FRIDAY EVENING PARADES, U.S. Marine Barracks, 8th and I streets SE. Tel. 433-6060, or 433-4011 for a 24-hour recording.
Dress parades Friday evenings from mid-May through August get underway at 2045 hours (8:45pm). Arrive no later than 8. It's a show and a half. That's why you have to call for reservations on the *Monday* three weeks before the parade you want to attend. You may also write for reservations; address your request to Adjutant, Marine Barracks, 8th and I streets SE, Washington, DC 20390.

MILITARY BAND SUMMER CONCERT SERIES, U.S. Capitol (west side), Sylvan Theatre (Washington Monument grounds). Tel. 475-1281 or 433-4011 (Marines).
Attend a free outdoor concert by a U.S. military band five evenings a week at either the U.S. Capitol (West Terrace) or Sylvan Theatre (Washington Monument grounds), at 8pm from Memorial Day through Labor Day.

Mondays:	U.S. Navy Band—Capitol
Tuesdays:	U.S. Army Band—Sylvan Theatre
	U.S. Air Force Band—Capitol
Wednesdays:	U.S. Marine Band—Capitol
Fridays:	U.S. Army Band—Capitol
	U.S. Air Force Band—Sylvan Theatre
Sundays:	U.S. Marine Band—Sylvan Theatre

SUNSET PARADE, Iwo Jima Memorial, near Arlington Cemetery. Tel. 433-4497.
It's first-come, first-served for lawn seats at the Marine Corps War Memorial, where you'll hear the 80-member Marine Drum & Bugle Corps and see precision drills Tuesday evenings at 7pm from late May through August. Shuttle buses run from the Visitors Center at Arlington Cemetery, starting at 6pm.

THE AMERICAN SAILOR, Washington Navy Yard waterfront, 9th and M streets SE. Tel. 433-2218.

Every Wednesday from the last Wednesday in May through early September, a multimedia presentation showcases the history of the U.S. Navy at 9pm. Reservations are required; call number listed above.

U.S. NAVY CONCERTS ON THE AVENUE SERIES, U.S. Navy Memorial, 701 Pennsylvania Ave. NW, between 7th and 9th streets. Tel. 737-2300, or 347-6327.

Beginning Memorial Day at 8pm and thereafter several times a week, get in tune with the U.S. Navy, Air Force, and Marine bands. Call for schedule.

TWILIGHT TATTOO, The Ellipse, between the White House and Washington Monument. Tel. 703/696-3147.

Watch intricate military drills and precision marching and enjoy selections by the U.S. Army Band Wednesday evenings from mid-July to mid-August at 7pm. Arrive early to get a good seat.

BLUES & JAZZ

BLUES ALLEY, 1073 Wisconsin Ave. NW, in an alley behind M St. Tel. 337-4141.

 Washington's first and foremost jazz club for more than a quarter of a century has played host to Charlie Byrd, Herbie Mann, George Shearing, Stan Getz, Dizzy Gillespie, Wynton Marsalis, and hundreds of other jazz greats. There are two shows weeknights, three on Friday and Saturday. Reservations are taken up to two weeks in advance, and seating is first-come, first served. Anyone over the age of 6 is welcome.

You'll have no trouble gobbling up the $5 minimum. For kids there are burgers and sandwiches in the lower registers ($5–$9), entrées (mostly beef and Créole-seafood dishes) from $14 to $19 in the upper. Drinks cost $2 to $7.

Admission: $10 to $35, depending on the performer, plus $5 food or drink minimum.

THE BARNS OF WOLF TRAP, 1624 Trap Rd., Vienna, VA. Tel. 703/938-2404, or 432-0200 to charge tickets.

Jazz, pop, country, and bluegrass predominate from October to May on the grounds of this well-known center for the performing arts. The 200-year-old barn has been restored and the horses are long gone. Not a place to bring babies, The Barns invites school-agers to come with their parents and absorb a little history along with the music in this charming, rustic setting.

Admission: $12–$20; kids pay full price. Free parking.

COUNTRY & FOLK

THE BARNS: see above listing

CONCERTS ON THE CANAL, C & O Canal, between 30th and Thomas Jefferson streets NW, below M Street Tel. 619-7225.

It's not surprising that this series of free Sunday afternoon concerts, sponsored by Mobil Oil, has a big following. The series runs from mid-June through August, every other week, and the music runs the gamut from folk to flamenco

to gospel. It's great fun for the whole family and a perfect occasion to picnic along the Canal. Watch toddlers carefully or restrain them; the Canal is a very real threat.
Admission: Free.

DUBLINER, 520 N. Capitol St. NW. Tel. 737-3773.

★ The Dubliner is so fond of kids, they even have highchairs, so wee leprechauns can enjoy the spirited Irish music (but not the Killian's Red) along with Mom and Dad.
Admission: No cover charge or minimum; food costs $6–$12 at lunch; $8–$16 at dinner.

POP & R-O-C-K

THE CAPITAL CENTRE, Exit 15A or 17A off the Capital Beltway, Landover, MD. Tel. 301/350-3400.

Sandwiched in between a multitude of sporting events, the Cap Centre presents a Prince-ly (yes, he's played there, as have Michael Jackson, Madonna, Eric Clapton, and the Rolling Stones) number of rock concerts every year. It's not unusual for groupies to camp out the night before tickets go on sale.
Admission: Varies according to performer.

DAR CONSTITUTION HALL, 18th and D streets NW. Tel. 638-2661.

Can you picture Rodney Dangerfield playing the national headquarters of the Daughters of the American Revolution? Well, he has. So too have Patti LaBelle, Whitney Houston, Barry Manilow, and Ray Charles. Many less-than strait-laced headliners have packed the nearly 4,000-seat hall. Tickets for most performances are sold through Instant Charge (tel. 432-0200). **Metro:** Farragust West.
Admission: Tickets $15–$30, depending on the act.

ROBERT F. KENNEDY MEMORIAL STADIUM, E. Capitol & 22nd streets NE. Tel. 547-9077 for information; 432-0200 to charge tickets.

What do Michael Jackson, Bob Dylan, New Kids on the Block, Paul McCartney, and Madonna have in common? Certainly not their costumer. Give up? They all filled this 55,000-plus-seat facility. Not too many acts, other than the Redskins, sell out this arena. **Metro:** Stadium/Armory.
Admission: Varies according to performer.

MERRIWEATHER POST PAVILION, 10475 Little Patuxent Pkwy., off Rte. 29, in Columbia, MD. Tel. 301/982-1800 for information; 202/ 432-0200 to reserve tickets.

Frank Sinatra, Huey Lewis, Liza Minnelli, Sting, Julio Iglesias, Willie Nelson, and Jimmie Buffett are just a sampling of the biggies who've performed at the open-air pavilion, about 45 minutes from downtown D.C. You'll need a car to get here. There are plenty of lawn seats, but no refunds are given if it rains. The open-air pavilion is roofed in and protected from the rain.
Prices: Pavilion tickets $17–$30; lawn tickets $13.50–$18.50; parking included.

THE PATRIOT CENTER, George Mason University, 4400 University Dr., Fairfax, VA. Tel. 703/323-2672.

Area teens are more than willing to get locked in massive traffic jams following concerts by their favorite performing artists at the Patriot Center. Since opening in 1985, the 10,000-seat facility on the grounds of George Mason University has drawn White Snake, Milli Vanilli (before their 1990 dubbing woes), Tom Petty, Wayne Newton, Don Henley, the Beach Boys, Kenny Rogers, and Miami Sound Machine. By car, take the Wilson Bridge to Route 623 (Braddock Road West) and continue west for about 8 miles to University Drive. Or take the Metro to the Vienna station and take any CUE Green or Gold no. 1 or 2 bus (35¢) to the university (tel. 703/385-7859 for information).

Admission: Varies according to performer.

4. COMEDY CLUBS

Comedy clubs are proliferating like an infectious case of the giggles, but many are open to adults only—and for good reason. If you want to die laughing, rather than of embarrassment, inquire when you make a reservation about the appropriateness of the show's material. No parent with kids in tow wants the shock of anticipating a Bill Cosby–type and finding Diceman instead.

THE CAPITOL STEPS, Chelsea's, The Foundry Mall, 1055 Thomas Jefferson St. NW. Tel. 298-8222.

The Capitol Steps present political satire regularly at Chelsea's in Georgetown. The cast puts their own spin on popular tunes and uses lots of props in their fast-paced musical numbers. The material is irreverent but suitable for older kids.

Admission: $15 cover; $10 food or drink minimum. **Metro:** Foggy Bottom.

THE COMEDY CAFE, 1520 K St. NW. Tel. 638-JOKE.

Local and nationally recognized comics (for example, Pat Paulsen, J.J. Walker, Larry Milla, Soupy Sales) take the mike at this popular downtown club Fridays at 8:30 and 10:30pm; Saturdays at 7, 9, and 11pm. Thursdays are the most spontaneous, when it's open-mike time from 8:30 to 10:30pm, when people are auditioning or pros are working out new material. Maybe one of your little clowns will be discovered. Cover is only $3.49 on Thursday night. **Metro:** McPherson Square.

Admission: $12.49 (except on Thursday); no minimum on food.

SCANDAL TOURS: see the listing in the "Theater & Performing Arts" section earlier in the chapter.

5. CINEMA

For film reviews, check the daily newspapers. The *Washington Post* has synopses of current movies in the Friday "Weekend" section. Happily for movie lovers, the number of discount movie houses in D.C. is on the rise, and at many theaters tickets to matinees and/or the first evening show are greatly reduced. One place you won't find bargains is at the refreshment stand. The prices are outrageous. You can buy a whole meal at a fast-food restaurant for what some theaters charge for a bucket of popcorn. Naturally, theater managers frown on patrons bringing in outside food, but if you're discreet and stuff your purse or pockets with candy before you enter, there's not a thing they can do. Maybe if enough family moviegoers boycott the stale, overpriced popcorn and $1.50 and up candy and drinks, theater owners will be forced to price snacks more realistically.

THE AMERICAN FILM INSTITUTE, Kennedy Center, New Hampshire Avenue NW and Rock Creek Parkway. Tel. 828-4000.

Many of AFI's regular series of classic and new films, both foreign and domestic, will appeal to young movie buffs 8 and older, depending on the subject matter. Movies are shown weeknights with some weekend matinees.

Underground parking at the Kennedy Center is $5 for the entire evening after 5pm. **Metro:** Foggy Bottom.

Admission: $6 for nonmembers, $5 for members (AFI memberships cost $15), senior citizens, and students under 18 with ID.

AIR AND SPACE MUSEUM, Samuel P. Langley Theater, Independence Avenue and 6th Street SW. Tel. 357-1686 or -1675.

If you're visiting the museum, stop at the box office first, preferably when it opens around 9:30am. Tickets may be purchased up to two weeks in advance.

The breathtaking films shown on the five-story IMAX screen frequently sell out, and after you've seen one you'll know why. *To Fly,* the first Langley Theater presentation in 1976, still packs 'em in. It's an aerial journey of America from a hot-air balloon, barnstormer, and spacecraft that is guaranteed to raise goosebumps on the toughest flesh. *Blue Planet* is an ecological examination of the earth from outer space, and some of the footage was shot during shuttle missions. Also worth seeing are *The Dream Is Alive, The Living Planet,* and *Ring of Fire.* The films alternate, and each is shown from one to four times daily. See them all if you can. Don't sit too close to the screen, as the huge images and booming soundtrack may frighten younger kids. Popcorn is not allowed, but you won't even miss it. **Metro:** L'Enfant Plaza.

Admission: $2.75 adults; $1.75 children, students, senior citizens.

A double-feature is presented some evenings at 5:35pm. **Admission:** $3.75 adults; $2.75 children.

On selected Friday, Saturday, and Sunday evenings at 7pm there's a Film Festival. **Admission:** $4.50 adults; $3.50 children.

HIRSHHORN MUSEUM, Independence Avenue at 8th Street SW. Tel. 357-2700.

The Hirshhorn hosts a free film series for kids under 12 most Saturdays during the school year at 11am in the lower-level auditorium. Call to find out what's on the big screen. **Metro:** L'Enfant Plaza.

Admission: Free.

MARTIN LUTHER KING MEMORIAL LIBRARY, 901 G St. NW. Tel. 727-1151.

Kids' films are shown every Wednesday during the school year at 4:15pm. **Metro:** Metro Center.
Admission: Free.

NATIONAL MUSEUM OF AFRICAN ART, 950 Independence Ave. SW. Tel. 357-4860.
Call for a schedule of animated and regular films on daily life, folk tales, and the art of Africa's rich and diverse culture, shown in the Learning Center Lecture Hall on the second level for kids ages 6 to 15. **Metro:** Smithsonian.
Admission: Free.

NATIONAL ZOO, opposite 3000 Connecticut Ave. NW. Tel. 357-2070.
Stop at the Education Building and see *Zoo—A Closer Look, Animals in the Wild,* or *Gorillas.* The three films, each about 40 minutes long, rotate throughout the day from 10:30am to 3pm. **Metro:** Cleveland Park or Woodley Park-Zoo.
Admission: Free.

6. PUPPET SHOWS

Puppet shows are given throughout the year, most frequently at Adventure Theater in Glen Echo Park, the Smithsonian's Discovery Theatre, and through the Kennedy Center's Theater for Young People. See the "Theater & Performing Arts" section earlier in the chapter for addresses and phone numbers. For a current listing of performances, check the Friday "Weekend" section of the *Washington Post.*

Several top-notch puppeteers live and work in the D.C. area. They have a knack for captivating and entertaining kids while slipping in important messages on moral issues. Most performances are timed for 45 minutes or less, just the right length for restless tykes. Like stand-up comedians, the puppeteers warm up their audiences first, and some perform cloaked in black in the Bunraku style. Call the following puppeteers to see if they'll be presenting a show during your visit. No strings attached.

AUGUST PUPPET THEATRE, 1202 S. Washington St., Alexandria, VA. Tel. 703/549-6657.

BLUE SKY PUPPET THEATRE, 5317 Taylor Rd., Riverdale, MD. Tel. 301/927-5599.

BOB BROWN PUPPET PRODUCTIONS, 1415 S. Queen St., Arlington, VA. Tel. 703/920-1040.

THE PUPPET CO. Tel. 234-6666.

For kids who would like to learn more about this ancient craft, puppet-making classes are offered by **The Puppet Co. at Glen Echo Park** (tel. 301/492-6229), **Bethesda Academy of Performing Arts** (tel. 301/320-2550), the **Kennedy Center's Adventures in the Arts program** (tel. 416-8810), and the **Smithsonian Residents Associates** (tel. 357-3255).

7. STORY HOURS

Story hours at the public library or area bookstores are fun and quiet times for pre-schoolers and young scholars—and their parents.

MARTIN LUTHER KING MEMORIAL LIBRARY, 901 G St. NW. Tel. 727-1151 for hours & information; 727-1248 for children's activities.
The main branch of the D.C. Public Library has story hours for pre-schoolers year round on Tuesday, Wednesday, and Friday mornings at 10 and 10:30am. Although the program is a magnet for day-care and pre-school groups, a spokesperson for the library said, "There's always room for visitors." To play it safe, call first. The "Saturday Special" program at 11am during the school year is for pre-schoolers and kids in grades 1–3. Lasting 30 to 45 minutes, it may include stories, films, songs, games, or crafts.

A monthly calendar of events is available at all library branches about the first of every month. Consult the phone book or ask your hotel concierge for the branch nearest you. To find out about the many free summer programs available to residents and visitors, call 727-1248.

From time to time, visiting authors speak at the following children's bookstores: **A Happy Thought,** 4836 MacArthur Blvd. NW (tel. 337-8300); **A Likely Story,** 1555 King St., Alexandria VA (tel. 703/836-2498); **Borders Book Shop for Kids,** 11520A Rockville Pike, Rockville, MD. (tel. 301/816-1067); **Cheshire Cat,** 5512 Connecticut Ave. NW (tel. 244-3956); and **Fairy Godmother,** 319 7th St. SE (tel. 547-5474). Check the monthly Literary Calendar that appears the Sunday before the first day of every month in the *Book World* magazine of the Sunday *Washington Post*.

8. CIRCUSES & RIDES FOR CHILDREN

While many circuses pitch their tents in Washington from time to time, only one—"The Greatest Show on Earth"—arrives as regularly as the daffodils every spring. If it's not spring, consider taking the kids for a ride—in a balloon, on a boat or ferry or train, or in a hay wagon.

CIRCUSES

RINGLING BROS. AND BARNUM & BAILEY CIRCUS, Feld Bros. Enterprises, Vienna, VA. Tel. 547-9077 or 432-0200.
The world's only three-ring circus takes over the D.C. Armory at 2001 E. Capitol St. SE (adjacent to RFK Stadium) in late March and early April for two weeks. If the 2½-hour spectacular is too long for your little ones, consider leaving at intermission. You remember that old saying, "Half a circus is better than none." While ticket prices are fair, most food and souvenirs are overpriced. To cut

costs and avoid arguments, eat before you go and put a lid on what kids spend on the extras.

For many kids, the best part of the circus takes place before the opening performance—and it's free! The parade of animals from the circus train to the Armory is even more exciting than their antics in the ring. There's something extra-special about watching lions, tigers, and elephants promenading down city streets. Watch local newspapers for the time and route.

Admission: Tickets $7.50–$14.50.

RIDES FOR CHILDREN

BALLOON RIDES   Go up, up, and away at several locations outside the Beltway. A balloon ride does not come cheaply, but if you're prepared to cough up $125 to $250 per person and there's not enough hot air in Washington to suit you, call one of the following: **Adventures Aloft** (tel. 301/881-6262), **Aeronaut Masters** (tel. 301/869-2FLY), **Fantasy Flights** (tel. 301/972-2839), or **Balloons Unlimited** (tel. 703/281-2300).

BOAT RIDES   During the warm weather months, take advantage of Washington's wonderful waterfront setting and enjoy the city from offshore with your kids. They'll rate a boat ride as one of the high-water marks of their visit. Rent a pedal boat on the Tidal Basin or a canoe or rowboat on the C&O Canal or Potomac River. For details on several D.C. boating centers, see the "Boating" entry in Chapter 4's "Letting off Steam" section.

If you like the feel of the wind at your back, rent a small sailboat from **Fletcher's** (tel. 244-0461) or **Thompson's** (tel. 333-4861). Experienced sailing families can rent a 21-foot sloop for about $20 an hour from the **Buzzard Point Marina** at the foot of 1st Street, NW. (tel. 488-8400). If you're feeling more ambitious, less than an hour's drive from downtown you and your crew can learn to sail on the Chesapeake Bay. For more information on sailing off into the sunset, see the "Sailing" entry in Chapter 4's "Letting off Steam" and the "Annapolis" entry in Chapter 9.

When charting your own course, make sure there are PFDs (personal flotation devices—"life vests") onboard for each family member, and try them on for size before you leave the dock.

If you prefer to sit back and let someone else play captain, board one of the many cruise boats that ply the Potomac's waters. The Mount Vernon cruise is especially popular with families. See the "Organized Tours" and "Cruises" sections of Chapter 4 for details.

CANAL BOAT RIDES ON THE C & O CANAL   Park Service guides in period dress will regale you with 19th-century canal lore and river songs as the mule-drawn boat makes its way slowly along the historic waterway. The *Canal Clipper* (tel. 301/299-2026) departs from Great Falls in Potomac, Maryland, on Saturday and Sunday from mid-April through mid-June and mid-September through October; Wednesday through Sunday from mid-June to mid-September. The *Georgetown,* berthed in the heart of Georgetown on the canal between 30th Street and Thomas Jefferson Street NW (tel. 472-4316), operates mid-April through October, Wednesday through Sunday. These two may look like barges, but they are actually boats, I was told by the Park Service, because they are steerable. The mules are the engine! A true barge has to be pulled and pushed; it cannot be steered. Live and learn. Anyway, the delightful and informative ride is 90 minutes long. Leave it to the Park Service.

They carry boxes filled with old-fashioned toys for restless little girls and boys. The cost for either ride is $4 for adults; $2.50 for kids 2 to 12; free for those under 2; $3 for senior citizens 62 and over.

CAROUSELS Families who enjoy going around together will want to take a ride on an antique carousel. Few excursions are as much fun or cost as little as these—only 50¢ to $1 per ride. The **carousel on the Mall,** 900 Jefferson Dr. SW., opposite the Smithsonian's Arts & Industries Building (tel. 357-2700), operates from 10am to 5:30pm daily, weather permitting, and has extended summer hours.

If you're a carousel freak, check out the following in Maryland and Virginia:

Burke Lake Park, 7315 Ox Rd., Fairfax Station, Virginia (tel. 703/323-6600), is open April through Labor Day, 11am to dusk; after Labor Day through October, weekends only.

✪ **Glen Echo Park,** MacArthur Boulevard at Goldsboro Road, Glen Echo, Maryland (tel. 301/492-8292), has a classic 1921 Dentzel carousel and it's our family's favorite. Ablaze with more than 1,200 lights, it has 52 carved wood figures and a 165-band Wurlitzer organ. It operates from May through September on weekends from noon to 6pm; on Wednesday and Thursday from 10am to 2pm. A park ranger gives a half-hour talk on the carousel's history Saturdays at 10:30am.

Lake Fairfax Carousel, 1400 Lake Fairfax Dr., Reston, Virginia (tel. 703/471-5415), opens Memorial Day weekend and closes Labor Day. You can ride from 10am to 8pm daily.

Lee District Park Carousel, 6601 Telegraph Rd., Alexandria, Virginia (tel. 703/922-9841), is open Memorial Day to Labor Day from 11am to 7pm.

FERRY RIDES About 30 miles northwest of the District of Columbia, the *Gen. Jubal Early,* an old cable ferry named after an even older Confederate general, crosses the Potomac from White's Ferry (tel. 301/349-5200) on the Maryland shore to just north of Leesburg, Virginia. Kids of all ages adore the *Jubal Early,* which operates seven days a week from 5am to 11pm. You can take your car on the ferry or go on foot. Take the Capital Beltway to I-270 to the Route 28 west exit, then continue on Route 28 west, and at Dawsonville take Route 107 and follow the signs.

HAYRIDES If you're visiting in the fall, especially around Halloween, treat your kids to a hayride. Afterward, stock up on apples, pumpkins, and fresh-pressed cider while you pick the hay out of each other's hair. Call for hours and special kids' activities. Here are two of the closer-in orchards with hayrides: **Butler's Orchard,** 22200 Davis Mill Rd., Germantown, Maryland (tel. 301/972-3299), and **Krop's Crops,** 11110 Georgetown Pike, Great Falls, Virginia (tel. 703/430-8933).

Check the Maryland and Virginia phone books for bushels more.

TRAIN RIDES If your youngsters have never been on a big choo-choo, board a northbound Amtrak train at Union Station, 50 Massachusetts Ave. NE (tel. toll-free 800/USA-RAIL) and ride to New Carrollton, Maryland, one stop away. Because it's only a 10-minute hop, they won't have time to raid the snack car. Trains operate hourly throughout the day, and the round-trip fare is $12 for adults, $6 for kids 2 through 11. If you'd like to make a day of it, go to Baltimore, where there are plenty of kid-pleasing things to do. It's a 40-minute ride from Union Station. Grownups pay $21; kids, $10.50.

Toddlers and pre-schoolers delight in riding the small-scale trains in the following regional parks: **Burke Lake Park,** 7315 Ox Rd., Fairfax Station, Virginia (tel. 703/323-6600); **Cabin John Regional Park,** Tuckerman Lane and Westlake Drive, Bethesda, Maryland (tel. 301/299-4555); and **Wheaton Regional Park,** Shorefield Road, Wheaton, Maryland (tel. 301/622-0056).

9. SPECTATOR SPORTS

D.C. is home to the Redskins (NFL football), the Bullets (NBA basketball), and the Capitals (NHL hockey). There's also plenty of sports action at American, Georgetown, and George Washington universities in D.C., and the University of Maryland in College Park, Md.

FOOTBALL

Although **Robert F. Kennedy Memorial Stadium** ("RFK"), East Capitol at 22nd Streets NE (tel. 547-9077), has 55,000 seats, chances are you won't be able to garner a single one for a Washington Redskins game, as seats are monopolized by season subscribers. Even when the 'Skins are playing poorly (something their loyal fans are reluctant to ever admit), it's next to impossible to get a ticket—unless you're prepared to pay a scalper's prices, you're well connected, or somebody dies and wills you a ticket. Check the *Washington Post* and *Washington Times* classifieds. You might get lucky.

BASKETBALL & HOCKEY

Almost without exception, other sporting events take place in the **Capital Centre,** Exit 15A or 17A off the Capital Beltway, 1 Harry S. Truman (was he a famous athlete?) Dr., Landover, Maryland (tel. 301/350-3400 for information; 202/432-0200, or toll free 800/448-9009 to charge tickets). The Cap Centre is home to the **Washington Bullets** (NBA) and **Washington Capitals** (NHL). The Georgetown University **Hoyas** (tel. 687-4692) also play many of their home basketball games in the 20,000-seat facility. Throughout the year, the Cap Centre hosts the **Washington International Horse Show** in October, the **Ice Capades, World Professional Figure-Skating Championships, rock concerts, wrestling,** the **Harlem Globetrotters,** and even **truck and tractor pulls.** The closest Metro stop is Landover, but you'll have to take a cab the rest of the way. The fare is about $7, according to **Blue Bird–Yellow Cab** (tel. 301/864-7700). Tickets can be purchased by phone about a month in advance or at the box office, near the Stars & Stripes entrance Monday through Saturday from 10am to 5pm.

BASEBALL

Washington has been without a professional baseball team since the Washington Senators vacated RFK Stadium in 1971, and a large contingent is working diligently to "Bring Baseball Back to Washington." In the meantime, fans travel to Oriole Stadium Camden Yards, site of the Baltimore Oriole's new stadium off I-95 near the Inner Harbor, to eat a lukewarm hot dog and see the O's play. Reserved seats are $6.50 and $7.50. General admission tickets are $4.75. Charge tickets over the phone (tel.

301/432-0200, or toll free 800/448-9009) or go to the Orioles Baseball Store, 914 17th St. NW (tel. 202/296-2473). It's about an hour's ride to the stadium. Check the newspapers for bus charters to and from the stadium.

GOLF

The Kemper Open is played at Avenel Tournament Players Club, 10000 Oaklyn Drive, Potomac, Maryland, the week immediately following the three-day Memorial Day weekend. In 1992 the dates are May 25–31. Special events for juniors are held Tuesday of tournament week. Take your kids to watch the pros practice in the morning and take part in a junior clinic in the afternoon. For specifics call 301/469-3737.

POLO

Polo anyone? The **National Capital Parks Polo Association-Lincoln Mall Club** plays on Sundays, beginning the last Sunday in April. Matches begin at 2pm in April and May, 3pm in June, 4pm in July. In August the ponies take a vacation. Play resumes the first Sunday after Labor Day. In September and October, the first chukker begins at 3pm. Matches take place in West Potomac Park across from the Lincoln Memorial, and general admission is free (tel. 202/362-3095 for information). If you're driving, there's parking on nearby Ohio Drive. The Federal Triangle, Foggy Bottom, and Smithsonian Metro stops are closest, but you'll still have about a 15-minute walk to the park.

TENNIS

Several professional tennis tournaments are played in the Washington area. The **Sovran Bank Classic** (men's) is held in July at the William H. G. FitzGerald Tennis Center off 16th Street NW. After years as a wintertime event, **The Virginia Slims of Washington** (women's) tournament switched in 1991 to August, and is also played at the FitzGerald Tennis Center. August is also the month for the **American Tennis Association Celebrity Tournament.** For the latest information, call the Washington Tennis Foundation (tel. 202/291-9888).

CHAPTER 7
WHERE KIDS LIKE TO EAT

1. **ON THE RUN**
2. **COOKIES, CANDIES & ICE CREAM**
3. **KID-RATED RESTAURANTS**

With nearly 3,500 restaurants of every ethnic persuasion to choose from, finding a place to eat is never a problem in Washington. The hard part is making a decision. You could get heartburn entertaining the endless possibilities. Be adventurous. Your kids' education doesn't end when you leave the Smithsonian. If you're raising them in a meat-and-potatoes environment, expand their gustatory horizons and try a Thai, Indian, or Ethiopian restaurant. And if your family has never tasted fresh crabmeat, here's your opportunity to savor this delicious local specialty that is harvested from the nearby Chesapeake Bay. After a taste test, you'll agree that crab cakes, crab imperial, and lump crabmeat cocktail are worth leaving home for.

Since space prohibits listing every family restaurant, consider this an hors d'oeuvrerie. Unless otherwise noted, the welcome mat is out for kids of all ages. Preteens and teenagers who are properly attired and like to dine rather than eat and run are welcome at any restaurant in the city. Most "grownup" places require reservations and appreciate an attempt at sartorial splendor a step or two beyond sweats and athletic shoes.

When deciding where to dine with a very young child, please consider the appropriateness of your choice. Some people persist in taking preschoolers to strictly adult places when everyone would have a much better time at a family-style establishment. Nobody with any sense wants to dress up and pay a lot of money in a fine restaurant to play peek-a-boo with an antsy, whining tot in the next booth. You might say this is a pet peeve of mine.

The drinking age in D.C. is 21. No exceptions are made for almost-21-year-olds dining with adults, so don't even think of offering your offspring a sip of your cocktail. A single violation could close the restaurant for good.

To save time on days when you want to pack in as much downtown sightseeing as possible, eat in a museum or federal building restaurant or cafeteria. Another option is to head for a food court in one of D.C.'s enclosed malls. Kids can exercise their freedom of choice at these popular eateries where the selections are consistent, inexpensive, and served with a smile. Feeling homesick? The nearest fast-food establishment is only a Golden Arch away. When you're rushed, take advantage of the many food vendors and pushcarts stationed strategically throughout the city. On a beautiful day, buy a movable feast at a carry-out shop and picnic on the grass.

Kids who would rather blow bubbles into their drink than eat a square meal are served better by fast food, take-out, or street food. Give them a break and don't make a federal case out of mealtime. Of course, it's always a good idea to have crackers or other snacks in your bag to pacify little ones who grow impatient waiting for the rolls to arrive.

Nothing can ruin an otherwise pleasant day faster than an interminable wait in a mobbed restaurant. Since there's a chance that sometimes service may be less than speedy, especially during peak times, always bring along some crayons, scrap paper, and a few playthings. For the most attentive service when you don't have reservations, be seated before noon or after 2pm for lunch and no later than 6 or 6:30pm for dinner. You don't have to act chic for your kids. They love you just the way you are.

1. ON THE RUN

In a hurry? For a quick bite when you're on the go, grab a snack from a street vendor. My kids were raised on hot dogs, soft pretzels, and ice cream without ill effect. They even got into college. Some vendors sell upscale treats like filled croissants and Chipwiches. Many hawk pizza and egg rolls, but these are usually less than satisfactory. My personal favorite—an addiction begun during numerous visits to New York City as a child—is a Sabrett's hot dog with "the works." It's a little bit of heaven for $1.25. Look for a pushcart with the blue and yellow umbrella bearing the Sabrett's logo. Accept no substitutes!

You'd have to travel to Mars to avoid Burger King, McDonald's, Hardee's (formerly Roy Rogers), Wendy's, Kentucky Fried Chicken, and Popeye's. Check the phone book for the nearest location, or, when hunger strikes and you yearn for a little grease, ask someone on the street to direct you to the nearest fast-food establishment. Chances are, there's one within a few blocks of wherever you are.

2. COOKIES, CANDIES & ICE CREAM

Now here's something I can really sink my teeth into. Researching this topic is an avocation at our house, so consider what you are about to read as sweet gospel.

COOKIES, ETC.

Wars have been started over nuttier things than who sells the best cookies in town. For my dough, Berger's and Mrs. Field's are as good as cookies get in this life. But, hey, don't take my word for it. Go out and try 'em all and then decide for yourself.

BERGER'S, Neam's, 3217 P St. NW. Tel. 338-4694.

Berger's cookies come from the Baltimore bakery of the same name, and, fortunately, you can buy them in D.C. Picture a little vanilla wafer—about the size of a hockey puck—that you can hardly see because it is almost totally encased in thick chocolate fudge. If you think you can stop at one, you're dead wrong.

Berger's are also sold at Ambrosia, Mazza Gallerie, 5300 Wisconsin Ave. NW (tel. 362-0677), and Traveling Gourmet, Union Station, 50 Massachusetts Ave. NE (tel. 842-1222).

BREAD & CHOCOLATE, 2301 M St NW. Tel. 833-8360.

Don't limit yourself to cookies here. Go ahead, sample the just-out-of-the-oven croissants and pastries. Eat in or take out.

There are other branches at 3251 Prospect St. NW in Georgetown (tel. 338-5722); 666 Pennsylvania Ave. SE on Capitol Hill (tel. 547-2875); 4200 Wisconsin Ave. NW (tel. 363-3744); and at 5542 Connecticut Ave. NW (tel. 966-7413).

DUNKIN' DONUTS, 85 S St. NW. Tel. 462-5612; 4531 Wisconsin Ave. NW. Tel. 364-8663.

Donuts. One of life's tastiest et ceteras. Is there a kid among us who can pass by without sampling the jelly- or cream-filled variety?

MRS. FIELD'S COOKIES, Union Station, 50 Massachusetts Ave. NW. Tel. 842-2360.

These soft, chewy, chip-laden cookies are nearly as good as homemade. They make an excellent bribe when a bribe is indicated (with kids, that's about every 7 minutes). I only wish they carried my name so I could retire to the Caribbean.

There are other Mrs. Field's branches at 1003 Connecticut Ave. NW (tel. 293-1945); 1706 Connecticut Ave. NW (tel. 667-7705); 1119 F St. NW (tel. 393-4712); and at Georgetown Park, Wisconsin & M streets NW (tel. 337-2050).

PÂTISSERIE CAFÉ DIDIER, 3206 Grace St. NW, off Wisconsin Avenue just below M Street. Tel. 342-9083.

This may be too good for your kids, but I'll mention it anyway. Tempting European pastries, baked by Dieter Schorner, the former pastry chef at New York's Le Cirque and La Côte Basque, are served in a sunny and inviting plant-filled Georgetown café. The setting could be the Left Bank instead of the left side of Wisconsin Avenue.

T.J. CINNAMON BAKERY, Union Station, 50 Massachusetts Ave. NE. Tel. 842-0752.

Follow the intoxicating aroma of cinnamon baking to the stand across from the movie-theater complex in Union Station's food court. Invest in a giant warm-from-the-oven cinnamon bun and take a few back to your room for later or tomorrow's breakfast.

WATERGATE PASTRY, 2354 Virginia Ave. NW. Tel. 342-1777.

Watergate supplies desserts to many restaurants, caterers, and VIP party-givers. Personally, I think the expensive baked goods look and smell a lot better than they taste. What's your opinion? Let me know.

CANDIES

There are times when everyone needs a little something sweet to make it through the next ten minutes. If you're out sightseeing and your time comes, try these.

CHOCOLATE CHOCOLATE, 1050 Connecticut Ave. NW. Tel. 466-2190.

Chocolate chocolate: my two favorite words in the English language. The shop carries a nicely balanced selection of imported and locally made confections. Gift baskets, too.

There's another branch at 3222 M St. NW (tel. 338-3356).

FANNIE MAE, 640 17th St. NW. Tel. 393-3883.

If it's sweet and loaded with calories, they have it. Stop in for a sugar rush.

THE FUDGERY, Old Post Office Pavilion, 1100 Pennsylvania Ave. NW. Tel. 371-9580.

Seven varieties of mouthwatering fudge are sold here, and the choices change from day to day. Stay a week and you can try them all.

KRON CHOCOLATIER, Mazza Gallerie, 5300 Wisconsin Ave. NW. Tel. 966-4946.

In a recurring dream, I fall into a vat of Kron's melted bittersweet chocolate and live happily ever after. Try the champagne truffles and chocolate-dipped strawberries and you too will have sweet dreams. Kids will find their own favorites.

ICE CREAM

An ice-cream break can be just what the doctor ordered when little spirits are sagging. While nothing I've sampled locally quite equals the ice cream scooped at Gruning's, the temple of my youth, many of the following establishments dish out some reasonable facsimiles. If you're interested, our family's vote for the best ice cream in D.C. is split—as in banana split—Ben & Jerry's, Bob's, Häagen-Dazs, and Gifford's.*

BASKIN-ROBBINS, 14th & K St. NW. Tel. 842-0707.

They must be doing something right. They sell more ice cream than any other retail dealer in the country. The franchises are kind of institutional, but, like an old friend, they're there when you need them.

There's another branch at 2604 Connecticut Ave. NW (tel. 483-4820).

BEN & JERRY'S, 2503 Champlain St. NW, near 18th Street and Columbia Road. Tel. 667-6677.

Eat in or take out some of the best ice cream produced anywhere on the planet. In the summer, drip your Cherry Garcia or Heath Bar Crunch on the outside tables while enjoying the mural of bike-riding, ice cream-eating cows.

There's another Ben & Jerry's branch in Alexandria, Virginia, and still another in Gaithersburg, Maryland.

BOB'S, 2416 Wisconsin Ave. NW. Tel. 965-4499.

Who can pass up the Oreo ice cream with its large, crunchy cookie chunks? Create your own sundae with one or more toppings. The ice cream is rich and creamy, and the portions are more generous than most other places.

There's another Bob's branch at 3510 Connecticut Ave. NW (tel. 244-4465).

CONE E ISLAND, 2000 Pennsylvania Ave. NW. Tel. 822-8460; and 2816 Pennsylvania Ave. NW. Tel. 338-6778.

Kids of all ages love the walk-away waffle cones, loaded with ice cream, hot fudge, and whipped cream. What's not to like? A bit pricey, but loyal fans will tell you well worth the cost and calories.

GELATO CLASSICO ITALIAN ICE CREAM, 1460 G St. NW. Tel. 628-4818.

*My daughter, Rachel Rubin, ice-cream lover *sine qua non*, helped with the research for this section.

You don't even want to know the butterfat content of the reverse chocolate chip flavor. This ice cream is really rich, and a little goes a long way. But as long as you're splurging, ask for a little hot fudge or caramel sauce on top.

GIFFORD'S, 7720 Wisconsin Ave., Bethesda, MD. Tel. 301/907-3436.

The family-owned Gifford's chain had a corner on the market before dying out in the '70s and '80s. Many of us went into prolonged mourning. Then along came Dolly Hunt, who, with the original recipes, reopened Gifford's on July 4, 1989. Thank you, Dolly! The Swiss chocolate and hot fudge sundaes are worth the trip (a short walk from the Bethesda Metro station) from wherever you are.

HÄAGEN-DAZS, 1438 Wisconsin Ave. NW, Georgetown. Tel. 333-7505; and The Shops at National Place, 1331 Pennsylvania Ave. NW. Tel. 737-9312.

This is first-class ice cream, and you don't have to play guessing games with the flavors. The mocha tastes like mocha, the vanilla like real vanilla, and so on. The chocolate-chocolate chip should be declared a national treasure.

I CAN'T BELIEVE IT'S YOGURT, 4000 Wisconsin Ave. NW. Tel. 363-8933.

The answer to a weight-watcher's prayer, each creamy ounce has only 27 calories; the nonfat, 20 calories. If you keep the ounces in the single digits and refrain from loading up on the candy toppings, you and yours will stay out of fat city. But what fun is that?

JOE & ANDY'S CAFE BEIGNET, Union Station, 50 Massachusetts Ave. NE. Tel. 682-2392.

Don't let the name throw you. This is ice-cream heaven, with beignets on the side. If you're dieting, sip an espresso while your kids inhale chocolate fudge mousse ice cream, frozen yogurt, a Dove Bar, or the Ridiculous Sundae for three.

LE SORBET, 1776 G St. NW. Tel. 789-1313.

The servings are a mite skimpy, but the ice cream is flavorful and satisfying. Try the butterscotch praline, or the fruit-flavored ices, which are especially refreshing on a hot summer's day. Le Sorbet also serves sandwiches and quiches.

SCOOPS, Old Post Office Pavilion, 1100 Pennsylvania Ave. NW. Tel. 789-4272.

Depending on your mood and capacity, go for the frozen yogurt (only 20 calories per ounce) or the large Sidewalk Sundae—two scoops, two toppings, and whipped cream in a homemade waffle cone (9 million calories). The 9 million calories probably won't bother your kids—they'll run them off. Maybe you'd better stick to the frozen yogurt.

SWENSEN'S ICE CREAM PARLORS, 1990 K St. NW. Tel. 833-1140; and 4200 Wisconsin Ave. NW. Tel. 244-5544.

To my tastes, Swensen's ice cream is adequate but lackluster, and it's hard to distinguish some of the flavors except by their colors. The sundaes are pricey and the table tops tend toward sticky. Otherwise, they're terrific.

AFTERNOON TEA

Many downtown hotels have adopted the veddy civilized British custom of serving afternoon tea. School-aged kids can practice their party manners while graciously wolfing down quantities of finger sandwiches, tea breads, scones, fruit tarts, petits fours, pastries, and fresh fruit. With a spread like this, who needs tea? While the kids sip their favorite soft drink and you enjoy steaming potfuls of Earl Grey, you can discuss the day's happenings while pretending you're to the manor born.

The price for full tea is $10–$12; some hotels also offer a light tea with sweet breads and scones for $6–$8. If you sip your cuppa late enough in the day, you may be able to skip dinner altogether. Dust off your white gloves, Vaseline your patent-leather shoes, and try one of these (do make advance reservations).

THE CARLTON HOTEL, 923 16th St. NW (tel. 638-2626).
Full and light tea are served in the Allegro restaurant Monday through Saturday from 2:30 to 5:30pm.

THE FOUR SEASONS HOTEL, 2800 M St. NW (tel. 342-0444)
Enjoy tea in the beautiful Garden Terrace overlooking Rock Creek Park from 3 to 4:30pm Monday through Friday and from 3 to 5pm on Saturday and Sunday.

THE MAYFLOWER HOTEL, 1127 Connecticut Ave. NW (tel. 347-3000)
The soothing setting of the Café Promenade is the scene for tea for two—or three or four or more—every day from 3 to 5pm.

THE PARK HYATT HOTEL, 24th and M streets NW (tel. 789-1234).
Fill your plate as many times as you like in the elegant lobby lounge from 3 to 5pm every day. You can also order à la carte. Palmist Jeannie Oliver is on hand Wednesdays and Thursdays—a mini-reading costs $5.

WASHINGTON NATIONAL CATHEDRAL, Massachusetts and Wisconsin avenue. NW (tel. 537-8993).
What a setting in which to enjoy tea every Tuesday and Wednesday afternoon after the special 1:45pm cathedral tour. Reservations are required.

THE WILLARD INTER-CONTINENTAL HOTEL, 1401 Pennsylvania Ave. NW (tel. 628-9100).
Full tea is served from 3 to 5pm daily in the Nest of this beautifully restored Old World–style hotel, where you'll feel like royalty because you'll be treated as such.

3. KID-RATED RESTAURANTS

Prices are difficult to categorize, except in broad terms, because so much depends on what you order. If you're traveling with very young children who share an entree or are content with an appetizer and dessert, your bill will be considerably less than noted here. Most of the places listed are in the moderate and budget ranges. If you want to spend more than $50 a head for your kids' meals, I'd like to meet your kids. On second thought, I'd like to be your kids. A few of D.C.'s top restaurants are included for big kids with big appetites. If you want more recommendations, ask people you meet while sightseeing or your concierge, or buy one of Prentice Hall's adult guides—*Frommer's Washington, D.C.; Frommer's Washington, D.C., on $40 A Day;* or *Gault-Millau's Washington, D.C.*

Generally, at expensive establishments expect to pay $30 to $50 per person; moderate, $15 to $30; and budget, below $15. At most budget-priced restaurants, you can stuff yourself for well under $15 if you choose wisely. Order an appetizer, salad, and dessert to cut costs. These are often better than the entrees anyway. Asian restaurants are an excellent choice when dining with kids. An order of crispy egg rolls or steamed dumplings and bowl of soup makes a hearty meal for under $6 at many places.

Washington is a big lunch town, and midday many establishments offer items from their dinner menu for substantially less. If you eat your main meal around noon and graze at dinner, you'll have more money left for shopping and baby-sitters. In an ongoing effort to entice value-conscious customers, more and more restaurants are offering fixed-price, pre-theater, and early-bird specials, to be enjoyed from about 5 to 6:30pm—an ideal time to dine with kids. Seek and ye shall find!

The sales tax on D.C. restaurant meals is 8%. To simplify tipping, merely double the tax. A few restaurants add a 15% gratuity to the bill, so be sure to look at your check or you may tip twice. For the adults in your party, expect to pay $3 to $5 for a glass of wine or a cocktail, $2 to $3 for a beer.

CAPITOL HILL

A host of casual and pleasing dining establishments fill the Hill. Of all D.C.'s dining neighborhoods, this one seems to be the most kid-friendly. If your stomach starts growling while you're touring the Capitol, Supreme Court, or Library of Congress, try one of their dining rooms or cafeterias for a quick meal or snack. Here are some of our favorites:

MODERATE

AMERICA, Union Station, 50 Massachusetts Ave. NE. Tel. 682-9555.
   Cuisine: AMERICAN. **Reservations:** Recommended. **Metro:** Union Station.
$ Prices: Main courses $6–$16. AE, DC, MC, V.
   Open: Mon–Fri 11:30am–midnight; Sat–Sun 11:30am–2am.
   Children's Services: Highchairs, boosters.
Try the San Diego fish tacos, New Orleans muffaleta (like a sub or hoagie), Kansas City steaks, or anything else from the ambitious menu in this cavernous, multilevel Union Station restaurant that diligently tries to be all things to all people. Opt for a balcony table—the views of the Main Hall are spectacular.

TORTILLA COAST, 201 Massachusetts Ave. NE. Tel. 546-6768.
   Cuisine: MEXICAN. **Reservations:** Accepted for 8 or more. **Metro:** Union Station.
$ Prices: $6–$12; child's plate $3.95. AE, MC, V.
   Open: Lunch Mon–Fri 11:45am–3pm; brunch Sat–Sun noon–3pm; dinner Mon–Thurs 3–10:30pm, Fri–Sat 11:45am–11pm, Sun noon–10pm.
   Children's Services: Highchairs, children's portions.
To avoid trouble (i.e., long waits) getting into this ever-popular Hill Margaritaville, the management suggests avoiding Friday nights when congressional employees take over

Adams Morgan Spaghetti Garden 1
Air & Space Museum 2
   Flight Line Cafeteria
   Wright Place Restaurant
America, Union Station 3
American Café 4a
American Café Market House 4b
American Café, the Shops,
   at National Place 5
Austin Grill 6
A.V. 7
Bangkok Orchid 8
Boogie's Diner 9
Brickskeller 10
Bullfeathers 11

Cafe Mozart 12
Chadwick's 13
Cheesecake Factory 14
China Inn 15
Clyde's 16
Crêpe A La Carte 17
Dirksen Senate Office Building,
   South Buffet Room 18
El Bodegon 19
El Pollo Primo 20
El Tamarindo 21
Enriqueta's 22
Filomena's 23
Food Court at the Old Post Office
   Pavilion 24

Food Hall at the Shops at
   National Place 25
Garrett's 26
Geppetto 27
Hamburger Hamlet 28
Hamburger Hamlet, Georgetown 29
Hard Rock Cafe 30
Hirshhorn Museum's
   Full Circle Plaza Cafe 31
Hogs on the Hill 32
House of Representatives
   Members Dining Room 33
Houston's 34
Hunan Chinatown 35
I Matti 36

WASHINGTON, D.C., DINING

Metro Stop **M** Information ⓘ

Jockey Club ③⑦
Kramerbooks & Afterwords Café ③⑧
Library of Congress Cafeteria ③⑨
Market Lunch ④⓪
Marrakesh ④①
Morton's of Chicago ④②
The National Gallery of Art: ④③
    Concourse Buffet
    Garden Cafe
    Terrace Cafe
National Museum of American History: ④④
    Cafeteria Carousel
    Palm Court (Victorian Ice Cream Parlor)

National Museum of Natural History
    Cafeteria ④⑤
National Portrait Gallery,
    Patent Pending ④⑥
Old Ebbitt Grill ④⑦
Otello ④⑧
Pan Asian Noodles & Grill ④⑨
Paolo's ⑤⓪
Philadelphia Mike's ⑤①
Pleasant Peasant ⑤②
Red Sea ⑤③
The Refectory ⑤④
Sea Catch ⑤⑤
Sherrill's ⑤⑥

Sholl's Colonial Cafeteria ⑤⑦
Sky Terrace ⑤⑧
The Supreme Court Cafeteria ⑤⑨
Szechuan ⑥⓪
T.G.I. Friday's ⑥①
Tandoor ⑥②
Thai Taste ⑥③
Thai 89 ⑥④
Tortilla Coast ⑥⑤
Tunnicliff's Tavern ⑥⑥
Union Station Food Court ⑥⑦

to toast T.G.I.F. The steak and chicken fajitas are standouts at this beachlike hangout. The child's plate holds a smaller serving of the grownup fare with rice and beans.

BUDGET

AMERICAN CAFÉ, 227 Massachusetts Ave. NE. Tel. 547-8500.
   Cuisine: AMERICAN. **Reservations:** For groups of 6 or more. **Metro:** Union Station.
   $ Prices: Entrees $5.95–$9.95, carryout less. AE, D, DC, MC, V.
   Open: Breakfast (self-service) Mon–Fri 7:30–9:30am, Sat–Sun 8:30–10am; Mon–Thurs 11am–midnight, Fri–Sat 11am–1am, Sun 10:30am–midnight; extended summer hours. Market House (takeout) Mon–Fri 7:30am–9pm, Sat–Sun 8:30am–9pm.
   Children's Services: Highchairs, boosters, children's menu.

★ Many say the food has slipped over the years, but the American Café is still a family favorite—bright, clean, and casual with friendly service. Ask for the award-winning children's menu; the kids will love it. The tarragon chicken salad on a croissant or baguette is delicious, and the chili and desserts are above average. You can sit inside or outside on a brick terrace with umbrella tables.

AMERICAN CAFÉ MARKET HOUSE, Union Station, 50 Massachusetts Ave. NW. Tel. 682-0937.
   Cuisine: AMERICAN. **Reservations:** Not accepted. **Metro:** Union Station.
   $ Prices: 75¢–$4.95. AE, MC, V.
   Open: Mon–Sat 7am–9pm; Sun 8am–6pm.
On the first level of Union Station, this is a good place to pick up a light meal when you're in a hurry, dashing for a train, or in the mood to picnic. There's ample seating in the food court downstairs.

BANGKOK ORCHID, 301 Massachusetts Ave. NE. Tel. 546-5900.
   Cuisine: THAI. **Reservations:** Recommended.
   $ Prices: Lunch $2.95–$8.25; dinner $4.25–$14.95. AE, MC, V.
   Open: Sun–Thurs 11am–10:30pm, Fri–Sat 11am–11pm.
   Children's Services: Highchairs.
Although relatively new, Bangkok Orchid already has its share of loyal fans who wax poetic over the seafood, chicken, and noodle dishes. Ask your server for non-spicy recommendations if you or yours can't stand the heat. In-season dining outside.

BULLFEATHERS, 410 1st St. SE. Tel. 543-5005.
   Cuisine: AMERICAN. **Reservations:** Anytime except noon–1:30pm.
   $ Prices: Entrees $5.25–$14.95; kids menu $1.95–$3.95. AE, D, MC, V.
   Open: Mon–Thurs and Sat 11:30am–11pm, Fri 11:30am–1am; Sun brunch 10:30am–3:30pm.
   Children's Services: Highchairs, children's menu.
Really good hamburgers, nachos, and a full menu of meat, pasta, and seafood specialties make this a popular spot for diners of all ages. The bargain children's menu includes peanut butter and jelly sandwiches, chicken, and a 3½-ounce kiddie burger. Light fare is served in the saloon.

DIRKSEN SENATE OFFICE BUILDING SOUTH BUFFET ROOM, 1st and C streets NE. Tel. 224-4249.

Cuisine: AMERICAN. **Reservations:** Accepted but not required. **Metro:** Capitol South or Union Station.

$ Prices: Lunch buffet $7.15 adults, $4.89 kids under 12, plus a 15% gratuity. No credit cards.

Open: Lunch Mon–Fri 11:30am–2:30pm.

Children's Services: Highchairs, boosters.

⭐ Getting here is half the fun. Take the free subway that runs under the Capitol to this all-you-can-eat buffet. There's a carvery station plus several steamer trays with additional hot entrees, side dishes, a full salad and fruit bar, a wide choice of desserts, and beverages included in the price of admission. A make-your-own-sundae bar will make the kids ecstatic.

HOGS ON THE HILL, 732 Maryland Ave. NE. Tel. 547-4553.

Cuisine: AMERICAN. **Reservations:** Accepted for 8 or more.

$ Prices: Lunch $5.95–$6.95, dinner $7.50–$13.50. AE, MC, V.

Open: Daily 11am–10:30pm.

Children's Services: Boosters.

Who needs fancy digs when you're chowing down on yummy slow-cooked ribs and chicken or tangy minced barbecue. Entrees come with two southern-style side dishes. Try the greens and cornbread. You won't leave here hungry. Oink. A second Hogs opened in May '91 at 14th and U streets NW.

HOUSE OF REPRESENTATIVES MEMBERS DINING ROOM, Room H118 at the south end of the Capitol. Tel. 225-6300.

Cuisine: AMERICAN. **Reservations:** Not accepted. **Metro:** Capitol South.

$ Prices: Entrees $4.20–$8.50. AE, DC, MC, V.

Open: Breakfast Mon–Fri 8–11am; lunch Mon–Fri 1:30–2:30pm; dinner 5–9pm when Congress is in session—you must be accompanied by a member at dinner.

Children's Services: Highchairs, boosters.

Fortify the family with a full breakfast here before touring the Hill. Sample the famous and infamous Senate bean soup at lunch. Sandwiches, burgers, and a few entrees are available for bean haters.

LIBRARY OF CONGRESS CAFETERIA, JAMES MADISON MEMORIAL BUILDING, 101 Independence Ave. SE, Sixth floor Tel. 554-4114, or 707-8300.

Cuisine: AMERICAN. **Reservations:** Not accepted. **Metro:** Capitol South.

$ Prices: Appetizers 80¢–$4; entrees $2–$4.25; sandwiches $1.85–$3.50. No credit cards.

Open: Breakfast Mon–Fri 9–10:30am; lunch Mon–Fri 12:30–2pm; light fare Mon–Fri 2–3:30pm.

Located on the sixth floor of the Madison Building, this handsome cafeteria has a wall of windows overlooking the city. There's always a salad bar at lunch, as well as hot entrees, carved meats, health food, pizza, fast food (fried chicken, burgers), deli sandwiches, and desserts—pies, cakes, and puddings.

The more formal Montpelier Room, adjoining the cafeteria, serves a marvelous $7.95 buffet lunch Monday through Friday between 11:30am and 2pm. Prime ribs are featured Fridays. Reservations are required for 4 or more. This place is definitely not for very young kids.

MARKET LUNCH. 225 Seventh St. SE. Tel. 547-8444.
Cuisine: ECLECTIC/AMERICAN. **Reservations:** Not accepted.
$ **Prices:** Breakfast $1–$3.95; lunch $2.75–$8.95. No credit cards.
Open: Breakfast Tues–Sat 7:30–10:55am, lunch Tues–Sat 11am–2:30pm.
Children's Services: Highchairs.
Try the mouthwatering blueberry buckwheat pancakes or french toast at breakfast at this restaurant in the heart of bustling Eastern Market. The softshell crab sandwich on homemade bread is a lunchtime specialty. Weather permitting, there's outdoor seating. Weekends the place jumps with live music and hordes of young people hunting for bargains at the nearby flea market.

THE REFECTORY, first floor, Senate side of the Capitol, Constitution Avenue and 1st Street NE. Tel. 224-4870.
Cuisine: AMERICAN. **Reservations:** Not accepted. **Metro:** Capitol South.
$ **Prices:** Appetizers $1.45–$5.70; entrees $2.50–$8.35. No credit cards.
Open: Mon–Fri 8am–4pm (later when Senate is in session).
Children's Services: Highchairs.
For a quick meal or snack at the Capitol, stop at the Refectory for breakfast, light fare, and desserts. There's seating for 75 in this appealing little place with vaulted ceilings and wainscotted walls.

SHERRILL'S, 233 Pennsylvania Ave. SE. Tel. 544-2480.
Cuisine: AMERICAN. **Reservations:** Not accepted. **Metro:** Capitol South.
$ **Prices:** Breakfast $1–$2.95; lunch (sandwiches) $1.10–$4.95; platters $5–$8.75. No credit cards.
Open: Mon–Fri 6am–8pm; Sat–Sun, hols 7am–8pm.
Children's Services: Sassy seats, boosters.
The subject of a 1989 documentary that was nominated for an Academy Award (it should have won!), Sherrill's has been serving home-cooked meals since 1922. The pastries (éclairs, napoleons, cream puffs, etc.) and soups are made in-house and are quite good. So is breakfast. The kids will get a kick out of the soda counter complete with old-fashioned malted machine. Take a trip back to the future at this colorful establishment.

THE SUPREME COURT CAFETERIA, 1st Street NE, between East Capitol Street and Maryland Avenue. Tel. 479-3246.
Cuisine: AMERICAN. **Reservations:** Not accepted. **Metro:** Capitol South.
$ **Prices:** Entrees $2.95–$6. No credit cards.
Open: Breakfast Mon–Fri 7:30–10:30am; lunch Mon–Fri 11:30am–2pm (closed to public noon to 12:15pm and 1–1:10pm).
Hear ye, hear ye. The decision is out on the food: It may not be supreme, but it's appealing. Fresh-baked muffins are featured at breakfast; soup, sandwiches, entrees, salad bar, ice cream and desserts at lunch. There's also a carry-out snackbar—homemade cakes and pies sell for just 95¢ to $1.25 per slice.

TUNNICLIFF'S TAVERN, 222 Seventh St. SE. Tel. 546-3663.
Cuisine: AMERICAN. **Reservations:** Strongly recommended.
$ **Prices:** $2–$16.50; special kids' menu. AE, D, MC, V.
Open: Mon–Fri 11am–11pm; brunch Sat–Sun 11am–3pm.
Children's Services: Highchairs, boosters, children's menu.

This is a fun family spot thanks to Lynne Breaux Cooper, who knows a thing or two about kids. At comfy and cozy Tunnicliff's, hamburgers and french fries star. Or try a turkey sandwich on pita, an engagin' Cajun specialty, or something from the grill. The kids' menu is in the form of a coloring book, and little ones enjoy their own happy hour in the toy-filled living room.

UNION STATION FOOD COURT, 50 Massachusetts Ave. NE. Tel. 371-9441.
  Cuisine: CAFETERIA FARE. **Reservations:** Not accepted.
$ Prices: $1–$8. No credit cards.
  Open: Mon–Sat 10am–9pm, Sun noon–6pm.
Kids of all ages love casing the many stands before making a selection at this bustling, booming food court. You can't go wrong with anything you choose. Some of the best bets for kids include the European Kosher #5 hot dog at Dogs Plus; the deep-dish pizza at Ilardo's; the charbroiled hamburger at Flamer's. Movable Feast packs delectable "express lunches" if you're rushing to catch a train or it's a nice day for a picnic.

MALL & MUSEUM RESTAURANTS

There are few restaurants close to the Mall, so days when you're concentrating your sightseeing in that area, save time by eating right in one of the museums. When the weather is good, buy lunch in a cafeteria or from a street vendor and park yourselves outside for an impromptu picnic. The fresh air will revive everyone's spirits and enthusiasm for the afternoon's activities.

AIR AND SPACE MUSEUM FLIGHT LINE CAFETERIA, Independence Avenue at 6th Street SW (or enter on the south side of the Mall near 4th Street SW). Tel. 357-2700.
  Cuisine: AMERICAN. **Reservations:** Not accepted. **Metro:** L'Enfant Plaza.
$ Prices: Entrees $3.95–$6.95; sandwiches and salads $1.50–$5. No credit cards.
  Open: Daily 10am–5pm; extended hours June–Aug.
  Children's Services: Highchairs, boosters.
Take a look at this stunning, futuristic dining complex, even if you're not hungry. Talk about letting the sunshine in . . . ! The 800-seat cafeteria, with its eye-catching tubular construction and expansive windows overlooking the Mall, National Gallery, and Capitol, is a knockout. Help yourself from several buffet stations where salads, sandwiches, hot entrees, soups, pizza, and dessert are appealingly displayed. Breads and pastries are baked fresh daily. The more-than-adequate fare and bright, airy setting combine to make this an ideal refueling spot.

AIR AND SPACE MUSEUM WRIGHT PLACE RESTAURANT, upstairs from Flight Line Cafeteria, Independence Avenue at 4th Street SW. Tel. 371-8777.
  Cuisine: AMERICAN. **Reservations:** Suggested. **Metro:** L'Enfant Plaza.
$ Prices: Entrees $5–$11; sandwiches and salads $5.25–$7.25 kids' menu $3.25–$3.95. AE, MC, V.
  Open: Daily 11am–3pm.
  Children's Services: Highchairs, boosters, children's menu.

Above the Flight Line is an attractive full-service continental café decorated with lots of greenery and aviation photographs. The ambiance outflies the trendy food, and the views are somewhat obstructed, but the grilled marinated chicken sandwich and children's menu (with such items as grilled cheese, hamburger, fried chicken fingers plus potatoes, vegetable, milk or soda, and a chocolate sundae) make up for the deficiencies.

HIRSHHORN MUSEUM'S FULL CIRCLE PLAZA CAFE, south side of the Mall at Independence Avenue and 8th Street SW. Tel. 357-2700.
    Cuisine: AMERICAN. **Reservations:** Not accepted. **Metro:** Smithsonian.
$ Prices: Not available at this writing.
    Open: Memorial Day–Labor Day; hours not available at this writing.
This delightful outdoor café, which has been closed for renovation for what seems like forever, is due to reopen in the spring of 1993. An oasis on a summer's day, the café has sheltered and shaded tables and a limited menu. In the old days kids could get PB & J, milk, and an apple for a nominal sum. Let's hope the new menu doesn't overlook those in the peanut gallery.

NATIONAL GALLERY OF ART CONCOURSE BUFFET, between the two wings of the National Gallery, north side of the Mall between 3rd and 7th streets. NW Tel. 737-4215 or 347-9401.
    Cuisine: AMERICAN. **Reservations:** Not accepted. **Metro:** Archives or Judiciary Square.
$ Prices: Entrees $3.50–$4.50. AE, MC, V.
    Open: Mon–Sat 10am–4pm; Sun noon–6pm; extended hours in summer.
    Children's Services: Highchairs.
The line moves quickly in this bright and cheery space with seating for 600. Create your own salad, choose a pre-made sandwich or one with hand-sliced deli meats from the carvery, or a hot entree. There are passable hot dogs, burgers, and fries that pose no threat to Mickey D's, and frozen yogurt with varied toppings for the kids. Try to snag a table near the waterfall.

NATIONAL GALLERY OF ART TERRACE CAFE, upper level, East Building, 4th St. and Constitution Ave. NW. Tel. 357-2700.
    Cuisine: AMERICAN. **Reservations:** Not accepted. **Metro:** Archives or Judiciary Square.
$ Prices: Entrees $6–$10.50. AE, MC, V.
    Open: Mon–Sat 11:30am–4pm, Sun noon–4pm; extended hours in summer.
    Children's Services: Highchairs, boosters.
The Terrace Cafe reopened in September 1991 after renovation. The menu, which changes seasonally, features a sandwich or two, like delicious grilled ham and Brie (ideal for the kids), several entrees, and a splendid assortment of desserts that includes cakes of carrot, cheese, or chocolate, pecan pie, and, especially for the munchkins, sundaes.

NATIONAL GALLERY OF ART GARDEN CAFE, West Building, 6th Street and Constitution Avenue NW. Tel. 357-2700.
    Cuisine: AMERICAN. **Reservations:** Not accepted. **Metro:** Archives or Judiciary Square.
$ Prices: Entrees $6–$8. AE, MC, V.

Open: Mon–Sat 11am–4:30pm, Sun 11am–6pm; extended hours in summer.
Children's Services: Highchairs.
Come to reflect, cool your heels, and have dessert or something simple at a fountainside table surrounded by ferns. Eating is incidental.

NATIONAL MUSEUM OF AMERICAN HISTORY, CAFETERIA CAROU-SEL, Constitution Avenue NW at 14th Street Tel. 357-2700.
Cuisine: AMERICAN. **Reservations:** Surely you jest. **Metro:** Federal Triangle.
$ Prices: 75¢–$5. No credit cards.
Open: Breakfast 10–11am; lunch and snacks 11am–5pm.
Children's Services: Highchairs.
Kids marvel at the mirrored carousel that dispenses hot dogs, sandwiches, and desserts in the belly of this treasure house of American social history. Many find it as mesmerizing as the Foucault Pendulum. This otherwise dreary cafeteria is open for breakfast, lunch, and snacks. Plenty of highchairs and nonsmoking areas here.

NATIONAL MUSEUM OF AMERICAN HISTORY, PALM COURT [VICTOR-IAN ICE CREAM PARLOR], 14th Street and Constitution Avenue NW. Tel. 357-1832.
Cuisine: MOSTLY SWEETS. **Reservations:** Only for 8 or more and private parties. **Metro:** Federal Triangle.
$ Prices: $2–$5. AE, MC, V.
Open: 11am–4pm.
Children's Services: Highchairs, boosters.
Once you've admired the etched-glass mirrors, potted palms, and wicker, you can get down to the business at hand in this carefully researched and executed turn-of-the-century ice cream parlor on the museum's first floor. You could start with something healthful like a sandwich or soup, but why bother. Dig right into the Double Devil (brownies, ice cream, fudge sauce, whipped cream, and sprinkles), a too-thick-to-sip-through-a-straw malt, or pie à la mode. Kids can order a junior-size sundae.

NATIONAL MUSEUM OF NATURAL HISTORY CAFETERIA, 10th Street and Constitution Avenue NW. Tel. 357-2700.
Cuisine: FAST FOOD. **Reservations:** None. **Metro:** Federal Triangle.
$ Prices: 75¢–$5. No credit cards.
Open: Light breakfast daily 10–11am; lunch and snacks daily 11am–5pm.
Children's Services: Highchairs, boosters.
The former dungeonlike atmosphere of this museum eatery is history. Renovation includes the welcome addition of skylights and greenery. Before or after your burger and shake stop at the adjacent Shop For Kids, a pint-sized souvenir emporium filled with affordable mementos.

NATIONAL PORTRAIT GALLERY PATENT PENDING CAFE, (don't you love the name?), off the courtyard between the Museum of American Art (8th and G Streets NW) and National Portrait Gallery (8th and F Streets NW). Tel. 357-2700.
Cuisine: AMERICAN. **Reservations:** Not accepted. **Metro:** Gallery Place.
$ Prices: Sandwiches $2.75–$3.75; salad bar 25¢ per ounce. No credit cards.
Open: Mon–Fri 11am–3:30pm, Sat–Sun 11:30am–4pm.
Children's Services: Highchairs, boosters.

The fountains and sculpture are food for the soul at this charming hideaway that is a secret to many. Sit at a table under the trees, weather permitting. Be an artist and create your own sandwich or follow the flocks to the salad bar and the frozen yogurt bar.

CONVENTION CENTER/DOWNTOWN

EXPENSIVE

MARRAKESH, 617 New York Ave. NW. Tel. 393-9393.
   Cuisine: MOROCCAN. **Reservations:** Required. **Metro:** Gallery Place.
   $ Prices: Fixed-price dinner $22.50 before 6:30pm, $25 after 6:30pm; kids under 10 half price Sun–Thurs. No credit cards; checks accepted with two pieces of ID.
   Open: Mon–Sat 6–11pm, Sun 5–11pm.

⭐ Celebrate a birthday or the summer solstice or whatever at this lively, colorful oasis. Snuggle into the pillowed banquettes and partake of the multicourse fixed-price dinner (eating is strictly a hands-on experience) while enjoying Middle Eastern music and belly dancing. Don't be surprised if someone in your party is asked to be part of the entertainment. A lot of fun for the money—an experience the kids are sure to tell their friends about.

MODERATE

CAFE MOZART, 1331 H St. NW. Tel. 347-5732.
   Cuisine: GERMAN/VIENNESE. **Reservations:** Recommended at dinner.
   Metro: Metro Center or McPherson Square.
   $ Prices: Breakfast $2–$8; lunch $4–$18; dinner $7–$20. AE, D, MC, V.
   Open: Mon–Fri 7:30am–10pm, Sat 9am–10pm, Sun 11am–10pm. **Closed:** Christmas and New Year's days.
   Children's Services: Boosters.

⭐ You could do a lot wurst than to dine at this gemütlich restaurant tucked behind a deli where the sauerbraten is almost as good as my grandmother's, and the mood is like Oktoberfest year round. The food is robust and tasty, service is warm and friendly, and there's live music Wednesday through Saturday. Kids of all ages are welcome for breakfast and lunch; older kids only in the evening. Free parking is provided Monday through Friday after 6pm.

CHINA INN, 631 H St. NW. Tel. 842-0909 or 842-0910.
   Cuisine: CHINESE. **Reservations:** Suggested at dinner. **Metro:** Gallery Place.
   $ Prices: Appetizers $3–$10; most entrees $7.50–$10, some as high as $22. AE, MC, V.
   Open: Mon–Thurs 11am–3am, Fri–Sat 11am–4am, Sun 11am–1:30am.
   Children's Services: Boosters.

While new restaurants spring up like bamboo in Chinatown, this oldie (in operation since 1937) is still a goodie. Small appetites can try something from the appetizer and soup offerings, while heartier appetites splurge on the Cantonese-style duck or seafood dishes. Don't let the institutional setting and sometimes perfunctory service put you off. China Inn is still a crowd pleaser. Whatever your children's preference in seasonings, the kitchen will gladly adjust them to suit their tastes. No high chairs are available here.

HUNAN CHINATOWN, 624 H St. NW. Tel. 783-5858.

Cuisine: CHINESE. **Reservations:** Suggested. **Metro:** Gallery Place.

$ **Prices:** Appetizers $2.40–$4.20 lunch, $2.50–$5.50 dinner; entrees $7–$11 lunch; $10–$15 dinner. AE, CB, DC, MC, V.

Open: Lunch Mon–Fri 11am–3pm; dinner Sun–Thurs 3–11pm, Fri–Sat 11am–1am. **Closed:** Thanksgiving and Christmas days.

Children's Services: Highchairs, boosters.

What you see is what you get at another of Chinatown's standbys, where the food is consistent if uninspired. Many of the dishes are Hunan hot, hot, hot—so, depending on your tolerance, ask the kitchen to go easy on the chili peppers and hot oil, especially on the kids' orders. Children will enjoy such appetizers as spring rolls, fried wonton, and meat-filled steamed or pan-fried dumplings.

OLD EBBITT GRILL, 675 15th St. NW, between F and G streets. Tel. 347-4801.

Cuisine: AMERICAN. **Reservations:** Recommended. **Metro:** Farragut West or McPherson Square.

$ **Prices:** Breakfast $1–$7; lunch entrees $6–$12; dinner entrees $6–$17; Sunday brunch $6–$10. AE, CB, D, DC, MC, V.

Open: Breakfast Mon–Fri 7:30–11am, Sat 8–11am; brunch Sun 11am–4pm; lunch Mon–Fri 11am–4pm, Sat 11am–5pm; dinner Mon–Fri 5pm–midnight, Sat–Sun 4pm–midnight; light fare daily till 1am. **Closed:** Christmas Day.

Children's Services: Highchairs, boosters.

Around the corner from the White House, the Ebbitt is a good choice anytime. Stick to the beef and pasta dishes at dinner. On my last visit, the crab cakes had enough shell bits in them to start a collection. Everyone enjoys the hustle-bustle of this large but cozy saloon with its polished wood, brass, and gaslights. It's easy to keep your tab in the budget range with something from the raw bar, a sandwich or hamburger, or a sumptuous dessert—how about a hot fudge sundae made with homemade vanilla ice cream or a chocolate brioche bread pudding topped with vanilla sauce, fresh whipped cream, and pecan-praline crumble.

PAN ASIAN NOODLES & GRILL, 1018 Vermont Ave. NW, between 14th and 15th streets. Tel. 783-8899.

Cuisine: EAST ASIAN. **Metro:** McPherson Square. **Reservations:** For large groups.

$ **Prices:** Entrees $5.95–$8.95. AE, MC, V.

Open: Lunch 11:30am–2:30pm; dinner 5–8pm.

Because it's very good and very reasonable, Pan Asian is also very crowded, especially at lunchtime. Go early or late for a quick, inexpensive meal of soup (the wonton is especially worthwhile), noodles, and grilled dishes derived from various Asian cuisines, real and imagined. Service is as crisp as a fried noodle.

There's another branch at 2020 P St. NW (**Metro:** Dupont Circle).

BUDGET

AMERICAN CAFÉ, The Shops at National Place, 1331 Pennsylvania Ave. NW. Tel. 626-0770.

Cuisine: AMERICAN. **Metro:** Metro Center.

$ **Prices:** Entrees $5.95–$9.95.

Children's Services: Highchairs, boosters, children's menu.

Behind the regular sit-down portion of the restaurant (see the listing in the "Capitol Hill" listings above) lies the Market Express (open Mon–Fri 7:30am–9pm, Sat–Sun 8:30am–9pm), where you can eat in or take out sandwiches, salads, and several entrees.

A.V., 607 New York Ave. NW. Tel. 737-0550.
    Cuisine: ITALIAN. **Reservations:** For 10 or more only. **Metro:** Gallery Place or Judiciary Square.
$ **Prices:** Appetizers $2–$7.50; entrees $5–$15. AE, CB, D, DC, MC, V.
    Open: Mon–Thurs 11:30am–11pm, Fri 11:30am–midnight, Sat 5pm–midnight.
    Closed: Sun.
    Children's Services: Highchairs, boosters.
A.V. has spawned a host of other trattorias in the area since sliding its first pizza from the oven 42 years ago. It still reigns supreme, however, when it comes to large servings of pasta smothered with no-nonsense sauces—a single portion enough for two in most cases. New Yorkers, native and otherwise, brighten to find their style of pizza, which is among the best anywhere south of the Mason–Dixon Line. If you avoid the sometimes pricey daily specials, you can eat like a Corleone for under $10.

FOOD COURT AT THE OLD POST OFFICE PAVILION, 1100 Pennsylvania Ave. NW. Tel. 289-4224.
    Cuisine: FAST FOOD. **Metro:** Federal Triangle.
$ **Prices:** $1.50–$7. No credit cards.
    Open: Hours change, so call ahead.
If you're sightseeing along Pennsylvania or Constitution avenues, duck in here for a quick meal or a snack. You'll find everything from Indian and Asian fare to burgers and fries. For a tasty treat, try the spicy chicken wings with celery sticks and blue-cheese dip at Wingmaster's. The kids are sure to find their own favorites.

FOOD HALL AT THE SHOPS AT NATIONAL PLACE, 1331 Pennsylvania Ave. NW (enter on Pennsylvania Avenue or F Street). Tel. 783-9090.
    Cuisine: ETHNIC FAST FOOD. **Metro:** Federal Triangle or Metro Center.
$ **Prices:** $1–$6. No credit cards.
    Open: Daily; call for new hours.
Nibble your way through the 18 stands selling ethnic food, pizza, subs, potatoes, yogurt, hot dogs, deli, cookies, and ice cream. There's plenty of seating, but you'll have to improvise a booster seat. Nobody calls this fine dining (except the kids), but it's not bad, and it's quick and cheap. Groups of 15 or more should call for information on discount group meal programs.

HARD ROCK CAFÉ, 999 E St. NW, next to Ford's Theatre. Tel. 737-ROCK.
    Cuisine: AMERICAN. **Reservations:** Not accepted. **Metro:** Metro Center.
$ **Prices:** Entrees $5.95–$12.95. AE, MC, V.
    Open: Sun–Thurs 11am–midnight, Fri–Sat 11am–1am.
    Children's Services: Highchairs, boosters.
Let the good times roll as you ogle a Michael Jackson costume with rhinestone kneepad, autographed Stones photo, and Chuck Berry's guitar. Stick to the basics: burgers, french fries, and chicken salads. The pulled pork should have been left on the pig, but don't miss the strawberry shortcake or hot fudge brownie sundae—they'll

make you feel like dancin'. Go at off-times unless you or yours don't mind standing in line.

PHILADELPHIA MIKE'S, 605 12th St. NW. Tel. 737-5326; 1426 L St. NW. Tel. 638-1390.
   Cuisine: AMERICAN. **Reservations:** Not accepted. **Metro:** Metro Center (12th Street location); McPherson Square (L Street location).
$ **Prices:** Sandwiches $2.19–$6.99. No credit cards.
   Open: Mon–Sat 11am–8pm. L Street location is closed on Saturday.

You won't mind ordering at the counter or sharing a table with strangers because Philadelphia Mike's makes the best cheese steak sandwich (on marvelous house-baked bread) this side of South Philly. Try one of the variations on a theme, but don't ruin it with mayonnaise.

Besides these two downtown locations, there's a branch in Bethesda, Maryland (check the phone directory and call for particulars).

SHOLL'S COLONIAL CAFETERIA, 1990 K St. NW, in the Esplanade Mall. Tel. 296-3065.
   Cuisine: AMERICAN. **Reservations:** Not accepted. **Metro:** Farragut West.
$ **Prices:** Appetizers 75¢–85¢; entrees $1.60–$4.95. No credit cards.
   Open: Breakfast Mon–Sat 7–10:30am; lunch Mon–Sat 11am–2:30pm; dinner Mon–Sat 4–8pm.
   Children's Services: Boosters.

S A Washington institution since 1928, Sholl's still dishes out freshly prepared quality vittles at low, low prices. Load your tray with a full breakfast (two eggs, bacon, home fries, juice, coffee or milk, and fresh baked biscuits) for less than $5. At lunch and dinner the hot meals cost less than $5. How about a dinner of roast beef, mashed potatoes, broccoli, coconut cream pie, and coffee or milk for $4.95? And the homemade pies and cakes are definitely a cut above average. Sholl's motto is "Live well for less money with quality food at reasonable prices." A great motto for families.

SKY TERRACE, Hotel Washington, 15th Street and Pennsylvania Avenue NW. Tel. 638-5900.
   Cuisine: LIGHT FARE. **Reservations:** Not accepted. **Metro:** Metro Center.
$ **Prices:** $5–$10. AE, DC, MC, V.
   Open: Mid-May–Oct 11:30am–1am.

Go anytime to graze on a sandwich, cheese and fruit, or dessert or to enjoy drinks on this very special rooftop. The extraordinary view of downtown and the environs is feast enough for most souls. You can almost touch the planes landing and taking off from National Airport. See how many buildings your kids can identify.

SZECHUAN, 615 I St. NW. Tel. 393-0130.
   Cuisine: CHINESE. **Reservations:** For 4 or more. **Metro:** Gallery Place.
$ **Prices:** Lunch $5.95–$8.95; dinner $5.45–$17.95. AE, MC, V.
   Open: Mon–Thurs 11am–11pm, Fri–Sat 11am–midnight, Sun 11am–10pm.
   Children's Services: Highchairs, boosters.

 The food has slipped a bit over the years, but the dim sum brunch on Saturday and Sunday from 11am to 2:30pm is still a respected and well-attended family tradition. Wait till your kids see the endless procession of carts rolling by laden with lots of good things to eat. Even the fussiest eater in your party will find something to savor.

DUPONT CIRCLE

VERY EXPENSIVE/EXPENSIVE

JOCKEY CLUB, Ritz-Carlton Hotel, 2100 Massachusetts Ave. NW. Tel. 659-8000.
   Cuisine: CONTINENTAL. **Reservations:** A must. **Metro:** Dupont Circle.
$ **Prices:** Entrees $15–$25 lunch, $25–$35 dinner. AE, CB, D, DC, MC, V.
   Open: Daily breakfast 6:30–11am; lunch noon–2:30pm; dinner 6–10:30pm; Sunday brunch noon–2:30pm.
   Children's Services: Highchairs, boosters, children's menu.

An in-spot with Washington politicoes and powerbrokers for 30 years, this elegantly clubby (as in old money) establishment wants the world to know that junior powerbrokers are welcome too. A kids' menu, in the form of a coloring book, lists hamburgers, chicken, spaghetti, and even peanut butter sandwiches. More mature appetites will want to sample one of the fish or veal entrees or outstanding crabcakes. Service is always special at the Jockey Club, even if you are not. On holidays there's a children's buffet and around Christmas a "Nutcracker" brunch.

MODERATE

EL BODEGON, 1637 R St. NW. Tel. 667-1710.
   Cuisine: SPANISH. **Reservations:** Recommended. **Metro:** Dupont Circle.
$ **Prices:** Tapas (appetizers) $3–$7 lunch, $6–$18 dinner; entrees $7–$13 lunch, $15–$30 dinner. AE, MC, V.
   Open: Lunch Mon–Fri 11:30am–2:30pm; dinner Mon–Thurs 5:30–10:30pm, Fri–Sat 5:30–11pm; closed Sun.

Maybe it is touristy. Who cares? It's festive, fun, and your family will love it. The tapas—tasty little hors d'oeuvres español—make a meal for hungry muchachos. At dinner, strolling guitarists and flamenco dancers do their respective things while waiters with goatskin porrons pour wine down the faces and into the mouths of customers over 21. Kids over 5 are welcome.

OTELLO, 1329 Connecticut Ave. NW. Tel. 429-0209.
   Cuisine: ITALIAN. **Reservations:** Accepted. **Metro:** Dupont Circle.
$ **Prices:** Lunch $7.75–$9.50; dinner $9.50–$11.50. AE, DC, MC, V.
   Open: Lunch Mon–Fri noon–2:30pm, dinner Mon–Sat 5:30–10:30pm; closed Sun.

Otello is a friendly, family-operated neighborhood trattoria, more typical of those found in New York than D.C. The flavorful sauces pack the right amount of punch, and the seafood and veal dishes are as fine as you'll find south of Little Italy. Not suitable for bambinos under 8.

BUDGET

BRICKSKELLER, 1523 22nd St. NW. Tel. 293-1885.
   Cuisine: AMERICAN. **Reservations:** Not accepted. **Metro:** Dupont Circle.

$ Prices: $4–$15. AE, D, MC, V.

Open: Mon–Thurs 11:30am–2am, Fri 11:30am–3am; Sat 6pm–3am, Sun 6pm–2am.

Children's Services: Boosters.

Pub fare is served in a tastefully tacky setting accessorized with dart boards, backgammon, and video games. More than 500 kinds of beer and an oldies-filled jukebox will nurture your nostalgia trip while the kids play electronic games and munch on chicken wings, burgers (regular and buffalo), and other light fare.

CRÊPE À LA CARTE, 1304 18th St. NW. Tel. 223-3300.

Cuisine: FRENCH. **Reservations:** Not accepted. **Metro:** Farragut North.

$ Prices: $1.35–$6.95. No credit cards.

Open: Mon–Fri 7:30am–7pm, Sat 10am–6pm, Sun 10am–3pm.

Kids like to watch their food being prepared right before their eyes, just like at home. You fix crêpes at home? In this tiny Moulin Rouge-ish café, choose from 10 "healthy" and 13 sweet fillings, as well as quiches, pâtés, *croque monsieurs,* and a Gallic hot dog with Dijon mustard on a baguette. Indoor space is tight, but on nice days tables are set up outside. **Good news:** In spring '91 the owners opened a full-service, bistro-style restaurant at 1301 Connecticut Ave. NW (behind the crêperie), where you can order the same delicious crêpes as well as several examples of country French cooking. Kids are welcome.

KRAMERBOOKS & AFTERWORDS CAFE, 1517 Connecticut Ave. NW, between Dupont Circle and Q Street. Tel. 387-1462.

Cuisine: AMERICAN. **Metro:** Dupont Circle.

$ Prices: Breakfast $1.75–$8.50; appetizers $3.50–$6.75; entrees $5.95–$11.75. AE, MC, V.

Open: Mon–Thurs 8am–1am; continuously from Fri 8am to Sun 1am.

After browsing at Kramerbooks, stop for a meal or snack at Afterwords, where the atmosphere is as close to Greenwich Village in its heyday as Washington allows itself to get. Try the quesadilla or bagels with smoked salmon and cream cheese at breakfast. The o.j. is fresh squeezed. At other times you'll find everything from salads, sandwiches, and fettuccine to calorie-packed desserts like sour cream blackout cake and banana splits. Grownups could indulge in margaritas ($17.50 for a huge pitcherful) while the kids enjoy ice cream treats.

GEORGETOWN/FOGGY BOTTOM

Georgetown is one of Washington's most-visited tourist areas, hence there are quite a few restaurants here. The Metro does not run into Georgetown, however, but you can take Friendship Heights buses (no. 30, 32, 34, and 36) from Pennsylvania Avenue to any point in Georgetown. If you are dining in Georgetown or Foggy Bottom, the closest Metro stop is the Foggy Bottom station.

VERY EXPENSIVE/EXPENSIVE

MORTON'S OF CHICAGO, 3251 Prospect St. NW, just off Wisconsin Avenue. Tel. 342-6258.

Cuisine: AMERICAN. **Reservations:** Recommended.

$ Prices: Entrees $14.95–$25.95. AE, CB, DC, MC, V.

Open: Mon–Sat 5:30–11pm, Sun 5–10pm. **Closed:** Most major holidays. Come here for the best steak in town, maybe in the world. While some Morton's fans prefer the veal chop or oversized lobsters, I say stick with the steak and side orders of hash-browns and fresh vegetables—enough for two or three servings. Well-mannered kids over 10 with healthy appetites are welcome. Check out the permanent collection of Leroy Neiman paintings.

There's a second Morton's branch in Tysons Corner, Virginia (tel. 703/883-0800). For complete details, see the entry in the "Virginia" section, later on in this chapter.

SEA CATCH, Canal Square, 1054 31st St. NW, at M Street. Tel. 337-8855.

Cuisine: SEAFOOD. **Reservations:** Recommended.

$ Prices: Entrees $13–$20 lunch, $15–$25 dinner. AE, CB, DC, MC, V.

Open: Daily 11:30am–5pm lunch; 5–11pm dinner.

Children's Services: Highchairs.

When you're in the mood to linger over a lovingly prepared seafood dinner, reserve a canal-side table at this attractive stone-and-brick restaurant, once a warehouse for goods transported on the C&O Canal. Pop some oysters or clams at the 40-foot marble raw bar to whet your appetite for seasonal specialties like Dover sole, softshell crabs, crab cakes, or lobster. Or try the sushi bar. Key lime pie or cheesecake are fitting finales. A jazz duo plays during dinner, Tuesday through Saturday. Well-behaved kids over 7 are welcome. There's free valet parking.

MODERATE

ENRIQUETA'S, 2811 M St. NW. Tel. 338-7772.

Cuisine: MEXICAN. **Reservations:** For 6 or more.

$ Prices: Entrees $6–$15. AE, MC, V.

Open: Lunch Mon–Thurs 11:30am–2:30pm; dinner Mon–Thurs 5–10pm, Fri–Sat 5–11pm, Sun 5–10pm.

Children's Services: Boosters.

The service is quick (some say too quick), the food is consistent and authentic (if undistinguished), and reasonable in this closet-sized cantina tucked between Georgetown and Foggy Bottom. Kids like it *con mucho gusto*. Stay away if you have a disk problem or hemorrhoids—the hard-backed chairs are unmerciful.

FILOMENA'S, 1063 Wisconsin Ave. NW, below M Street. Tel. 338-8800.

Cuisine: ITALIAN. **Reservations:** Recommended.

$ Prices: Lunch entrees $4.50–$11.95; dinner entrees $10.95–$31.95.

Open: Wed–Sat 11:30am–11:30pm; Mon–Tues 5–11:30pm; Sun brunch 11am–3pm, dinner 3–11:30pm. **Closed:** Jan 1, July 4, Dec 24–25.

Children's Services: Highchairs.

Even with a reservation, on Friday and Saturday nights you may have to wait, so eat early or go on a weeknight. Filomena's is fun and serves delicious pasta (made daily on the premises) with a variety of interesting sauces. For a real treat, try the lobster-laden Cardinale-sauced pasta, and don't bypass the bread. Two kids can share a portion of pasta while enjoying the Italian garden-like atmosphere. Everybody's friendly and it's not unusual to hear your neighbor's life story before the espresso arrives. Don't miss the home-baked desserts.

GARRETT'S, 3003 M St. NW. Tel. 333-8282.

Cuisine: AMERICAN. **Reservations:** Accepted.

$ Prices: Entrees $6–$8 lunch, $9–$15 dinner; appetizers $3.50–$4.95; sandwiches $4.75–$7.75. AE, CB, DC, MC, V.

Open: Lunch Mon–Fri 11:30am–2:30pm; dinner daily 6–10:30pm.

Children's Services: Boosters.

Shhhhhh! If you like Garrett's, please don't tell anyone else. Bypass the noisy bar scene downstairs for a table on the charming enclosed second-floor terrace. Nice, huh? Kids can make a meal out of the nachos appetizer or a quesadilla. The burgers are generous and juicy, the roast beef sandwich lean and tasty. Check out the seafood chowder and grilled shrimp at this casual eatery.

PAOLO'S, 1303 Wisconsin Ave. NW, between N and Dumbarton streets. Tel. 333-7353.

Cuisine: ITALIAN (CALIFORNIAN-STYLE). **Reservations:** Not accepted.

$ Prices: Lunch $5.95–$12.95, dinner $7.95–$18.95; Sunday brunch $5.95–$8.95.

Open: Mon–Sat 11:30am–midnight; Sun 11am–midnight (brunch 11am–4pm).

Children's Services: Highchairs, boosters, sassy seats.

Paolo's is not just another pretty face on the restaurant scene, but it is a looker. After devouring the crisp breadsticks, try the pastas, pizzas, or a salad—all well-prepared and attractively served. My friend Ellen, the chicken expert, raves about the roasted capon. Since Paolo's is a current hot spot, try it at off times. The kitchen will split orders for children.

There are Paolo branches in Rockville, Maryland; Reston, Virginia, and at Baltimore's Inner Harbor—check them out if you are in the neighborhood.

BUDGET

AUSTIN GRILL, 2404 Wisconsin Ave., south of Calvert Street. Tel. 337-8080.

Cuisine: TEX-MEX. **Reservations:** Not accepted.

$ Prices: $5.25–$11.95. AE, M, V.

Open: Mon 5:30–11pm, Tues–Thurs 11:30am–11pm, Fri–Sat 11:30am–midnight; Sun 11:30am–10:30pm.

Children's Services: Highchairs, boosters.

Since the Austin Grill is just north of Georgetown in Glover Park, you'll have to walk, drive, or take a bus up Wisconsin Avenue for the good, inexpensive Tex-Mex fare served in a totally unpretentious setting. There's no kids' menu here, but children's portions are available. Things can get lively—some would venture to say boisterous—with the mostly under-30 crowd. The kids will love it, but you may end up with a headache.

When in Alexandria, Virginia, visit the **South Austin Grill** at 801 King St. (tel. 703/684-8969).

BOOGIE'S DINER, 1229 Wisconsin Ave. NW. Tel. 298-6060.

Cuisine: AMERICAN. **Reservations:** Not accepted.

$ Prices: $4.50–$7.95. AE, D, MC, V.

Open: Sun–Thurs 11:30am–11pm, Fri–Sat 11:30am–1am.

Children's Services: Highchairs, boosters.

"Eat heavy, dress cool" is Boogie's motto. Not bad words to live by. Inspired by a character in Barry Levinson's movie "Diner," Boogie's is a clothing store downstairs, a booth-filled eatery upstairs. Oldies fill the air as diners enjoy potato skins, burgers, soups, sandwiches, chili, or meatloaf with mashed potatoes and gravy. Save room for dessert. Besides several fountain creations, there's an 8-inch-high chocolate layer cake (I measured it!). Boogie on down. The kids will love it here.

CLYDE'S, 3236 M St. NW. Tel. 333-9180.

Cuisine: AMERICAN. **Reservations:** Strongly suggested.

$ Prices: Bar food and lunch $6–$10; dinner entrees $12–$20. AE, CB, DC, MC, V.

Open: Mon–Thurs 11am–2am, Fri 11am–3am, Sat 9am–3am, Sun 9am–2am.

Children's Services: Highchairs, boosters.

The granddaddy of Georgetown saloons, Clyde's has been SRO since opening in 1963. Have brunch in the sunny Omelette Room or head for the bright and breezy Patio Room for a burger, sandwich, salad, or something more substantial. Don't miss the cottage fries (ask for them well done). Stay out of the bar area if you bring the kids—or if you want to retain your hearing and sanity. The 4-to-7pm "Afternoon Delights" snack menu inspired the Starland Vocal Band to write their hit song. Look for the gold record in the Patio Room.

GEPPETTO, 2917 M St. NW. Tel. 333-2602.

Cuisine: PIZZA. **Reservations:** Not accepted.

$ Prices: Pies $7.45–$23.25. AE, DC, MC.

Open: Mon–Thurs noon–11:30pm, Fri–Sat noon–1:30am, Sun 4–11:30pm.

Children's Services: Boosters.

Some pizza mavens grow dewy-eyed describing the white pizza, loaded with garlic, onion, and fontina cheese. Others engage in heated discussions over the merits of the deep-dish versus regular crust variety. Life is not easy. Kids like the decorative cuckoo clocks and puppets almost as much as the food. The restaurant is not much larger than a pizza itself, so you may want to eat your pie in the comfort of your hotel room, or down by the C & O Canal.

You'll find a Geppetto branch in Bethesda, Maryland, as well.

HAMBURGER HAMLET, 3125 M St. NW. Tel. 965-6970.

Cuisine: AMERICAN. **Reservations:** Accepted for large parties only.

$ Prices: $1.95–$12.95. AE, CB, D, DC, MC.

Open: Sun–Thurs 11am–1am, Fri–Sat 11am–3pm.

Children's Services: Highchairs, boosters, children's menu.

It's kind of pricey for glorified fast food, the kitchen is erratic, the hamburgers rarely come out cooked as ordered, and the service can be very slow. So why does everyone keep coming back for more? Beats me. But it's still a good place for kids, who amuse themselves with the restaurant-supplied crayons and are less fussy than their parents. Stick to the burgers (maybe you'll hit the jackpot and get one medium-rare), Zucchini Zircles, chicken wings, fries, and shakes.

There's another Hamlet branch at 5225 Wisconsin Ave. NW, and one at 10400 Old Georgetown Rd. in Bethesda, Maryland.

HOUSTON'S, 1065 Wisconsin Ave. NW, below M Street. Tel. 338-7760.

Cuisine: AMERICAN. **Reservations:** Not accepted.

$ Prices: Appetizers $1.25–$6.45; most entrees $6.25–$17.95. AE, MC, V.
Open: Sun–Thurs 11:15am–11pm; Fri–Sat 11:15 am–1am.
Children's Services: Highchairs, boosters.

★ Absolutely and positively, Houston's serves the best hickory-grilled hamburgers in Washington. You could die waiting for a table, but it's worth it. When the line is long (at peak lunch and dinner hours), put your name on the list and walk around Georgetown; or solve the problem by eating early or late. The ribs and salads are outstanding, washed down with a no-cal (just kidding!) extra-thick chocolate milkshake. Portions are large enough for little ones to share. This attractive restaurant is part of a chain extending from Atlanta to Phoenix to Chicago. Its popularity is easily understood: Houston's ambience is simpático (kids love it here) and the food is fresh and first quality.

T.G.I. FRIDAY'S, 2100 Pennsylvania Ave. NW, entrance on 21st Street at I Street. Tel. 872-4344.
Cuisine: AMERICAN. **Reservations:** Accepted for 10 or more.
$ Prices: $5.75–$13; kids' menu $1.95–$2.75 AE, D, DC, MC, V.
Open: Sun–Tues 11am–midnight, Wed–Sat 11am–2am.
Children's Services: Highchairs, boosters, children's menu.

★ A welcome addition to Foggy Bottom on the campus of George Washington University, Friday's is a family-friendly link in the popular national chain. The servers are enthusiastic and young (you remember young?) and the place looks like a before picture of a garage sale with Tiffany lamps, hanging plants, antiques, and photos *everywhere.* Those 12 and under can choose from standbys like grilled cheese, hamburgers, and hot dogs on the kids' menu. The grownups' menu is 10 pages long. Try any of the chicken dishes (I wish they'd call chicken fingers something else) or one of the enormous salads or sandwiches. Save room for the mocha mud pie. Try Friday's any day of the week, including the branches in Maryland and Virginia as well.

ADAMS-MORGAN

Note: Parking is next to impossible in the Adams-Morgan area, especially on weekends, and the nearest Metro stop is a hefty walk. Take a taxi, and enjoy the many ethnic eateries.

MODERATE

I MATTI, 2436 18th St. NW. Tel. 462-8844.
Cuisine: ITALIAN. **Reservations:** Recommended. **Metro:** Woodley Park-Zoo (area not safe after dark—recommend taking a taxi)
$ Prices: Entrees $7.95–$13.95. AE, DC, MC, V.
Open: Lunch Mon–Fri noon–2:30pm, Sat noon–4:30pm; Sun brunch 11:30am–3pm; dinner Mon–Thurs 6–10:30pm, Fri–Sat 6–11pm plus light menu after 11pm, Sun 5:30–9:30pm.

Head for the second, quieter floor at this popular trattoria, where the lines may lead you to believe they're giving the pizza away. Best choices are pasta, pizza, and fish. Don't miss the polenta. It comes with most entrees, but can also be ordered as a side dish. The breads are outstanding, especially the crusty, salt-topped variety. Some kids make a meal of the mixed antipasto. If you know what's good for you, stay away on Saturday nights.

BUDGET

ADAMS MORGAN SPAGHETTI GARDEN, 2317 18th St. NW, near Columbia Road. Tel. 265-6665.

Cuisine: ITALIAN. **Reservations:** Recommended. **Metro:** Woodley Park-Zoo.
$ Prices: Appetizers $1.95–$4.75, pasta entrees $4.75–$7.25, meat entrees $7.45–$11.95; children's spaghetti portions $2.95.
Open: Mon–Thurs noon–midnight, Fri–Sat noon–1am, Sun noon–11pm.
Closed: Thanksgiving, Dec 25, Jan 1.
Children's Services: Highchairs, boosters.

The Garden is a family favorite known for its zesty Italian cooking and homey atmosphere. All ages are welcome. Don't try anything too ambitious, but stick to hearty, generously sauced, cooked-to-order pasta standbys like spaghetti, ravioli, and lasagna (rich in meat, ricotta, and mozzarella, light on noodles—an award-winner). And what's an Italian meal without garlic bread—here topped with crushed red peppers and freshly minced garlic. Children's portions of spaghetti are available for $2.95.

EL POLLO PRIMO, 2471 18th St. NW. Tel. 232-5151.

Cuisine: CHICKEN. **Reservations:** Not accepted. **Metro:** Woodley Park-Zoo.
$ Prices: $3.30–$18.25 (20 pieces). No credit cards.
Open: Mon–Fri 11am–9pm, Sat–Sun 11am–10pm.

The chicken at this no-frills eat-in, carry-out establishment is marinated before grilling, and the results are skin that is crispy and meat that is moist and lip-smacking good. Side dishes of Mexican rice, corn on the cob, potato salad, and cole slaw are nice complements, and prices are cheap, cheap, cheap.

There are branches also in Langley Park and Rockville, Maryland. Check the phone book for locations.

RED SEA, 2463 18th St. NW, near Columbia Road. Tel. 483-5000.

Cuisine: ETHIOPIAN. **Reservations:** Recommended. **Metro:** Woodley Park-Zoo.
$ Prices: Appetizers $1.50–$2.95; entrees $5–$9.75. AE, MC, V.
Open: Sun–Thurs 11:30am–midnight, Fri–Sat 11:30am–2am.
Children's Services: Highchairs, boosters.

Select an Ethiopian tune from the jukebox to get in the proper mood, and roll up your sleeves, as your silverware is dangling at the ends of your arms. You'd probably yell if your kids ate like this at home, and that's why they'll love scooping up the stew-like entrees with pieces of *injera* (spongy pancakelike Ethiopian bread made with wheat, buckwheat, and flour). One of the sampler platters will amply feed two little ones. A word of caution: *wat* items are hot and spicy, *alecha* dishes are milder.

THAI 89, 2427 18th St. NW. Tel. 232-8989.

Cuisine: THAI. **Reservations:** Accepted for 6 or more. **Metro:** Woodley Park-Zoo.
$ Prices: Entrees $6.95–$10.95. AE, MC, V.

Open: Sun–Thurs 5–10pm, Fri–Sat 5–11pm.

Here's an example of a child doing its parent proud. Thai 89 was spawned by Pan Asian Noodles and Grill in 1990, and the whole family is flourishing. Your own offspring will have a field day with the crispy fried tofu, steamed rolls (not unlike dim sum), and spicy grilled chicken strips from the appetizer menu. You'll find the pud thai—a mélange of rice noodles, shrimp, and vegetables—subtler in flavor than some of the peppery chicken, beef, and shrimp dishes. Try the flan for dessert. It's as smooth as silk.

UPPER NORTHWEST

EXPENSIVE

PLEASANT PEASANT, Mazza Gallerie, 5300 Wisconsin Ave. NW, main entrance on Jenifer Street. Tel. 364-2500.
    Cuisine: AMERICAN. **Reservations:** Accepted for 8 or more. **Metro:** Friendship Heights.
$ Prices: Entrees $4.95–$9.50 lunch, $9.95–$24.95 dinner. AE, CB, MC, V.
    Open: Lunch daily 11:30am–3pm; dinner Sun–Thurs 5:30–11pm, Fri–Sat 5:30–midnight.
    Children's Services: Boosters.

Bring older children (this is no place for infants and toddlers) to the Pleasant Peasant when you're celebrating a special event or you've had it up to here with fast food. Light fare is served in a café setting downstairs, accompanied by piano music. In the upstairs dining room, smartly done in black and white, choose from the entrees chalked on your menu board. We haven't hit a loser yet. Younger family members, intimidated by so much food, may be better served by ordering an appetizer and/or soup to go with the complimentary warm fried bread and poppyseed herb butter. Save room for some of the best desserts in the city. The Chocolate Intemperance is heaven. Valet parking.

MODERATE

TANDOOR, 2623 Connecticut Ave. NW, at Calvert Street. Tel. 483-1115.
    Cuisine: INDIAN. **Reservations:** Accepted. **Metro:** Woodley Park-Zoo.
$ Prices: Entrees $5.50–$8 lunch, $6.95–$12 dinner. AE, MC, V.
    Open: Daily 11:30am–2:30pm and 5:30–11pm.
    Children's Services: Boosters.

Delicious tandoori chicken is prepared in a charcoal-fired clay oven. The curries, vegetarian dishes, and wonderful breads all merit attention at the area's oldest Indian restaurant. Most kids like the samosas (delectable pastry wrappers filled with a variety of meat and vegetable combinations—sort of an Indian eggroll) and pakoras (batter-dipped vegetable fritters). There are Tandoor branches in Georgetown; Rockville, Maryland; and Alexandria, Virginia, as well.

THAI TASTE, 2606 Connecticut Ave. NW, at Calvert Street. Tel. 387-8876.
    Cuisine: THAI. **Reservations:** Not accepted on Fri or Sat. **Metro:** Woodley Park-Zoo.

$ Prices: Appetizers $4.25–$6.95; entrees $6.50–$14.95. AE, CB, DC, MC, V.
Open: Mon–Thurs 11:30am–10:30pm, Fri–Sat 11:30am–11pm, Sun 5–10:30pm.
Children's Services: Highchairs, boosters.

If your innards are heat-sensitive, ask your server to recommend some of the milder dishes. Younger children can feast on appetizers, like barbecued pork in peanut sauce and spring rolls, while you try the coconut chicken soup and make up your mind from among the many fish, chicken, and pork entrees. If you don't mind bus fumes, there's sidewalk dining in nice weather.

There's a Thai Taste branch in Rockville, Maryland; check the telephone directory for specifics.

BUDGET

CHADWICK'S, 5247 Wisconsin Ave. NW, at Jenifer Street. Tel. 362-8040.
Cuisine: AMERICAN. **Reservations:** Not accepted. **Metro:** Friendship Heights.
$ Prices: Entrees $4.95–$7.95 lunch, $4.95–$11.95 dinner; children's menu. AE, CB, DC, MC, V.
Open: Lunch Mon–Sat 11:30am–4pm, Sun brunch 10am–4pm; dinner Sun–Thurs 4pm–midnight, Fri–Sat 4pm–1am.
Children's Services: Highchairs, boosters, children's menu.

Going to Chadwick's is like visiting an old friend. Kids get balloons, crayons, and their own menu, and the service is friendly and prompt. The hamburgers and sandwiches are ample and tasty, and Sunday brunch is a bargain.

If you're visiting Georgetown or Alexandria, Virginia, look for Chadwick's too.

CHEESECAKE FACTORY, 5345 Wisconsin Ave. NW. Tel. 364-0500.
Cuisine: AMERICAN. **Metro:** Friendship Heights.
$ Prices: Entrees $5.95–$15.95. AE, MC, V.
Open: Sun–Thurs 11:30am–11:30pm, Fri–Sat 11:30am–12:30am.
Children's Services: Highchairs, boosters.

The California-based Cheesecake Factory blew in like a Santa Ana, and judging by the lines this is no ill wind. The first-class french fries are crunchy and greaseless, the salads and chicken dishes tasty though humongous (two kids could easily share one portion). The extensive menu is worth framing. Some complain about the noise and the wait. I can't say it often enough: Go early, especially with easily tired young'uns. Don't forget to try at least one of the 35 kinds of cheesecake.

EL TAMARINDO, 4910 Wisconsin Ave., NW, at 42nd Street. Tel. 244-8888.
Cuisine: SALVADORAN. **Metro:** Tenleytown.
$ Prices: Entrees $5.25–$8.95. CB, DC, MC, V.
Open: Daily 11am–2am.
Children's Services: Highchairs, boosters.

S Weather permitting, eat on the patio at this friendly neighborhood spot whose specialty is chicken, beef, or shrimp fajitas. Those in the know say the dishes are authentically prepared. All I know is everything tastes good, the kids like the place, and the prices are ridiculously low. The congenial atmosphere is gratis.

HAMBURGER HAMLET, 5225 Wisconsin Ave. NW, at Jenifer Street. Tel. 244-2037.

For complete details, see Georgetown listing above.

Children's Services: Highchairs, boosters, children's menu.

ZEBRA ROOM, 3238 Wisconsin Ave. NW. Tel. 362-8307.

Cuisine: PIZZA/PASTA. **Reservations:** Accepted for 6 or more. **Metro:** Tenleytown, then take any 30 bus.

$ Prices: Pizza $5–$34 (36″ special!) MC, V.

Open: Daily 8:30am–11:30pm.

Children's Services: Boosters, child's portion.

Families have been flocking here since 1955 for one thing, and one thing only: Pizza. Eat it plain, dress it up with one or more toppings, or splurge on the "Royal" with the works. The spaghetti and burgers aren't bad, but you can get those anyplace. Tuesday and Thursday evenings are half-price nights. Translation: You get two pizzas for the price of one. Now, aren't you glad you came to Washington? Take your hungry kids and queue up early. In good weather, sit outside and listen to the traffic.

SUBURBAN MARYLAND

Years ago if you lived in or visited the suburbs and wanted a decent meal, you had to venture downtown. Now there are so many good restaurants ringing the Beltway that most diners are content—as well they should be—to stay put. Here are a few (my editor will holler if I list too many) of Maryland's many family-friendly restaurants.

EXPENSIVE

THE RESTAURANT, 7820 Norfolk Ave., Bethesda. Tel. 301/657-1607.

Cuisine: FRENCH. **Reservations:** Recommended. **Metro:** Bethesda.

$ Prices: Entrees $5.50–$12.95 lunch, $13.95–$20.95 dinner. Tuesday kids' menu $12.95. AE, MC, V.

Open: Lunch Mon–Fri 11:30am–2pm; dinner Mon–Sat 5:30–10pm, Sun 5:30–9pm.

Children's Services: Boosters.

Youngsters can brush up on their manners and sample fine French cuisine on Tuesday evenings when The Restaurant offers a special fixed-price menu for kids 6 and over that includes mini-portions of some of The Restaurant's outstanding appetizers and entrees. The rack of lamb and crabmeat-stuffed salmon in phyllo are prizewinners. Part of Tuesday night's proceeds are donated to the National Institutes of Health's Children's Inn, which houses children being treated at NIH.

MODERATE

CRISFIELD, 8012 Georgia Ave., Silver Spring. Tel. 301/589-1306.

Cuisine: SEAFOOD. **Reservations:** Not accepted. **Metro:** Silver Spring.

$ Prices: Entrees $4–$12 lunch, $11.50–$39 dinner; kids' (under 12) platters $8. No credit cards.

Open: Tues–Thurs 11am–10pm, Fri–Sat 11am–10:30pm, Sun noon–9pm.

Closed: Mon.

Children's Services: Highchairs, boosters, children's menu.

The decor may be early restroom, but don't let the cinderblock turn you off. Crisfield's serves some of the freshest seafood west of the Chesapeake Bay. Try the crab imperial, crab cakes, or baked stuffed fish or shrimp. The sinfully rich and delicious seafood bisque of shrimp, lobster, and crabmeat in a tomato-cream base is a steal at $5.50. Kids under 12 can order a crab cake, fried shrimp, or fried chicken platter for $8. Avoid dinnertime on weekends or go early. No arguing that the menu is larger (and includes beef) and the digs are fancier at the 8606 Colesville Rd. location, but that branch lacks the charm of the original.

FOONG LIN, 7710 Norfolk Ave., Bethesda. Tel. 301/656-3427.

Cuisine: CHINESE. **Reservations:** Accepted. **Metro:** Bethesda.

$ **Prices:** Lunch $4.50–$7.50, dinner $6.50–$17.95. AE, MC, V.

Open: Sun–Thurs 11am–10pm, Fri–Sat 11am–11pm. **Closed:** Thanksgiving

Children's Services: Highchairs, boosters.

This family-oriented neighborhood restaurant has a staff of friendly waiters who are especially kind and considerate to kids. Foong Lin turns out a host of above-average Cantonese, Hunan, and Szechuan favorites, and the crispy whole fish is exceptional (see if you can talk the kids into trying it). What more do you want? Guaranteed good news in your fortune cookie?

FUDDRUCKER'S, 1300 Rockville Pike, Rockville. Tel. 301/468-3501.

Cuisine: AMERICAN. **Reservations:** Not accepted. **Metro:** Twinbrook.

$ **Prices:** $3–$6.25. AE, MC, V.

Open: Sun–Thurs 11am–10pm, Sat–Sun 11am–11pm.

Children's Services: Highchairs, boosters.

It's strictly self-service, appropriately noisy, and almost always crowded; but the burgers are yummy and actually grilled to the degree you desire, the lines move quickly, and kids 12 and under eat free after 4pm. Can you beat that? The kids'll have fun drowning their burgers with all the toppings. The taco salad is tasty and filling; hot dogs and desserts are only so-so.

HOUSTON'S, 12256 Rockville Pike, Rockville. Tel. 301/468-3535.

Metro: Twinbrook (1 mile south).

Children's Services: Highchairs, boosters.

See Georgetown listing, above, for complete details. Try the french fries here. Arrive by 11:30am for lunch or 5:30pm for dinner, or don't bother.

IL FORNO, 4926 Cordell Ave., Bethesda. Tel. 301/652-7757.

Cuisine: PIZZA. **Reservations:** Not accepted. **Metro:** Bethesda.

$ **Prices:** Pizza pies $4.75–$14.95. MC, V.

Open: Mon–Thurs 11am–10pm, Fri 11am–11pm, Sat noon–11pm, Sun noon–10pm.

Children's Services: Boosters.

You can't get pizzas like these delivered. They're baked in huge wood-burning ovens, so the thin, New York–style crust has just the right amount of bite and doesn't collapse under the weight of the very fresh toppings. The garlic bread and calzone are worth trying too. Space is tight indoors, so opt for a seat outside in favorable weather.

Il Forno also has a Gaithersburg location—check the phone book for location.

LOTTA BULL, 891 Rockville Pike, Rockville. Tel. 301/340-8700.

Cuisine: AMERICAN. **Reservations:** Not accepted. **Metro:** Twinbrook or Rockville.

$ Prices: $3.50–$12.95. MC, V.
Open: Daily 11am–10pm.
Children's Services: Highchairs.

The barnlike setting is apt for devouring a juicy and flavorful roast beef or steak sandwich with a side of boardwalk-style french fries. If you're off beef, order the chicken breast platter. Room left? Force yourselves to try the carrot cake. Burp.

LOUISIANA EXPRESS, 4921 Bethesda Ave., Bethesda. Tel. 301/652-6945.
Cuisine: CAJUN/CREOLE. **Reservations:** Not accepted. **Metro:** Bethesda.
$ Prices: Appetizers $2.75–$3.25; entrees $2.50–$6 for small portions, $4.50–$9.75 for large; salads, sandwiches, omelets $2.25–$6.25. MC, V.
Open: Daily 11am–10pm.
Children's Services: Boosters.

⑤ Cajun, casual, and cheap, Louisiana Express excels at New Orleans-style po-boys (a.k.a. subs, hoagies, grinders), fish fritters, and gumbos. There's unspicy chicken and french fries for the kiddies. Any of the "small portions" would be suitable for the young ones in your family. You can stuff your craws with some mighty good eats for less than $10. Seating is limited, and service is cafeteria-style.

O'BRIEN'S PIT BARBECUE, 387 E. Gude Dr., Rockville. Tel. 301/340-8596.
Cuisine: RIBS/BBQ. **Reservations:** Not accepted.
$ Prices: $2.15–$12.25. AE, MC, V.
Open: Sun–Thurs 11am–10pm, Fri–Sat 11am–11pm.
Children's Services: Highchairs, boosters.

While Texas ribs and barbecued beef brisket are top draws in this ersatz Western-style cafeteria, the best offering by far is the wonderful chopped pork sandwich with plenty of barbecue sauce and a side of smoky baked beans and cole slaw. Mmmm mmmm good! Junior cowpokes will feel right at home.

There's another branch in Springfield, Va.

PHILADELPHIA MIKE'S, 7732 Wisconsin Ave., Bethesda. Tel. 301/656-0103.
Open: Mon–Sat 7am–10pm, Sun 7am–9pm. **Metro:** Bethesda.
Children's Services: Highchairs, boosters.

For other details see the branch listing in the Convention Center/Downtown section, above.

RIO GRANDE CAFE, 4919 Fairmont Ave., Bethesda. Tel. 301/656-2981.
Cuisine: MEXICAN. **Reservations:** Not accepted. **Metro:** Bethesda.
$ Prices: Entrees $2.95–$10.95 lunch, $7.25–$12.95 dinner; appetizers $2.25–$8.25. AE, MC, V.
Open: Mon–Thurs 11am–10:30pm, Fri–Sat 11:30am–11:30pm, Sun 11:30am–10:30pm.
Children's Services: Highchairs, boosters.

Build a better burrito and the world will beat a path to your door. Dig into the warm tortilla chips and chunky salsa while the kids watch the weird Rube Goldberg contraption that produces around 400 tortillas an hour. The "Fajitas Al Carbon" are numero uno for big appetites, while an appetizer or an à la carte taco or burrito will most likely fill *los niños*. Finish with honey-drenched sopapillas. *¡Que bueno!* Go at off-times, especially on weekends or holidays. Don't say I didn't warn you. There's a branch in Arlington, Virginia (tel. 703/528-3131). For complete details, see the entry in the "Virginia" section, later on in this chapter.

ROY'S PLACE, 2 East Diamond Ave., Gaithersburg. Tel. 301/948-5548.

Cuisine: SANDWICHES. **Reservations:** Not accepted.

$ **Prices:** 57¢ (ice-cube sandwich)–$15. AE, DC, MC, V.

Open: Mon–Thurs 11am–11pm, Fri–Sat 11am–midnight, Sun noon–11pm.

Children's Services: Highchairs, boosters.

It may be a trip from downtown D.C., but it's worth it, and kids of all ages love it. Allow extra time to digest the 16-page menu of sandwich combinations, variations, and permutations. We bought a menu 20 years ago so we could study the choices in the car. That menu has survived wars, braces, broken bones, broken hearts, puberty, and numerous pets. So has Roy's.

SHOOTZ, 4915 St. Elmo Ave., Bethesda. Tel. 301/654-8288.

Cuisine: ECLECTIC. **Reservations:** Not accepted. **Metro:** Bethesda.

$ **Prices:** $3.75–$7.95. MC, V.

Open: Sat noon–7pm, Sun 2–7pm to kids with adults. The rest of the time it's grownups only.

Children's Services: Boosters.

Attention Minnesota Fats fans: Saturdays and Sundays during daylight hours, this unique billiard parlor/café welcomes families to try their luck with a cue stick while they munch a chicken drumstick or corn dog on a stick; or stick to something else on the brief, irreverent menu. Table time is $10 an hour on Saturday, $12 on Sunday.

TASTEE DINER, 7731 Woodmont Ave., Bethesda. Tel. 301/652-3970.

Cuisine: AMERICAN. **Reservations:** Not accepted. **Metro:** Bethesda.

$ **Prices:** Breakfast $1.75–$3.50 (Kiddie Breakfast $1.50); lunch and dinner $1.75–$7.95. No credit cards.

Open: Always.

Children's Services: Highchairs, boosters.

Round the clock, 7 days a week, 365 days a year, 366 days in leap years, are the hours of the Tastee Diner. None of the new neon and chrome establishments calling themselves diners holds a candle to the Tastee, which served its first creamed chipped beef on toast in 1942. Come here for the hearty breakfasts, homemade chili and soups, sandwiches, and desserts. The tired leatherette booths, individual jukeboxes, colorful regulars, chatty short-order cooks, and beehived waitresses spell "Happy Days." You and the kids can't not love it.

There are Tastee Diners in Silver Spring and Laurel, Maryland, and Fairfax, Virginia, too.

SUBURBAN VIRGINIA

With so many restaurants in Northern Virginia, you well may wonder where all the patrons come from. The area near and beyond the Beltway, which a generation ago was considered the "boonies," continues adding to an ever-growing list of ethnic restaurants. Along with an overabundance of fast-food, pizza, pubby, and fine dining establishments, you won't have far to search for your next meal.

EXPENSIVE

MORTON'S, Fairfax Square at Tysons Corner, 8075 Leesburg Pike, Vienna. Tel. 703/883-0800.

Cuisine: AMERICAN. **Reservations:** Recommended.

$ **Prices:** Entrees $6.95–$18.95 lunch, $16.95–$28.95 dinner. AE, CB, DC, MC, V.

Open: Lunch Mon–Fri 11:30am–2:30pm; dinner Mon–Sat 5:30–11pm, Sun 5–10pm.

Most steak lovers concur that Morton's serves the area's best prime beef. This congenial steakhouse is tastefully decorated and invites leisurely dining. Certainly not your typical kids' restaurant, Morton's has a more relaxed policy than its Georgetown progenitor and welcomes all ages, though parental discretion is advised and there are no highchairs. Stick to the broiled-to-perfection steaks and chops, and expect to pay $40 to $50 for dinner, without wine. What do you expect of a restaurant whose neighbors are Gucci, Hermès, and Tiffany?

MODERATE

BISTRO BISTRO, Village at Shirlington, 4021 South 28th St., Arlington. Tel. 703/379-0300.

Cuisine: NEW AMERICAN. **Reservations:** Recommended at dinner. **Metro:** Pentagon then take 7A or 7F bus.

$ **Prices:** Entrees $5.95–$8.95 lunch, $8.95–$14.95 dinner; children's portions available. AE, MC, V.

Open: Sun–Thurs 11am–10pm, Fri–Sat 11am–11pm.

Children's Services: Highchairs, boosters.

The menu changes every few months at this inviting, family-friendly café where the burgers, onion rings, and desserts will keep juniors who play it safe satisfied while you sample something more innovative. The kitchen gladly serves pint-size portions of anything on the menu, and encourages using the crayons on the disposable tablecloths.

CLYDE'S, 8332 Leesburg Pike, Vienna. Tel. 703/734-1901.

Cuisine: AMERICAN/CONTINENTAL. **Reservations:** Recommended.

$ **Prices:** Entrees $5.95–$9.95 lunch, $8.95–$16.95 dinner; children's half-portions. AE, MC, V.

Open: Mon–Sat 11am–2am, Sun 10am–2am.

Children's Services: Highchairs, boosters, children's menu.

The burgers (especially the blue cheese and bacon variety), ribs, pasta dishes, and salads are delish and kids can offer half-portions of any entree. Try the prime rib on Friday and Saturday. A visual stunner, Clyde's merits a look around on your way in or out. Kids dig the giant palms and the naked ladies (don't worry, they're just paintings) in the main dining room.

FEDORA CAFE, 8521 Leesburg Pike, Tysons Corner. Tel. 703/556-0100.

Cuisine: AMERICAN. **Reservations:** Recommended.

$ Prices: Entrees $5.95–$8.75 lunch, $15.95–$22.95 dinner; children's portions of pasta. AE, D, DC, MC, V.

Open: Mon–Sat 11:30am–3pm and 5:30–11:30pm, Sun 10:30am–2:30pm (brunch) and 4:30–9:30pm.

Children's Services: Highchairs, boosters.

For openers, try the pizza topped with goat cheese and sun-dried tomatoes or fried zucchini. The varied menu changes seasonally, and kids can enjoy half-portions of pasta. You can't go wrong with the rôtisserie chicken or one of the fish specials in this attractive spot frequented by local Yuppies. We tip our hats—and forks—to Fedora's homemade pastries and desserts.

BUDGET

CARNEGIE DELI, Embassy Suites Hotel, 8517 Leesburg Pike, Vienna. Tel. 703/790-5001.

Cuisine: DELI. **Reservations:** Not accepted.

$ Prices: $6.25–$20.95; kids' menu available. AE, DC, MC, V.

Open: Sun–Thurs 11am–10pm, Fri–Sat 11am–midnight.

Children's Services: Highchairs, boosters, children's menu.

A kids' menu is available, but corned beef isn't on it. Let your kids share an oversized corned beef, pastrami, or combination sandwich. They'll never ask for grilled cheese again. This offshoot of the famed New York City delicatessan/restaurant also serves sinfully rich desserts. Go for the cheesecake if you have the room.

CHILI'S, 8051 Leesburg Pike, Vienna. Tel. 703/734-9512.

Cuisine: SOUTHWESTERN/AMERICAN. **Reservations:** Not accepted.

$ Prices: Entrees $3.25–$9.95. MC, V.

Open: Mon–Thurs 11am–11pm, Fri–Sat 11am–midnight, Sun noon–10pm.

Children's Services: Highchairs, boosters, children's menu.

Elegant it ain't, but Chili's serves good food and loves families, which is probably why so many families love Chili's. It's the kind of place where you don't have to keep reminding your kids to keep their voices down. Many fajitas freaks—young and old—say these are the best in town. The burgers, french fries, and salads are all above average. Kids especially like it here 'cuz the soda is served in pitchers. When you're in Maryland, try the Chili's in Rockville.

GENEROUS GEORGE'S PIZZA, 3006 Duke St., Alexandria. Tel. 703/370-4303.

Cuisine: PIZZA/PASTA. **Reservations:** Lunch only.

$ Prices: $3.75–$16.95. MC, V.

Open: Mon–Thurs 11am–midnight, Fri–Sat 11am–1am, Sun 11am–11pm.

Children's Services: Highchairs, boosters.

George's has been doing right by kids for 15 years. No wonder it is consistently voted one of the best family restaurants in the metropolitan area. A foursome can enjoy superior pizza in a super-casual, funky '50s setting and escape for $20. And you won't have to "shush" your little pepperonis once. Try George's ingenious creation, a Positive Pasta Pie—linguine, fettuccine, seafood or chicken served on a pizza crust.

There's another George's branch at 6131 Backlick Rd. in Springfield (tel. 703/451-7111).

RED HOT & BLUE, 1600 Wilson Blvd., Arlington. Tel. 703/276-7427.

Cuisine: BARBECUE. **Reservations:** Not accepted. **Metro:** Rosslyn or Court House.

$ Prices: Entrees $4.50–$10.95. MC, V.

Open: Mon–Thurs 11am–10pm, Fri 11am–11pm, Sat noon–11pm, Sun 1–10pm (summer 5pm–1am). **Closed:** Thanksgiving, Dec 25.

Children's Services: Boosters.

MmmmmmMmmmmmm good. Some think it's easier to get into heaven than to get a table at Red Hot & Blue. The Memphis ribs, pulled-pig sandwiches, and onion rings are fast becoming a legend in these parts. The place is nothing to look at, but if you want beauty, go to the National Gallery. If you want great BBQ, come here. Take home a souvenir bottle of the tangy barbecue sauce. Avoid a wait by arriving before 6pm.

There are branches also at 3014 Wilson Blvd. (tel. 703/243-1510, carry-out only), Manassas, Virginia (tel. 703/330-4847), and Laurel, Maryland (tel. 301/953-1943).

RIO GRANDE CAFE, 4031 N. Fairfax Dr., Arlington. Tel. 703/528-3131.

Cuisine: MEXICAN. **Reservations:** Not accepted. **Metro:** Ballston.

$ Prices: Entrees $5.95–$10.95 lunch, $6.50–$12.95 dinner. AE, DC, MC, V.

Open: Mon–Thurs 11am–10:30pm, Fri 11am–11:30pm, Sat 11:30am–11:30pm, Sun noon–10:30pm (brunch 11:30am–3pm).

Children's Services: Highchairs, boosters.

Warm tortilla chips and chunky salsa are served as soon as you sit down. While you contemplate gorging your adult selves on the "Fajitas Al Carbon," suggest to your youngest niños an appetizer or a taco or burrito for their smaller appetite. Finish with honey-drenched sopapillas.

T.G.I. FRIDAY'S, 2070 Chain Bridge Rd., Tysons Corner. Tel. 703/556-6173.

Cuisine: AMERICAN. **Reservations:** Not accepted.

$ Prices: $5.75–$13; kids' menu $1.95–$2.75. AE, CB, D, DC, MC, V.

Open: Daily 11:30am–2am.

Children's Services: Highchairs, boosters, children's menu.

T.G.I. Friday's is a family-friendly link in the popular national chain. The servers are enthusiastic and young. Those in your family under 12 can choose from such standbys as grilled-cheese sandwiches, hamburgers, and hot dogs on the kids' menu. The 10-page-long grownups' menu is filled with possibilities, but save room for the mocha mud pie.

CHAPTER 8

WHERE KIDS PREFER TO STAY

- **FROMMER'S SMART FAMILY TRAVELER: HOTELS**
1. **VERY EXPENSIVE**
2. **EXPENSIVE**
3. **MODERATE**
4. **INEXPENSIVE**
5. **BUDGET**
6. **BED & BREAKFAST**
7. **CAMPGROUNDS**

When it comes to choosing accommodations when traveling with kids, stick to the basics, and since Washington, D.C., is your destination, look for a hotel that is convenient to the Metro, sightseeing attractions, restaurants, and amusements. Everything else is whipped cream. While you may be turned on by complimentary terry-cloth robes and 24-hour room service, such amenities are of little consequence to most youngsters. In fact, comfortable beds, large closets, and au courant décor are all secondary—what's important to them is whether there's a refrigerator, restaurant, or snack machine; whether there's a pool, video games, or shopping close by.

Depending on your budget, the selection of places to stay in Washington, D.C., is wide indeed. For those who like to exit the city at night, several hotels in the Maryland and Virginia suburbs are included. The following suggestions cover a broad spectrum, from super-duper luxury hotels to budget alternatives. All—with a couple of exceptions in Virginia—are within walking distance of the Metro, and all have something (in most cases, several somethings) that make them attractive to kids. If you can't swing a $1,000-a-night Presidential Suite or room with a view of the Capitol, don't despair. You won't be spending that much time in your room anyway. At day's end, flopping into a bed—even one with a few lumps—will spell relief.

GETTING THE MOST FOR YOUR DOLLAR

To get the best value for your travel dollar, here are a few tips from the experts. First, you'll pay top dollar during the high season, which runs from late March to mid-June. Rates typically fall in summer when Congress is on vacation and during the winter months. January is especially slow. If you can live without cherry blossoms, avoid April, not only the cruelest but also the most expensive month.

Your kids may be your ticket to special room rates and weekend packages. Aren't you glad you decided to bring them? Hotels clamor for family business, especially on weekends and during the summer. At most places, children under a certain age (usually 16 or 18) stay free in their parents' room. Weekday rates may drop 30% to 50% on weekends and, depending on occupancy, you may cash in on weekdays as well. Hotels sometimes run unadvertised special promotions, but you won't find out about them if you don't ask.

Many experienced travelers believe you'll be quoted a better rate if you call the hotel directly rather than reserving through the toll-free number. Try it. What have you got to lose? Don't be afraid to ask (as if you're hard of hearing), "Don't you have something for less?" In some circles, this is considered chutzpah, but in most, it's considered just plain good sense. Better the money in your pocket than in theirs. There's no point trying this around cherry blossom time, but it's amazing what reservations clerks will come up with when you tell them you're going to shop around.

For a brochure on hotels offering special weekend packages, write the **Hotel Association of Washington,** P.O. Box 33578, Washington, DC 20033, or the **D.C. Committee to Promote Washington,** P.O. Box 27489, Washington, DC 20038-7489—ask for "Washington Weekends."

If you're more comfortable with someone else doing the negotiating for you, write or call **Capitol Reservations,** 1730 Rhode Island Ave. NW, Suite 302, Washington, DC 20036 (tel. 202/452-1270, or toll free 800/VISIT-DC). They handle hotels in all price ranges and are privy to discounts because of their high-volume business. This free service has listings that begin at $55 a night, and—important to families—they've all been screened for cleanliness and they're all in safe neighborhoods.

Groups who will occupy 10 or more rooms should know about **U.S.A. Groups** (tel. 202/861-1900, or toll free 800/872-4777). The free service represents hotel rooms at almost every property in the Washington, D.C., and suburban Virginia/Maryland region and will work hard to find the best accommodations at the rates you request, saving your group valuable time and money.

Presented below are those establishments in all price categories that are "kid-friendly" and offer the best value for the money in the D.C. area. The prices for a double room per night during the week (remember, weekends are less expensive) are roughly as follows: "very expensive" accommodations cost $175 and up per day; "expensive" rooms range from $125 to $175; "moderate" cost from $75 to $125; "inexpensive," from $50 to $75; and "budget" run less than $50.

1. VERY EXPENSIVE

GRAND HYATT WASHINGTON AT WASHINGTON CENTER, 1000 H St. NW, Washington, DC 20001. Tel. 202/582-1234, or toll free 800/233-1234. Fax 202/637-4781. 891 rms, 60 suites. A/C MINIBAR TEL TV **Metro:** Metro Center.

$ Rates: Weekday $209 single, $234 double, $425–$1,250 suites; weekend $99–$119 single or double. Children under 18 stay free in parents' room; crib free; Camp Hyatt, special family weekend rates, and Regency Club available. Ask about AAA discounts. AE, CB, DC, DISC, MC, V.

Parking: $14 valet; $12 self-parking.

Your kids won't want to go home after they see this place! Just one block from Metro Center, with underground access, the Grand Hyatt is within walking distance of the FBI, Ford's Theatre, Chinatown, the Old Post Office Pavilion, and shopping. The large, well-appointed rooms are located on 12 floors surrounding a

FROMMER'S SMART FAMILY TRAVELERS:
HOTELS

1. Use reservations services such as **Capitol Reservations** (details above); they obtain lower rates by booking rooms in volume.
2. Take advantage of reduced weekend rates, often offered Friday through Sunday and sometimes off-season weekdays as well. They may be as much as 50% lower.
3. Bargain with the reservations clerk. An unoccupied room nets a hotel zero dollars, and whatever you offer to pay is better than that. This works best on the afternoon of your arrival, when the desk knows there will be empty rooms. Adventurous families may try this approach; less adventurous ones may prefer confirmed reservations.
4. Ask about special discounts for families.

stunning glass-enclosed atrium filled with abundant light and greenery. There's plenty of action and razzle-dazzle here for the entire family.

As part of the weekend Camp Hyatt program, kids 15 and under get their own room at half-price, as well as special room-service and restaurant menus and supervised evening activities ($4 per child per hour) that will allow you to slip off for a little quality adult time. Kids can swim in the indoor pool (accompanied by an adult), play mini-basketball, feel the spray from the two-story waterfall, or watch an in-room movie or Camp Hyatt videos. Board the Old Town Trolley outside the 10th Street door. One ticket will buy you a guided tour of 12 attractions and you'll be allowed to board and reboard as often as you like.

Dining/Entertainment: While the kids are enjoying Camp Hyatt activities (Friday and Saturday from 5 to 9pm), unwind with a cocktail in Palladio's multilevel lounge. Dine in the open-air Grand Café (open daily from 6:30am to 11pm) at the edge of a lagoon, where kids 3 and under eat free; those 15 and under can order smaller portions for half price or items from the Camp Hyatt menu. Relax while the pianist at the white grand piano atop a glass-and-stone "lily pad" sends soothing sounds your way. Have sandwiches in the casual Zephyr Deli (open Monday through Saturday from 7am to 6pm) or take them up to your room. In the Grand Slam sports bar, kids, with an adult, can shoot a few hoops or play miniature hockey and video games while downing burgers, hot dogs, and nachos. Entertainment and dancing are on tap nightly for grown-ups at Impulse.

Services: 24-hour concierge and room service, laundry/valet, coin-op laundry, baby-sitting can be arranged through the concierge. Regency Club weekend package includes breakfast, tea and cookies, cocktails and hors d'oeuvres served in a private lounge.

Facilities: Junior Olympic-size pool (kids under 16 must be accompanied by an adult); steamroom, sauna, health club (free on weekends), Jacuzzi, exercise/aerobics room, massage room, Juice Bar; Izod LaCoste shop and gift shop; beauty shop (next door).

HYATT REGENCY WASHINGTON, 400 New Jersey Ave. NW, Washington, DC 20001. Tel. 202/737-1234, or toll free 800/233-1234. Fax 202/393-7927. 834 rms, 31 suites. A/C MINIBAR TV TEL **Metro:** Union Station.

$ **Rates:** Weekday $200–$215 single, $225–$240 double, suites from $350 weekdays. Weekend $89–$119 single or double. Children under 18 stay free in parents' room; crib free. Weekend and seasonal packages, Gold Passport and Regency Club available. Ask about AAA discounts. AE, DC, DISC, MC, V. **Parking:** $14.

⭐ The wonderful Camp Hyatt program was born at this Hyatt on Capitol Hill in 1986. Summer weekends on Friday and Saturday evenings from 6 to 11pm, kids 4 to 12 are kept busy in the Children's Suite with movies, crafts, games, and food. What a boon to parents! The charge is $4 per hour per child, with a discount after the second child. Also, as part of Camp Hyatt, families can book a second room at half-price for the kids, the restaurants and room service have special kids menus, and discount coupons for the Capital Children's Museum are issued at check-in.

This Hyatt caused quite a stir with its five-story atrium lobby and luxurious rooms and facilities when it opened in 1976. Renovation of all the guest floors was completed in March of 1991, and Hugo's restaurant on the top floor reopened in Fall '91 as the Capitol View Club (and what a view it has!) after a complete facelift.

Some Hyatt extras include in-room movies, three restaurants (where kids 15 and under can order smaller portions for half-price), a large pool in a beautiful two-story glass atrium, poolside juice and snack bar, health club (kids 18 and under must be accompanied by an adult), large gift and sundries shop, unisex hairstyling salon (no appointment necessary and lots of celebrity photos on the wall), and a shoeshine stand. You can arrange an Old Town Trolley Tour at the sightseeing desk near the entrance or borrow games at the concierge desk.

Dining/Entertainment: The sunny Park Promenade off the lobby is the best choice for families, as there's something for everyone at reasonable prices. It's open daily from 6:30am to midnight. Jonah's Oyster Kitchen is open for lunch, Monday through Friday, and dinner nightly until midnight. There are a few non-seafood items on the tempting menu, and reservations are recommended. The Capitol View Club, part lounge/part restaurant, is okay for teenagers on up. Kids with an adult are welcome in the lobby-level Spy's Eye cocktail lounge, which features music videos and dancing.

Services: 24-hour room service, concierge, shoeshine, laundry/valet, babysitting.

Facilities: Indoor heated pool with deck and juice/snack bar (kids 16 and under must be accompanied by an adult), fully equipped health club with sauna and steam room (kids 18 and under must be accompanied by an adult), sightseeing desk, game room, gift shop, hair salon.

J.W. MARRIOTT, 1331 Pennsylvania Ave. NW at E St., Washington, DC 20004. Tel. 202/393-2000, or toll free 800/228-9290. Fax 202/626-6991. 772 rms, 51 suites. A/C MINIBAR TV TEL **Metro:** Metro Center.

$ **Rates:** Weekday $224 single; $244 double; weekend $244 concierge level single or double; $119 single or double with breakfast. Children under 18 stay free in parents' room; crib free. Extra person $20. Weekend packages and family plan available. AE, DC, DISC, ER, JCB, MC, V. **Parking:** $14.

One look at the lobby and you know Marriott has come a long way since the family opened a root beer stand on 14th Street more than 50 years ago. The expansive space—all peach and mauve and seafoam with opulent crystal chandeliers, towering ficus trees, and fresh flower arrangements—is a sight for sore eyes, as my grandmother used to say. Pretty as it is, it's easy to become disoriented. One end of the lobby flows into The Shops at National Place, making things a bit more confusing, so keep a sharp eye on younger kids. If you send them for a newspaper, they may be gone for days.

If you're looking for luxury and location, you've arrived. Rooms are light and bright, and well-coordinated furnishings carry out the lobby's color scheme. Rooms overlook Pennsylvania Avenue and the Washington Monument or the hotel's courtyard. Guess which costs more. Furnishings include a king or two double beds, a good-size dresser, desk and chair, remote-control TV with cable and HBO, and a minibar. Bathrooms are generous in size, and a basket of amenities awaits guests.

Kids will no doubt bypass the health club and maybe the indoor pool in their haste to reach the video arcade with Atari's Pole Position and Teenage Mutant Ninja Turtles games. (For this you traveled to Washington?) While they're playing you can work out, swim 100 laps, or slip into the Garden Terrace lounge for a cocktail.

Nobody goes hungry at the Marriott, where you can choose from four restaurants that run from very elegant to très casual (see below). Kids also love the Food Hall next door at The Shops at National Place; and a host of good restaurants are within a short walk or Metro ride.

Dining/Entertainment: East meets West at Celadon, where French and Asian dishes are served in elegant surroundings. Kids over 12 with sophisticated tastebuds will like the atmosphere and food; those younger will consider it a punishment. Look into the four-course pre-theater menu, served from 5:30 to 6:30pm. Off the lobby, the Garden Terrace has a family-pleasing luncheon buffet weekdays and a Sunday brunch buffet with a Dixieland band and Mardi Gras masks for the kids. Try to get a window table for a primo view of Pennsylvania Avenue. The National Café is open on the lower level from very early until 11pm. Buffet and menu items are available and the atmosphere is less stiff than at Celadon. Best bet: "early bird" dinners (soup, salad, entrée, and dessert) for under $15. There's also a children's menu with stuff they like (pancakes, burgers, grilled cheese sandwiches, etc.), and nothing is more than $6. Catch the action and grab a snack at SRO, a New York–style deli next to the National Café. Kids are welcome to watch their favorite team on TV as long as they don't stand at the bar or drink. Light fare is served from 11:30am until 11pm.

Services: 24-hour room service, concierge, laundry/valet.

Facilities: Health club (with exercise room with Universal equipment, indoor swimming pool, hydrotherapy pool, sun deck, and video arcade), a connecting mall with 85 shops and restaurants, car rental/airline/travel desks, gift shop.

OMNI SHOREHAM HOTEL, 2500 Calvert St. NW at Connecticut Avenue, Washington, DC 20008. Tel. 202/234-0700, or toll free 800/THE-OMNI. Fax 202/332-1372. Telex 710/822-0412. 770 rms, 55 suites. A/C MINIBAR TV TEL **Metro:** Woodley Park-Zoo.

$ Rates: Weekday $175–$255 single, $195–$275 double, suites from $350; off-season and weekend $79 single or double. Children under 18 stay free in parents' room; crib free, cots $20. Extra person $20. Family and weekend packages available. Ask about the spectacular "First Family Vacation Packages." AE, CB, DC, DISC, MC, V.

WASHINGTON, D.C.

The Bellevue Hotel **1**
Brickskeller Inn **2**
The Carlyle Suites **3**
Connecticut Avenue Days Inn **4**
The Days Inn Downtown **5**
Embassy Suites **6**
Embassy Square Suites **7**
Grand Hyatt Washington,
    at Washington Center **8**
Guest Quarters, New Hampshire Avenue **9**
Guest Quarters, Pennsylvania Avenue **10**

WASHINGTON, D.C., ACCOMMODATIONS

Hotel Anthony **11**
Hotel Harrington **12**
Hyatt Regency Washington **13**
J.W. Marriott **14**
Omni Shoreham Hotel **15**
Quality Hotel Capitol Hill **16**
Ramada Renaissance Techworld **17**
University Inn **18**
Washington International Youth Hostel (WIYH) **19**
Waterfront Villas **20**

Parking: $12.

If you think bigger is better, your pockets are deep, and you've a family of fitness freaks who like to jump from sightseeing to tennis to jogging to swimming, look no further. The OMNI Shoreham is a self-contained 14-acre resort in a residential neighborhood off Connecticut Avenue, two blocks from the Metro and less than 15 minutes from downtown. Play tennis on three lighted Har-Tru courts, swim in the two outdoor pools—one just for kids—or work out in the health club. If that's not enough exercise for you, the hotel's back door opens onto Rock Creek Park, with hiking, biking, riding, and jogging trails, and a fitness course.

The 60-year-old dowager, who looks remarkably youthful after several facelifts has, in her lifetime, provided the setting for Perle Mesta's celebrated parties, numerous inaugural balls, and Harry Truman's poker games. The cavernous lobby is usually filled with conventioneers weekdays and there's plenty of nighttime activity centered around the art deco Marquee Cabaret, Parisian-style Monique Café et Brasserie, and Garden Court cocktail lounge.

As you might expect, the guest rooms are large and elegantly furnished, and snacking kids should avoid picnicking on the bedspreads while they watch in-room movies. Despite the marble-floored bathrooms, glitzy lobby, and amenities, the best thing about the OMNI Shoreham is its location—you can walk to the National Zoo.

Dining/Entertainment: Have breakfast, lunch, or dinner (or all three) in the Monique Café (open from 6:30am to 11pm), where the menu favors French brasserie fare but also includes several American selections. As hotel restaurants go, Monique rates well above average. Dinner entrees are $13–$20; lunch/brunch less pricey. Drink in the scene that is The Garden Court, with its tropical trees, beveled-mirror walls and 35-foot vaulted ceiling. Older kids with their parents can enjoy nightly entertainment in the Marquee Cabaret, the former Marquee Lounge once presided over by political satirist Mark Russell. On Saturday, "Now This Kids," invites youngsters to participate in a show by a musical comedy improvisation group. Showtime is 12:30pm; and tickets are $5 for kids 4–12, $7 for adults.

Services: Room service 6am–1am, concierge, laundry/valet, video checkout, limousine rental, baby-sitting.

Facilities: Two outdoor pools; three lighted Har-Tru tennis courts; on-premises health club (kids must be accompanied by an adult); 10 miles of jogging, hiking, and bicycle trails (winding off into Rock Creek Park), plus a 1.5-mile Perrier parcourse with 18 exercise stations; sauna; shops; newsstand; travel/sightseeing desk.

RAMADA RENAISSANCE TECHWORLD, 999 9th St. NW, at K Street NW, Washington, DC 20001. Tel. 202/898-9000, or toll free 800/228-9898. Fax 202/789-4213. 800 rms. A/C MINIBAR TV TEL **Metro:** Gallery Place.

$ Rates: Weekday $185 single; $205 club single; $205 double; $225 club double. Weekend $79–$110 single or double, $89–$119 club. Children 18 and under stay free in parents' room; crib free. Seasonal and weekend packages available. Ask about the $79 "Washington Weekend" package. AE, CB, DC, DISC, MC, V.

Parking: $14.

There's plenty of hustle and bustle weekdays at the 800-room Ramada Techworld, which mainly serves conventioneers attending functions at the Convention Center across the street. The location is excellent and, on weekends when the place is relatively quiet, families can take advantage of huge savings and enjoy all the extras on a shoestring.

Everything is spanking clean and fresh in the three-year-old hotel, and the attractive, well-equipped rooms have remote-control color TVs with cable and pay movie options and video message retrieval. Stocked minibars are locked for everyone's peace of mind, and there are ice and soft-drink machines on every floor.

An entire 15-story tower with 166 rooms constitutes the Renaissance Club, where guests are pampered with extra amenities. Club guests also have a private concierge-staffed lounge, a cozy domain where you may enjoy sharing a complimentary continental breakfast with the kids. Afternoon hors d'oeuvres for grownups too.

Adjacent to the third-floor health club is a 60-foot pool and juice machines. If you forget to bring a bathing suit, T-shirt, or shorts, pick up what you need at the desk (adult sizes only). Two gift shops and a newsstand are right off the large atrium lobby, which is broken up into small sitting areas—ideal for kids who need a little space and want to have a hot game of cards or checkers. The Chinese rock garden outside is something to see and may inspire a game of hide-and-seek. Take kids over 8 to Holography World, in the Tech World Plaza south lobby (across from the Ramada's Plaza Café). It's open Monday through Friday. Don't miss it!

Dining/Entertainment: Two restaurants, a lounge, and outdoor cafe serve everything from gourmet fare to pizza. Floreale is the Ramada's upscale gourmet restaurant featuring American regional cuisine. Families can order à la carte or dig into the sumptuous buffets at the more casual and kid-friendly Café Florentine, where little ones order from their own adorable, environmentally inspired souvenir menu. For an after-dinner drink, the Marco Polo Lounge has nightly entertainment in an exotic palm-filled setting. In warm weather, the most picturesque dining spot is the outdoor Plaza Café, where salads, sandwiches, and finger food are served from 11:30am to 2am, weather permitting.

Services: 24-hour room service, concierge daily 7am–11pm, laundry/valet.

Facilities: Indoor pool, fully equipped health club (with lap pool, whirlpool, steamrooms, treadmills, StairMasters, bikes, rowing machines) aerobics classes, gift shops, boutiques, hairdresser, newsstand, Tech 2000 museum of interactive videos.

2. EXPENSIVE

EMBASSY SQUARE SUITES, 2000 N St. NW, Washington, DC 20036. **Tel. 202/659-9000,** or toll free 800/424-2999. Fax 202/429-9546. 250 suites. A/C MINIBAR TV TEL VCR **Metro:** Dupont Circle.

$ Rates (including continental breakfast): Weekday $139 single; $169 double. Children 18 and under stay free in parents' room; crib free. Weekend, weekly and monthly rates available. Ask about AAA rates, if you are a member. AE, DC, DISC, MC, V.

Parking: $9 (no vans).

At the Embassy Square Suites (not to be confused with Embassy Suites—they are different chains), the accommodations are comfy and commodious. It's ideal for families, as everyone is afforded space and privacy. The separate living room is equipped with a wet bar, refrigerator, and a second TV to prevent arguments over who watches what. Kids will be delighted with the videocassette player, and movies can be rented at the front desk. Kitchens come fully equipped, in case you miss cooking.

You want more? The rates include a complimentary continental breakfast, there's a pool in the center of an open-air courtyard, and adults have free use of health club facilities nearby. All this, and you're only a few blocks from the Dupont Circle Metro stop. It's one stop to Connecticut Avenue and K Street NW; two to Metro Center, where you can transfer to trains on the other lines.

Dining/Entertainment: The recently remodeled Rhapsody Restaurant, the setting for your complimentary breakfast, is also open for lunch and Happy Hour Monday through Friday.

Services: 24-hour front-desk assistance, concierge in summer, free in-room coffee, laundry/valet.

Facilities: Outdoor pool, complimentary use of off-premises health club, coin-op laundry.

EMBASSY SUITES, Chevy Chase Pavilion, 4300 Military Rd. NW, at Wisconsin Avenue, Washington, DC 20015. Tel. 202/362-9300, or toll free 800/EMBASSY. Fax 202/686-3405. 198 suites. A/C TV TEL VCP **Metro:** Friendship Heights (Western Avenue exit).

$ Rates (including complimentary breakfast): Weekday $140 single, $155 double; weekend $109–$119 single or double. Children 18 and under stay free in parents' room; crib free. Weekend and seasonal promotions available. AE, DC, DISC, MC, V.

Parking: $8.

Our family several times has been on the verge of selling our house and moving to an Embassy Suites. Breakfast alone is sufficient reason to relocate. At this property, which opened its doors in October 1990, the delicious complimentary cooked-to-order breakfast is served in the pleasant second-floor Willows Restaurant.

Spacious suites consist of a bedroom with a king-sized bed and a separate living room with a sofa bed. There are two TVs, a wet bar and refrigerator (so the munchkins need never go hungry), and videocassette player. You can rent movies at the front desk. There's underground access to the Metro, and it's only a 15-minute ride to downtown. The hotel is within walking distance of scores of restaurants as well as excellent shopping at Mazza Gallerie, Woodward & Lothrop, Lord & Taylor, and Saks.

After a tough day sightseeing, swim in the indoor pool, unwind in the Jacuzzi, or work out in the fully equipped health club (kids must be accompanied by an adult). Cocktails are complimentary weeknights during the Happy Hour.

Dining/Entertainment: The Willows Restaurant is open for breakfast, lunch, and dinner. The lunch and dinner menus are heavy on seafood dishes; entrees average $7 to $16.

Services: Suite service, 24-hour front-desk assistance, valet/cleaning.

Facilities: Indoor pool, Jacuzzi, on-premises health club, coin-operated laundry.

EMBASSY SUITES CRYSTAL CITY, 1300 Jefferson Davis Highway, Arlington, VA 22202. Tel. 703/979-9799, or toll free 800/EMBASSY. Fax 703/920-5946. 267 suites. A/C MINIBAR TV TEL **Metro:** Crystal City.

$ Rates (including complimentary breakfast and cocktails): Weekday $129–$174;

weekend $94–$114. Children 12 and under stay free in parents' room; crib free. Special weekend packages ($79 up) available at certain times. Ask about AAA rates, if you are a member. AE, DC, DISC, MC, V.

Parking: Free.

Walk or take the hotel's free transportation to the Crystal City Metro stop. You can be downtown in 10 to 15 minutes on the Yellow or Blue line, depending on the day's agenda.

The suites are nicely decorated in pleasing mauve tones, and the double sink outside the bath will help to speed everyone on their way in the morning. Ask for a microwave if you want one; there's no extra charge. Not enough can be said about the merits of having the kids sleep in a separate room with their own TV—worth twice the price.

If you have the time, snoop around Crystal City Underground, filled with shops and restaurants, or take the Metro one stop to The Fashion Centre at Pentagon City, where you won't need security clearance, just lots of moolah. While Macy's and Nordstrom are the anchors here, of greater interest to kids are Record World, the Disney Store, the Nature Company, The Gap, and GapKids. There are 13 eateries in the Food Court, a number of "proper" sit-down restaurants, and six movie theaters. The mall, open Monday through Saturday from 10am to 9:30pm, Sunday from 11am to 6pm, is a great escape if you run into foul weather.

Dining/Entertainment: Breakfast and late-afternoon cocktails are complimentary. Ellington's (open daily) has a children's menu for the 12-and-under set, featuring burger, hot dog, fried chicken, and grilled-cheese baskets with french fries. The regular menu lists beef, veal, and pasta entrées—all come with soup or salad, potato, and vegetable. On Friday and Saturday from 6 to 8:30pm, there's an All-American Buffet with roast beef, several other entrées, and all the trimmings. Kids under 6 eat free; kids 6–12 are charged $5.95, and adults pay $14.95.

Services: Room service, laundry/valet, free transportation to National Airport.

Facilities: Indoor pool with lifeguard, sundeck, coffee maker in all rooms.

EMBASSY SUITES TYSONS CORNER, 8517 Leesburg Pike, Vienna, VA 22182. Tel. 703/883-0707, or toll free 800/EMBASSY. Fax 703/883-0694. 232 suites; 14 2-bedroom suites. **Metro:** Dunn Loring.

$ Rates: Weekday $99–$179, single or double, 2-bedroom suites $250; weekend $69–$129. Children 12 and under stay free in parents' room; crib free. Extra person $15. Several packages available. AE, CB, D, DC, MC, V.

Parking: Free.

By now you know that if you stay at an Embassy Suites you and your kids won't be tripping over one another. There's a lot to be said for that, especially when you're spending every waking moment in each other's company. The separate bedroom and living room each have a TV, and there's a double sink outside the bathroom. A delicious cooked-to-order breakfast and pre-dinner cocktails (for those over 21) are included in your room rate.

Although the Metro is not within walking distance, and you're about 12 miles from the city, the hotel provides free transportation to the Dunn Loring station as well as anywhere within a 5-mile radius of the hotel. Some of the more expensive hostelries in the area should take note of this. Serious shoppers won't want to miss visiting nearby Tysons Corner and/or Tysons II.

Dining/Entertainment: The Embassy Suites has only one restaurant, but one is more than enough when it's the Carnegie Deli, an offshoot of the well-known restaurant on Seventh Avenue in New York. How they arranged such a coup is the mystery of the century. Lovers of corned beef, pastrami, potato pancakes, and other exquisite taste sensations will have a field day. It's the best New York–style deli between Virginia (that includes D.C.) and Baltimore. The last couple of times I rounded the Beltway for a C.B. fix, the pickles were disappointing. If yours are limp and tired, ask the waitress for fresh ones. Medals should be given to those who can finish a whole sandwich. Take my advice and share with a loved one. If you're still hungry, you can always order something else. Like a side of blintzes or slab of cheesecake. There's a kids' menu too. Swim a few laps in the pool, then come back for more. The Deli is open Sunday through Thursday from 11am to 10pm, Friday and Saturday till midnight. A full cooked-to-order breakfast and Happy Hour drinks are complimentary.

Services: Room service, transportation to Metro and shopping.

Facilities: Heated indoor pool, sundeck, Jacuzzi, saunas, exercise room; Thrifty car rental desk on premises.

GUEST QUARTERS–PENNSYLVANIA AVENUE, 2500 Pennsylvania Ave. NW, Washington, DC 20037. Tel. 202/333-8060, or toll-free 800/424-2900. Fax 202/338-3818. 123 suites. A/C MINIBAR TV TEL **Metro:** Foggy Bottom.

$ Rates: Weekday $185–$200 single or double; weekend $109 up for up to 4 family members. Children under 18 stay free in parents' room; crib free. Extra person $15. Weekend and special packages available. Monthly rates. Ask about AAA Value Rates, if you are a member. AE, DC, DISC, MC, V.

Parking: $13 (valet).

Walk to Georgetown, the Kennedy Center, George Washington University, and the White House from this Foggy Bottom location. The Metro is a few blocks away. The contemporary suites are spacious and have a living room, separate bedroom, full kitchen, and bath. There's a pleasant tree-lined patio off the rear of the lobby, and numerous restaurants are within a couple of blocks. Donatello's, a few doors down, is one of the best Italian restaurants in the city, but I don't recommend it for very young children. The West End Market, a block away, has everything you'll need to set up housekeeping during your stay, and it's open every day. Room service is also available—from 6am to 10pm. The big pluses at Guest Quarters are space and privacy. It's also a good choice if you're shopping for colleges, as George Washington and Georgetown University are nearby. Additional amenities include a coin-op laundry, vending machines, game and book rental from the front desk, and complimentary use of an off-premises health club (adults only).

GUEST QUARTERS–NEW HAMPSHIRE AVENUE, 801 New Hampshire Ave., Washington, DC 20037. Tel. 202/785-2000, or toll free 800/424-2900. Fax 202/785-9485. 101 suites. A/C MINI-BAR TV TEL **Metro:** Foggy Bottom.

$ Rates: See the preceding entry. AE, DC, DISC, MC

Parking: $13 (valet).

No, you're not seeing double. This Guest Quarters is in Foggy Bottom also. The suites are nearly identical and amenities are the same, with one exception—this location has a small rooftop pool but no patio, so if your kids prefer swimming to sitting, this is a logical choice. By the way, this GQ location will welcome Fido or Fluffy for a $12 daily fee.

HYATT REGENCY BETHESDA, One Bethesda Metro Center, (Wisconsin Avenue and Old Georgetown Road), Bethesda, MD 20814. Tel. 301/657-1234, or toll free 800/233-1234. Fax 301/657-6478. 380 rms and suites. A/C MINIBAR (by request) TV TEL **Metro:** Bethesda.

$ Rates: Weekday $162 single, $187 double, suites from $400. Weekend $79 up single or double; suites $175 up. Children 18 and under stay free in parents' room; crib free. Special weekend, family, Regency Club, and Camp Hyatt packages available. AE, CB, D, DC, MC, V.

Parking: $10 weekdays, $7 weekends.

⭐ Providing top-notch facilities at a convenient suburban location next to the Bethesda Metro, the Hyatt knows how to deliver the goods to vacationing families. As part of Camp Hyatt, families benefit from 50% savings on a second room, and kids may take part in organized activities weekend evenings for a nominal sum. There's a special Camp Hyatt menu with nothing priced over $3, and kids 12 and under can always order smaller portions at reduced rates in the Plaza Café.

As Yogi Berra used to say, you'll get "déjà vu all over again" when you enter the large, plant-filled open atrium lobby with its requisite bar. There is a definite tendency—obviously intentional—toward repetition among Hyatts, and this location is no exception. You have to admit, though, it's eye-catching and, refreshingly, the Southwestern look is given a welcome reprieve.

The rooms are large and sumptuous with either a king or two double beds, plenty of closet and drawer space, and marble baths. A one-bedroom suite that goes for $400 during the week is only $175 on weekends, when the rate for a regular room sometimes dips as low as $79. Always ask the reservationist for the best family rate available.

Your kids will spend nary a dull moment here. There's a large glass-enclosed indoor pool (open daily during the summer, weekends the rest of the year), fully equipped health club (you'll have to go with them) and workout area, as well as gift shops and a family-style restaurant. Lowen's, one of the biggest and best toy stores anywhere, is just down the street.

Adjacent to the hotel at Bethesda Metro Center is a skating rink (open from Thanksgiving through February), a playground, and Food Court selling pizza, barbecue, Chinese food, chicken prepared many ways, and Mrs. Field's cookies. Friday evenings from May to September there's big band dancing at an outdoor ballroom, and all ages are welcome. Bethesda Metro Center also sponsors special family events throughout the year. Usually once during the summer, 30 tons of sand are dumped on the ice rink for a beach party blast.

Bethesda abounds with restaurants of every persuasion, and Mazza Gallerie and White Flint mall (with Bloomies, Lord & Taylor, and I. Magnin) are about equidistant.

Dining/Entertainment: The kid-friendly Plaza Café, overlooking the skating rink and playground, is open for breakfast, lunch, and dinner (6:30am–midnight). Half portions ($3–$11) are available for kids 12 and under. The extensive weekday luncheon buffet and weekend dinner buffet are finds. Take advantage of the "early-bird special" from 5 to 6pm Friday and Saturday, when adults pay $9.95 and kids 12 and under can gorge themselves for $4.95. Fellini's is the Hyatt's upscale dining spot serving northern Italian and continental fare. I wouldn't step foot in here with kids under 12. It's rather starched and expensive, and well-heeled patrons might take exception.

Services: Room service, concierge, limousine service to airports, laundry/valet, baby-sitting may be arranged through the front desk.

Facilities: Indoor pool, fully equipped health club, workout area, gift shops.

SHERATON PREMIERE AT TYSONS CORNER, 8661 **Leesburg Pike, Tysons Corner, VA 22182. Tel. 703/448-1234,** or toll free 800/325-3535. Fax 703/893-8193. 455 rms. A/C MINIBAR TV TEL **Metro:** Dunn Loring.

$ Rates: Weekday $115–$150 single, $130–$165 double, suites $250–$300; weekend $79 single or double. Children under 12 stay free in parents' room; crib free. Extra person $15. Weekly rates; also special promotional packages (Value Rates) sometimes available. AE, D, DC, ER, MC, V.

Parking: Free.

The Sheraton Premiere offers luxury accommodations with all the frills. Our family has attended several functions at the Sheraton, and the facilities, service, and food are first class. The location is convenient to Tysons Corner and Tysons II, Toys Я Us, 18 movie theaters, and numerous restaurants. One big drawback is the lack of complimentary transportation to the Metro. One hopes this oversight will be rectified sometime in the future. If you don't have a car, a taxi to the Dunn Loring Metro station will set you back $7 or more, depending on the number in your party.

On the bright side, there are three restaurants and two bars on the premises to serve you, plus great recreational facilities. The weekend package includes 15% off food and beverage service in the hotel, and the so-called Value Rates, when available, are a steal. Be sure to ask!

Dining/Entertainment: Ashgrove's is the Sheraton's family-friendly restaurant for informal dining. The children's menu, in the form of a clown mask, lists six main courses plus three desserts for kids under 12. Baron's is open for fine dining (entrées $16–$27), and First Impressions serves sandwiches and light fare in the lobby, along with piano music starting at 5pm. The Capital Club has a D.J. every day but Sunday for your listening pleasure—or displeasure, as the case may be.

Services: 24-hour room service, concierge, poolside service, laundry/valet, baby-sitting services, free weekend shopping transportation, free Dulles Airport transportation.

Facilities: Indoor and outdoor pools with lifeguard, exercise equipment, weights, Jacuzzi, sauna, bicycles, 3 racquetball courts, lighted tennis privileges, 18-hole golf privileges (greens fees), hair salon, drugstore, gift shop.

WATERFRONT VILLAS, 1100 6th St. SW., Suite 510, Washington, DC 20024. Tel. 202/554-1250. 2 floating villas. A/C TV TEL **Metro:** L'Enfant Plaza.

$ Rates: Winter $130; April–Dec $165 (for 3–4 persons). Extra person $20. Weekly rates available. AE, CB, DC.

Parking: Free.

Watch the sunset over the Potomac without moving a muscle. You'll be rocked to sleep by the gentle motion of the water if you opt to stay on one of two 38-foot Coast Guard–approved floating homes docked at the Gangplank Marina on Water Street. Both the *Serendipity* and *La Paz* have one bedroom, a loft area, kitchen, living room with color TV, bath and patio/deck, and each can accommodate 4 persons.

Shop for fresh fish along Maine Avenue just up the street and prepare it onboard for dinner. Safeway, Arena Stage, and several waterfront restaurants are within a few blocks, and you're a 15-minute walk or short taxi ride to the L'Enfant Plaza Metro station. Stay here and give the kids an experience they'll never forget.

3. MODERATE

THE BELLEVUE HOTEL, 15 E St. NW, Washington, DC 20001. Tel. 202/638-0900, or toll free 800/DC-ROOMS. Fax 202/638-5132. 138 rms. A/C TV TEL. **Metro:** Union Station.

$ Rates: Weekday $99.50 single, $114.50 double; weekend $75 single or double. Children under 16 stay free in parents' room; free crib. Extra person $15. Weekend packages available. AE, CB, DC, MC, V.

Parking: $8 from 9am to 4pm, complimentary from 4pm to 9am.

Kids and anyone else with a flair for the dramatic will love the lobby, which is pure 1930s Hollywood with Moorish windows, wrought-iron railings, palms, and Corinthian columns against a two-tone pink background. A stone's throw from Union Station and the Capitol, the Bellevue is on a quiet block, a short walk from Mall attractions and the Metro.

The ambiance of this intimate, European-style hotel comforts those seeking solitude and old-world charm over hoopla and high-tech glitz. They've been here since 1928, so you know they're doing things right. Service is personalized and there's a delightful restaurant on the premises. Kids love the comic-book menu and snack selections at the Tiber Creek Pub. The spacious, attractively furnished rooms recently underwent major renovations, and each has a queen-size bed, small pull-out couch, and plenty of room to spare for a rollaway. Corner rooms are largest and, while the bathrooms are "old-world" small, there's an extra sink and vanity.

Dining/Entertainment: The Tiber Creek Pub, off the lobby, welcomes kids to settle into the same highback leather chairs frequently occupied by congressional leaders. Named for the creek that ran through D.C. 200 years ago, it's open for breakfast Monday through Friday and lunch and dinner daily. You can order anything from boardwalk fries and nachos to an 18-ounce T-bone steak.

Services: Room service, 24-hour front-desk assistance, valet service, baby-sitting arrangements.

THE CARLYLE SUITES, 1731 New Hampshire Ave. NW, between R and S Streets, Washington, DC 20009. Tel. 202/234-3200. Fax 202/387-0085. 170 suites. A/C TV TEL **Metro:** Dupont Circle (Q Street exit).

$ Rates: Weekday $69–$99 single, $79–$109 double, $125 suite. Weekend $24.50 per person double. Children under 18 stay free in parents' room; crib $10. Extra person $10. Weekend packages available. AE, DC, MC, V.

Parking: Free but limited.

This 8-story all-suite hotel, three blocks from the Dupont Circle Metro, sits on a quiet residential street and has lots going for it besides its location. First and foremost, it's service-oriented, with 24-hour assistance available at the front desk.

Elements of the art-deco exterior are reflected in the attractive lobby and stylish Neon Café. Rooms (with two double beds and a sofabed, or a king and sofabed) are spacious with overly large closets, dining and sitting areas, and well-equipped kitchenettes. You can even request a microwave for the kids' popcorn. Best of all, there's a Safeway market two blocks away, where you can load up on supplies so your youngsters can snack to their hearts' content while enjoying a movie on SpectraVision. Do shop, because there's no room service here.

Dining/Entertainment: The Neon Café, so named because of the purple neon tubing accenting the trendy black, white, and gray decor, is open daily for breakfast, lunch, dinner, and weekend brunch. Choose from salads, sandwiches, and a nice selection of entrees at lunch and dinner while listening to hits from the 1930s and 1940s.

Services: 24-hour front-desk assistance, food shopping service, baby-sitting sources.

Facilities: Coin-op laundry, vending/game room, gratis access to nearby Office Health Center (1990 M St. NW) with Nautilus and Universal exercise equipment, Lifecycles, treadmills, rowing machines, StairMasters, whirlpool, sauna, steam room—adults only.

CONNECTICUT AVENUE DAYS INN, 4400 Connecticut Ave. NW, between Yuma and Albemarle streets, Washington, DC 20008. Tel. 202/244-5600, or toll free 800/325-2525. Fax 202/244-6794. 155 rms. A/C TV TEL **Metro:** Van Ness.

$ Rates (including continental breakfast): Weekday $69–$99 single, $69–$109 double, $99–$125 quad suite. Weekend $49–$79 single or double. Children under 18 stay free in parents' room. Super-Saver rates and specials available. AE, CB, DC, DISC, MC, V.

Parking: Free.

You don't have to pinch yourself; you're not dreaming. This well-maintained hotel in the upper northwest, just two blocks from Metro, is *almost* too good to be true. It's one Metro stop—or a pleasant walk—to the zoo, and a 15-minute ride to most downtown attractions. You don't pay a penny more for the complimentary continental breakfast, cable TV with HBO, and free parking. The rooms are in mint condition, there's a gift shop on the premises, and it's a short walk to numerous neighborhood restaurants and shops.

Many families opt for a parlor suite with an extra room to give everyone breathing space—and an extra TV. To take advantage of the Simple Super-Saver, you must book at least 30 days in advance through the toll-free number.

The hotel has direct-billing privileges with the Espresso Café, a casual carryout/sitdown restaurant one block away that serves breakfast, lunch, and dinner inside or on the patio. The emphasis is on deli fare with some American and Italian entrées at dinner. Room service is provided by Vie de France. There's a gift shop in the rather plush lobby.

DAYS HOTEL CRYSTAL CITY, 2000 Jefferson Davis Highway (US1),

Arlington, VA 22202. Tel. 703/920-8600, or toll free 800/325-2525. Fax 703/920-2840. 247 rms, 3 suites. A/C TV TEL **Metro:** Crystal City.

$ Rates: Weekday $79 and up; weekend $65 and up. Children under 17 stay free in parents' room. Weekend and seasonal packages available. AE, D, DC, MC, V. **Parking:** Free.

Walk two blocks to the Metro from this family-pleasing hotel close to National Airport. It may not be fancy, but it's clean, and there's a homey, pleasant feeling about the place. The lobby was recently remodeled, and what the rooms lack in panache they make up for in amenities. Every room has a coffee maker, and for $4 a day you can request a room with a combination microwave/refrigerator/freezer. Think of all the money you'll save on breakfast and snacks!

A lifeguard is on duty at the outdoor pool (open Memorial Day to Labor Day), and there's complimentary transportation to National Airport weekdays from 7am to 11pm and weekends from 6am to 11pm. A children's menu, with word puzzles on the back, is available for all meals in Gatwick's Restaurant for those 10 and under. Your kids will like the "S'cetti" (spaghetti and garlic bread).

Get your fill of shopping and eating at the Crystal City Underground (within walking distance) and The Fashion Centre at Pentagon City (a quick Metro ride). All the downtown sights and Old Town, Alexandria, are 10 to 15 minutes away via the Metro. You can also get off at the Rosslyn stop and walk over the Key Bridge to Georgetown.

Dining/Entertainment: As mentioned above, Gatwicks is open daily and has a children's menu with reasonably priced items they like. Adults will enjoy cocktails and listening to the jukebox in The Brass Lantern.

Services: Front-desk assistance, laundry/valet, free transportation to National Airport.

Facilities: Outdoor pool with lifeguard, gift shop.

THE DAYS INN DOWNTOWN, 1201 K St. NW, Washington, DC 20005. Tel. 202/842-1020, or toll free 800/562-3350. Fax 202/289-0336. 220 rms. A/C TV TEL **Metro:** Metro Center.

$ Rates: Weekday $77–$87 single; $87–$97 double; weekend $75 single or double. Extra person $6. Children under 18 stay free in parents' room. Super-Saver rate ($59 single or double) available if you reserve 30 days in advance via the toll-free number 800/325-2525. AE, CB, DC, DISC, MC, V. **Parking:** $7 (doesn't include in-and-out service).

The rooms and hallways have been spruced up, and the results are exceedingly pleasing. Although this isn't the most picturesque block in the city, the location can't be beat. It's four blocks to Metro Center, where you can hop a train for anywhere on Metro's five lines. Walk to Ford's Theatre, the FBI, the Shops at National Place, the Mall, and downtown shopping. A small rooftop swimming pool with a sundeck and video game room is more than adequate for cooling off after pounding the summertime pavement. Kids can watch free movies on TV or the channel airing tourism information. There are ice and soda machines on every floor; snacks and candy on the second floor. Additional amenities: room service from 7am to 9pm and car rental agencies just across the street, plus there's a Domino's Pizza (for you know who) across the street at 1108 K St.

Dining/Entertainment: Buckley's Grill, with its fish tanks, nautical paintings, and big-screen TV, welcomes kids with open arms. It serves lunch Monday through

Friday, breakfast and dinner daily. Load up on the all-you-can-eat $6 breakfast buffet and you can probably skip lunch. At dinner kids have a choice of fried chicken wings or fish strips for $3.25 if they can't tackle the regular menu. Parents will enjoy the excellent and competitively priced New American fare plus Créole specialties, fresh seafood, and gourmet pizzas. The adjoining Buckley's Lounge is the scene of happy-hour buffets Monday through Friday from 5 to 7pm, perfect after the wee ones have been retired for the evening.

HOLIDAY INN CHEVY CHASE, 5520 Wisconsin Ave., Chevy Chase, MD 20815. Tel. 301/656-1500, or toll free 800/HOLIDAY. Fax 301/656-5045. 214 rms; 12 suites. A/C TV TEL **Metro:** Friendship Heights.

$ Rates: Weekday $89 and up single, $99 and up double; weekend $62 single or double. Children 18 and under stay free in parents' room. "Great Rates" packages (from $59 per room per night) are available through the toll-free reservation number. AE, CB, D, DC, MC, V.

Parking: Free.

This Holiday Inn is ideal for those whose families want to mix heavy doses of shopping in with their sightseeing. Stroll over to Saks Fifth Avenue, Lord & Taylor, Woodward & Lothrop, Gucci, Brooks Brothers, Yves St. Laurent, and Mazza Gallerie (with Neiman Marcus and many upscale boutiques and specialty stores). When you run out of money and want to head downtown for some free sightseeing, the Friendship Heights Metro is only a block away.

The third-floor outdoor pool is watched over by a lifeguard from Memorial Day to Labor Day, and guests (over 18) have free use of a fitness center up the street. All you have to do is flash your room key. While you're working out, the younger kids can enjoy an in-room movie on HBO or Showtime or watch their favorite sports on ESPN. The family pooch can room here for free with the kids.

There's a slew of family restaurants within walking distance too. Tila's, The Cheesecake Factory, Chadwicks', and Hamburger Hamlet all welcome families. The Pleasant Peasant is perfect for leisurely dining with older kids.

Dining/Entertainment: The Avenue Deli is open for breakfast and lunch and has a children's menu with plenty of good things to eat for hungry girls and boys, and an adult menu for those footing the bills. Next door at Julian's (basically a steak and seafood restaurant), families can enjoy lunch and dinner specials like grilled salmon and prime rib in a more formal dining room setting. Kids are welcome here, but if yours can't sit still for more than 20 minutes, this is probably not the best choice.

Services: Room service, front-desk assistance.

Facilities: Outdoor pool with lifeguard, coin-op laundry, free access to nearby fitness center.

HOTEL ANTHONY, 1823 L St. NW, Washington, DC 20036. Tel. 202/ 223-4320, or toll free 800/424-2970. Fax 202/223-8546. 99 efficiency suites. A/C TV TEL **Metro:** Farragut North or Farragut West.

$ Rates: Weekday $99–$123 single, $109–$133 double; weekend $60–$70 single or double. Children under 16 stay free in parents' room. Extra person $10. Weekend packages available. AE, CB, D, DC, MC, V.

Parking: $10–$15 at public garages.

Walk to the White House, National Geographic, Renwick and Corcoran galleries from this rather elegant-looking residential hotel two blocks from the Connecticut Avenue business corridor lined with upscale dining and shopping establishments. At the Hotel Anthony, visitors enjoy the comforts of home just four Metro stops from the Smithsonian museums.

All kitchens have sinks, refrigerators, a coffee maker, cutlery, china, and cookware. Some have stoves, microwaves, and wet bars. The rooms, closets, and baths are spacious and the decor is tasteful and inviting.

Samantha's, next door, is open daily from 11:30am to 2am for deli sandwiches, omelets, salads, burgers, and daily specials such as steamed mussels in garlic and white wine sauce. The ambiance is casual at this family-friendly restaurant, which is a popular watering hole during the happy hour. Tables are set up outside in good weather. The Royal Frontier, an exotic stone-walled restaurant, is on the premises. It's open for American breakfasts, Indian lunches and dinners. It's suitable for older children especially. There's music and dancing on Friday and Saturday nights.

Anthony extras include a copy of the *Washington Post* each weekday morning, room service, laundry/valet service, and gratis use of the nearby Office Health Center, which has Nautilus and Universal exercise equipment, Lifecycles, exercise bikes, treadmills, rowing machines, StairMasters, whirlpool, sauna, steam, and more (kids must be accompanied by an adult). A unisex hairstyling salon is on the premises.

HOTEL HARRINGTON, 11th and E St. NW, Washington, DC 20004. Tel. 202/628-8140, or toll free 800/424-8532. Fax 202/347-3924. 284 rms. A/C TV TEL **Metro:** Metro Center.

$ Rates: Weekday $65 single, $69–$75 double; weekend $59 single or double. Family, weekend, and summer packages available. AE, D, DC, MC, V.

Parking: $5.

Still family owned after 75 years, the Harrington is within walking distance of the FBI, Ford's Theatre, The Shops at National Place, the Old Post Office Pavilion, the National Aquarium, and several Smithsonian museums. The Metro Center stop is only two blocks away. The high-ceilinged rooms, although clean and modernized, are showing their age. The beds are firm; closets and bathrooms are small. All rooms have a desk, chair, and TV (no cable); some have minibars. Family suites, consisting of two rooms (one with a queen bed, the other with two twins) and two baths, are ideal for a family of four.

Two restaurants serving home-style cooking are on the premises (see below). The hotel has a lobby gift shop and tour office and offers limousine service to Dulles Airport.

Little wonder this oldtimer is still going strong after three quarters of a century. The price is right and the location is prime. The Harrington doesn't pretend to be what it is not, and it's the only hotel that hasn't succumbed to inflation in this pricey neighborhood.

Dining/Entertainment: Ollie's Trolley, a bargain, is open for full breakfast and lunch, perfect for family dining. The Harrington Café is open year-round for complimentary continental breakfast, seasonally for dinner, and other times for sanwiches and light fare.

QUALITY HOTEL CAPITOL HILL, 415 New Jersey Ave. NW, Washington, DC 20001. Tel. 202/638-1616, or toll free 800/228-5151. Fax 202/638-0707. 341 rms. A/C TV TEL **Metro:** Union Station.

$ Rates: Sept–Nov and Feb–May $108–$135 single, $118–$150 double, $130–

$375 suites. Higher rates Cherry Blossom Festival; lower rates rest of year. Kids 18 and under stay free in parents' room, crib free. Weekend and Children's Museum Packages $68 and up. AE, D, DC, MC, V.

Parking: Free.

At this prime Capitol Hill location for 20 years, the Quality Hotel is a find, especially on weekends when the rates dip as low as $68. Underground parking is always free, and Union Station and Amtrak are a 5-minute walk away. Rooms are clean, large, and comfortable, with an extra sink outside the bathroom. If you want more space, request a room with an adjoining parlor—a large TV/sitting room with a Murphy bed.

The Children's Museum Package includes discounts to the Capital Children's Museum and Washington Doll and Toy Museum, both big hits with kids. The remote-control TVs have SpectraVision, and there are soda and ice machines on every floor; snack machines on some. In summer, take the young ones swimming in the rooftop pool—one of the largest in the city—with its adjacent sundeck and snack bar with a view.

There's a small gift/sundries shop off the lobby, as well as the clubby Coach & Parlor restaurant, which has a "Young Engineer's Menu" for kids. The all-you-can-eat breakfast and lunch buffets are a bargain, and dinner is just fine too. Parents will enjoy stopping in for libations at the Whistlestop cocktail lounge.

If you don't want to leave Rover at home, you'll be pleased to learn he's welcome here. Everyone is welcome, for service is key here; 80% of the employees have been with the hotel for five or more years. How many hotels can make that claim? Other amenities include concierge service, room service, baby-sitting arrangements, coin-op laundry, and gift shop.

4. INEXPENSIVE

BRICKSKELLER INN, 1523 22nd St. NW, Washington, DC 20036. Tel. 202/293-1885. 44 rms. A/C TV TEL **Metro:** Dupont Circle (Q St. exit), walk 2 blocks to left at 22nd St.

$ Rates: $45 with shared bath; $65 with private bath. Weekly rates available. AE, DC, MC, V.

Parking: None on premises; $6–$8 at public lot.

What you see is what you get at the European-style Brickskeller Inn (formerly the Marifex). The hotel is on a quiet residential street a few blocks from the Dupont Circle Metro station and has a casual, family-friendly restaurant downstairs. Rooms are small and spartan, but clean and neat with a bed, dresser, and TV. Some rooms have private baths; most have sinks.

On the outskirts of Rock Creek Park, the Brickskeller lies within the colorful Dupont Circle neighborhood, known for its galleries, shops, and restaurants. It's an easy walk to the Phillips Collection and Embassy Row (Massachusetts Avenue), and only six blocks to the eastern "border" of Georgetown. "Quiet" is the operative word here. The weekly rate for two with a private bath is under $300. Better reserve early, particularly if you want a room with a private bath.

Dining/Entertainment: Play a video game or darts or pop a coin into the oldies jukebox downstairs at the cozy, family-friendly Brickskeller. There's plenty for the kids to do while waiting for their burgers or chicken wings (see the writeup in Chapter 7, "Where Kids Like to Eat").

UNIVERSITY INN, 2134 G St. NW, Washington, DC 20037. Tel. 202/ 342-8020, or toll free 800/842-1012. 118 rms, 1 suite. A/C TV TEL **Metro:** Foggy Bottom.

$ Rates: $57–$79 per room. AE, DC, MC, V.

Parking: None on premises; public garage at 22nd & I St.

The University Inn is a clean, well-lighted place three blocks from the Metro on the campus of George Washington University. Rooms are modest yet comfortable, ranging from a single with a bed and dresser to a double with two twin beds, a dresser, and desk. Suite 204 has two bedrooms and is suitable for a family of three. A complimentary breakfast of juice, coffee, and pastry is served in the lobby, and D.J.'s deli/restaurant across the street is open every day but Sunday.

The paint may be tired, but the hotel is quiet and the atmosphere is friendly. The White House is five blocks away, and you can walk to restaurants, Georgetown, and some downtown sightseeing. At 2000 Pennsylvania Avenue, there's a small shopping/ restaurant complex with Tower Records and Video.

5. BUDGET

WASHINGTON INTERNATIONAL YOUTH HOSTEL (WIYH), 1009 11th St. NW at K Street, Washington, DC 20001. Tel. 202/737-2333. 250 beds. A/C **Metro:** Metro Center.

$ Rates: $14 AYH members; $17 nonmembers. With a $35 family membership (good for one year), children under 17 pay $7 per night. No credit cards.

Parking: None; public lots in area.

The Washington International Youth Hostel's (WIYH) dorm-style rooms in this renovated downtown apartment building are strictly no-frills, but the location just three blocks from the Metro Center stop can't be beat. The big question is: Can your kids survive without TV? The freshly painted dorm rooms have from 4 to 14 beds and are comfortable; there are clean baths down the hall. The best deal for families is to pay the $35 annual family membership, which allows kids under 17 to stay for half-price—a staggering $7 (yes, that's U.S. currency) per night. Some family rooms, accommodating 4 to 5 persons, are available in the winter. Otherwise, remember the dorms are for men or women only and thus couples are separated, with sons sleeping in the same dorm as fathers, and daughters with their mothers.

Guests must provide their own towels, soap, and linens—blankets and pillows are provided. Sleeping bags are not allowed. You can rent the requisite sleep sheets here for $1 per night or buy one.

Upon registering, you'll be given an information sheet detailing local services. WIYH offers special activities for guests—volleyball games, cookouts, movies, and more. And near the entrance, knowledgeable volunteers staff a comprehensive information desk to help guests with sightseeing and other travel questions.

To cut costs further, shop for groceries at the smallish Capitol Market, 1231 11th

St. NW (three blocks away), or the Giant supermarket at 9th and O St. NW. You can prepare your meals in the huge self-service kitchen, and eat in the dining room. Just like home! There's a comfortable lounge, coin-op laundry machines, storage lockers, and indoor parking for bicycles.

Reserve as far in advance as possible and plan to check in after 2:30pm. Remember the maximum stay is three nights, but that limit may be extended with permission, subject to available space. At these prices, there are few vacancies. With the money you save by staying here, you can plan a return trip next year.

Note: The hostel has a midnight curfew, which is strictly enforced. The hostel is also closed daily from 11am to 2:30pm for cleaning and maintenance.

6. BED & BREAKFAST

Staying in a B&B will enhance your family's visit because you'll receive personalized service and have a chance to meet and greet locals and other visitors in an intimate setting. Rooms in B&Bs run the gamut from inexpensive cubicles in out-of-the-way locations to ornately furnished suites in historic buildings.

In addition to my specific B&B recommendation, I've listed several services under whose umbrellas are numerous homes renting out rooms on this basis. Reserve as early as possible to get the greatest selection of locations and lowest rates, and do specify your needs and preferences: for instance, discuss children, pets, smoking policy, preferred locations (do you require convenient public transportation?), parking, availability of TV and/or phone, preferred breakfast, and choice of payment.

B&B RESERVATION SERVICES

The **Bed and Breakfast League/Sweet Dreams & Toast,** P.O. Box 9490, Washington, DC 20016 (tel. 202/363-7767), is a reservation service representing over 85 B&B accommodations in the District and adjoining Maryland and Virginia suburbs. Through them, you might find a room in a mid-1800s Federal-style Capitol Hill mansion, a Georgetown home with a lovely garden, or a turn-of-the-century Dupont Circle town house filled with Victorian furnishings. Those are just a few of the many possibilities. Accommodations are all screened, and guest reports are given serious consideration. Hosts are encouraged, though not required, to offer such niceties as fresh-baked muffins at breakfast. All listings are convenient to public transportation. Rates for most range from $35 to $100 single, from $50 to $110 double, and from $10 to $25 per additional person. There's a two-night minimum-stay requirement and a booking fee of $10 (per reservation, not per night). AE, DC, MC, V.

Similarly, there's **Bed 'n' Breakfast Ltd. of Washington, D.C.,** P.O. Box 12011, Washington, DC 20005 (tel. 202/328-3510), with about 80 homes, inns, guesthouses, and unhosted furnished apartments in its files. Some are in historic District homes. Its current roster offers, among many others, a Georgian-style Colonial brick home on a tree-lined avenue near Tenley Circle; an 1899 Victorian home on Capitol Hill owned by a network news producer (a well-stocked library is a plus); and a former embassy on upper 16th Street with an attractive modern interior. Rates are from $45 to $125 single, from $50 to $150 double, $15 for an extra person, and from $60 for a full apartment. At guesthouses and inns, rates run the gamut from $70 to $175 single, $80 to $200 double. AE, DC, MC, V.

B&B RECOMMENDATION

MORRISON CLARK INN, Massachusetts Avenue NW, at 11th Street, Washington, DC 20001. Tel. 202/898-1200, or toll free 800/332-7898. Fax 202/289-8576. 54 rms (includes 12 Victorian suites). A/C TV TEL VCR **Metro:** Metro Center.

$ Rates (including continental breakfast): Weekday $115–$155 single, $135–$175 double; weekend $89–$135 single or double. Children under 12 stay free. Extra person $20. Family rates available. AE, CB, DC, MC, V.

Parking: $10.

Even if you have no intention of staying here, add the Morrison Clark Inn to your sightseeing list when you visit. It's magnificent. The original twin buildings were erected in 1865 and it is on the National Register of Historic Places. The interior is worthy of an *Architectural Digest* spread, from the Victorian entry parlor to the beautifully decorated guest rooms, individualized with wicker, antiques, original art, and fresh bouquets. All rooms have private baths, two phones (bed and bath), remote-control color TVs, and VCRs (tapes are available at the desk). Some accommodations have bougainvillea-draped trellised balconies or private porches surrounding a fountained courtyard garden.

A complimentary continental breakfast of fresh-baked breads, muffins, croissants, brioches, and pastries is served in the delightful Club Room. Gratis daily newspapers, twice-a-day maid service with Belgian chocolates at bed turndown, and complimentary overnight shoeshines are but a few of the extras at the Morrison Clark, which takes the B&B concept to new heights of luxury. The management is very gracious about accepting children of all ages, but because there are so many pretty things to break, consider staying here only if your kids are at least 11 or 12.

Dining/Entertainment: The hotel's noted restaurant of the same name is open daily, except Monday, for highly acclaimed regional American cuisine at lunch, dinner, and Sunday brunch. Reservations are a must. This place is strictly for older kids who appreciate fine dining and elegant trappings. Barbara Bush has enjoyed the food and hospitality here, but without her grandchildren.

7. CAMPGROUNDS

Maybe you're a family of campers? If so, consider staying in one of Maryland or Virginia's many campgrounds. Here are two of the closest and best equipped.

AQUIA PINES CAMPGROUND, 3071 Jefferson Davis Highway, Stafford, VA 22554. Tel. 703/659-3447.

$ Rates: $20 per recreational vehicle (includes 2 persons); $2.50 each additional person; $15 no hook-up; air-conditioner $2.50. MC, V.

Billed as "The Campground Most Convenient to the White House," Aquia Pines lies off I-95, about 35 miles south of D.C. and 10 miles north of George Washington's boyhood home, Fredericksburg. The campground is heavily treed and the bathrooms are so clean they were photographed by the National Campground Association for a training film. Now that's clean! Amenities for the kids include a large pool, game room, mini-golf course, basketball court, and playground. There are also hot showers, picnic tables, and a general store. Guided tours of Washington and historic Fredericksburg pick up passengers at the campground, and rental cars are available.

CHERRY HILL PARK, 9800 Cherry Hill Rd., College Park, MD 20740. Tel. **301/937-7116.** Fax 301/595-7181. **Metrobus:** no. 82 from park to Rhode Island Avenue Metro.

$ Rates: $30 per recreational vehicle (includes 2 persons); $2 each additional person; $25 tent campers (2). D, MC, V.

Just 10 miles from downtown Washington, at the intersection of I-95 and the Capital Beltway, lies this 53-acre campground. Staying here can hardly be considered a back-to-nature experience. When was the last time you roughed it with an outdoor pool, large-screen TV room, video games, fitness classes, 30-some-odd washers and dryers, and tour options? The Gurevich family runs the place like a southern-style Borscht Belt resort. In summer, your kids will love the location, as Wild World Amusement Park, with its many water attractions, is only 20 minutes away. The only drawback to Cherry Hill Park is the incessant traffic noise. But that's why earplugs were invented.

CHAPTER 9

EASY EXCURSIONS

1. AMUSEMENT PARKS
2. BARNSTORMING
3. MOUNT VERNON
4. OLD TOWN,
ALEXANDRIA
5. ANNAPOLIS
6. BALTIMORE
7. HARPERS FERRY,
WEST VIRGINIA

I f time permits, plan a side trip to one or more of the following attractions. Using your hotel as a base, you can visit most of these in a day and be back in D.C. for the nightly news on TV.

---

1. AMUSEMENT PARKS

With the exception of Wild World, which is off the Beltway, the following parks are an hour or more from D.C. If you have the time and the kids plead long and loud enough, you're bound to give in. It may seem like a waste of time and money to drive a long distance to lose your lunch on a giant roller coaster, but remember, they're only young once. Since the food is expensive and mediocre, and outside rations may not be brought in, you may want to keep a cooler filled with drinks and snacks in your car to cut costs.

BUSCH GARDENS ("The Old Country"), Williamsburg, VA. Tel. toll free 800/772-8886.

The emphasis at this 360-acre theme park in an ersatz-European setting is on family entertainment, as in musical revues, celebrity concerts, and hokey variety acts. Most kids prefer getting soaked on the Roman Rapids, riding the Questor flight simulator, or screaming their heads off on the Loch Ness Monster to watching a musical. The park is 165 miles south of Washington, D.C.

Admission: $22.95 3 years and up; $28.95 for a two-day ticket.

Open: Late March–mid-May weekends only, Sat 10am–10pm, Sun 10am–7pm; mid-May–mid-June Sat 10am–10pm, Sun–Fri 10am–7pm; mid-June–mid-July daily 10am–10pm; mid-July–Aug 31 Sat 10am–midnight, Sun–Fri 10am–10pm; Labor Day weekend 10 am–10 pm; rest of Sept–Oct, Fri–Tues 10am–7pm. **Directions:** Take I-95 south to Route 295 east (circling Richmond) to I-64. Take exit 57A and follow signs.

HERSHEYPARK, Hershey, PA. Tel. toll free 800/437-7439.

Take the family to "The sweetest place on earth," and between wolfing Hershey bars and Reese's, catch the dolphin and sea lion show. Ride the Sidewinder—guaranteed to make you nauseated and leave your kids squealing for more—and 49 other rides. Entry to Zoo America, home to many native American species, is included in your admission to Hersheypark and is right next door. Hersheypark is 150 miles north of Washington, D.C.

Admission: $20.95 adults, $17.95 kids 3–8, $13.75 seniors over 62.

Open: Mid-May–Memorial Day, weekends only 10:30am–8pm; Memorial

Day–mid-June, open daily, hours vary; mid–June through Aug, daily 10:30am–10pm; September weekends only 10:30am–8pm. **Directions:** Take I-95 north to Baltimore, then take either Rte 695 around the city to I-83 or pick up I-83 as you enter the city. Take I-83 to the Harrisburg exit and follow Route 332 E to the Hersheypark Drive exit and follow the signs.

KINGS DOMINION, Doswell, VA. Tel. 804/876-5000.

Don't wrestle with the Anaconda after a full meal. Brand new in '91, this roller coaster turns upside down four times and makes a 14-story dive that's sure to jar your dentures. If you're not up to the experience, there are 100 other rides and attractions. The Avalanche bobsled still packs 'em in, but you may need a Dramamine beforehand. Younger kids will meet their favorite cartoon and TV characters in Hanna-Barbera Land. This park is 75 miles south of Washington, D.C.

Admission: $21.95 adults; $13.95 kids 3–6; $16.95 adults 55 and over.

Open: Late Mar to Memorial Day weekends only, hours vary; Memorial Day to Labor Day, 9:30am–8pm weekdays, extended weekend hours; Sept to mid-Oct weekends only, 9:30am–8pm. **Directions:** Take I-95 south to exit 40. You can't miss it from there.

WILD WORLD, 13710 Central Ave., Mitchelville, MD. Tel. 301/249-1500.

There's water, water, everywhere, and still plenty to drink at this popular Prince George's County theme park. Older kids thrill to The Double Rampage, a wet-and-wild roller coaster, while younger siblings splash around in the Tadpool. The Wild Wave pool is said to be the world's largest, and you can work on your tan and scratch your back at the same time while reclining on tickly Astroturf. Plenty of mechanical rides, a children's play area, and video arcade are available for those who prefer terra firma. There are several snack bars on the premises and a picnic area just outside the park if you want to BYO.

Admission: $15.95 adults and kids over 8; $13.95 kids 3–8.

Open: Memorial Day weekend 11am–8pm; June 1 to Labor Day daily 11am–8pm, some extended hours. **Directions:** Take I-95 north (the Beltway) to exit 15A at Central Avenue. Wild World is 5 miles east on the left.

2. BARNSTORMING

THE FLYING CIRCUS AERODROME, Bealeton, VA., Tel. 703/439-8661.

Have you or your kids ever seen antique biplanes and World War I fighters perform heart-stopping aerial stunts, other than in the movies? If the answer is no, fly over to Bealeton any Sunday between May and November for an afternoon of barnstorming, dogfights, and wing walkings. It's well worth the 1½-hour drive from D.C. to watch seasoned pilots put vintage planes through their paces. Open cockpit rides begin at 1pm. The actual air show begins at 2:30—and what a show it is! There's a concession stand for drinks and snacks and picnic tables on the premises. For a treat your kids won't forget, pack your lunch, leather helmet, and goggles and pretend you're the Red Baron for the day. The aerodrome is about 60 miles southwest of Washington, D.C.

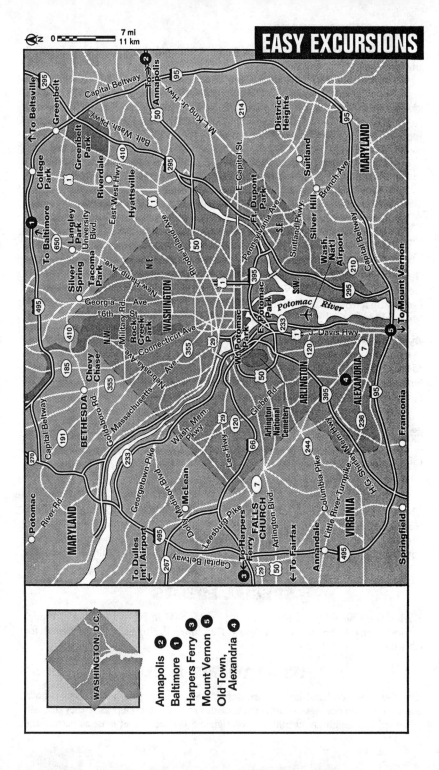

Admission: $8 adults; $3 kids under 12. Additional charge for rides before and after the show.

Open: May–October, Sundays 11am–dusk. Show at 2:30pm. **Directions:** Take Route 66 West to Route 28, the Dulles/Centerville exit. Follow Route 28 through Manassass to Route 17 at Bealeton. Turn left (south) on Route 17 (towards Fredericksburg) and continue 5 miles until you see a wind sock flying on your left. If you get to a roller rink, you've gone too far.

3. MOUNT VERNON

16 miles of Washington, D.C.

GETTING THERE   By Car   Take any of the bridges over the Potomac into Virginia to the George Washington Memorial Parkway going south. The parkway ends at Mount Vernon.

By Tourmobile   **Tourmobile** buses (tel. 554-7950) depart daily April through October from Arlington National Cemetery and the Washington Monument. Round-trip fare is $16.50 for adults, $8 for children 3 to 11, and includes admission to Mount Vernon. Call ahead for departure hours.

By Riverboat   From late March through October, the *Spirit of Mount Vernon* riverboat travels down the Potomac from Pier 4, at 6th and Water streets SW (tel. 554-8000 for departure hours). There are two sailings daily. Round-trip fares are $18 for adults, $16 for senior citizens, $10.75 for children 6 to 11, $7.75 for children 2 to 5, under 2 free. Fares include admission to Mount Vernon.

George Washington's estate, just 16 miles from the District, has been lovingly restored to its original appearance, down to the paint colors on the walls. No visit to Washington, D.C., is complete without a visit here.

INFORMATION

Mount Vernon is owned and maintained by the **Mount Vernon Ladies' Association.** For a brochure, write to them at Mount Vernon, VA 22121 (tel. 703/780-2000). Mount Vernon is open daily, including Christmas, March through October 9am to 5pm; November through February 9am to 4pm. Admission is $6 adults; $5.50 seniors 62 and older; $3 kids 6–11.

SPECIAL EVENTS

Washington's Birthday is celebrated the third Monday in February with a memorial service open to the public, and every December the mansion is decorated for Christmas.

WHAT TO SEE & DO

If you've ever wondered how an aristocratic 18th century family lived, this is how. Some of the furnishings are original, and the rooms are set up as if they are still inhabited. Although about 500 of the original 8,000 acres still exist as part of the estate, 30 are yours to explore. The plantation dates back to 1674 when the land was granted to Washington's great-grandfather. Washington spent two years in retirement here before he died in 1799.

As you tour at your own pace, docents are on hand to supplement what you see. They take pride and a personal interest in Mount Vernon's story and are extremely knowledgeable, so don't be bashful with your questions. Children are usually less interested in the period furnishings than the family kitchen and outbuildings where everyday tasks—baking, weaving, and washing—took place.

A short walk from the mansion is the tomb where George, his wife Martha, and other family members are buried. On the third Monday of February a memorial service, commemorating Washington's birthday, is held at the estate.

Also of interest is the slave burial ground and the museum where the family's personal possessions are displayed. There's a Museum Shop on the grounds and Mount Vernon Inn Gift Shop outside the main gate. Allow time for a stroll through the grounds and gardens. Wait 'til you see the view from the front lawn. Talk about prime waterfront property!

WHERE TO DINE

Just outside the main gate are a **snack bar,** open for breakfast, lunch, and light fare, and the **Mount Vernon Inn** restaurant, open daily for lunch, Monday through Saturday for dinner (tel. 703/780-0011). Reservations are recommended at the Inn. You can **picnic** one mile north of Mount Vernon at Riverside Park or, on your way back to D.C., stop in Old Town, Alexandria, where there are scores of restaurants. If you choose the *Spirit of Mt. Vernon* as your mode of travel, there's a snack bar onboard.

4. OLD TOWN, ALEXANDRIA

6 miles S of Washington, D.C.

GETTING THERE   By Metro   The easiest way to do the trip is via Metro. And the sights of Old Town are so compact, you won't need your car once you arrive. Take the Yellow Line to the King Street station. From the station, board a DASH bus (70¢) to King and Fairfax—right to the door of the Visitors Center. Take a transfer, and you can board any DASH bus within a 3-hour period. It's a short ride from the station; in fact you could walk it, but better to save your feet for sightseeing.

By Car   If you're driving, take the Arlington Memorial or 14th Street Bridge to the scenic George Washington Memorial Parkway, which will take you right into King Street, Alexandria's main thoroughfare. It's about a 6-mile trip. Parking permits are available from the Ramsay House Visitors Center (see below).

Everyone enjoys a visit to Old Town. What's not to like? The once-thriving colonial port on the western shore of the Potomac River, about 6 miles south of D.C., is picturesque, made for walking, and steeped in history, with many fine restorations of 18th and 19th century buildings dotting its cobblestone streets.

George Washington was a teenage surveyor's assistant when Alexandria became a city in 1749. The original 60 acres now comprise Old Town. Explore the waterfront and board a tall ship, watch artisans at work in the Torpedo Factory Art Center, and shop for up-to-date stuff in old-style buildings.

INFORMATION

Make the **Ramsay House Visitors Center,** 221 King Street (tel. 703/838-4200), your first stop. It's a faithful reconstruction of Alexandria's first house, and is open every day but Thanksgiving, December 25, and January 1, from 9am to 5pm. Pick up a brochure (available in several languages), "Discovery Sheets" outlining self-guided walking tours for families with kids in three age groups, and "Cheap Treats," suggestions for stretching your vacation dollars. If your kids are old enough to appreciate such things, purchase admission tickets to historic homes and sights. For information on costumed historic tours, call "Doorways to Old Virginia" (tel. 703/548-0100). Of special interest to kids is The Graveyards and Ghosts tour, available in the fall by appointment.

SPECIAL EVENTS

Inquire about special events, some of which require tickets, at the Visitors Center. There's always something doing in Old Town! If you're planning ahead and can't reach the phone numbers listed below, call the Visitors Center (tel. 703/838-4200).

January The **birthdays of Robert E. Lee** and his father, **"Light Horse Harry" Lee,** are celebrated with house tours, music, and refreshments.

February Festivities marking **George Washington's birthday** include the nation's largest George Washington Day parade, a 10-kilometer race, and special tours in honor of Alexandria's most famous former resident.

March Alexandria's origin may be Scottish, but you wouldn't know it when **Saint Patrick's Day** rolls around. The town grows greener than a field of shamrocks, and there's a parade and plenty of entertainment.

April Tours of historic homes and gardens are featured during **Historic Garden Week.**

May From May to September, narrated **Lantern Tours** leave from the Visitors Center Saturdays at 8pm. Purchase your tickets right before the tour. School-age kids on up enjoy the anecdotal narration about Alexandria's history. For information call 703/838-4200 or 703/548-0100.

June Don't miss the **Red Cross Waterfront Festival,** an outstanding family event held the second week of June. Boat rides and races, historic tall ships, children's games, entertainment, and food are featured at the harbor. Since the event draws around 100,000 people, arrive early. For information call 703/838-4200.

Drive or taxi over to Fort Ward on selected days for Civil War drills, concerts, and lectures. During one weekend, **Civil War Living History** features authentically dressed military units performing drills and period music. For information call 703/838-4848.

July Alexandria's Scottish heritage is celebrated with **Virginia Scottish Games**

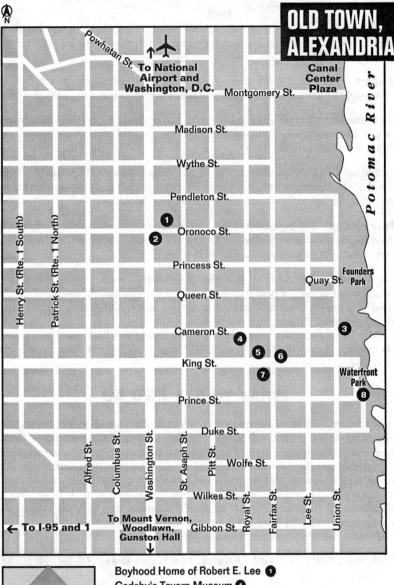

OLD TOWN, ALEXANDRIA

N

Powhatan St.

To National
Airport and
Washington, D.C.

Montgomery St.

Canal
Center
Plaza

Potomac River

Madison St.

Wythe St.

Pendleton St.

Oronoco St.

Princess St.

Quay St.

Founders
Park

Queen St.

Cameron St.

King St.

Prince St.

Waterfront
Park

Henry St. (Rte. 1 South)

Patrick St. (Rte. 1 North)

Duke St.

Wolfe St.

Alfred St.

Columbus St.

Washington St.

St. Asaph St.

Pitt St.

Wilkes St.

Royal St.

Fairfax St.

Lee St.

Union St.

← To I-95 and 1

To Mount Vernon,
Woodlawn,
Gunston Hall

Gibbon St.

WASHINGTON, D.C.

Old Town
Alexandria

Boyhood Home of Robert E. Lee ❶

Gadsby's Tavern Museum ❹

Lee-Fendall House ❷

Market Square ❺

Ramsay House Visitors Center ❻

Stabler-Leadbetter Apothecary Shop ❼

Torpedo Factory Art Center ❸

Waterfront Park ❽

the fourth weekend of the month. Athletic events, a parade of tartan-clad clans, Highland dancing, and storytelling are some of the events. For information call 703/838-5005.

August An 18th century tavern is the scene for music, entertainment, food—1700s-style—during **August Tavern Days.** For information call 703/838-4200.

September Storytellers, jugglers, crafts, and people in period dress are featured at the **Colonial Fair.** Kids especially like the glassblowing demonstration. For information call 703/838-4200.

October The competition is stiff at the **War Between The States Chili Cookoff** in Waterfront Park. For a small admission fee you can sample all the entries and enjoy fiddling contests and country music. For information call 703/548-0100.

November Maybe your older kids will accompany you willingly to the **Historic Alexandria Antiques Show,** with dozens of dealers from several states showing their wares. For information call 703/838-4554.

December The **Annual Scottish Christmas Walk** heralds the holiday season with bagpipers, a parade of the clans, puppet and magic shows and, of course, food. Children's games and Scottish dogs and horses (probably not in kilts) will please the bonnie ones.

Visit historic Alexandria homes and a tavern, decked with holly and other seasonal decorations, during the **Old Town Christmas Candlelight Tour,** usually the second week of the month.

WHAT TO SEE AND DO

Take younger children to Waterfront Park, where they can run loose, feed the pigeons, and look at the boats. Board the 125-foot schooner **Alexandria,** a classic Scandinavian cargo vessel berthed here. Tour the decks, main salon, and a stateroom of this tall ship Saturday and Sunday from noon to 5pm. The tour is free, but donations are appreciated. Everyone enjoys a stroll through Old Town's quaint streets to browse in the area's enticing **shops.** Of special interest to kids are: Bearly Believable, 13 King St.; Granny's Place, 303 Cameron St.; John Davy Toys, 301 Cameron St.; and Why No?, 200 King St.

Note: Some properties are closed on Monday.

TORPEDO FACTORY ART CENTER, 105 North Union St. Tel. 703/838-4565.

This is a must see for all ages. In a Navy-built torpedo shell-case factory, circa World War I, the only thing fired these days is the clay. Catch sculptors, painters, weavers, potters, and numerous other craftspeople and artisans in the act of creating. Since most items are priced reasonably, it's an excellent opportunity to stock up on one-of-a-kind gifts. Kids seem most fascinated watching clay take shape on the potter's wheel. Self-guided tours, available at the information desk, will help you structure your visit. Alexandria Archeology is also centered here, and many unearthed artifacts are on display.

Admission: Free.

Open: Torpedo Factory daily 10am–5pm. Alexandria Archeology and research lab Tues–Fri 10am–3pm, Sat 10am–5pm. **Closed** Thanksgiving, Christmas, New Year's Day, and Easter Sunday.

STABLER-LEADBETTER APOTHECARY SHOP, 105-107 South Fairfax St. Tel. 703/836-3713.

Stop here on your travels and look for the handwritten request for cod liver oil, signed by "Mrs. Washington"—not Martha, as many think, but Mrs. Bushrod Washington, the wife of George Washington's nephew. On display are hand-blown medicine bottles and blood-letting paraphernalia. Extensive restoration is due to be completed early in 1992, and guided tours are planned for the near future.

Admission: Free.

Open: Mon–Sat 10am–4pm and Sun noon–4pm.

GADSBY'S TAVERN MUSEUM, 134 North Royal St. Tel. 703/838-4242.

Older kids may want to see the tavern visited (but not recently) by Washington, Madison, and Jefferson. Originally two buildings that were joined in 1796 by innkeeper John Gadsby, it is now a museum of colonial furnishings and artifacts. Half-hour tours are conducted 15 minutes before and after the hour.

Admission: $3 adults, $1 kids 11–17; kids 10 and under free with paying adult.

Open: Tues–Sat 10am–5pm, Sun 1–5pm.

BOYHOOD HOME OF ROBERT E. LEE, 607 Oronoco St. Tel. 703/548-8454.

This Federal-style mansion was home to "Light Horse Harry" Lee, his wife, and brood of five. History comes alive in every room; the Lafayette Room marks the occasion when that prominent gentleman visited Robert E. Lee's widowed mother in 1824. Tours are ongoing.

Admission: $3 adults, $2 kids 11–17; kids under 11 free.

Open: Mon–Sat 10am–3:30pm, Sun 1–3:30pm.

LEE-FENDALL HOUSE, 614 Oronoco St. Tel. 703/548-1789.

Many Lees called this home over the years, but Robert E. never hung his clothes in the closet. Built in 1785, the original structure was renovated in 1850. Kids like the antique dollhouse collection and boxwood garden better than the home, which serves as a museum of Lee furniture and memorabilia. The half-hour tour paints an impressionistic picture of family life in the Victorian age.

Admission: $3 adults; $2 kids 11–17, free kids under 11.

Open: Tues–Sat 10am–4pm, Sun noon–4pm.

FORT WARD MUSEUM AND PARK, 4301 West Braddock Rd. Tel. 703/838-4848.

This 45-acre park, a short drive from Old Town, boasts an extensive Civil War research library and is the site of one of the forts erected to defend Washington during the Civil War. Explore the fort, six mounted guns, and reproduction of an officer's hut. Civil War weapons and other war-related exhibits can be found in the museum. Picnic areas surround the fort, and outdoor concerts are given during the summer. Every year during Living History Day (usually on the hottest day in August), visitors flock to the Civil War encampment where uniformed regiments perform drills. Tell the kids, no battles allowed.

Admission: Free; donations appreciated for special events.

Open: Park, daily 9am–sunset; museum Tues–Sat 9am–5pm, Sun noon–5pm.

WHERE TO STAY

HOLIDAY INN OLD TOWN, 480 King St., Alexandria, VA. 22314 Tel. 703/549-6080. 227 rms. A/C TV TEL

$ Rates: $99 single; $99–$150 double; $88 Great Rate based on availability.

If you want to stay overnight in Old Town, you can't get any closer than this. There's a large indoor pool open year 'round. The 101, a casual restaurant serving breakfast, lunch, and dinner, and two lounges are on the premises. Ask about the Washington Weekend Package that includes coupons for food and drinks.

WHERE TO EAT

Most of the nearly 100 restaurants in Old Town fall under the mantle of American cooking. If you want to enjoy the sun with your salami, try one of the deli-style carryouts with outside seating. Ask shopkeepers and locals if you're after formality and five courses. Otherwise, try these.

MODERATE/BUDGET

WAREHOUSE BAR & GRILL, 214 King St. Tel. 703/683-6868.

    Cuisine: Seafood. **Reservations:** Recommended.

    $ Prices: Sandwiches $6.95–$9.95; dinner entrees $12.95–$19.95. AE, DC, MC, V.

    Open: Mon–Thurs 11am–10:30pm, Fri and Sat 11–11, Sun 10am–11pm.

The fried shrimp and clams are done to a turn—crunchy and greaseless—at this popular seafood house, but more ambitious fish selections sometimes fall flat as a flounder. Fish haters crying "where's the beef?" are in luck—the steaks are surprisingly good.

BUDGET

CHADWICK'S, 203 S. Strand St. Tel. 703/836-4442.

    Cuisine: American. **Reservations:** No.

    $ Prices: $4.95–$11.95. AE, DC, MC, V.

    Open: Mon–Sat 11:30am–2am, Sun 10am–2am.

Eat in or carry out at good old reliable Chadwick's, a stylish pub opposite the waterfront. The salads, burgers, homemade soups and Sunday brunch are all standouts, and kids always receive VIP treatment.

HARD TIMES CAFE, 1404 King St. Tel. 703/683-5340.

    Cuisine: American. **Reservations:** For 10 or more.

    $ Prices: $3.75–$5.25. MC, V.

    Open: Mon–Thurs 11am–10pm, Fri–Sat 11am–11pm, Sun 4–10pm.

You could live on the onion rings here, but it'd be a shame not to leave room for the chili. Kids usually prefer the milder, tomatoey Cincinnati variety to the spicy, mostly-meat Texas style. There's also veggie chili, the weakest of the three. The chiliburger is sensational.

UNION STREET PUBLIC HOUSE, 121 South Union St. Tel. 703/548-1785.

    Cuisine: American. **Reservations:** No.

    $ Prices: $5.50–$14. AE, CB, DC, MC, V.

Open: Mon–Thurs 11:30am–10:30pm, Fri–Sat 11:30am–11:30pm, Sun 11am–10:30pm.

Try the burger topped with cheddar on toasted rye, ribs, or small filet on an English muffin at this lively pub known for consistently good food and service. Sample one of the local beers while you're here.

5. ANNAPOLIS

30 miles NE of Washington, D.C.

GETTING THERE By Bus Bus transport is available via **Dillon's Bus Service** (tel. 410/647-2321), which picks up passengers at various points throughout the District and makes several stops in Annapolis, including the Navy Marine Corps Stadium parking area. One-way fare is $3.25. Call for departure times and to find the most convenient departure point.

By Car Annapolis is easily reached in about 40 minutes by car via U.S. 50, an eastern extension of New York Avenue. Take the Rowe (rhymes with cow) Boulevard exit and follow signs.

Set off with your crew for Annapolis, the 300-year-old jewel of the Chesapeake, less than an hour's drive—as the gull flies—from downtown D.C. Explore the many facets of this friendly and charming 18th century seaport on the Severn River, dubbed "the sailing capital of the world." Annapolis is home to the U.S. Naval Academy, Maryland State House, St. John's College, beautifully restored historic homes, and about 30,000 pleasure craft.

INFORMATION

Stock up on brochures at the **Visitor Information Center** at the City Dock in the heart of town. It's open daily from 10am to 5pm (tel. 410/268-8687). Information is also available from the City of Annapolis' **Office of Public Information and Tourism,** 160 Duke of Gloucester St., Annapolis, MD. (tel. 410/263-7940). For a list of upcoming events, call 410/268-TOUR or send a self addressed legal-size envelope to: Annapolis Visitors Bureau, 1 Annapolis St., Annapolis MD 21401. Stop at the City Dock or call for information on **Chesapeake Marine Tours'** cruises (tel. 410/268-7600). *Hint:* To see Annapolis at its best, avoid summer Saturdays and Sundays, unless you plan on arriving before noon. Afterward it's a zoo.

The **area code** for Annapolis changed from 301 to 410 in November '91. The **zip code** for Annapolis is 21401.

SPECIAL EVENTS

Tours of historic homes and gardens are ongoing throughout the year (tel. 410/263-7940). During **Commissioning Week** in late May, the public is invited to many events celebrating the graduation of the Naval Academy's first class (seniors to us civvies). Dress parades and a stunning air show by the Blue Angels are part of the festivities (tel. 410/263-6933). On Tuesday evenings in summer, the Naval Academy Band gives **free concerts** at the City Dock. Every fall, in-water **power and sailboat shows** draw boating enthusiasts from all over the world (tel. 410/268-

8828). To usher in the holidays, area boaters spend months decorating their crafts for the spectacular **Christmas Parade of Lights,** which takes place on a Saturday evening in mid-December (tel. 410/267-8986). During the holiday season, the entire downtown area is decked with holly, evergreen boughs, and twinkling lights. It out-Dickens Dickens.

WHAT TO SEE AND DO

Unwind on the seawall with an ice cream cone from **Storm Bros.,** 130 Dock Street, and plan your day as pleasure craft parade up "Ego Alley." Despite a small-town population of 35,000, Annapolis encompasses 16 miles of waterfront. Not surprisingly, one of the best vantage points is from the water, so board one of the **charter boats** or water taxis berthed at the dock or **learn to sail**—it's a breeze at one of the area's sailing schools. Sightseeing, shopping, and restaurants are all an easy walk from the heart of the historic district. Among the **shops** on little shoppers' lists are Be Beep (toy shop) at 14 Market Space, Fit To a Tee at 162 Main Street, The Ship & Soldier Shop (toy soldiers, trains, and boat models) at 58 Maryland Avenue, and Annapolis Pottery, 61 Cornill Street, where potters are usually at work, and you can pick up an attractive hand-crafted reminder of your visit.

ANNAPOLIS SAILING SCHOOL, 601 6th St. Tel. 410/267-7205 or toll free from D.C. 800/261-1947.

Before you go overboard for sailing, this is a good place to start. In two days of concentrated instruction alternating between the classroom and the school's fleet of 24-foot Rainbow sloops, families can learn enough to skipper a small boat. Honest! I've done it. Kids over 6 with an adult are welcome.

Admission: $185 and up; packages with hotel room available.
Open: Late March–Oct.

CHESAPEAKE MARINE TOURS, City Dock. Tel. 410/268-7600.

Board a sightseeing boat for a 40- or 90-minute Severn River cruise spring through fall. When time permits, take an all-day trip to St. Michael's on the Eastern Shore. There are snack bars aboard all boats; music on some.

Admission: $5–$28 (St. Michael's).
Open: May–Oct 10am–dusk.

CHESAPEAKE SAILING SCHOOL, Port Annapolis Marina, 7074 Bembe Beach Rd. Tel. 410/269-1594 or toll free 800/776-0012.

If you get queasy in the bathtub, your kids can learn to sail without you in Kidship. Summer courses for 6- to 16-year-olds run from 3 to 10 days on weekdays 9:30am–3:30pm. Sailing classes for the rest of the family are offered spring through fall.

Admission: $150 and up
Open: Kidship June–Aug; Chesapeake Sailing School Apr–Nov.

MARYLAND STATE HOUSE, State Circle. Tel. 410/974-3400.

The oldest state capitol in continuous legislative use served as the nation's capitol from November 1783 to June 1784. Here George Washington resigned his commission in 1783 and the Treaty of Paris was ratified. Tours are scheduled from 11am to 4pm.

ANNAPOLIS

ACCOMMODATIONS:
Annapolis Marriott
Waterfront **1**
Chez Amis B&B **2**
Scotlaur Inn **3**

DINING:
Cafe Normandie **1**
Chick and Ruth's **2**
Riordan's **3**

ATTRACTIONS:
Annapolis Sailing School **1**
Chesapeake Marine
Tours **2**
Chesapeake Sailing
School **3**
Maryland State House **4**
Miss Anne or Miss
Anne II **5**
U.S. Naval Academy **6**
William Paca House and
Gardens **7**

Church **✝**   Post Office **⊠**   Information **①**

Admission: Free.
Open: Daily 9am–5pm.

MISS ANNE OR MISS ANNE II, City Dock. Tel. 410/261-2719.

These smallish sightseeing boats cast off every half hour for a tour of the harbor.
Open: Daily 12:15–9:45pm.
Admission: $5.

WILLIAM PACA HOUSE AND GARDENS, 186 Prince George St. (garden at 1 Martin St.). Tel. 410/263-5553.

William Paca, a signer of the Declaration of Independence and governor of Maryland during the Revolution, built this five-part Georgian mansion between 1763 and 1765. In the early 1900s the house became a hostelry for legislators and visitors to the U.S. Naval Academy. When the wrecker's ball threatened in 1965, the Historic Annapolis Foundation stepped in and restored the house and 2-acre garden to their former grandeur. While older kids generally find the house of interest, *everyone* delights in the garden with its intricate parterres, terraces, and waterway. The flower enclosure is abloom from March to November.

Admission: $5 adults, $3 kids 8–18; garden only, $2 adults, $1 kids.
Open: Apr–Oct, Tues–Sat 10am–5pm, Sun noon–5pm; Nov–Mar, Mon–Sat 11am–4pm; Sun noon–4pm. Closed Thanksgiving and Christmas.

U.S. NAVAL ACADEMY, Visitors Gate at foot of King George St. Tel. 410/267-6100.

★ It's only a 5-minute walk from town to the Naval Academy, founded in 1845. Take the hour-long tour that departs from Ricketts Hall from March through November (tel. 410/263-6933), or visit on your own the Navy Chapel with John Paul Jones's crypt, and Preble Hall, filled with 200 years of naval art and artifacts (tel. 410/267-6656). In fall and spring, watch noon formation outside Bancroft Hall, the "dormitory" for all 4,500 midshipmen. Would your kids be willing to line up like this for their macaroni and cheese? Stroll the beautiful grounds, walk along the Dewey seawall for a wide-angle view of the harbor and, perhaps, catch a band concert in the gazebo.

Admission: Free self-guided tour; guided tour $3 adults, $1 kids first–sixth grade, free kids under first grade.
Open: Academy grounds open 9am–5pm; tours March–Thanksgiving, Mon–Sat 9:30am–4pm, Sun 11am–4pm. Group tours year-round by appointment.

WHERE TO STAY

If you're planning an overnight stay, take your pick of historic inns, B&Bs, and luxury hotels. Hotels outside the historic district often offer complimentary shuttle service. For a brochure describing B&Bs in Annapolis, write the **Annapolis Association of Licensed Bed and Breakfast Owners,** P.O. Box 744, Annapolis, Md. 21404. You may also make reservations through the **Maryland Reservation Center** (tel. 410/263-9084).

ANNAPOLIS MARRIOTT WATERFRONT, Compromise and St. Mary's streets, Annapolis, Md. 21401. Tel. 410/268-7555 or toll free 800/336-0072. 139 rooms. A/C TV TEL

$ **Rates:** $140–$290. Ask about Breakfast Special and other packages.

Overlooking the harbor and Spa Creek, the Marriott enjoys a prime downtown location and is looking very spiffy indeed after renovation and a change of hands to the Marriott organization. Juan Alfredo's restaurant and dockside bar/lounge is on the premises, and scores of Annapolis eateries (not to mention shopping and sightseeing) are within a few blocks. Room service is available around the clock and the hotel has an arrangement with a local health club. I'm sure they have their reasons, but I think they goofed when they eliminated the swimming pool.

CHEZ AMIS B&B, 85 East St., Annapolis, Md. 21401. Tel. 410/263-6631. 3 rooms. A/C TV TEL
$ Rates: $65–$85; special off-season rates.
Chez Amis is a family-friendly B&B on a quiet block in the heart of the historic district. This former corner store is enchanting, and the original tin ceilings, pine floors, and oak counters were retained in the recent renovation. Rooms have private baths (one with a clawfoot tub), and the extended continental breakfast includes freshly squeezed juice, homemade breads and buns. Children can bunk in the same or separate rooms. You know the owners are kid-considerate; all rooms have TVs.

SCOTLAUR INN, 165 Main St. Annapolis, Md. 21401. Tel. 410/268-5665. 10 rooms. A/C TV TEL
$ Rates: $60–$75; ask about special mid-week rates.
Roll out of bed onto Main Street—literally! Stay at what may be the world's only "Bed and Bagel" and enjoy complimentary breakfast in Chick and Ruth's Delly downstairs. The 10 distinctive rooms are charmingly done in turn-of-the-century furnishings, and the walls are so thick, you'll think you're in the country. When you go downstairs for breakfast, ask Ted to do magic tricks for your kids. You won't have to ask twice.

WHERE TO EAT

MODERATE

CAFE NORMANDIE, 185 Main St. Tel. 410/280-6470.
  Cuisine: French. **Reservations:** Recommended.
  $ Prices: Lunch and dinner entrees $5.95–$19; breakfast less. AE, MC, V.
  Open: Daily 8–11am (breakfast); 11am–5pm (lunch); 5–10pm (dinner).
I would have no problem dining at this cozy, plant-filled bistro three times a day. Don't try all these at one sitting, but the cream of crab soup, Caesar salad, veal and fish entrees, crepes, and fresh fruit tarts are especially noteworthy. If your kids are finicky, they're bound to dig the crepes.

BUDGET

RIORDAN'S, 26 Market Space. Tel. 410/263-5449.
  Cuisine: American. **Reservations:** No.
  $ Prices: $3.25–$18 (sandwiches $5–$9). AE, DC, MC, V.
  Open: Sun–Thurs 11am–1am, Fri and Sat 11am–2am. Sun brunch 10am–1pm.
Close your eyes and picture a friendly neighborhood saloon with lots of wood, brass, and tchotchkas on the walls. That's Riordan's. No wonder locals introduce their kids early on to the potato skins with the works, burgers, sandwiches (especially the roast

beef and Reuben), and such. The food is consistent, and the friendly servers know how to hustle. Sunday brunch is an Annapolis tradition ($6.50–$9 for grownups, $4.50 for kids).

CHICK AND RUTH'S DELLY, 165 Main St. Tel. 410/269-6737.

Cuisine: Deli. **Reservations:** No

$ Prices: $1–$6.25. No credit cards.

Open: Daily, round the clock, but closed between Christmas and New Year's.

The Levitts moved from Baltimore and established their deli restaurant on Main Street back in the 50s, before Annapolis became a Yuppie outpost. Chick's son Ted helps run the place (when he isn't entertaining customers with sleight of hand), and the grandchildren are in training. Breakfast platters are served all day, and 28 tasty sandwiches are named for Maryland pols and locals. You'll love the funky 50s decor, fountain treats, and cheeky waitresses at this friendly eatery. Don't dress up.

---

6. BALTIMORE

38 miles NNE of Washington, D.C.

GETTING THERE   By Train   Frequent daily train service via **Amtrak** (tel. 800/USA-RAIL) is available between Washington and Baltimore. Fare is $11 one-way, $19 round-trip, half price for children.

There are also **MARC commuter trains** (tel. 800/325-RAIL) Monday through Friday; fare is $5 one-way, $9 round-trip, ages 6 to 11 pay half price, under 6 free. Call for departure times. Both train services leave from Union Station and arrive at Baltimore's Penn Station, the latter about 15 blocks from Inner Harbor.

By Bus   Greyhound/Trailways (tel. 301/565-2662) provides frequent service between the Washington bus terminal at 1st and L streets NE and 210 West Fayette Street in Baltimore. Fare is $8.50 one-way, $16 round-trip, half price for children 5 to 11, 10% for ages 2 to 4, under 2 free.

By Car   To get to Baltimore, take I-95 to I-395 north to Pratt Street, make a right and another right at President Street. You'll find many parking lots near the harbor.

Where to start? Only an hour's drive or 40-minute train ride from D.C., Crab Town offers families such an abundance of sights and experiences that you could easily spend several days and leave begging for more. Home of Babe Ruth, H. L. Mencken, and the Baltimore Orioles, and birthplace of our national anthem and Baltimore clipper ships, the city is enlivened by its rich ethnic heritage. Myriad activities are centered at the Inner Harbor, a revitalized complex of businesses, sightseeing attractions, shops, restaurants, and hotels built around the city's natural harbor. Not the least of Baltimore's claims to fame are steamed Chesapeake Bay blue crabs and the best corned beef south of New York City. Don't leave without sampling both.

INFORMATION

For maps and information on sightseeing and walking tours, contact the **Baltimore Visitors Information Center** (tel. 410/837-4636 or toll free 800/282-6632).

Baltimore Good Time Tours (tel. 410/539-3330) and **About Town Tours** (tel. 410/592-7770) operate city tours.

SPECIAL EVENTS

Every February more than 500 artisans fill Festival Hall for the **Baltimore Craft Show**, one of the nation's largest and most prestigious. The **Preakness** is celebrated with concerts, parades, and balloon festivals during the third week of May preceding the race at Pimlico. A **Maritime Festival** is held at the Inner Harbor in June, and **Flag Day** (June 14) is celebrated at Fort McHenry and other sites. Throughout the summer, weekend **Ethnic Festivals** are held near the harbor, an area often visited by tall ships from around the world. Fireworks light up the sky over the Inner Harbor on the **4th of July** and, in October, the **Fells Point Funfest** street festival features clowns, jugglers, music and, of course, good things to eat. Baltimoreans ring in the New Year with a dazzling pyrotechnic display at the Inner Harbor on **New Year's Eve.**

WHAT TO DO AND SEE

BALTIMORE ZOO, Druid Hill Park. Tel. 410/396-7102

The innovative Baltimore Zoo has been trading cages for natural habitats that enable animal lovers to come face to face with their favorite creatures. After a visit, kids come away with a greater appreciation of an animal's point of view. In the Maryland Wilderness section of the zoo, more than 100 local species are exhibited. Your little bipeds can climb into a huge oriole's nest, scale a tree like a bear, or crawl woodchuck-style through an acrylic tunnel under a dam. In the Maryland Farmyard, kids are invited to ride a pony, pet a sheep, or breeze down the silo slide. Lunch with the Kodiak bears at 2pm or watch the African black-footed penguins dive for an early dinner of raw fish at 3pm. Cap your visit with a ride on the antique carousel and Zoo Choo train.

Admission: $6.50 adults, $3.50 kids 2–15; free under 2.

Open: Daily 10am–4:30pm. **Directions:** Take I-95 north to 695 west (toward Towson) to I-83 south (Jones Falls Expressway). Exit 7 west off the Expressway to Druid Park Lake Drive and follow signs to the zoo. In the summer, a shuttle runs to the zoo a few times a day from the Stouffer Harborplace, 202 E. Pratt Street (tel. 410/366-LION).

BALTIMORE AND OHIO RAILROAD MUSEUM, 901 W. Pratt St. (at Poppleton). Tel. 410/752-2490.

Train buffs make tracks for this museum on the site of the country's first train station. The comprehensive exhibits are a must see for little toots who get steamed up over trains and railroad memorabilia.

Admission: $5 adults, $3 kids 5–18.

Open: Wed–Sun 10am–4pm. **Directions:** Take I-95 north to Russell St. exit, left at Lombard, go three blocks to left at Poppleton to museum parking.

CLOISTER CHILDREN'S MUSEUM, 10440 Falls Rd, Brooklandville, Md. 21022. Tel. 410/823-2550.

The rooms of this 1930 Tudor mansion abound with antique toys, clothing, and collectibles, most of which are touchable. The emphasis is on creativity as children interact with the exhibits, rather than push buttons on a video screen. Kids are encouraged to rummage through the trunks of old clothes, play with the sock puppets, and make tombstone rubbings. Farm animals are penned outside, and weekend workshops and entertainment are a tradition. *Note:* Strollers are not permitted.

Admission: $3.

Open: Wed–Sat 10am–4pm. **Directions:** Take I-95 north to 695 west to exit 23B (Falls Road south). Left at first traffic light, then ½ mile to museum on right.

FORT MC HENRY NATIONAL MONUMENT AND HISTORIC SHRINE, E. Fort Avenue (at the very end). Tel. 410/962-4290.

✪ Francis Scott Key was so moved on the night of September 11, 1814, as the British fired on Fort McHenry (missing their target repeatedly, I might add), he wrote a poem that became our national anthem in 1931. Visit the spot where the bombs were bursting in air while Key was waxing poetic on a boat in the harbor. A movie about the War of 1812 battle that inspired Francis Scott Key plays at the exhibit center. The gun collection and underground dungeons are of interest to most kids.

Admission: $1 everyone 17–61.

Open: Winter 8am–5pm, summer 8am–8pm. **Directions:** Take I-95 north to exit 55 (before the tunnel) and follow signs.

GENERAL MOTORS BALTIMORE ASSEMBLY PLANT, 2122 Broening Highway. Tel. 410/631-2142.

If your kids are over 10 (or at least in 5th grade), and they can stand the grinding noise and smell of metal that's worse than in an orthodontist's office, press the pedal to the metal and hightail it up to "Bawlmer" (the local pronunciation) to witness the 15-minute birth of a Chevy. On a good day, nearly 4,000 United Auto Workers at this GM plant play midwife to seemingly unrelated stacks of parts that exit the assembly line with frightening rapidity as living, breathing Chevrolets. Since tours are given only to groups of eight or more, carpool with another family or two.

Admission: Free.

Open: Tours Mon–Fri 9am and 7pm, except for several weeks in mid-summer. Call and reserve 3–4 weeks ahead. **Directions:** Take I-95 north to Fort McHenry Tunnel; right at first exit after tunnel (Boston Street) to right on Broening Highway.

HARBORPLACE, Pratt and Light streets. Tel. 410/332-4191.

✪ Baltimore's top tourist draw at the Inner Harbor consists of two pavilions that, after 12 years, still do their seductive best to lure visitors into their shops, restaurants, and food stalls. The Light Street Pavilion is primarily food-oriented, and kids love the second-floor Food Hall, which draws locals and visitors with a wide array of American-style and ethnic fast food. Weather permitting, consume your selection on a bench overlooking the harbor. At the information kiosk, find out about special events which, in the past, have included rowing regattas, band concerts, and crab races. Shoppers head for the Pratt Street Pavilion, filled with big-name retail stores and one-of-a kind boutiques. Especially for kids are Arthur Watson's Zoo, What's Your Game, Arcadia (games and gimmicks), and Crabtree & Evelyn if they're into bathing with scented soap. Even on dismal non-holidays, the air

is festive around Harborplace. Without spending a cent, you can have a rich time watching the other tourists, strolling the waterfront promenades, and window shopping.

Open: Shops, Food Hall 10am–10pm; restaurants with separate entrances stay open later. **Directions:** Take I-95 north and follow signs to Harborplace.

LEXINGTON MARKET, West Lexington St. (between Paca and Eutaw). Tel. 410/685-6169.

Skip breakfast; it's pig-out time! Eat your way through this former open-air market that blew out 200 birthday candles in 1982. The oldest continuously open U.S. market began humbly in 1782 when farmers in Conestogas arrived from outlying areas to barter produce, game, fowl, and dairy goods. The first shed was raised in 1803, and the market grew in fits and starts until it was wiped out by fire in 1949. The bulk of the market, as you see it today, reopened in 1952.

More than 130 merchants hawk produce, seafood, poultry, and a variety of prepared foods and baked goods from row upon row of stalls in two buildings. An information kiosk is located in the center of the Arcade, the sight of entertainment and special events. Seating for 500 is available on the Arcade's second level. Recommendations (diligently researched over many years) include Polock Johnny's sausage sandwiches (with the works), Barron's deli for corned beef, Faidley's for seafood, Utz potato chips, and Berger's for cookies and doughnuts. Who remembered the Tums?

Open: Mon–Sat 8:30am–6pm. **Directions:** Take I-95 north to Russell Street exit. Russell runs into Paca; continue 5 blocks.

LIGHTSHIP CHESAPEAKE AND U.S.S. TORSK, Pier 3, Inner Harbor, Pratt and Light sts. Tel. 410/396-3854.

Kids will get an idea of how sailors live and work on this guided tour of a lightship and submarine.

Admission: $3 adults, $2.50 seniors, $1.50 kids 5–12, free 4 and under.

Open: Daily 9:30am–4:30pm. **Closed:** Major holidays. **Directions:** Take I-95 north and follow signs to Inner Harbor.

MARYLAND SCIENCE CENTER, Inner Harbor, 601 Light St. (at Key Highway). Tel. 410/685-5225.

Time passes quickly in this facility established by the Maryland Academy of Sciences. Scores of hands-on exhibits invite kids of all ages to touch, to explore, to learn. Enter a distorted room, make friends with a computer, and delve into physics, geology, and the human mind.

Watch a movie on the five-story-high Imax screen or reach for the stars in the Davis Planetarium. Both are recommended for kids 4 and over. Two movies alternate in the Imax theater, and planetarium shows air twice a day on weekdays, numerous times on weekends. Friday and Saturday at 7:30pm, a double feature is shown in the Imax.

While tickets may seem steep, admission includes all exhibits, one Imax movie, and a planetarium show. The exhibits alone are worth the price of admission. Strollers are not allowed in the theaters.

Admission: $7.50 adults, $5 kids 4–17 and seniors, free 3 and under.

Open: Mon–Fri 10am–5pm, Sat and Sun 10am–6pm; extended summer hours.

Directions: Take I-95 north and follow signs.

NATIONAL AQUARIUM, Pier 3, 501 E. Pratt St. (adjacent to Harborplace). Tel. 410/576-3810.

⭐ You'll feel like you're underwater the minute you enter this multi-story aquarium that towers over the harbor. Set aside at least 2½ to 3 hours *early in the day* to do justice to the main Aquarium building and Marine Mammal Pavilion. I once made the mistake of visiting in the afternoon and the experience was totally frustrating because of the crowds.

Moving ramps and escalators transport visitors through various aquatic habitats. The various ring tanks contain rays, tropical fish, and sharks. The Maryland exhibit follows a raindrop from pond to ocean. Kids like to hunt for protectively colored species in Surviving Through Adaptation and inspect the touch pool in Children's Cove. Hands-down, the steamy and exotic Rain Forest, where small animals and tropic birds roam freely, is the most popular exhibit.

Very young kids may bore easily in the main Aquarium, especially if their view is blocked by tourists three-deep, but they'll surely wake up in the Marine Mammal Pavilion where beluga whales and bottlenose dolphins entertain several times a day during half-hour shows. Unlike shows at many other seaquariums, which are strictly for entertainment's sake, these are highly instructional. The 1,300 seat, $40-million pavilion, which opened to rave reviews in December 1990, features two multi-screen video monitors that strikingly supplement the antics in the pool.

Outside the main Aquarium, the seals are fed at 10am, 1 and 4pm. Check the sign over the lobby information desk to find out when the sharks (mercifully, indoors) will be fed.

Admission: $11.50 adults, $8.75 kids 12–18 and college students with ID, $6.75 kids 3–11, free under 3. Purchase advance tickets a day ahead through Ticketron (tel. 800/448-9009).

Open: Sept. 16–May 14 Sun–Thurs 10am–5pm, Fri 10am–8pm; May 15–Sept 15 Mon–Thurs 9am–5pm, Fri–Sun 9am–8pm. **Directions:** Take I-95 north and follow signs to Harborplace.

BABE RUTH MUSEUM, 216 Emory St. Tel. 410/727-1539.

Stand in the very room where George Herman Ruth drew his first breath. The sultan of swat's career record of 714 homers remained unbroken for more than 40 years until Hank Aaron settled the score in 1974. Displays in this downtown row house chronicle the Babe's life, and there's a healthy dose of Baltimore Oriole memorabilia too. Don't miss the photo of the 3-year-old slugger playing ball.

Admission: $4 adults, $1.50 kids infant–15, $2.50 seniors; reduced admission for AAA members.

Open: Daily 10am–5pm. **Closed:** Thanksgiving, Christmas, New Year's. **Directions:** Take I-95 north to Rte 395/Downtown. At fork, take Martin Luther King Jr. Boulevard. Turn right on Pratt, go two blocks, and then turn right on Emory. Go one block further to museum.

TOP OF THE WORLD, Inner Harbor, 27th floor of World Trade Center, 401 E. Pratt St. Tel. 410/837-4515.

On a clear day you can see forever; well, almost. Would you settle for the harbor, the O's new stadium, and north to Towson 13 miles away?

Admission: $2 adults, $1 kids 5–15 and seniors 60 and over, free 4 and under.

Open: Mon–Sat 10am–4:30pm, Sun noon–4:30pm; extended summer hours.

Directions: Take I-95 north and follow signs to Inner Harbor.

U.S. FRIGATE CONSTELLATION, Inner Harbor, Pier 1, Pratt & Light streets. Tel. 410/539-1797.

The first ship commissioned by the U.S. Navy was launched from nearby Fells Point in 1797 and wasn't retired until 1945. She never enjoyed the notoriety of her sister ship, the *Constitution,* and was used for many years as a training vessel. Tour at your own pace, and be sure to give the captain's cabin a white-glove inspection.

Admission: $3 adults, $1.50 kids 6–15, free kids under 6, $2 seniors.

Open: Daily, June 15–Labor Day 10am–7:30pm; Labor Day–Oct 15 and May 15–June 14 10am–6pm; Oct 16–May 14 10am–4pm. **Directions:** Take I-95 north and follow signs.

CRUISES

Of the numerous cruise boats plying the Inner Harbor during the warm weather months, here are a few that are particularly appealing to tiny tars.

BALTIMORE PATRIOT, Pratt Street side of Harborplace. Tel. 410/685-4288.

In a 1½-hour tour, travel the 8-mile length of the harbor on the *Baltimore Patriot,* which sails from Constellation Dock daily from April through October. Cruise past Fort McHenry, Fells Point, Federal Hill, and Fort Carroll (a six-sided island in the middle of the Patapsco River), before returning to port.

Admission: $6 adults, $3.30 kids 3–12.

Open: May–Sept, hourly 11am–4pm; Apr and Oct 11am, 1 and 3pm.

THE HALF SHELL, Harrison Pier 5 at Harborplace. Tel. 410/522-4214.

The Half Shell, a 54-foot working oyster boat, clears its deck of oyster shells to ferry tourists around the harbor on summer weekends.

Admission: $7 adults, $3 kids under 12.

Open: May–Sept; call for departure times, which vary.

THE CLIPPER CITY, Light Street Finger Pier at Harborplace. Tel. 410/575-7930.

This 150-foot replica of a 19th century top-sail schooner leaves port almost daily from April through mid-October. Cruises are of varying lengths, and you must call for reservations a week or more in advance.

Admission: Varies according to cruise.

Open: Apr–Oct 15.

WHERE TO STAY

STOUFFER'S HARBORPLACE, 202 E. Pratt St., Baltimore, MD. 21202. Tel. 410/547-1200 or toll free 800/468-3571. 622 rooms. A/C MINIBAR TV TEL.

$ Rates: $165 single; $185 double; weekend and other packages from $125. Children 18 and under stay free in parents room. **Parking:** $8 self-park, $11 valet.

Go for it! Stouffer's location is prime, and rooms are spacious and nicely appointed. Morning coffee and a newspaper are gratis; turn-down service as well, if you so desire. Windows, the hotel's restaurant and lounge overlooking the harbor, welcomes families. There's an indoor pool, Jacuzzi, sauna, and Nautilus equipment on the seventh floor, and the hotel is attached to the Gallery, a multi-level mall with scores of shops and food stands. Harborplace is just across Pratt Street, and reachable by a skywalk from the hotel. The concierge will secure tickets for local attractions and arrange a bonded babysitter if you want to enjoy Baltimore's night life *sans* kiddies.

DAYS INN, 100 Hopkins Place, Baltimore, MD. 21201 Tel. 410/576-1000 or toll free 800/325-2525. 250 rooms. A/C TV TEL.
$ Rates: $70 and up single; $100 and up double. Kids 18 and under stay free in parents room. Ask about Family Packages.
Parking: $4.50.
The Days Inn is only 1½ blocks from the Inner Harbor and offers families a special weekend rate in summers of $55 a night for a double room, plus $25 per child. Included are tickets to the Aquarium or Baltimore Zoo, a buffet breakfast, and picnic lunch. An outdoor pool is open from Memorial Day to Labor Day.

WHERE TO EAT

MODERATE

CHIAPPERELLI'S, 237 S. High St. Tel. 410/837-0309.
Cuisine: Italian **Reservations:** Recommended.
$ Prices: Dinner entrees $9.95–$27. AE, CB, D, DC, MC, V.
Open: Mon–Thurs 11am–11pm, Fri and Sun 11am–midnight, Sat 11am–2am.
Bring the bambinos for heartily sauced pastas (nothing subtle or bland here), seafood, and veal. The ravioli is *bellisima,* and the hot antipasto appetizer is an appetizing meal in itself. You may have trouble finishing your entree after the large house salad, deliciously drenched in a creamy, garlicky dressing. Go ahead, force yourselves to try the homemade bread. Child's portions are available.

GUNNING'S, 3901 S. Hanover St. Tel. 410/354-0085.
Cuisine: Seafood **Reservations:** Needed for 8 or more.
$ Prices: Entrees $11–$13.70; crabs $20–$40 a dozen, depending on size. AE, MC, V.
Open: Sun–Thurs 11am–11pm, Fri and Sat 11am–midnight.
When in Rome . . . Well, this is crab territory, so roll up your sleeves and dig into a pile of steamed crabs. If picking crabs seems too much like work, try one of Gunning's award-winning crabcakes or one of several other seafood offerings. A few non-seafood items are listed for spoil sports. Eat in one of the dining rooms or large, enclosed "garden" room, or outdoors when the weather cooperates. Crabs are also available for carryout. A friendly tip: Buy the largest size crabs—less work and more meat.

BUDGET

FOOD HALL, Light Street Pavilion at Harborplace, Pratt and Light streets. 410/332-4191.
Cuisine: Everything!
$ Prices: $1–$6 No credit cards.
Open: 10am–10pm.

Pizza, french fries, milk shakes, tempura, cookies, roast beef, crabcakes, hot dogs, gyros, fried chicken, fruit drinks, sushi, egg roll, tacos, oysters, calzone, barbecue, ice cream. Did I skip something? Eat lunch early or late or you may have to stand. Take your ticket to heartburn city outside and grab a seat with a harbor view.

JACK'S, 1150 E. Lombard St. Tel. 410/327-1177.
   Cuisine: Deli **Reservations:** No way.
   $ Prices: $2–$4. No credit cards.
   Open: Mon–Sat 7:30am–6pm, Sun 8am–5pm.
Jack's is far from a pretty face, and the location leaves something to be desired, but these minor irritations disappear with the first bite into a corned beef or pastrami sandwich. The corned beef comes two ways: regular for true C.B. lovers ($2.89) and lean for sissies ($3.19). Someday nutritionists will add this to their list of essential foods. Don't forget a half-done or well-done (sour) pickle to go with your C.B. fix. While Jack's has several other locations, sandwiches taste better at this one. Maybe it's the decor.

PAOLO'S, Light Street Pavilion at Harborplace, Pratt and Light Sts. Tel. 410/539-7060.
   Cuisine: Italian/American. **Reservations:** No.
   $ Prices: Grown-up entrees $6.95–$16.95. AE, D, MC, V.
   Open: Mon–Fri 11am–midnight (pizza 'til 1 am), Sat and Sun 10:30am–midnight.
This place has plenty going for it: atmosphere, friendly service, reasonable prices, and very good food to boot. Kids are given crayons while waiting for wagon wheel pasta, pizza, or a hot dog from their very own menu. You won't go wrong with pizza, pasta, or a giant salad, but the chicken (grilled or oven-roasted) is really special. Come for brunch on Saturday and Sunday.

7. HARPERS FERRY, WEST VIRGINIA

70 miles NW of Washington, D.C.

GETTING THERE By car Take I-270 north to Rte. 340 west for about 15 miles. Parking is available at the National Park's main entrance off Rte. 340. Shuttle buses operate every 10 minutes to transport visitors the 2 miles into town. Street parking is almost nonexistent.

Harpers Ferry sits on a bluff at the confluence of the Shenandoah and Potomac Rivers. Few places combine as much beauty and history as this scenic town poised in a natural gap in the Blue Ridge Mountains where John Brown and his cohorts took possession of the U.S. Armory in 1859 in an attempt to put an end to slavery. At "The Point" visitors marvel over the vista where the two rivers and three states (Maryland, Virginia, and West Virginia) come together. History and Civil War buffs have a field day as Park Service guides and local historians regale them with tales and reenactments of a bygone era.

It's hard to resist the sense of continuity in a town where merchants still trade in century-old buildings constructed of Harpers shale, quarried from close-by cliffs. From Potomac Street, you can watch trains "disappear" into these same cliffs. Allow time to enjoy the outdoors. The rivers, mountains, and forests offer families limitless recreational possibilities.

INFORMATION

Contact the **National Park Service** at Harpers Ferry National Historical Park, P.O. Box 65, Harpers Ferry, WV 25425 for park information and a map (tel. 304/535-6298). For "A Guide to Shops, Eating Establishments, and Places to Stay," write **The Harpers Ferry Merchants Association,** P.O. Box 262, Harpers Ferry, WV 25425 (tel. toll free 800/848-TOUR). If you're interested in whitewater rafting, canoeing, tubing, or fishing, contact **River & Trail Outfitters,** about 2 miles east of Harpers Ferry on the Maryland side of the river (tel. 304/695-5177). Call for information on area **campgrounds** (tel. 800/Call-WVA). After you arrive, the **information center** is located in the Stagecoach Inn bookstore on Shenandoah Street.

SPECIAL EVENTS

The Merchants Association sponsors family festivals and entertainment throughout the year. Hike and enjoy an Easter dinner buffet over **Family Easter Weekend** in April. In October, **Fantastic Fall Foliage weekends** spotlight the magnificent display of the changing leaves. **Old Tyme Christmas** is celebrated the first and second weekends of December when the town glows under the light of yuletide lanterns and flickering luminarias, and costumed troops and townspeople parade through the streets. Caroling, breakfast with St. Nick himself, and puppet shows are part of the festivities (tel. toll free 800/848-TOUR).

WHAT TO DO AND SEE

HARPERS FERRY NATIONAL HISTORICAL PARK, Rte 340. Tel. 340/535-6298.

Tours depart the Visitors Center at 10 and 11am, noon, 1, and 2pm from June through Labor Day. The rest of the year tours are self-guided, except by reservation. Guides in period dress take visitors on a historic journey past the armory and fort where John Brown and his boys created a stir, the John Brown Museum, gunmaking museums, and other historic buildings. As tours go, this one rates high for school-age kids. It's quick paced, fun, and informative. Be sure to see the exhibits and enjoy the park's many splendors before you leave. Shuttle buses operate every 10 minutes between the park and town.

Admission: $5 per vehicle (good for 7 consecutive days); $2 per person cyclists and walk-ins.

Open: Daily Memorial Day–Labor Day 8:30am–6pm; rest of year 8:30am–5pm.

HISTORIC DISTRICT SHOPPING AREA, along High and Potomac streets. Tel. toll free 800/848-TOUR.

Before you begin your climb up High or Potomac Street, note the high-water marks floods have left on Shenandoah Street buildings. Stop also at the **National Park Bookshop** on Shenandoah Street next to the Visitors Center for a good selection of children's books, posters, and postcards. On High Street, **shops** of special interest to young people include: The Cookie Shop (for dolls, dollhouses, miniatures, and homemade cookies); The Hodge Podge (souvenir T-shirts and collectibles); and Old Tyme Portraits, where you can have your picture taken dressed as a gunslinger, belle, or Civil War officer.

When visiting over a weekend between May and November, be sure to stop on Potomac Street at **Ghost Tours** of Harpers Ferry (tel. 304/725-8019). The "ghost lady" escorts groups through town on Friday, Saturday, and Sunday evenings at 8pm and shares stories of haunted history that you won't find in the guidebooks. A longtime resident assures me that you'll return a little wiser and a little warier than when you began.

ST. PETER'S CATHOLIC CHURCH, off High St.

During your exploration of town, climb—and I do mean climb—the stone steps cut into natural rock off High Street (adjacent to the Civil War Museums) to St. Peter's. The church was built in the 1830s and is still in use. Take in the vista from the stone patio, then continue along the footpath beyond the church to Jefferson Rock. On a visit here in 1783, Jefferson thought the view "worth a voyage across the Atlantic." Smart man, that Jefferson. *Warning:* Use caution, as the uneven steps are slippery sometimes.

WHERE TO STAY

HILLTOP HOUSE HOTEL, 400 E. Ridge St. (P.O. Box 930), Harpers Ferry, WV 25425. Tel. 304/535-2132 or toll free 800/338-8319. 73 rooms. A/C TV TEL.

$ Rates: $59–$85 (room with parlor); kids 12 and under $3 extra in same room. Hilltop is undergoing restoration and expansion that should be completed in time for your stay. The hotel dates back to 1888 and has hosted Mark Twain, Alexander Graham Bell, and Woodrow Wilson, so you'll be in good company. A quiet, relaxed atmosphere pervades, and the surrounding scenery acts as a tonic, especially if you've just come from the city. The weekend buffets are legendary.

THE VIEW, 700 E. Ridge St. Harpers Ferry, WV 25425. Tel. 304/535-2688. 2 rooms. A/C TV TEL.

$ Rates: $60–$75 (weekends).
You'll practically have the whole place to yourself if you stay here. This modern B&B overlooking the Potomac welcomes kids and offers families reduced weekday rates. Private baths, continental breakfast, and a common area with TV, VCR, and Jacuzzi are included. It's a pleasant walk to the historical district and shops.

WHERE TO EAT

MODERATE

THE ANVIL, Washington St. (border of Harpers Ferry and Bolivar). Tel. 304/535-2582.
    Cuisine: American/seafood. **Reservations:** Recommended.
$ Prices: Dinner entrees $13.95–$26.50. AE D MC V.
    Open: Sun–Thurs 11am–9pm, Fri and Sat 11am–10pm. **Closed:** Mon.
The Anvil has the feel of a country inn, yet the kitchen turns out dishes more indicative of big-city restaurants. This is not a bad combination! Try any of the house specialties among the seafood, steak, and veal entrees. Weather permitting, there's

dining on the screened porch. While all ages are welcome at lunch and nobody is ever turned away, at dinner this is not an appropriate restaurant for the very young.

CLIFFSIDE INN, 1 mile south of Harpers Ferry on Route 340. Tel. 304/535-6302.

Cuisine: American. **Reservations:** Recommended.

$ Prices: Dinner entrees $8–$15. AE D DC MC V.

Open: Sun–Thurs 7am–9pm, Fri and Sat 7am–10pm.

Families come first in the restaurant of this resort inn/conference center just outside of town. Children's-size helpings are always available, with half-price portions offered at the weekend buffets. The regular menu is varied and includes many kids' favorite dish: spaghetti. How refreshing—it's called spaghetti, not pasta. If you dine here on a Friday night, try the seafood crêpes. Breads and pastries are baked on the premises by Cliffside's pastry chef.

BUDGET

BACK STREET CAFE, Potomac St. Tel. 304/535-2772.

Cuisine: American. **Reservations:** No.

$ Prices: $1.50–$3. No credit cards.

Open: 10am–6pm (later on weekends).

Grab a frank, burger, or bowl of homemade soup or chili while you're visiting the shops along Potomac Street. Kids always enjoy the nachos. Back Street is ultra-casual, and there's outdoor seating.

LITTLE PONDEROSA BEEF & PORK BBQ, Potomac St. Tel. 304/535-2186.

Cuisine: BBQ. **Reservations:** No.

$ Prices: Under $5. No credit cards.

Open: 10am–5pm (later on weekends).

Kids enjoy eating in the little red caboose restaurant across from the train station. The meat is smoked on the premises and the beef barbecue is mighty tasty. Little Ponderosa is also open for breakfast and serves other light fare throughout the day.

YESTERDAYS, High St. (near the bottom). Tel. 304/535-2738.

Cuisine: Baked goods and other sweet delights.

$ Prices: 5¢–$1.95. No credit cards.

Open: 10am–dark.

Mmmmmmm. . . . Your brood will want to return to the past again and again after sampling the apple dumplings, cinnamon rolls, and homemade fudge at Yesterday's carryout. Take your ice cream and candy to the bench out front.

CHAPTER 10

IF KIDS ARE COMING TO STAY

**1. PREPARING FOR
YOUR GUESTS**

2. AIRPORT ARRIVALS

3. SOME PRECAUTIONS

So, you're expecting houseguests. Little ones. Maybe your grandchildren are coming to visit for a week so Mom and Dad can slip off to an undisclosed location for some much-needed R & R. Maybe a friend is going through a crisis, and you offered to care for her brood—short term. If the pitter patter of little feet is but a faded melody, and you've forgotten the tune, help is on the way.

HOW TO GUARANTEE A SPLENDID VISIT

If you haven't been around kids in a while, you may have forgotten that things don't always run smoothly. But some little tricks will help you make the most of your time together. For openers, to ensure a successful visit, follow three simple rules: Plan, plan, plan. Confine your activities to one general area per day and don't overschedule. Let kids over 6 toss in their two cents to help plan each day, but don't offer too many choices.

Don't build yourself a booby trap by announcing tomorrow's plans today. Kids handle surprises a lot better than last-minute disappointments. Don't do what will later have to be undone.

1. PREPARING FOR YOUR GUESTS

Any travelers worth their weight in American Tourister will tell you that anticipation is half the joy of traveling. Your young visitors may not have experienced this yet, so help them along. Send picture postcards of D.C. or an "I Love Washington" T-shirt or hat. Devise a multiple-choice questionnaire. Sample questions might include:

1. I love (train, boat, pony, subway) rides.
2. I would rather eat (hot dogs, Chinese food, fajitas, cold cereal).
3. I like (animals, movies, whining, parks).

To make your visitors feel welcome and at-home right away, do any or all of the following before they arrive. Hang a "Welcome" sign on your front door or in the guest room. Tie a helium balloon to the toilet handle. Display their photos and/or art work on the refrigerator or a bulletin board. Have their favorite cookies, candy, or other treat on hand.

If you really want to make a statement, have a large poster made of your guest. **Colorfax,** with 11 D.C. locations and more in the suburbs, will take a 35mm negative and turn it into a 20 x 30 inch poster in five working days for $22.95. Check the phone book for the nearest location or call Colorfax's main office (tel. 301/622-1500).

A special present is also a nice way to say "I'm glad you're here." **S.W.A.K. (Sealed With a Kiss)** sends colorfully wrapped gift packages to kids all over the world. Each box contains 10 to 20 items and is customized according to the child's age and sex. Founded 10 years ago by local entrepreneur Julie Winston, who had a knack for sending the right stuff to her kids and their bunk mates at camp, S.W.A.K. has won accolades coast-to-coast. S.W.A.K. gift packages are $30 (tel. 800/888-SWAK).

PLAYTHINGS TO HAVE ON HAND

FOR LITTLE ONES (Infant to 3 years old) Use extra care when choosing playthings for this most vulnerable age group. Avoid toys with small or easily removable pieces. If parts are small enough for babies or toddlers to put in their mouths, they probably will. Avoid things with points or sharp edges. If a toy looks fragile, it probably is. To find out the safety of any toy for any age group, call the U.S. Consumer Products Safety Commission Hotline (tel. 800/638-CPSC), Monday through Friday from 8:30am to 5pm.

Aside from all the seductive items available at your local toy store, here are a few things you probably already have that never go out of style.

1. Metal pots and pans, aluminum or plastic mixing bowls; a wooden spoon. Toddlers can make their own pretend meals while you prepare yours.

2. Books: cloth books for baby; waterproof books for bathtime; and storybooks for naptime, bedtime, or anytime.

3. A large rubber ball or plastic blow-up beach ball with nonremovable stopper.

4. Records or tapes of nursery rhymes and fairy tales.

5. Bathtub toys.

FOR 3- TO 10-YEAR-OLDS The best playthings for kids in this age group are each other. If you're entertaining one child, call friends who have children or grandchildren about the same age and arrange an introduction. Or head for the nearest park or playground. Acquaintances are easily made on a jungle gym or in a sandbox. Meanwhile, stock your makeshift hotel with the following:

1. Gather coloring books, construction paper, crayons, markers, round-tipped scissors, Elmer's glue, and Scotch tape in one large shopping bag. For collages, put old magazines, catalogues, gift wrap and ribbons, paper plates, and scraps of material in another.

2. Scour your closest for old clothes, pocketbooks, shoes, and jewelry. Put everything in a suitcase so the kids can play dress-up whenever the spirit moves them.

3. Games may come, and games may go, but cards, checkers, Scrabble (there's a children's version), and Monopoly—like love—are here to stay.

VIDEOCASSETTE RECORDERS Pop a tape into the VCR and buy yourself time to make a phone call, fix dinner, or wash your hair. If you don't own a VCR, borrow or rent one. Installation is child's play. If I, who have trouble opening my front door, can do it, so can you. Check your neighborhood video store or public library for age-appropriate tapes. Thus far, Blockbuster's and Tower Video have the best selection in D.C. See Chapter 5.

KIDSNET, P.O. Box 5959, Takoma Park, MD 20912, a nonprofit organization serving the educational community, categorizes videotapes by age, evaluations, and NEA recommendations. KIDSNET has plans to produce a parents' guide in the near future. They ask that you write, not call, to see if the guide is currently available.

KIDPROOFING YOUR HOME

Get out your grubbiest work clothes and put on your knee pads. Most of your efforts will be geared to those 5 and under. But remember: kids over 5 can be trouble too, so keep a clear head and anticipate every potential hazard as you begin your search-and-destroy operation.

KITCHEN Keep the dishwasher locked at all times. Harmful caustics adhere to all machine surfaces, and toddlers are non-discriminatory about what they eat. (If it's a pretty color, in the mouth it goes.) Move step stools and ladders to someplace far away, or at least out of reach. They could be an inducement for a junior explorer to climb onto a hot stove top. OUCH! Twist a sturdy elastic band around the knobs or handles of under-sink cabinet doors, home to so many poisonous and injurious liquids and powders. Do the same to all cabinets containing breakables, heavy pots, and serving dishes. If you're out of rubber bands or have contemporary-style cabinets, buy plastic safety latches at the hardware store. There are two types: the loop for cabinets with knobs; the latch for knobless.

BATHROOMS Keep the door closed. If you have a clothes hamper, move it. It's an ideal stepping-stone to the medicine cabinet. Of course, the toilet seat serves the same purpose, but it stays. Pack away a shopping bag or shoe box with razors and blades, medications, creams, and cosmetics. Ditto for hot rollers, hair dryers, and radios (unless the waterproof variety). If you have a TV or phone in the W.C. remove them too. You'll muddle through without them for a few days.

NIGHT TABLES Clean off the tops and clean out the drawers. Amazing what accumulates, isn't it?

DOORS AND WINDOWS Put masking tape over all but the top (i.e., unreachable by little people) front door lock. If you have push-in doorknob locks, cover them with plastic doorknob covers from the hardware store or Five and Ten. Make sure all windows are locked. If it's between heating and air-conditioning seasons, open double-hung sash windows from the top. If they're stuck, holler for somebody strong to come and help.

OTHER CHOICES, OTHER ROOMS It's knee pad time! Down on your knees. Tackle one room at a time. If you spot sharp corners on tables, sofas, cabinets, or shelves at eye level, cover them. Invest in "Kinder-gards" at the hardware store. These inexpensive corner protectors could safeguard your visitors' eyes during a heated touch football game in the living room. While you're at the hardware store, buy a bunch of plastic outlet covers. Some kids take perverse pleasure in seeing what will happen if they stick something, like the dog's tail or a piece of wire, into those inviting little outlets. If your visitor's parents refer to him or her as "knob nutty," move quickly. Tape closed all tuning knobs on TVs, VCRs, and stereos or you're apt to spend quality sightseeing time waiting for the repairman.

With valuables and breakables you have a choice: Leave them out and die everytime your guest comes within 10 feet of them, or put them away for the duration. Get rid of lighters and match strikers too. If you're in the dark after stowing heirloom porcelain lamps, borrow a sturdy lamp from another room or pick up something ugly but functional at a thrift shop.

When you think you've completely kid-proofed your house, take a deep breath, hitch up the knee pads, and look again.

SETTLING IN: FURNITURE, EQUIPMENT & FOOD

Sleeping in a new bed in a strange place is an adjustment. To help ensure an easy transition for your visitor, urge the parents to pack a favorite crib toy, blanket, or stuffed animal. If they forget, everyone will spend a sleepless night.

The U.S. Consumer Product Safety Commission (tel. 800/638-CPSC) dispenses information on recalled children's toys, furniture, outdoor playground equipment, and clothes. To receive free pamphlets on "Safety of Children" and *It Hurts When They Cry,* a buyer's guide to selecting children's furnishings, write to: Public Request, CPSC, Washington, D.C. 20207.

Crib gyms or other cute-looking gizmos that hang from the sides of cribs are hazards, and most mobiles are no-nos too. Eventually, babies can reach them, pull off parts, and choke. When buying a toy, evaluate it carefully. Just because a toy is on the market is no guarantee that it has been tested and proven safe.

Crib graduates of all ages like to sleep on futons. They are comfortable, easily stored, and especially practical for young kids, who won't have far to fall if they get restless during the night. If your pint-size friend is a recent convert to a big bed, consider bed guards, which fold flat when not in use. You can order bed guards from Lillian Vernon (tel. 914/633-6300). One is $16.98; two are $29.98. The catalogue number is 661708.

Highchairs must be steady, well balanced, and have a seatbelt. The Sassy Seat, with side clamps that attach to a table, is good for home and restaurant use. To create a makeshift booster seat, put the D.C. *Yellow Pages* on an armchair, and use an old belt as a seatbelt.

Playpens. I hated them when my kids put up with being confined in them, and I hate them now. The old mesh ones with collapsible sides are bloody dangerous, and it's back-breaking trying to lift little ones (many of whom weigh the same as a professional linebacker) in and out. Besides, if you've childproofed your abode, you won't need one. If you have one, use it for storing toys.

Don't fret if you're out of drawer space. Use the bottoms of large dress boxes or cartons from the grocery store for kids' clothes. If you're into artsy-craftsy projects, line the boxes with shelf or Contact paper or colorful material and attach it with masking tape or glue, not staples. I'm an expert at this; I once covered my kitchen pencils to match the wallpaper.

B.Y.O. is the rule in my house for visitors who use strollers. If they forget their own wheels, you can always rent. But why should you have to?

In the D.C. area, you can buy (good), rent (better), or borrow (best) all the equipment you could possibly need to entertain a Lilliputian army. Buying doesn't make sense, unless the visitor happens to be a regular. To rent a crib, rollaway bed, or highchair, call A-Allied Rentals (tel. 301/229-5400) They deliver.

LOADING THE LARDER

Kids are more interested in what they eat than where they sleep or watch TV. At least a week before the big day—so you have ample time to bring in a supply of their favorite grub—have the honored guest's parent send you a list of liked, tolerated, hated, and allergy-producing foods. Ask for specifics. For example, should juice be natural, frozen, or bottled? This is more important than sleeping schedules and almost as important as the indispensable "bankee." Some kids eat like grown-ups; others subsist on air. This is no time to play guessing games.

2. AIRPORT ARRIVALS

If your visitor is arriving by plane, make sure you get to the gate early. A little person's entire visit could be sabotaged by not being met promptly.

When meeting an under-12 unaccompanied passenger, you become a predesignated adult, the only person to whom airline personnel will release the child. Make sure you have proper proof of identification. The airport sign "Only Passengers with Tickets Beyond This Point" does not apply to you. Explain that you must meet and sign for your V.I.C. (very important cargo) at the arrival gate. All this takes time.

Greet young children with a balloon or welcome sign and, of course, a hug. If you're meeting kids between 10 and 16, don't make any loud noises or sudden movements. Be cool. If they're over 16, just give 'em a map and the keys to the car.

3. SOME PRECAUTIONS

Of course you're not going to do everything your guest's parents do. Kids need a break once in a while too. Establish reasonable rules and stick to them, hard as it may be. Don't go overboard with gifts or the child will henceforth greet you with an outstretched hand. In my family, this is known as "the gimmes," as in "gimme this;" "gimme that." You'll do everyone a disservice if you send a spoiled brat back to Mom and Dad, who will think twice before requesting an encore. Don't overload the kid with activities. Set aside a portion of every day to do nothing. Quiet time is as important to them as it is to you.

INDEX

GENERAL INFORMATION

SIGHTS & ATTRACTIONS

WASHINGTON, D.C., AND ENVIRONS

NOTE: An asterisk (*) indicates an Author's Favorite

MARYLAND

PENNSYLVANIA

VIRGINIA

ACCOMMODATIONS

WASHINGTON, D.C.

KEY TO ABBREVIATIONS: * = an Author's Favorite; $ = Special Value; *B&B* = Bed & Breakfast; *B* = Budget; *CG* = Campground; *E* = Expensive; *I* = Inexpensive; *M* = Moderate; *VE* = Very Expensive; *YH* = Youth Hostel

MARYLAND

VIRGINIA

WEST VIRGINIA

RESTAURANTS

WASHINGTON, D.C.

AFTERNOON TEA

AMERICAN

KEY TO ABBREVIATIONS: * = an Author's Favorite; $ = Special value; *B* = Budget; *E* = Expensive; *M* = Moderate; *VE* = Very Expensive

MARYLAND

FROMMER'S CITY GUIDES

(Pocket-size guides to sightseeing and tourist accommodations and facilities in all price ranges)

☐ Amsterdam/Holland $8.95	☐ Minneapolis/St. Paul $8.95
☐ Athens. $8.95	☐ Montréal/Québec City. $8.95
☐ Atlanta $8.95	☐ New Orleans. $8.95
☐ Atlantic City/Cape May $8.95	☐ New York $12.00
☐ Bangkok. $12.00	☐ Orlando $12.00
☐ Barcelona $12.00	☐ Paris $8.95
☐ Belgium $7.95	☐ Philadelphia $11.00
☐ Berlin. $10.00	☐ Rio $8.95
☐ Boston. $8.95	☐ Rome. $8.95
☐ Cancún/Cozumel/Yucatán. $8.95	☐ Salt Lake City $8.95
☐ Chicago. $9.95	☐ San Diego. $8.95
☐ Denver/Boulder/Colorado Springs. . . .$8.95	☐ San Francisco $12.00
☐ Dublin/Ireland. $10.00	☐ Santa Fe/Taos/Albuquerque. $10.95
☐ Hawaii $12.00	☐ Seattle/Portland $12.00
☐ Hong Kong. $7.95	☐ St. Louis/Kansas City $9.95
☐ Las Vegas. $8.95	☐ Sydney. $8.95
☐ Lisbon/Madrid/Costa del Sol $8.95	☐ Tampa/St. Petersburg $8.95
☐ London $12.00	☐ Tokyo. $8.95
☐ Los Angeles $8.95	☐ Toronto $8.95
☐ Mexico City/Acapulco $8.95	☐ Vancouver/Victoria $7.95
☐ Miami $8.95	☐ Washington, D.C. $12.00

FROMMER'S $-A-DAY® GUIDES

(Guides to low-cost tourist accommodations and facilities)

☐ Australia on $40 a Day $13.95	☐ Israel on $40 a Day. $13.95
☐ Costa Rica, Guatemala & Belize	☐ Mexico on $45 a Day $18.00
on $35 a Day. $15.95	☐ New York on $65 a Day. $15.00
☐ Eastern Europe on $25 a Day $16.95	☐ New Zealand on $45 a Day $16.00
☐ England on $50 a Day. $17.00	☐ Scotland & Wales on $40 a Day $18.00
☐ Europe on $45 a Day $19.00	☐ South America on $40 a Day $15.95
☐ Greece on $35 a Day $14.95	☐ Spain on $50 a Day $15.95
☐ Hawaii on $70 a Day. $18.00	☐ Turkey on $40 a Day. $22.00
☐ India on $40 a Day. $20.00	☐ Washington, D.C., on $45 a Day. $17.00
☐ Ireland on $40 a Day. $17.00	

FROMMER'S CITY $-A-DAY GUIDES

☐ Berlin on $40 a Day $12.00	☐ Madrid on $50 a Day (avail. Jan '92) . .$13.00
☐ Copenhagen on $50 a Day $12.00	☐ Paris on $45 a Day $12.00
☐ London on $45 a Day $12.00	☐ Stockholm on $50 a Day (avail. Dec. '91)$13.00

FROMMER'S FAMILY GUIDES

☐ California with Kids $16.95	☐ San Francisco with Kids. $17.00
☐ Los Angeles with Kids $17.00	☐ Washington, D.C., with Kids (avail. Jan
☐ New York City with Kids (avail. Jan '92) $18.00	'92). $17.00

SPECIAL EDITIONS

☐ Beat the High Cost of Travel. $6.95	☐ Marilyn Wood's Wonderful Weekends
☐ Bed & Breakfast—N. America $14.95	(CT, DE, MA, NH, NJ, NY, PA, RI, VT) . .$11.95
☐ Caribbean Hideaways. $16.00	☐ Motorist's Phrase Book (Fr/Ger/Sp) . . .$4.95
☐ Honeymoon Destinations (US, Mex &	☐ The New World of Travel (annual by
Carib). $14.95	Arthur Frommer for savvy travelers) . . .$16.95

(TURN PAGE FOR ADDITONAL BOOKS AND ORDER FORM)

0891492

☐ Paris Rendez-Vous	$10.95	☐ Travel Diary and Record Book	$5.95
☐ Swap and Go (Home Exchanging)	$10.95	☐ Where to Stay USA (from $3 to $30 a night)	$13.95

FROMMER'S TOURING GUIDES
(Color illustrated guides that include walking tours, cultural and historic sites, and practical information)

☐ Amsterdam	$10.95	☐ New York	$10.95
☐ Australia	$12.95	☐ Paris	$8.95
☐ Brazil	$10.95	☐ Rome	$10.95
☐ Egypt	$8.95	☐ Scotland	$9.95
☐ Florence	$8.95	☐ Thailand	$12.95
☐ Hong Kong	$10.95	☐ Turkey	$10.95
☐ London	$12.95	☐ Venice	$8.95

GAULT MILLAU
(The only guides that distinguish the truly superlative from the merely overrated)

☐ The Best of Chicago	$15.95	☐ The Best of Los Angeles	$16.95
☐ The Best of Florida	$17.00	☐ The Best of New England	$15.95
☐ The Best of France	$16.95	☐ The Best of New Orleans	$16.95
☐ The Best of Germany	$18.00	☐ The Best of New York	$16.95
☐ The Best of Hawaii	$16.95	☐ The Best of Paris	$16.95
☐ The Best of Hong Kong	$16.95	☐ The Best of San Francisco	$16.95
☐ The Best of Italy	$16.95	☐ The Best of Thailand	$17.95
☐ The Best of London	$16.95	☐ The Best of Toronto	$17.00

☐ The Best of Washington, D.C. $16.95

THE REAL GUIDES
(Opinionated, politically aware guides for youthful budget-minded travelers)

☐ Amsterdam	$9.95	☐ Mexico	$11.95
☐ Berlin	$11.95	☐ Morocco	$12.95
☐ Brazil	$13.95	☐ New York	$9.95
☐ California & the West Coast	$11.95	☐ Paris	$9.95
☐ Czechoslovakia	$13.95	☐ Peru	$12.95
☐ France	$12.95	☐ Poland	$13.95
☐ Germany	$13.95	☐ Portugal	$10.95
☐ Greece	$13.95	☐ San Francisco	$11.95
☐ Guatemala	$13.95	☐ Scandinavia	$14.95
☐ Hong Kong	$11.95	☐ Spain	$12.95
☐ Hungary	$12.95	☐ Turkey	$12.95
☐ Ireland	$12.95	☐ Venice	$11.95
☐ Italy	$13.95	☐ Women Travel	$12.95
☐ Kenya	$12.95	☐ Yugoslavia	$12.95

ORDER NOW!

In U.S. include $2 shipping UPS for 1st book; $1 ea. add'l book. Outside U.S. $3 and $1, respectively.

Allow four to six weeks for delivery in U.S., longer outside U.S. We discourage rush order service, but orders arriving with shipping fees plus a $15 surcharge will be handled as rush orders.

Enclosed is my check or money order for $_____

NAME_____

ADDRESS_____

CITY_____ STATE_____ ZIP_____

0891492